Counseling Gay Men & Lesbians: Journey to the End of the Rainbow

Edited by

Sari H. Dworkin, PhD
Fernando J. Gutiérrez, EdD

AMERICAN
COUNSELING
ASSOCIATION

5999 Stevenson Avenue
Alexandria, VA 22304-3300

American Counseling Association
5999 Stevenson Avenue
Alexandria, VA 22304

Cover design by Sarah Jane Valdez

Library of Congress Cataloging-in-Publication Data

Counseling gay men and lesbians: journey to the end of the rainbow
    /Sari H. Dworkin and Fernando J. Gutiérrez, editors.
        p. cm.
    Includes bibliographical references.
    ISBN 1-55620-089-7
    1. Gays—Counseling of—United States.   2. Gay couples—Counseling
of—United States.   3. Victims of family violence—Counseling of—United
States.   4. Counseling—Methodology.   I. Dworkin, Sari H.
    II. Gutiérrez, Fernando J.
HQ76.25.J68   1992
158'.3'08664—dc20   91-27262
                                                                                                        CIP

Printed in the United States of America (Third Printing)

Fernando Gutiérrez dedicates this book to his parents Mariana and Alberto, and to his brother Albert and sister Mariana, for being accepting of his gayness; and to his lover John for his unconditional love.

Sari Dworkin dedicates this book to her parents Selma and Philip, her teachers, and her friends, whose love and support gave her the courage to be who she is; and to her lover Kathryn for enriching her life.

Jointly we dedicate this book to the gay men and lesbians who have died of AIDS, who have died or been victims of antigay and lesbian hate crimes; and to the lesbian and gay community in general, in our struggle to attain human rights.

Contents

Foreword

It was with pleasure that I accepted Drs. Dworkin and Gutiérrez' invitation to write this foreword to their edited volume. Reading the manuscript in preparation to write the piece has been something of a tour down memory lane, a reminder of what has come before and its significance for the work we, as psychotherapists and counselors, must do to attain the future.

Twenty years ago, when lesbians and gay men in the helping professions first began to emerge from our own closets and bring the liberating awareness of the lesbian and gay rights movements to our professions, we did not possess the complexity of vision that informs this volume. We simply knew that the oppression and stigmatization of lesbian women and gay men, which we had begun to call by the clinical term *homophobia*, was no longer an acceptable aspect of the work of counseling and psychotherapy.

Many of us in that first wave had had the experience, never to be forgotten and long in the healing, of being on the receiving end of misguided or hateful attempts by the therapists to "convert" our sexual orientations to heterosexual ones, or to deny our sexuality because it distressed the therapist and challenged his or her assumptions about how lesbians and gay men were as human beings. So in that first light of awareness, we could simply say that therapy with lesbians and gay men, to be efficacious and ethical, needed to be free of homophobia and affirming of lesbian and gay lives.

This book demonstrates the diversity and complexity of that vision as it has developed over the past two decades. A lesbian- and gay-affirmative stance in counseling and psychotherapy has come to be seen as a necessary, but not sufficient, component of psychotherapy with sexual minority clients (an overarching term used to describe any nonheterosexually identified person).

Our perspectives on our clients have broadened as we have been able to see more fully and clearly the range of people making up the lesbian and gay communities of North America. As the various populations addressed by this book suggest, counselors and psychotherapists *must* assume that they will come into contact with sexual minority clients during their careers—as school counselors, therapists in health care delivery settings, vocational specialists, childbirth educators, family therapists. The list of possible settings in which to encounter sexual minority clients grows continuously. In tandem with the expanded awareness of the extensive and pervasive presence of lesbians and gay men in all aspects of society, there is a growth of sophistication in regard to work with sexual minorities that is also observable in these pages.

Two decades ago, we lacked the experience of working with lesbian and gay male clients who lived in an open and supportive community in which there was an option to lead a fully integrated life as an out lesbian or gay man. Consequently, we did not know how to differentiate the impact of internalized oppression and mandatory hiding of one's identity from genuine psychopathology. As this volume points out in several places, we are now in a position to begin such a process of distinguishing that which is the wound of the culture with its processes of stigmatization and violence, and that which would be problematic for a person regardless of his or her sexuality. We are also able to address problems that were previously deeply hidden, even within sexual minority communities, because of their tendency to reinforce stigma, such as the problems of same-sex battering relationships and the needs and concerns of lesbians and gay men who are adult survivors of childhood sexual abuse.

Because we are free to move away from valorizing lesbian and gay lives as a corrective against unremitting homophobia and heterosexism, we can follow the lead of these authors in exploring the special clinical needs of sexual minority clients without the constant fear that these clinical vignettes will serve as some kind of "proof" of psychopathology of homosexuality.

This volume is important for both psychotherapists and counselors of all sexual orientations. The lesbian, gay, or bisexual counselor will be reminded that her or his life experiences as a sexual minority person by themselves do not provide an adequate basis for working in his or her community, that the supplement of solid information and an awareness of our diversity are also required.

The heterosexual therapist will find this a rich resource for information as well as for confrontation with her or his own values and attitudes in regard to homosexuality and bisexuality. As chapters 21 and 22 on supervision and ethics point out, we cannot assume that our clients are heterosexual, but we can assume that all of us have been affected by the homophobia and heterosexism of the cultures in which we were raised. The authors in this volume present lesbians and gay men living their lives, working, raising children, being in families, growing old, dying, and participating fully in the human experience in ways that are absent in homophobic stereotypes of sexual minority existence.

You, as the reader, are invited to learn about the unique needs of this culture—as well as its banal humanness—and to integrate the duality of difference and similarity into your work as a counselor or psychotherapist working with lesbian, gay, and bisexual clients.

Laura Brown, PhD

Contributors

Sari H. Dworkin, PhD—is an associate professor of counselor education at California State University-Fresno and a Licensed Marriage, Family, and Child Counselor. Her private practice is primarily with gay and lesbian clients. She is a long-time activist in the gay and lesbian rights movement. Dr. Dworkin has served as chair of AACD's Committee on Gay, Lesbian, and Bisexual Issues in Counseling; co-chair for the Association for Gay, Lesbian, and Bisexual Issues in Counseling; co-editor of the special issue of the *Journal of Counseling and Development* on gay, lesbian, and bisexual issues; and member of the steering committee of the Association of Lesbian and Gay Psychologists. She is currently on the executive committee for Division 44 of the American Psychological Association. Locally, Dr. Dworkin does training for clinicians on working with gay and lesbian clients and is on the board of directors for the Central Valley AIDS Team.

Fernando J. Gutiérrez, EdD—is in private practice in San Jose and San Francisco. He received a BA in psychology from Michigan State University, an MS in education in counseling from Purdue University, and an EdD in counseling and community psychology from Boston University. He was the founder of the AACD Committee on Gay, Lesbian, and Bisexual Issues in Counseling and former chair of the Association for Gay, Lesbian, and Bisexual Issues in Counseling. He was also co-editor of the special issue of the *Journal of Counseling and Development* on gay, lesbian, and bisexual issues. Dr. Gutiérrez is currently working on a doctor of jurisprudence degree at Santa Clara University Law School in order to pursue his interest in constitutional law as it relates to gays, lesbians, and bisexuals.

Jane Ariel, PhD—sees families, couples, and individuals in private practice in Oakland, California, and is involved in teaching and training therapists through John F. Kennedy University. She has a doctorate in family therapy from the California Graduate School of Family Psychology. Dr. Ariel was formerly the executive director of an institute in Israel dealing with the family as educator. She lives in a blended family with her female partner and their four sons.

Ricki Boden, LCSW, MFCC—is the director of women's services at Operation Concern, a lesbian- and gay-identified clinic affiliated with the California Pacific Medical Center in San Francisco. She is also the director of intern training. Ms. Boden has been in private practice since 1976 and, in addition, serves on the adjunct and clinical faculties of various institutions within the San Francisco area.

Elaine Brady, MFCC—is in private practice in San Jose, California, and has been a therapist for over 10 years. She obtained her master's degree at California State University-Hayward and is currently working on her doctorate through Union Institute. She also teaches classes on the issues of adult survivors of dysfunctional families through local junior colleges.

Dee Bridgewater, PhD—is a licensed psychologist working in a private practice setting in Beverly Hills, California.

Connie S. Chan, PhD—is associate professor of human services, College of Public and Community Service, University of Massachusetts at Boston. She is also a clinical psychologist specializing in work with the lesbian, gay, and Asian-American communities.

Barbara G. Faltz, RN, MS—is the manager of the Gay and Lesbian Psychiatry Unit and the Dual Diagnosis (Psychiatry and Chemical Dependency) Unit at Belmont Hills Hospital, Belmont, California. Her master's degree is in psychiatric nursing.

Ned Farley, MA, CMHC—is currently the clinical director of the Seattle Counseling Service for Sexual Minorities in Seattle, Washington. He has worked in the field of domestic violence for over 10 years, 8 of them focused on gay and lesbian domestic violence. He holds a master's degree in clinical psychology and mental health administration, and he is currently a doctoral student in counseling psychology.

Ronald L. Hawkins, PhD—is in private practice in Los Angeles. He has taught at both the California School for Professional Psychology, Los Angeles, and the California Family Studies Center in North Hollywood. He received his doctorate from the California School of Professional Psychology in 1982. Dr. Hawkins was involved with the founding of the AIDS Project in Los Angeles and has worked closely with the Gay and Lesbian Community Services Center of Los Angeles in supervising interns in the counseling department at the center.

Elizabeth L. Holloway, PhD—is associate professor in the Division of Counseling Psychology at the University of Oregon, Eugene. She is a diplomate in counseling psychology, American Board of Professional Psychology. She specializes in training counselors and conducting workshops in supervision.

Reese M. House, PhD—is professor and chair of the Department of Counseling at Oregon State University, Corvallis. He has worked in the counseling profession for 30 years and currently specializes in death and dying issues and educating people about AIDS.

A. Michael Hutchins, PhD—is a psychotherapist in private practice in Tucson, Arizona, where he specializes in working with adolescent and adult males and their families. Hutchins has conducted national workshops addressing sexual development and coming out issues for gay men, lesbians, and counselors. He is the editor of the newsletter of the Association for Specialists in Group Work; chair of the ASGW Commission on Gay, Lesbian, and Bisexual Issues in Group Work; the 1990–1991 chair of the AACD Committee on Gay, Lesbian, and Bisexual Issues in Counseling; and co-chair of the Association for Gay, Lesbian, and Bisexual Issues in Counseling. He is also a single, gay father.

Eduardo S. Morales, PhD—is a clinical and consulting psychologist in the area of counseling and mental health issues of lesbian and gay people of color. He is a core faculty member of the California School of Professional Psychology at the Berkeley/Alameda campus. He was a co-founder and director of the University of California-San Francisco AIDS Health Project in San Francisco and of multicultural inquiry and research on AIDS (MIRA) at the the UCSF Center for AIDS Prevention Studies. He has also served on various APA committees related to gays, lesbians, and people of color.

Bianca Cody Murphy, EdD—is assistant professor of psychology at Wheaton College in Massachusetts and currently a visiting research scholar at the Wellesley College Center for Research on Women. She is a clinician and educator whose previous publications include articles on lesbian couples and training mental health professionals about gay and lesbian issues.

Michael F. O'Connor, PhD—practices in Palo Alto, California, and is a member of the clinical faculty at Stanford Medical School. He received his doctorate from the University of Colorado at Boulder in 1984 and has studied clinical psychology training regimens and their impact on the clinician vis-à-vis the gay minority. He has been active locally and nationally in developing AIDS prevention programs for adolescents.

Ann M. Orzek, PhD—is a licensed psychologist and coordinator of training at the Counseling and Testing Center, Southwest Missouri State University, Springfield. She received her doctorate in counseling psychology from the University of Kansas in 1986. She currently serves on the board of directors for the AIDS Project of the Ozarks.

Marcia Perlstein, MFCC—is a practicing psychotherapist in Berkeley, California; director of psychotherapy services for North Berkeley Psychiatric Institute; and coordinator of the East Bay Volunteer Therapist AIDS Project. She is a national consultant, trainer, and supervisor with special expertise in suicide, depression, posttraumatic stress, and women's aspirations.

Mark Pope, EdD—is president of Career Decisions (a career counseling and consulting firm) and an adjunct professor at San Francisco State University, the University of San Francisco, Golden Gate University, and John F. Kennedy University. He is also clinical supervisor in Stanford University's doctoral program in counseling and health psychology.

Barbara E. Sang, PhD—is a clinical psychologist in private practice in New York City. She is a member of the Artist Therapy Service and the Women's Psychotherapy Referral Service. Recently Sang co-edited an anthology with Joyce Warshow and Adrienne Smith entitled *Lesbians at Midlife: The Creative Transition*.

Sarah M. Stearns, PhD—is a clinical psychologist from Duke University who has practiced in San Francisco and Oakland since 1980. She teaches couples therapy at New College of California and supervises trainees at the Family Therapy Clinic of the California Pacific Medical Center. She is also a consultant with Visions, a national organization that conducts multicultural workshops involving a personal approach to unlearning racism, sexism, homophobia, and other forms of oppression. She is currently in the process of beginning her own family.

Timothy J. Wolf, PhD—is a therapist in private practice in San Diego, California. He is a Licensed Marriage, Family, and Child Counselor.

Introduction: Opening the Closet Door

Sari H. Dworkin, PhD
Fernando J. Gutiérrez, EdD

The history of psychology's treatment of gays and lesbians has been well documented in recent issues of the *Journal of Counseling and Development* (Dworkin & Gutiérrez, 1989) and *The Counseling Psychologist* (Fassinger, 1991).

A content analysis of some of the studies and volumes from the 1950s to the present reveals that counselors have moved from an interest in documenting the healthy status of gays and lesbians (Hooker, 1957; Martin & Lyon, 1972; Weinberg, 1972) to documenting heterosexual bias in psychological research with lesbians and gay men (Morin, 1977) and to accepting and understanding those who are lesbian or gay (Bell & Weinberg, 1979; Clark, 1977). The focus then moved to gay and lesbian identity (Cass, 1979; Troiden, 1979) and the coming out process (Cass, 1979; Coleman, 1982).

At the beginning of the last decade, several books were written on counseling issues with gays and lesbians (e.g., Boston Lesbian Psychologies Collective, 1987; Coleman, 1987; Gonsiorek, 1982; Hidalgo, Peterson, & Woodman, 1985; Moses & Hawkins, 1982; Woodman & Lenna, 1980). Woodman and Lenna (1980) focused on counselors assisting gay and lesbian clients in their development of positive gay and lesbian identities and the coming out process. Gonsiorek (1982) focused on gay affirmative counseling models, predominantly with male clients; Moses and Hawkins (1982) expanded on various life issues within the lesbian and gay communities; Hidalgo, Peterson, and Woodman (1985) provided an anthology of articles, including people of color and the disabled; and Coleman (1987) focused on integrated identity approaches and contemporary treatment modalities. The Boston Lesbian Psychologies Collective's work (1987) moves beyond the closet and attempts to capture the experience of lesbian life.

These books have made a significant contribution to the field, bringing the topic of homosexuality out of the closet. The closet metaphor has served to illustrate the invisibility of gay and lesbian people throughout recent history. To expand this imagery further: When you, the reader, are called upon to deal with an emergency, you rush to the closet to get your coat. You open the closet door, focus on the more obvious items, and scan hurriedly to find the item that you need. You are goal oriented, and by necessity, you become oblivious to what else is in the closet.

In the past decade, assisting clients with the coming out process, helping clients to manage stigmatized identities, and assisting counselors in removing their homophobic attitudes were the first priorities in dealing with homosexuality from an affirmative developmental perspective. Clients and counselors needed to understand the process that gays and lesbians were going through in coming to terms with who they were.

Now that basic needs are met, there is an opportunity to slow down, to go back to the closet as well as to the other rooms in the gay and lesbian house and explore what else is there and what other needs gays and lesbians have that counselors must address.

In these rooms, counselors discover the complexity and enriching qualities of persons whose sexual orientations are nonheterosexual. As counselors we need to take these newly discovered qualities into consideration when working with clients. But because there has been a lack of information, which has created a void between the clients' needs and counselors' knowledge and training, we are frustrated in our attempts to journey beyond the closet with our clients.

Counselor educators, supervisors, and practitioners must develop techniques to deal with the needs of gays, lesbians, and bisexuals who have come out of the closet and are going through a journey that is uncharted. We propose that this journey leads to the end of the rainbow; and at the end of this rainbow is not a pot of gold but the gift of self-acceptance and self-actualization.

The choosing of the symbol of the rainbow by oppressed groups has biblical origins. When it appeared after the 40 days and 40 nights of rain, the rainbow symbolized a promise from God that there would be no more revenge upon God's creatures (Genesis 9:13–17). Gays and lesbians adopted this symbol to remind society that we are God's creatures and that we have also been spared from God's revenge.

In its modern day symbolism, the rainbow is a band of colors representing the spectrum of diversity of people that inhabit the Earth, including people of color and persons of diverse sexual orientations. The title of this book carries on the use of this symbol.

In the past, homosexuality and bisexuality have been treated as abnormal, as anomalies of nature. There is scientific evidence (Gonsiorek, 1982; Hart, Roback, Tittler, Weitz, Walston, & McKee, 1978; Hooker, 1957) as well as new psychoanalytic theory (Isay, 1989) that has challenged this illness model. Gutiérrez (1989) argued that the gay, lesbian, and bisexual's journey is a natural instinct to achieve harmony with nature, a natural proclivity toward one's sexual orientation. The goal for practitioners now is to assist clients not only in accepting their sexual identity but also in dealing with the day-to-day stresses of living in a homophobic world.

It is the purpose of this book to outline some of the issues that gays, lesbians, and bisexuals must deal with beyond the coming out process and to demonstrate, through the case method approach, effective techniques utilized by gay-, lesbian-, and bisexual-affirmative practitioners. This book will help counselors understand the complexity of gay, lesbian, and bisexual lifestyles and the demands that these lifestyles place on them as counselors.

This book goes beyond theory and research findings and focuses on the practical aspects of working with gay, lesbian, and, to a lesser extent, bisexual clients who face such issues as raising children, coupling, and dealing with physical disabilities, career issues, aging, and death and dying. These everyday concerns are made more difficult because they occur within a heterosexist and homophobic environment (Morin, 1991).

Format of the Book

As editors, we instructed authors to use case material, either specific or composite, to illustrate the techniques of gay- and lesbian-affirmative psychotherapy. Names are changed to ensure confidentiality, and except where noted, the clients discussed are White and able-bodied.

Theory is kept to a minimum and woven into the case material as appropriate. Authors refer readers to key sources illustrating theoretical principles. A rigid format is not used: Authors designed their chapters in the way that worked best for them. The selection of content areas emerged from our own clinical needs and those of our colleagues, and from our desire to cover areas not thus far addressed in the literature. It was our intent to compile the most comprehensive data and cover the widest range of issues possible within the limitations of book length and author availability.

Terminology

Some terminology particular to therapy with gay and lesbian clients is used throughout this book:

- *Heterosexism.* Heterosexism is the belief that everyone is heterosexual and that heterosexual relationships are necessary for the preservation of the family, particularly the nuclear family. Heterosexism is institutionalized through religion, education, and the media and leads to homophobia (Pharr, 1988).
- *Homophobia.* Homophobia is the irrational fear of anyone gay or lesbian, or of anyone perceived to be gay or lesbian. Homophobia is a weapon of sexism because it works to keep men and women in rigidly defined gender roles (Pharr, 1988).
- *Internalized homophobia.* Internalized homophobia is produced by the negative messages about homosexuality that gay men and lesbians hear from early childhood on. Because gay men and lesbians are stereotyped, kept isolated and uninformed, or fed inaccurate, distorted information about homosexuality, the messages are internalized and result in low self-esteem. Internalized homophobia leads to self-hatred and often to psychological problems.
- *Coming out.* Coming out is the process whereby a gay man or lesbian comes to accept a gay or lesbian identity as his or her identity. There are numerous developmental models that discuss the stages of the coming out process. The most well-known model is that of Cass (1979), which involves the following six stages: Identity Confusion—previously accepted heterosexual identity is questioned; Identity Comparison—the possibility of a gay or lesbian identity is accepted; Identity Tolerance—the person seeks out others who are gay or lesbian, but public and private identities are kept separate; Identity Acceptance—gay or lesbian identity is accepted, and selective disclosure to others is begun; Identity Pride—the person immerses in gay and lesbian culture and rejects people with nongay or nonles-

bian identity and values; and, finally, Identity Synthesis—the person accepts his or her gay or lesbian orientation as one part of the person's identity.

The developmental process of coming out can take several years. O'Bear and Reynolds (1985, p. 82) presented the following developmental process for lesbians and gay men (adapted from the November 1977 *APA Monitor*):

	Age of lesbians	Age of gay men
Awareness of homosexual feelings	13.8	12.8
Understood what *homosexual* was	15.6	17.2
Had the first same-sex sexual experience	19.9	14.9
Had first homosexual relationship	22.8	21.9
Considered self homosexual	23.2	21.1
Acquired positive gay identity	29.7	28.5
Disclosed identity to spouse	26.7	33.3
Disclosed identity to friends	28.2	28.0
Disclosed identity to parents	30.2	28.0
Disclosed identity professionally	32.4	31.2

O'Bear and Reynolds pointed out that there seems to be a 16-year gap between awareness of homosexual feelings and the development of a positive gay or lesbian identity. They noted an 8- to 10-year gap between first awareness of same-sex feelings and self-labeling as *homosexual*. Coming out professionally seems to be the most difficult process, occurring almost 18 years after first awareness of one's orientation.

For consistency, we asked authors to use certain terms rather than others. Brief definitions of these terms and explanations of the rationale for their use are as follows:

- *Gay and lesbian*—rather than *homosexual*. The term *homosexual* defines attraction to the same sex and is one orientation on the continuum from homosexual to bisexual and heterosexual. This term has become associated with the historical belief that homosexuality is unnatural, a sin and a sickness. Where the term *homosexual* represents an orientation along a continuum, it has been maintained within the chapters; where the term *homosexual* might be construed to represent sin or sickness, it has been replaced by the more affirming *gay* or *lesbian*.

Because of the Women's Movement, there has been recognition that women, and lesbians as women, have issues differently defined than those of heterosexual and gay men. There has also been recognition that lesbians, as all women of whatever orientation, have been historically invisible. This invisibility caused us to reject using *gay* to refer to both men and women; therefore, this book uses *gay* *and lesbian* to refer collectively to male and female homosexuals.

- *Sexual orientation*—rather than *sexual preference*. The understanding of sexual orientation is limited (see chapter 22 on ethical considerations). Gay and lesbian people have struggled throughout history with the notion that their sexual identity was a choice—and the wrong choice because of socialization in a world in which only heterosexuality was allowed. Gays and lesbians have behaved heterosexually, although their identity was gay or lesbian. They remember feeling different from an early age and see this as stemming from their gay and lesbian orientation. By owning this orientation, gays and lesbians make a conscious choice to let their behavior conform to their orientation, just as a heterosexually oriented person makes a choice not to behave in a homosexual manner.

There are some, especially women influenced by the feminist movement, who feel that their lesbianism is a choice, a preference, an alternative to a patriarchally controlled society. We believe that the clients we see are struggling with the fact that they have a gay or lesbian orientation that is not their choice but their natural orientation; and we believe that they are being forced through prejudice, ostracism, and discrimination to behave incongruently in a heterosexual manner.

Sections

This book is divided into five sections:

Section I, Developmental Issues, focuses on the periods of adolescence, young adulthood, and midlife and the issues of aging in the gay and lesbian communities. Young and old people are ignored in American culture because they are perceived as nonproductive and powerless members of our society.

Adolescents cannot vote and older people may come to a point where they are no longer economically and physically powerful. The overlay of being gay or lesbian during developmental periods when individuals need the most support from their biological families creates unique stresses with which counselors need to familiarize themselves.

O'Connor (in chapter 1) looks at the stresses that a young male adolescent goes through in his coming out process and in owning his sexual identity. Orzek (in chapter 2) discusses issues that gays and lesbians encounter in trying to translate their sexual identity into an expression of self through work, in an attempt to become economically viable in the community. To conclude this section, Sang (in chapter 3) and Gutiérrez (in chapter 4) address issues of aging lesbians and gay men in their attempts to find integrity in their lives.

In Section II, Marriage and Family Counseling, Murphy (in chapter 5) and Hawkins (in chapter 6) address same-sex male and female couple relationships. These chapters concentrate on the impact of the socialization process, heterosexism, and homophobia. Murphy also addresses issues of sexism, Hawkins the impact of AIDS in forming relationships among men.

Ariel and Stearns (in chapter 7) focus on issues that lesbians and gay men face in raising families in a world in which heterosexual couples and nuclear families are the only relationship constellations considered by the heterosexual society to be normal and valued. They describe, nonexhaustively, various configurations of family structure within the gay and lesbian worlds and their inherent issues. The sexist view that only women can be good parents is challenged in the highlighting of Ariel and Stearns' citation of Bigner and Bozett's (1989) work on parenting by gay fathers.

Section III, Diverse Populations, looks at Asians, Latinas and Latinos, African Americans, and bisexuals. Chan (in chapter 8) addresses guidelines to consider when working with Asian clients in regard to levels of acculturation, traditional versus modern values, and the role of family in these cultures. She also addresses the incorporation of gayness and lesbianism into a client's identity development as an adult individual within the Asian cultures.

Morales (in chapter 9) focuses on psychosocial factors, commonalities and differences, and the stresses Latinos and Latinas face in trying to participate in three worlds: Latino or Latina, gay or lesbian, and heterosexual.

Chapter 10's focus is on African Americans. Gutiérrez and Dworkin tap into their experience in working with African American gay and lesbian clients to demonstrate how counselors work with clients around these specific issues.

It is important to comment about the difficulty in obtaining an author for the chapter on African Americans. We contacted several potential authors: Many were reluctant to write a chapter on lesbian or gay sexual orientation for fear of coming out. Others were over-burdened because African American and other minority professionals are few, and the issues confronting minorities that these professionals are being called upon to address are many. Further, homophobia does not escape even oppressed minorities: For example, when contact was made with a leading heterosexual African American authority, we were told that gay and lesbian issues were low in African American profes-sionals' priorities, that other issues took precedence. Minority com-munities, however, need to see homophobia as another form of oppression that leads to prejudice against a group because of their characteristics. When people accept oppression of one group, people accept oppression of any group as justifiable, thus legitimizing oppression. In this chapter Gutiérrez and Dworkin tapped into their experience in working with African American gay and lesbian clients to demonstrate how counselors work with clients on these specific issues.

In chapter 11, the focus is on the physically disabled. Here Boden emphasizes the need to stop denying a person's disability by couching the term *disabled* with other euphemisms. She discusses the impor-tance of role modeling by physically disabled lesbian or gay therapists in working with clients whose self-esteem has been shattered by their disability as well as the homophobia they encounter in the world.

To conclude this section, Wolf (in chapter 12) addresses bisexuality, one of the elements on the sexual orientation continuum. Bisexuals are often stigmatized by the heterosexual as well as the gay and lesbian communities. The gay and lesbian communities often erroneously perceive bisexuals as closeted gays and lesbians attempting to build a facade of heterosexuality. A chapter on bisexuality in a gay and lesbian book is an important step in acknowledging the fact that al-though many closeted gays and lesbians do opt for the facade, bi-sexuality as a sexual orientation is a valid orientation for many individuals. Wolf addresses the application of specific intervention models in work-ing with bisexuals.

In Section IV, Incidents of Violence, the focus is on actions and situations that stem primarily from the oppression of gays and lesbians during their struggle to survive in a homophobic world.

Gutiérrez (in chapter 13) addresses incest and issues of memory retrieval, feeling responsible for the incest, and grieving the losses by gay male incest survivors. Brady (in chapter 14) discusses eight key issues faced by lesbian incest survivors, including the questioning of the possible cause-and-effect nature of childhood molestation in later homosexual orientation development and dual survivor lesbian relationships.

Bridgewater (in chapter 15) provides practical information on how to assess effectively the negative impact of antigay violence on gay men and initiate appropriate therapeutic interventions. Farley (in chapter 16) defines domestic violence and describes techniques of working with the gay and lesbian perpetrator as well as the victim of violence.

Section V, Counseling Techniques for Specific Issues, addresses such counseling issues as substance abuse, death and dying, coming out in groups, and bias in testing as well as such training issues as supervision and ethical considerations. These issues represent areas in which all counselors receive training, but rarely with an emphasis on the needs of gay and lesbian clients.

Faltz (in chapter 17) examines chemical dependency within the gay and lesbian community. She highlights particular areas such as shame around a gay or lesbian identity and the countertransference that must be addressed when treating chemically dependent gay and lesbian clients.

Gutiérrez and Perlstein (in chapter 18) discuss the need to recognize how Kubler-Ross's grief stages interact with developmental stages of clients. They discuss hospice care as an alternative to traditional settings for the terminally ill, and the need for flexibility on the part of the counselor in the provision of services.

Pope (in chapter 19) addresses the fears gay and lesbian clients may have around the use of psychological tests and gives guidelines for counselors in the interpretation of tests with this population.

Disclosing one's sexual orientation is difficult in any situation but may be even more difficult within a group. Hutchins (in chapter 20) discusses the thoughts and experiences such disclosure brings forth in a men's group both for the other group participants and for the group counselor.

Using vignettes rather than cases, House and Holloway (in chapter 21) illustrate dilemmas faced by supervisors and supervisees when sexual orientation is a factor.

Concluding the section, Dworkin (in chapter 22) addresses ethical issues of diagnosis, confidentiality, discrimination of clients who fit gay and lesbian stereotypes, transference and countertransference, and boundary violations.

xxv

Finally, the epilogue focuses on where the field needs to go from here, not only in the counseling sphere but also in the political sphere in demanding human rights for gays and lesbians.

Acknowledgments

Putting together this anthology takes the collaboration of many individuals. We would like to thank the authors for their insightful contributions to the field of counseling and to society as well as for patiently enduring all of the changes necessary throughout the process.

We would also like to thank Laura Brown, PhD, clinical psychologist in private practice and associate professor at the University of Washington for her support of this project. We thank Mark Hamilton of the Media Office and the Media Committee at AACD for believing in us and in the importance of this project.

The ability of Elaine Pirrone, AACD acquisitions and development editor, to bolster our morale when the process seemed overwhelming, to walk us through step by step, and to be optimistic and encouraging is truly phenomenal.

We would also like to thank Robin Buhrke, PhD, associate professor of counseling psychology at the University of Miami in Coral Gables, Florida, and Stephen Lenton, PhD, private practitioner in Richmond, Virginia, who served as reviewers for the book.

Fernando Gutiérrez would like to thank his lover, John Dawson, for tolerating the time away from the relationship to do this book as well as for his editorial comments and proofreading.

Sari Dworkin would like to thank her lover, Kathryn Bumpass, for putting up with her lack of attention and irritability and for not leaving her.

We hope that this book will be a valuable addition for the counselor's collection.

References

Bell, A., & Weinberg, M. (1979). *Homosexualities: A study of diversity among men and women.* New York: Simon & Schuster.

Boston Lesbian Psychologies Collective. (1987). *Lesbian psychologies: Explorations and challenges.* Urbana, IL: University of Illinois Press.

Cass, V. (1979). Homosexual identity formation: A theoretical model. *Journal of Homosexuality, 4,* 219–235.

Clark, D. (1977). *Loving someone gay.* New York: New American Library.

Coleman, E. (1982). Developmental stages of the coming out process. *Journal of Homosexuality, 7,* 31–43.

Coleman, E. (Ed.). (1982). *Psychotherapy with homosexual men and women: Integrated identity approaches for clinical practice.* New York: Haworth.

Dworkin, S., & Gutiérrez, F. (1989). Counselors be aware: Clients come in every size, shape, color, and sexual orientation. *Journal of Counseling and Development, 68,* 6–8.

Fassinger, R. (1991). The hidden minority: Issues and challenges in working with lesbian women and gay men. *The Counseling Psychologist, 19,* 157–176.

Gonsiorek, J. (1982). *Homosexuality and psychotherapy: A practitioner's handbook of affirmative models.* New York: Haworth.

Gutiérrez, F. (1989, August). *Gays and lesbians: An ethnic minority identity.* Paper presented at the annual convention of the American Psychological Association, New Orleans.

Hart, M., Roback, H., Tittler, B., Weitz, L., Walston, B., & McKee, E. (1978). Psychological adjustment of nonpatient homosexuals: Critical review of the research literature. *Journal of Clinical Psychiatry, 39,* 604–608.

Hidalgo, H., Peterson, T., & Woodman, N. (Eds.). (1985). *Lesbian and gay issues: A resource manual for social workers.* Silver Spring, MD: National Association of Social Workers.

Hooker, E. (1957). The adjustment of the male homosexual. *Journal of Projective Techniques, 21,* 18–31.

Isay, R. (1989). *Being homosexual: Gay men and their development.* New York: Giroux.

Martin, D., & Lyon, P. (1972). *Lesbian/woman.* New York: Bantam.

Morin, S. (1977). Heterosexual bias in psychological research on lesbianism and male homosexuality. *American Psychologist, 32,* 629–637.

Morin, S. (1991). Removing the stigma: Lesbian and gay affirmative counseling. *The Counseling Psychologist, 19,* 245–247.

Moses, A., & Hawkins, R. (1982). *Counseling lesbian women and gay men.* St. Louis, MO: Mosby.

O'Bear, K., & Reynolds, A. (1985, March). *Opening doors to understanding and acceptance: A facilitator's guide for presenting workshops on lesbian and gay issues.* Workshop and manual presented at the American College Personnel Association convention, Boston.

Pharr, S. (1988). *Homophobia: A weapon of sexism.* Inverness, CA: Chardon Press.

Troiden, R. (1979). Becoming homosexual: A model of gay identity acquisition. *Psychiatry, 42,* 362–373.

Weinberg, G. (1972). *Society and the healthy homosexual.* New York: Anchor.

Woodman, N., & Lenna, H. (1980). *Counseling with gay men and women.* San Francisco: Jossey-Bass.

Section I
Developmental Issues

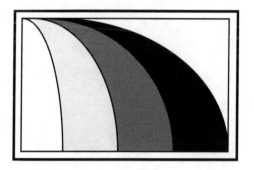

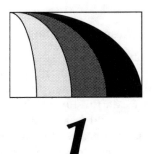

1

Psychotherapy With Gay and Lesbian Adolescents

Michael F. O'Connor, PhD

The lesbian or gay adolescent is perhaps the least visible member of a minority population for whom invisibility is a significant problem. Clinicians are thus likely to overlook even the least subtle indications of a teenager's struggle with sexual orientation. Particularly because nearly one-third of successful adolescent suicides are thought to be homosexual youth, the need for more adequately informed clinical services for this population is clear.

This chapter opens with a brief review of essential research findings related to homosexual adolescents. A discussion of relevant theoretical foundations in relation to development and treatment models follows. These set the stage for a clinical application, a look at an adolescent who began to develop an integrated homosexual identity in the course of psychotherapeutic treatment. His struggle typically involves issues beyond that of sexual identity. His case was chosen because of its lack of a predictable process and outcome, because of the frank resistance, fear, and flight it exemplifies, and because of its illustration of the damage that can be wrought by an insensitive culture. The presentation throughout the chapter reflects the author's psychodynamic and systems orientation to development and treatment.

Research Findings

Researchers, theorists, and clinicians have recently developed models of experience (Feldman, 1989; Herdt, 1989; Martin & Hetrick, 1988; Paroski, 1987), development (Anderson, 1987; Cass, 1979; Coleman & Remafedi, 1989; Hetrick & Martin, 1987; Malyon, 1982; Remafedi, 1987; Slater, 1988; Troiden, 1989), and treatment (Gonsiorek, 1988; Malyon, 1982; Remafedi, 1987; Slater, 1988) relating to gay and lesbian adolescents. Whereas the vacuum created by the removal of homosexuality from the psychopathology nomenclature in the early 1970s was substantial, gay-affirmative models of psychotherapeutic treatment for adults and adolescents are now available (Gonsiorek, 1988; Malyon, 1982; Slater, 1988).

A number of models for the treatment of gay and lesbian adolescents call for a priority to be placed on counselor awareness and education (Coleman & Remafedi, 1989; Malyon, 1982; Slater, 1988). Gays and lesbians are in their origins, and in frequent practice, an invisible minority who often do not disclose their sexual orientation, or concerns about it, to others (Voeller, 1980; Warren, 1980). This means that gays and lesbians, particularly as adolescents, are not likely to get accurate information or timely assistance in perhaps their most formidable personal struggle. According to one investigator, homosexual adolescent males sampled were most often informed about homosexual lifestyles through sexual encounters (96%), TV and media, (91%), word of mouth (87%), and by going to gay hangouts (81%). Lesbian adolescents were found to be likewise informed by TV and media (88%), word of mouth (81%), and by associating with other lesbians (50%). Only 20% of males and 13% of females in this study learned about gay and lesbian lifestyles from health care facilities or professionals, and between 50% and 80% believed common myths about homosexuals, for example, that homosexuals always have gender-opposite identifications, dislike the opposite sex, and are bound to lead unhappy lives (Paroski, 1987).

It is clearly time for therapists to become especially attuned to the needs of these individuals in clinical settings. The inaccessibliity of accurate information for homosexually oriented youth adds to the difficulties of a disrupted identity formation. Mental health providers can benefit these individuals by sharing and utilizing such information where it is needed.

Developmental Models

Some 3 million male and female adolescents in this country are thought to have a homosexual orientation (Gonsiorek, 1988; Herdt, 1989). These estimates are encumbered by the fact that gay and lesbian adolescents are unlikely to identify themselves as gay, either to themselves or others, at least in the earlier phases of adolescence (Cass, 1979; Coleman, 1989; Coleman & Remafedi, 1989; Herdt, 1989; Hetrick & Martin, 1987; Remafedi, 1987; Troiden, 1989).

It is important to note that adaptation to a homosexual identity is likely to be a prolonged process (Remafedi, 1987; Slater, 1988; Troiden, 1989). The adolescent may struggle with orientation-related conflicts well before he or she is able to label him- or herself as homosexual to a helper or other adult.

Several models have been formulated to describe the development of gay and lesbian individuals. A partial review of these models is presented by Slater (1988). Most are stage models, and few, if any, argue in favor of discreet and orderly progression through all stages for the average individual. Theorists typically see homosexual identity adaptation as a process that may include regressions to earlier phases, stalling or incomplete movement through stages, and a tendency to repeat efforts at tasks not completed in a particular stage. Troiden (1989) has integrated previous efforts in this area, including the classic work of Cass (1979), and formulated a four-stage model of homosexual identity formation that is relatively representative of theories in this area.

Descriptions of Troiden's stages—Sensitization, Identity Confusion, Identity Assumption, and Commitment—follow. For each stage pertinent findings of other investigators and comments as relevant are included in order to further elucidate the adolescent homosexual's developmental process. Note that any individual may resolve only portions of the tasks of each stage at any one time and may return to these issues later. The stages may also vary for the individual based on socioeconomic status, family environment, gender identity, and other issues (Slater, 1988; Troiden, 1989).

The discussion here of homosexual identity formation is not intended to be exhaustive but rather to provide a context for the discussion of treatment models and an appropriate theoretical template for discussion of the specific case described in the last section of this chapter. For further elaboration of the finer points of theory in the area of homosexual identity formation, the reader is directed to the authors cited.

Stage 1: Sensitization

According to Troiden, this stage occurs before puberty and involves the social experiences of marginality and difference from peers that form the basis for later difficulties in identity formation. Troiden noted that in this phase the child is more concerned with gender identification than with sexuality, and that sexuality is not yet likely to be related to a sense of "differentness."

Many investigators suggest a preadolescent experience of differentness consistent with later same-sex sexual orientation (Anderson, 1987; Coleman, 1988; Malyon, 1982; Remafedi, 1987; Troiden, 1989). It should be noted that although cross-gender identification in childhood is apparently correlated with adult homosexual orientation (Anderson, 1987; Green, 1985), the reverse is not true. That is, not all homosexually oriented adults displayed cross-gender typical behaviors as children (Paul, Weinrich, Gonsiorek, & Hotvedt, 1982; Slater, 1988).

Teasing and negative labeling for marginal or cross-gender traits and interests, whether experienced directly or witnessed, contributes to the internalization of a negative self-concept. Negative introjects, resulting from the experience of marginality and a typically homophobic socialization in the latency and adolescent periods, are thought to have significant disruptive influences on the child's continued socialization process, development of identity, self-esteem, defenses, cognitions, psychological integrity, and object relations (Malyon, 1982) as well as affect and interpersonal skill development (Gonsiorek, 1988).

The experiences of the Sensitization stage prepare individuals, for better or worse, to make adjustments in their view of themselves relative to others. Cass (1979) noted that a stable homosexual identity arises from the interaction between individuals and their environment. Thus perceptions of self and others are thought to be fundamentally related to the individual's developmental movement. The homosexual individual is typically unable to maintain a stable, congruent identity beyond a certain point, given the factors discussed here. She or he is thus likely to be compelled to enter a second phase.

Stage 2: Identity Confusion

According to Troiden, this stage occurs usually sometime in adolescence as individuals begin to recognize feelings and behaviors that could be labeled *homosexual*. It occurs on average for females at around age 18 and for males at around age 17. Troiden noted a shift from the social focus of latency to a genital focus of development at this stage. The youth may experience conflict between the identity adopted as a child and that demanded as an adolescent. He or she is without evidence of a clear category for his or her inclusion in the world and, according to Troiden, resorts to one of four strategies to cope. The first strategy is one of continued "denial" of impulses and feelings. The second strategy involves an awareness of homosexual impulses and feelings as well as an "avoidance" of situations in which these must be confronted. The third strategy involves attempts to "repair" the individual's make-up and thus to become heterosexual in behavior if not in fact. In the fourth and final strategy, the individual has the option to "accept" his or her impulses as a part of who he or she is.

The adolescent at this stage may experience conflicts between his or her former identity—either a false identity or one focused on positive nonsexual attributes of the latency period—and the newly emerging genital impulses, known to be socially denigrated. In addition, the adolescent is faced with the developmental task of formulating an identity for the self and of developing intimacy with others, as are adolescents generally (Erikson, 1963).

These tasks become difficult if not impossible for the gay or lesbian adolescent. Several investigators note that it is the additional burdens that accompany homosexual orientation, and not otherwise inherent intrapsychic conflicts, that create the majority of adjustment difficulties for these individuals (Gonsiorek, 1988; Hetrick & Martin, 1987; Slater, 1988). Peer relations, an important avenue for mirroring and social skill development, are disrupted by the youth's awareness of, and concern about, differentness. Adolescents in this stage notice that they do not have the same level of sexual arousal for the opposite sex as most of their peers. Yet, according to Troiden, such arousal does occur to some extent for the majority of female and male homosexuals during adolescence and may further confuse them. Teasing and harassment continue to be experienced or witnessed. The adolescent is at an impasse. He or she faces adjustment to a socially stigmatized role at a time when social expectations of sameness and belonging are keenly felt. The experience of being a minority of one is common (Anderson, 1987; Paul et al., 1982). The heterosexual socialization of childhood has not prepared the youth for homosexual life adaptations, and indeed, the adolescent is likely to have little positive knowledge of such options (Hetrick & Martin, 1987).

The negative consequences of this situation for the adolescent can be great. Ego defense at this stage is accomplished at the cost of increased rigidity, constricted affect, reduced interpersonal contact, heightened superego functioning, and the formation of a false identity in many, if not most, cases (Gonsiorek, 1988; Malyon, 1982). Malyon has noted that intimate and erotic capacities, interpersonal skills, and, hence, identity formation are stalled by an elaboration of the defenses necessary to bind chronic anxiety. He also noted that the normal transfer in object relatedness from parent to peer is disrupted. In addition, psychological, emotional, and interpersonal development is delayed until the coming out period. Gonsiorek noted that individuals may retreat to conflict-free areas, such as academics, and to risk reaction formations that include the adoption of perfectionist norms, a loss of self-interest and self-identity, and increased caretaking of others.

The stress of this adaptation can be enormous and lead to a state of crisis. Herdt (1989) noted that stigma and oppression make the homosexually oriented adolescent even more invisible and thus less likely to receive help. Yet Remafedi (1987) cited evidence that 40% of gay adolescents interviewed had sought previous psychiatric help, though not necessarily disclosing their sexual orientation at the time.

A most startling finding relates to the extent of distress these young people may be facing. An estimated 20% to 35% of gay and lesbian adolescents attempt suicide (Anderson, 1987; Bell & Weinberg, 1978; Herdt, 1989). Recently, the U.S. Department of Health and Human Services released a report indicating that homosexual youth are two to three times more likely than other youth to attempt suicide and may comprise 30% of successful youth suicide attempts annually in this country (Freiberg, 1990).

The stage of Identity Confusion may thus be the most difficult and dangerous phase for homosexual adolescents. These individuals can be expected to present for treatment in large numbers, however. The clinician's ability to screen individuals who may be struggling with this phase of development is obviously crucial. Despite the many difficulties inherent in the process, most individuals are able to move to the next, dramatically transformative phase.

Stage 3: Identity Assumption

According to Troiden, this stage of adaptation for homosexual individuals occurs on average at 19 to 21 years for males and 21 to 23 years for females and is related to a reduction in social isolation and increased contact with other homosexual individuals. A primary task in this phase is the management of stigma.

Troiden noted a variety of ways that this task is accomplished: One is "capitualization," in which the individual capitulates to a negative view of homosexuality but also acknowledges his or her membership in this group. Another is "minstralization," marked by the adoption of stereotypically and often exaggerated homosexual mannerisms and behavior. "Passing" is the selective concealment of one's homosexuality while acknowledging membership in this group, at least inwardly, to a limited group of associates. Yet another way is adaptation by "group alignment," which involves immersion of the individual in the homosexual community, often to the exclusion of most heterosexual contexts.

Cass (1979) broke this period down into the two stages of Identity Tolerance and Identity Acceptance. Initial motivation for this transition is thus thought to be based on pragmatic necessity, only later becoming ego-syntonic. Individuals may arrive at this phase of development in early or mid-adolescence (Herdt, 1989; Remafedi, 1987), but the options for such adolescents, usually still residing in their family home, are limited. Males at this stage are likely to make initial contacts in the homosexual world via sexual activity, with consequential exposure to sexually transmitted diseases often before receiving any education about these diseases (Slater, 1988; Troiden, 1989). Lesbian youth tend to enter this world via social or romantic involvements with other lesbian women, but there is evidence that some young lesbians become pregnant as a way of reassuring themselves and their families that they are heterosexually oriented (Paroski, 1987; Slater, 1988).

The importance of a supportive family context for the survival and psychological well-being of the minority individual has been noted (Jenkins, 1982; Nobles, 1974; Smith, Burlew, Mosley, & Whitney, 1978). Yet lesbian and gay individuals frequently do not enjoy a supportive family environment either because they have disclosed their sexual orientation or because they have not (Bell & Weinberg, 1979; Marmor, 1980; Voeller, 1980).

As a result of family dynamics, the lesbian or gay adolescent may be lacking an important ingredient for the successful resolution of the important issue of separation, and of individuation process in particular. Erikson (1963) noted that adolescence reflects an earlier developmental stage, also known as rapprochement, and appears to involve similar dynamics and needs. Mahler (1971), in describing the individuation and separation processes that occur in rapprochement, noted the importance of parental availability throughout this phase and the debilitating effects of parental rejection as the child moves toward independence.

We can expect that parental rejection of the adolescent may therefore have serious negative consequences. A survey of 329 homosexual adolescents ages 12 to 21 by Hetrick and Martin (1987) showed that the two most important problems reported by these youth were isolation and family rejection. These investigators also reported that 40% of these subjects had experienced violence, often at the hands of their families (Martin & Hetrick, 1988).

Investigators of male prostitution (Boyer, 1989; Coleman, 1989) noted that the majority (70%) of these prostitutes are homosexual, come from troubled family backgrounds, and report feeling unwanted at home. Family conflicts over the youth's homosexuality are frequently the precipitant for the youth's ejection onto the street.

Homosexually oriented youth are prone to become runaways, to engage in drug use and truancy, to experience academic problems, and to drop out of school as they are struggling with homosexual identity assumption (Coleman & Remafedi, 1989; Hetrick & Martin, 1987; Hunter & Schaecher, 1987). Hunter and Schaecher (1987) reported that one-fifth of female and one-half of male homosexual adolescents surveyed had experienced harassment, been threatened, or were assaulted in junior high or high school as a result of being perceived as homosexual.

The desire to behave in a manner consistent with an autonomous identity, combined with some level of self-hatred, may result in behavior that is self-destructive or destined to elicit responses that confirm the youth's poor self-image (Gonsiorek, 1988).

Coming out to individuals or in settings known to be antagonistic to homosexuals is but one example. Flaunting of homosexuality has also been noted as an adaptation to the management of stigma (Martin & Hetrick, 1988).

A final and daunting consideration in homosexual identity assumption for the adolescent is the issue of AIDS. AIDS is likely to delay and add to the adversity of the coming out process for adolescents (Feldman, 1989; Herdt, 1989). Infection rates are even more troubling, however. Feldman (1989), for example, has noted that, given the long incubation period of the disease, the most accurate evidence of teenage infection can be found in the symptomatology of individuals in their mid-20s. According to Feldman, these individuals account for one-fifth of all AIDS cases in the United States. As of August 1988, the incidence of AIDS cases among adolescents was doubling each year. The combination of psychosocial stress and low self-esteem, typical entry processes for the coming out adolescent, typically invulnerable attitudes and independent and experimental behaviors of adolescents generally, and a virulent disease make the AIDS epidemic an overwhelmingly dangerous one for gay youth.

Lesbian youth may be similarly impacted by the increased negativity that AIDS connotes for homosexuality per se, as well as by the relative closeness of this disease and its ramifications to the lesbian community.

The Identity Assumption stage is thus a period of enormous potential difficulty. It is also a crucially important and potentially positive time for the lesbian or gay person because the identity is more fully integrated and the individual is able to experience a personal wholeness heretofore impossible.

Stage 4: Commitment

According to Troiden, this final stage involves the integration of homosexuality to the extent that it becomes a state or way of being, rather than a description of sexual behavior, and is consequently consistently reflected in both love and life choices. Thus this stage includes the accomplishment of a same-sex love commitment and is marked by the identification of oneself as homosexual to nonhomosexual individuals. There is an increased level of self-satisfaction and happiness, and homosexuality per se may become a relatively less important part of one's overall identity. Stigma management strategies may shift in this stage with a decreased use of passing behaviors and an increased blending of one's sexuality into one's identity and lifestyle. According to Troiden, this stage occurs at ages 21 to 24 for males and at ages 22 to 23 for females on average. The overlap of this stage 4 age range for lesbian women with that of stage 3 is accounted for by the fact that early sexual relationships for these women are typically committed involvements. Gay men tend to engage in less committed sexual involvements in the Identity Assumption stage.

Thus Troiden's final stage does not fully integrate the fact that lesbian women appear to accomplish relational commitments at an earlier period. This and other likely differences in lesbian and gay male development are beyond the scope of this discussion but should be noted. Commitment to the lifestyle and identity of a gay or lesbian person may be a better way to conceptualize the task of stage 4.

Treatment Models

Treatment models for gay and lesbian adolescents consistently stress the importance of an awareness on the part of the provider of typical adjustments to homosexual identity (Coleman & Remafedi, 1989; Gonsiorek, 1988; Slater, 1988). These models are also consistent in stating that homosexual identity is not linked to psychopathology per se (Gonsiorek, 1988; Malyon, 1982; Slater, 1988).

Malyon (1982) has described a four-phase treatment model that stresses a careful building of the therapeutic alliance. The first phase is designed to gather data and formulate hypotheses. Malyon noted that it is important that the therapist be clear about his or her own values about homosexuality as well as about the pros and cons of coming out to the client if the clinician is homosexual. Such information about the therapist can provide a positive model for the client, but if shared precipitously, it may engender a failure to attach to the therapist, and even a flight from treatment.

The second, or analytic, phase of treatment, according to Malyon, involves conflict resolution and cognitive restructuring. This is accomplished via resolution of transference reactions and defenses, slowly and cyclically allowing the emergence of repressed material that can then be resolved. Integration of earlier experiences and memories prepares the individual for the third, or identity consolidation phase, in which a positive identity formation ultimately sets the stage for intimacy to occur.

The final, or existential, phase is thought to occur much later for lesbian or gay persons, often in their 40s or 50s according to Malyon. His description of this period is consistent with a focus away from one's sexuality and an expansion into other realms of life concerns. Malyon noted the importance of recognizing that homophobia has a differential effect on individuals and may not be the only pathogenic element deserving attention in treatment.

Other investigators have offered additional insights into effective treatment. Slater (1988) noted that the experience and consequences of a homophobic socialization must be made conscious for both the client and therapist. She also noted the need to counter myths with accurate information and recommended bibliotherapy as one important option. Remafedi (1987) cautioned counselors to watch assumptions of heterosexuality when working with an adolescent. He argued that treatment should focus on the results of stigmatization, including psychological and psychosocial maladjustment, family alienation, and drug abuse. He also noted that the promotion of abstinence in regard to sex and drugs is unrealistic and should be replaced with active educational efforts. Gonsiorek (1988) encouraged the clinician not to minimize sexual orientation, not to press for premature resolution of this question, and to offer sound and complete information about sexuality to young clients. He further recommended support groups and family support as well as the development of positive role models and advocacy efforts.

Families of lesbian or gay adolescents also need attention. Coleman and Remafedi (1989) argued that families must go through their own coming out process and may be better understood and helped with this in mind. They echo the need for support and resources for these families. Anderson (1987) likened parental reaction to the homosexual adolescent to a grief process, with the consequent stages of denial, anger, bargaining, and acknowledgment if not acceptance. He also encouraged the provider to obtain and give parents information to help them make sense of these events.

Clinical Application

We can now discuss the development and treatment issues as they apply to a 17-year-old male adolescent. The individual has been disguised in certain respects to protect confidentiality, although the client's presentation, treatment issues, and treatment course are substantially accurate. This individual's treatment occurred over a period of 11 months and involved outpatient therapy sessions on a weekly or twice weekly basis. The case raises issues other than those of homosexual identity adaptation, as is often the case for adolescents who seek or are referred for treatment. Because the client is male, generalizability of this discussion to the lesbian adolescent is in some respects limited.

The client herein described was chosen in part because so many of the issues relevant to the successful treatment of gay adolescents are demonstrated in his experience. Psychodynamic, object relations, and systems perspectives formed the theoretical basis for his treatment. It should be noted that, despite the data presented here, each adolescent presents an individual picture and set of problems.

The psychodynamic model of treatment is preferred because of its flexibility, its amenability to individual differences, and its utilization of the development and resolution of transference reactions thought to stem from the individual's actual experience. I believe a systems perspective is crucial in the effective treatment of any adolescent, in part because of his or her close developmental and physical proximity to the family.

The description that follows of the process and outcome of this individual's treatment may present the strongest argument here reviewed for realizing the importance of limited goals and for progressive, cyclical healing over an individually suited treatment period.

Paul was a 17-year-old White male and a senior at a prominent school when he presented for treatment. He was referred by the school following a year of poor academic performance and conflicts with teachers and his mother in regard to his lack of motivation for work and responsibility. At intake, he resided with a neighborhood family friend, Bill, aged 28. Bill had apparently been like a brother to Paul for some time. Paul was an only child. His parents were divorced when Paul was 5. His father resided in another part of the state. Paul's mother lived with a man, Gene, who had moved in a year earlier.

Paul had come to live with the couple 8 months previously, the culmination of several moves to relatives and schools since the divorce. He moved into Bill's house a few months later, after difficulties developed between Paul and Gene. Paul's mother and father were quite well off, and neither parent worked. Paul described his father as selfish and uninterested in him. His mother was described as irresponsible and more of a peer than a mom. He stated in the first interview that he wished his mother worked and maintained the house like other mothers he knew. Both sets of grandparents were wealthy and prominent citizens. He had only occasional contact with them, by choice.

Paul offered limited verbalization and little eye contact in our initial meetings. He was well oriented and appeared to have superior-range intelligence. His affect was notably flat, and his mood was depressed. Alcohol and drug use were denied.

Paul was concerned about how he was perceived by others. He reported that he had never been athletic and that he liked more passive activities. He had been teased about this as a child, and his father was critical of these characteristics. He felt isolated from his peers. He feared that others liked him only for his money and car. He noted that he was often more generous than he really wanted to be with both. He had a girlfriend of 1 month and had had a brief relationship with another girl before that. Paul had one close male friend whom he spoke of often.

Paul seemed disinterested when asked about his school difficulties. He noted that he found nothing very interesting and had little motivation to find a career because he stood to inherit a sum adequate to insure his future comfort. His mother disputed this fact, but despite multiple cautions about the value of money, she often caved in to Paul's demand for money or items he felt were crucial to acquire.

Paul's initial presentation was consistent in many respects with that noted in adolescents who will eventually assume a homosexual identity (Anderson, 1987; Coleman & Remafedi, 1989; Gonsiorek, 1988; Herdt, 1989; Remafedi, 1987; Slater, 1988; Troiden, 1989). He reported a feeling of differentness as a child; he appeared withdrawn; and he had concerns about belonging with his peers. He engaged in the kind of codependent behavior noted by Gonsiorek (1988) to be likely for the gay or lesbian adolescent. And he seemed to have stalled in his identity formation as exemplified by a lack of drive and self-esteem. He also engaged in covering behavior, that is, in dating girls without real interest in them. He reported cross-gender traits, at least in childhood, and, on closer inspection, worked hard to cover such traits as a young man. His mother reported him to be a shy child, and he had been denigrated as a child for being unathletic and passive.

Paul arrived a few minutes late for his third session. He had had a fight with his girlfriend, who had told him he was selfish. This feedback upset Paul, and he denied it. He said he did not wish to discuss his girlfriend and withdrew into himself in silence. I suggested that dating was often tricky and that people had different interests and attractions. I also suggested that some boys liked to date girls and others did not so much, and wondered if he'd thought about that at all. He began to talk about his friend Matt. Matt was a popular boy at school, and he and Paul had been "best" friends this year. He felt Matt had lately neglected him in favor of a girlfriend, and he was angry about that. He wondered whether he should wait for Matt to call him, or call him first and tell him he was a jerk. I told him that it was clear Matt was pretty important to him, and he denied this. Then I suggested that it was very hard to like someone a lot and sense they didn't feel the same way. He responded by saying that that was the way it always was. As the discussion continued he began to explain how much his being different bothered him. I told

Paul that many people have that feeling and gave examples, including those of gay people. Sensing interest, I gave him some additional information about homosexuality. He responded that he was not gay, but that he had thought about other men sexually.

This session reflects the stage of Identity Confusion described by Troiden (1989). Paul was not ready to describe himself as gay, but he was able to admit to having homosexual fantasies. He had notified me early in the session that direct interpretations could turn him off completely. Instead, a general discussion that included phrases like "some people ..." could be used to present important factual information as well as a model for homosexual identity.

Paul arrived on time for the next meeting. He seemed quite agitated and had great difficulty beginning. What eventually emerged was a report of 5 years of sexual abuse at the hands of Bill, the family friend with whom he lived. Bill's inducements of money, alcohol, cocaine, and other adult "privileges" were compelling. Paul knew that the arrangement was "wrong," and he felt immense guilt about it. He seemed faced with the conflict of giving in to Bill's demands or losing his primary support and friend, the only person who accepted him totally.

Needless to say, this session impacted the course of Paul's treatment powerfully. Paul, overwhelmed by his situation, decided to take an indirect step that would allow someone else to intervene. It is notable that this did not occur until it was suggested to him that homosexual behavior was an acceptable aspect of human behavior.

The following period was a tumultuous and difficult one for Paul. His mother was informed of the abuse at the following session. She was clearly shocked and at first doubted the veracity of Paul's charges. It emerged that to accept the seriousness of Paul's abuse, she would have to consider the issue of Paul's sexuality. She asked Paul whether he had in some way invited the sexual encounters with Bill. He vehemently denied this. She expressed both relief and some doubt, in response. She noted that one would have to agree to participate in such actions as a man, she thought. I attempted to clarify the dynamics of sexual abuse, but she seemed undeterred. I then asked her what she might feel if she were to find that her son was gay, noting that was not a determination

I had made. She responded that she would be disgusted and would be unable to accept it. At this point she and Paul colluded to avoid the issue by laughing it off. Paul had certainly heard every word, however.

The coming months included a number of difficult periods for Paul. Evidence of a drug problem emerged. The abuse, having been reported, led to a grueling experience for Paul involving lawyers, relatives, police officers, social workers, and the court. Paul's experience of abuse became the primary focus of treatment. He was also grappling with his sexual feelings, however, and his feelings for Matt, whom Paul had eventually told about the abuse.

Paul's transference reaction to me was at times troubling for him. He was often surprised by my understanding of his experience but was suspicious of my motives in helping him to explore his feelings. The biggest challenge was to find the level of work he could tolerate without adding to his experience of intrusion. Respecting his boundaries in this regard led to an increased level of trust on his part and was crucial to the corrective experience of therapy.

Paul continued to date girls, seeming to enjoy their support but frequently feeling too much demanded of him and fleeing the relationship. He could not accept his homosexual impulses, which he continued to experience. He was able to discuss these feelings and fantasies with me, but only briefly and always with a negative conclusion or qualifier. He finally decided he might be bisexual, but that in any case, homosexual behavior was impossible for him to act on.

Gonsiorek (1988) has cautioned against pushing prematurely for the resolution of an individual's sexual identity. He has also suggested that when sexual identity remains in question after several months of treatment sexual abuse must be suspected. Paul was not yet within the typical time line for Identity Assumption in Troiden's model. There seems little doubt that his sexual identity assumption was significantly hindered by the experience of abuse, however. The consequences of the reporting and prosecution procedures also interfered with a more private exploration of his sexual inclinations and provided him with negative feedback that was extremely difficult to manage. It was striking to me to realize the extent to which others—police, parents, doctors—saw him as a likely provocateur in the abuse sequence.

Paul continued to grapple with his sexuality and eventually found a place to rest: in a bisexual identity that acknowledged sexual feelings for other men but decried such behavior. This position is consistent with Troiden's avoidance strategy, which provided Paul with several advantages. He could bind some of the anxiety he was experiencing regarding his sexuality. He could continue to date girls, who provided him with relatively safe companionship and a cover. He could also in this way maintain a safe distance from both sex and intimacy. His impaired ability to trust others would therefore not be challenged.

An additional consideration of great concern was Paul's drug use. I chose to pursue this issue slowly, since Paul's need for support at this time was great, and he was prone to drop out of treatment if pushed too far.

Paul began to acknowledge his drug problem and to abstain. Drug treatment options were discussed (see chapter 15 on counseling chemically dependent gays and lesbians). His self-esteem and peer interactions began to improve. But Paul terminated his therapy abruptly, however. Bill was convicted but given only probation for his offenses. Paul was angry and scared, and he had been told of a psychiatrist who could "make him straight." It seemed clear that he had staked much of his acceptance of himself in the situation on a severe punishment of Bill. Paul was noticeably distanced from me in the last session. He mentioned that the family was moving to Arizona.

Paul's treatment ended in a truly unfortunate way. He had been tenuously clinging to a palatable image of himself as bisexual. The lenient action of the court with regard to Bill sent the message that Bill's behavior was not so important, that Paul's painful circumstances were not Bill's doing. This left Paul to carry the responsibility for the pain and anxiety of his recent existence and for all the failed attempts to make himself "normal."

Paul, in full view of the public, had shifted from a *discreditable* person to one *discredited*, to use the terms of some investigators (Hetrick & Martin, 1987). He had managed dissonant homosexual impulses and experiences by adopting an inactive bisexual stance. In this way he could not be discredited. The court's finding forced Paul and those around him to reconsider his role as victim in the sexual activity with Bill, and he was thereby discredited. Given his stage of Identity Confusion, he was unable to tolerate this position. He thus reverted to denial as a defensive strategy.

Paul was unfortunately encouraged to seek help from someone who could "change" him, a process he very much wished to involve magic rather than more pain. Many investigators and clinicians believe that offering therapies to change sexual orientation is unethical (Coleman & Remafedi, 1989; Gonsiorek, 1988; Malyon, 1982). The family colluded with Paul in attempting to escape to another location. His mother was apologetic on the phone for disrupting his treatment but felt he could start up again when they were settled in Arizona. She also stated that the move would help him "get away from all this." Paul lived in a world where escape was the answer to life's problems. I suspect that Paul's anger with me was also a way to end our relationship, knowing that he would be moving soon. It is notable that Paul chose to move to another state with his mother. He had just completed high school and would have been allowed to live independently elsewhere. He was still quite angry with his mother. Malyon's contention that the object-relational shift from parent to peer is disrupted for the gay or lesbian adolescent may apply in this situation.

Paul contacted me 1 year after the move to Arizona. He had not seen the recommended psychiatrist after all, but did get into treatment with another therapist and eventually sought drug treatment as well. He was in therapy at the time we talked. He sounded animated and much more open. He stated that he was sorry he had left treatment angrily and didn't really know why this had happened. About 1 year after this communication he referred a former friend into treatment with me. This individual related that Paul had come out earlier that year and was doing well. He was now 20 years old.

Conclusion

This chapter delineates issues and intervention strategies, in both theoretical and practical terms, as relevant to the treatment of the homosexual adolescent. Case considerations presented here may apply to the treatment of the lesbian adolescent as well, although gender and social differences from the case presented suggest caution in generalization to this population.

References

Anderson, D. (1987). Family and peer relations of gay adolescents. *Adolescent Psychiatry, 14*, 162–178.

Bell, A.P., & Weinberg, M.S. (1978). *Homosexualities: A study of diversity among men and women.* New York: Simon & Schuster.

Boyer, D. (1989). Male prostitution and homosexual identity. *Journal of Homosexuality, 17*(1/2), 151–184.

Cass, V.C. (1979). Homosexual identity formation: A theoretical model. *Journal of Homosexuality, 4,* 219–234.

Coleman, E. (1989). The development of male prostitution among gay and bisexual adolescents. *Journal of Homosexuality, 17*(1/2), 131–150.

Coleman, E. (Ed.). (1988). *Psychotherapy with homosexual men and women.* New York: Haworth.

Coleman, E., & Remafedi, G. (1989). Gay, lesbian and bisexual adolescents: A critical challenge to counselors. *Journal of Counseling and Development, 68,* 36–40.

Erikson, E. (1963). *Childhood and society* (2nd ed.). New York: Norton.

Feldman, D.A. (1989). Gay youth and AIDS. *Journal of Homosexuality, 17*(1/2), 185–193.

Freiberg, P. (1990, July). Sullivan is criticized by APA over report. *APA Monitor,* p. 41.

Gonsiorek, J.C. (1988). Mental health issues of gay and lesbian adolescents. *Journal of Adolescent Health Care, 9,* 114–122.

Green, R. (1985). Gender identity in childhood and later sexual orientation: Follow-up of 78 males. *American Journal of Psychiatry, 142,* 339–341.

Herdt, G. (1989). Gay and lesbian youth: Emergent identities and cultural scenes at home and abroad. *Journal of Homosexuality, 17*(1/2), 1–42.

Hetrick, E.S., & Martin, A.D. (1987). Developmental issues and their resolution for gay and lesbian adolescents. *Journal of Homosexuality, 14*(1/2), 25–43.

Hunter, J., & Schaecher, R. (1987). Stresses on lesbian and gay adolescents in schools. *Social Work in Education, 9*(3), 180–190.

Jenkins, A.H. (1982). *The psychology of the Afro-American: A humanistic approach.* New York: Pergamon Press.

Malyon, A.K. (1982). Psychotherapeutic implications of internalized homophobia in gay men. *Journal of Homosexuality, 7*(2/3), 59–69.

Mahler, M. (1971). A study of the separation-individuation process and its possible application to borderline phenomena in the psychoanalytic situation. In M. Mahler (Ed.), *The selected papers of Margaret S. Mahler, MD,* Vol. II. New York: Jason Aronson.

Marmor, J. (1980). Homosexuality and the issue of mental illness. In J. Marmor (Ed.), *Homosexual behavior: A modern reappraisal.* New York: Basic Books.

Martin, A.D., & Hetrick, E.S. (1988). The stigmatization of the gay and lesbian adolescent. *Journal of Homosexuality, 15*(1/2), 163–183.

Nobles, W. (1974). Africanity: Its role in Black families. *Black Scholar, 5*(9), 10–17.

Paroski, P.A. (1987). Health care delivery and the concerns of gay and lesbian adolescents. *Journal of Adolescent Health Care, 8,* 188–192.

Paul, W., Weinrich, J., Gonsiorek, J., & Hotvedt, M. (1982). *Homosexuality: Social, psychological, and biological Issues.* Beverley Hills, CA: Sage.

Remafedi, G. (1987). Homosexual youth: A challenge to contemporary society. *Journal of the American Medical Association, 258*(2), 222–225.

Slater, B.R. (1988). Essential issues in working with lesbian and gay male youths. *Professional Psychology: Research and Practice, 19*(2), 226–235.

Smith, W.D., Burlew, A.K., Mosley, M.H., & Whitney, W.M. (1978). *Minority issues in mental health.* Menlo Park, CA: Addison-Wesley.

Troiden, R.R. (1989). The formation of homosexual identities. *Journal of Homosexuality, 17*(1/2), 43–73.

Voeller, B. (1980). Society and the gay movement. In J. Marmor (Ed.), *Homosexual behavior: A modern reappraisal.* New York: Basic Books.

Warren, C.A.B. (1980). Homosexuality and stigma. In J. Marmor (Ed.), *Homosexual behavior: A modern reappraisal.* New York: Basic Books.

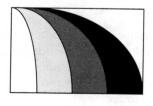

2

Career Counseling for the Gay and Lesbian Community

Ann M. Orzek, PhD

Career decision making is a lifelong process. Factors such as needs, values, beliefs, family, and priorities may change in their importance over the years. There is no reason to believe these issues are any less important for the gay, lesbian, or bisexual client who seeks counseling for vocational concerns. These individuals, however, have the additional variable of sexual orientation to consider when making choices in work and lifestyle.

The purpose of this chapter is to examine some of the issues involved in the career decision-making process for gays, lesbians, and bisexuals, including influences of identity development, family, values, and beliefs as well as how the counselor can facilitate this process. Illustrative case studies are also presented.

As groups, gay men, lesbian women, and bisexual people have been discriminated against in certain fields due to stereotypes held by the general public. Some individuals erroneously consider these groups mentally ill and therefore inept in performing their jobs. For example, working with children or adults in any job requiring close personal contact has been considered closed to these groups by many employers, despite the fact that most child molesters are heterosexual

(Lew, 1988). Other negative stereotypes and discrimination practices are covered more completely by Hetherington, Hillerbrand, and Etringer (1989) in their work on career counseling with gay men and by Hetherington and Orzek (1989) in their work on career counseling and life planning with lesbian women.

In the past, gays, lesbians, and bisexuals have responded to the discrimination in several ways. First, these clients did not even consider certain professions as viable options. Second, they may have chosen to enter a profession that may not be accepting and never reveal their orientation. Third, they entered a profession and were selective of whom they chose to tell about the orientation. Another alternative was to choose a profession that was not open to their lifestyle, yet choose to be open and deal with the discrimination. Some have chosen not to deal with the possibility of discrimination by trying to find a profession open to their lifestyle. It is difficult to say which professions actually fit each of the above categories. Choices are based more on perceptions, experiences, and role models from the past. In addition, these choices are not discrete categories, and they do not necessarily hold across an individual's life span. What the choices indicate is an attempt to blend personal identity needs with the needs met by one's career. This is a process unique to each individual, heterosexual or gay. For the sexual orientation minority, however, the extent to which personal needs may impact on career decision making is based somewhat on the role sexual orientation has in one's life. For some, it may be the primary factor in identity formation, but for others it may have less impact.

Another factor is the particular definition the person attaches to the concept of sexual orientation. Although this varies from individual to individual, it is important for the counselor to realize that sexual orientation does not mean the same to all clients. Each associates certain values, philosophies, political statements, sexual practices, and gender issues with the term. Therefore, in blending sexual orientation and career choice, the occupation needs to allow for an expression of these factors at some level in order to find career satisfaction. As stated by Holland (1973), "people search for environments that will let them exercise their skills and abilities, express their attitudes and values, and take on agreeable problems and roles" (p. 4). For those individuals whose lifestyle includes a sexual orientation not readily accepted by society at large, finding a work environment that will allow both the exercising of abilities and the tolerance of beliefs and values may be difficult.

Identity

Defining oneself is based on a number of variables. The importance of each variable may change, for example, because of personal development, age, and relationship status. How sexual orientation factors into one's identity is important for the counselor to establish early. (See chapter 1 for a discussion of a model of gay and lesbian identity development.) It may be a factor in choosing a career that is supportive or at least tolerant of his or her sexual orientation.

Case Study 1: Russell

Russell is a 22-year-old college senior and math major who identifies himself as a gay man, although he is currently not in a relationship. He has been active in college clubs supportive of sexual orientation minorities. He is worried he will not have a choice over the job he chooses because he has been quite open about his sexual orientation. At this stage of his career decision making, he wonders if his career and his openness about his lifestyle can indeed be combined, or if instead he will have to "settle" on a less desirable job while his primary vocation will be obtaining certain rights for minority sexual orientation people.

When Russell entered career counseling, his counselor first assessed the importance of sexual orientation to Russell in the formation of his identity as a whole. Russell related that being gay contributed more to his sense of self than what he chose to do for a living and verbalized that whatever career he chose, he would be open about his lifestyle.

Despite his stated recognition that he may experience discrimination, there appeared to be a great deal of unresolved anger concerning this injustice. The counselor explored this initially with Russell by reflecting his observations of how Russell's voice tone and presentation changed when he spoke about his fear of discrimination. Russell became more in touch with the affective component of his career decision-making process. This gave him additional information with which to work.

After several sessions, Russell became aware of incidents throughout his life that reflected discrimination. He felt certain professors devalued his opinion because he admitted his sexual orientation in their classes. He also felt that some of his heterosexual male friends hesitated in initiating activities for fear Russell would interpret it as their showing sexual interest. Russell began dealing with the anger he felt over the misperceptions of others.

Throughout this process, the counselor realized that although Russell originally presented for career counseling, much of what he was dealing with were unresolved personal concerns. Several times Russell met an impasse. This became obvious when Russell felt powerless over changing the perceptions and behaviors of others. The counselor saw these as extremely critical times because it was possible Russell could drop out of counseling because of his frustration. The counselor chose interventions that could help empower Russ. Initially the counselor suggested homework assignments, such as writing a piece for the school newspaper on sexual orientations. When Russell failed to complete this assignment, they processed this the next session. Part of the resistance was that Russell had tried to educate people before, but he saw no change and this only added to his frustration. The counselor had made the error of working from his frame of reference rather than the client's. He realized this when Russell volunteered that the most powerful he felt that week was when a heterosexual female acquaintance sought his help with her math. To Russell this translated as her seeing him as credible in other areas besides his sexual orientation. The counselor used this information to suggest that perhaps Russell's presentation as an effective role model for gays was the most powerful way he could educate others about homosexuality. Russell was then able to recall other incidents in which he served as an effective role model.

This information was extremely important for Russell in his career search. He had originally thought that the only way he could make an impact was directly working for the rights of sexual orientation minorities. He decided that he could also educate others by serving as a competent role model in mainstream society.

Russell decided to expand his job search and consider working for companies that would use his degree in math and computer science and not limit his search to jobs specifically involved with the rights of gays and lesbians or gay and lesbian issues. He decided to keep his work with Gay Pride Week and the college gay support group in his resume, feeling that he wants any company he works for to know about his sexual orientation. On the surface, Russell had not made many changes in his career plans, but his ability to perceive himself as a role model for others broadened his career options and added to his identity.

Case Study 2: Martha

Martha is a 20-year-old college junior who has had no overt sexual experience at this point but has felt since high school that she has been attracted to women. She is feeling pressure to declare her academic major. Although she has always envisioned herself a teacher, she is unsure of her chances of getting a job if indeed she chooses to act on her orientation and it becomes known to others.

When Martha presented for counseling, she appeared confused both as to her sexual identity and to her career choice. She was hesitant even to articulate the possibility she might be lesbian. Although she may have become somewhat aware of her orientation, she has not yet begun to explore it as part of her identity.

This was a situation in which the counselor felt that a deep trust needed to be established in the counseling relationship before Martha would be able to discuss her sexual identity concerns. In order to accomplish this, the counselor was more nondirective and supportive than task oriented so that Martha could feel accepted and safe and then explore the issues surrounding her orientation. Her confusion was manifested verbally by the questions she asked and behaviorally by an appointment she "forgot," but the counselor was able to summarize and reflect the concerns she observed. For example, with the missed appointment, the counselor asked, "I'm wondering what was going on with you that distracted you from remembering our appointment."

Martha became aware 4 weeks into counseling how overwhelmed she was feeling by asking herself to make two major decisions in her life: sexual orientation and career choice. Martha had been dealing with the decisions from a cognitive perspective and felt frustrated that no "logical" conclusion had been reached. Although the counselor had initially helped Martha with the problem-solving approach in order to join with her, it became apparent Martha needed to deal with affect surrounding the decision-making issues. Because of the trust developed with her therapist, the explorations of emotions became easier. The counselor began phrasing questions in more affective terms: "How would it feel to you to be in a lesbian relationship?" "When you say 'scared,' where do you feel it?"

With increased trust, the counselor was able to become somewhat more confrontive with Martha. When Martha became "stuck" in exploring issues, in the past she became angry or looked to the counselor to give her answers. For example, early in counseling, she asked the counselor which decision should she make first: her sexual orientation or her career. This was an indication of the level of personal development from which she was operating. Being dualistic in her thinking suggested there was a right and a wrong way to proceed. She also saw the counselor as an authority with the "correct" answer. By being supportive yet confrontive with Martha, the counselor was able to move to a multiplistic frame of operation in which Martha saw more possibilities. For example, when Martha asked which decision should be made, the counselor asked, "Are you able to see any issues common to both?" or "It sounds like you must be certain about one of the decisions before moving on to the next. Can you see any way the two are related?"

Throughout the course of counseling, Martha became more aware of the many issues involved in making her decisions. Her need for recognition through her profession became paramount. She was able to verbalize her need to choose her career and work toward completing her coursework in education. Although she was able to admit her sexual orientation is important, Martha verbalized that she was not ready to act on or further explore her sexual attraction to women.

In one of their final sessions, the counselor explored these questions with Martha: "What type of information would help you make the decision of whether or not to act on your sexual attraction to women?" "What are you feeling currently about your decision not to act at this time?" "How will you know when you are ready?"

Through these and other open-ended questions, Martha became aware of the type of information necessary for her to make the decision concerning her movement toward a lesbian orientation. She became aware of the need to see lesbian role models in her chosen career, the need to feel established with her identity as an educator before making any other decision, and her need to find a lesbian support group. Through her work with her counselor, she also feels comfortable about returning to counseling at a later time should she feel the need.

Family

The role of the family in influencing an individual's career choice has long been explored. In research by Roe (as cited in Amatea, 1975), vocation was found to be related to personality development, and this development in turn was a result of early parent-child interaction. In a broader sense, as the individual progresses through adolescence and young adulthood, careers may be chosen or rejected as a means of gaining approval from one or both parents. An individual who is gay, lesbian, or bisexual has also to consider the issue of whether or not to disclose to family and to deal with the impact on family dynamics. Gays, lesbians, and bisexuals are often rejected by their families. The pursuit of a career may thus be jeopardized due to lack of financial and emotional support.

Case Study 3: Sandy

Sandy is a 33-year-old bookkeeper with a regional corporation. She has been asked by management to relocate to another city to accept a position she considers a major career move. She is excited about the prospect of advancement, but a relocation will force her to leave a lesbian-women's community that she considers her family of choice. Although she currently is not in a committed relationship, she remains close to several former partners. She is unsure of a comparable community in the new city and how politically active she could be in her new position.

For Sandy, the concerns appeared to be family versus career. Although she may be uncoupled at this time, the lesbian-women's community acted as a support and as a potential source for partners. When Sandy presented for career counseling, she described it as "probably being just a couple of sessions because I need to make a decision in 2 weeks." The counselor assumed a sense of urgency, but Sandy presented in a logical, coherent manner, saying that she had thought quite a bit about the options. Sandy said that she "knew" what she needed to do, but it didn't "feel" right. At that point, the counselor was able to assess that Sandy uses both cognitive and affective information when making a decision. She related that, logically, the move would be good in that she would increase her salary by 50%; and because she had little contact with her family of origin, she knew she could not rely on them financially. Sandy volunteered that she had been in college when she came out to her family and they immediately withdrew financial support. She had taken on several part-time jobs to put herself through college but eventually dropped out after getting the position she has now. She has worked for this firm for 6 years. They knew about her sexual orientation, and she perceived it as not being a problem.

Sandy defined her problem as job security (career) versus potential loss of lesbian support group (sexual orientation) and talked about it in terms of logic versus emotions. The counselor pointed out that there were cognitive and affective elements in each alternative. In choosing to stay, Sandy would have her emotional support. In moving she could not be sure of finding a women's community. The counselor pointed out that this decision was not being made from the logical perspective that Sandy valued. They discussed ways she could explore the resources of the new city. She decided to ask in her current community if anyone knew someone with whom she could network. It was at this point that the counselor realized Sandy had not even discussed with her friends the possibility of her move. When the counselor questioned her, she reported she did not want them to influence her decision. The counselor became aware that Sandy was attempting to make a decision with partial information and pointed that out to her.

Although Sandy initially presented her dilemma as career versus friends, the counselor realized it became more a matter of the meaning Sandy gave each. The counselor then began to explore with her what needs would get met by her new job and what needs get met currently by her community. She was given the assignment to complete the list for next week. When Sandy returned the next week, she presented a list to the counselor and seemed distressed. The counselor began the session by asking what she learned from the assignment. Sandy's distress was a result of what the new job really meant to her. She discovered the job would give her new status, and somehow this would compensate for her sexual orientation in the hope that her family would invite her back. The counselor then reframed Sandy's decision from "career versus community" to "family of origin versus family of choice." Sandy was able to articulate that reframing it in that context "felt" right and "seemed" logical.

The issue of a possible career move made Sandy aware of unresolved abandonment issues with her family of origin. At the end of the session, she resolved to stay in her present position. She decided also to remain in counseling to help sort through her family issues.

Career Decision Making Throughout The Lifetime

Career decision making is an on-going process throughout one's life. Even if a person remains in the job for which he or she was trained, there is a continuous decision being made to remain in that position. Non-traditional-age college students and non-college-educated individuals who are in an alternate lifestyle may experience concerns specific to their state of personal development, career development, and identity development as gay, lesbian, or bisexual.

Case Study 4: Lionel

Lionel is a 40-year-old gay man who has been involved in a monogamous relationship with Roger for 5 years. Lionel has worked with a small electrical contracting firm for 7 years after serving in the army for 15 years. He is considering opening his own contracting firm but realizes Roger may need to have a majority of the financial responsibility for their household until he is established in business. Roger, who owns a small clothing store, is supportive of Lionel's decision to become self-employed but also realizes several of Lionel's closest gay male friends work with him and to leave them would be a great loss. Lionel realizes that starting a new business may take energy away from his relationship, and with the long hours each puts in, they may seldom spend time together. Lionel is concerned about the impact that changing jobs may have on his relationship.

When Lionel initially came in for counseling he realized his concerns were not entirely career oriented. He had thought through the impact of his career change on his relationship. The first issue that the counselor explored with Lionel was whether the changes he saw were his own perceptions or a result from input from Roger. It became apparent that Lionel was making assumptions based on his own frame of reference because he found it difficult to discuss his concerns with his partner. He admitted that this was his own bias because he did not want to alarm Roger, rather than because Roger did not want to discuss these issues with him. Because the concerns Lionel was dealing with centered around being in a dual career relationship, the counselor suggested a few sessions of couples counseling. Although Lionel was initially hesitant, because his interpretation was that the counselor saw them as having relationship problems, he agreed to ask Roger to participate.

Both Lionel and Roger participated in the next session. The counselor began by asking each how they perceived the relationship changing because of Lionel's career move. At this point, each perceived it differently. Lionel focused on the potential destructiveness (for example, because of long hours and a cut in pay), whereas Roger saw it as an opportunity for growth both for Lionel and for the relationship. Roger's perceptions were the result of his own career change from retail sales to owning a business. It was difficult for Lionel to understand Roger's frame of reference, and he interpreted it as Roger not caring if they had less time together and that his lack of financial contributions would be an excuse for Roger to terminate the relationship. Based on Lionel's interpretation of Roger's reaction and his hesitancy to enter couples work, the counselor moved from the career issue to further assessment of the relationship. The counselor asked each to state what they appreciated most about the other. Roger expressed an appreciation most for Lionel's caring nature and his commitment. Lionel stated he appreciated Roger's patience and his intelligence. The counselor then asked each to predict how he saw Lionel's career change impact on what he appreciated about the other. Roger stated that because of lack of time and finances, Lionel would not be able to demonstrate his caring as much as in the past but that he understood the modifications that needed to be made. Lionel feared Roger would lose his patience with his lack of time and money. The two men were able then to begin discussing alternative means of expressing to the other what he appreciated most. In essence, the major impact of the session was the reassurance to Lionel that he would not "lose" Roger because of the career decision he made. In the next session, in which both men were present, Lionel discussed the other losses in his life: father at an early age, loss of support from mother, and change in status when he was discharged from the service. Lionel had been viewing his career change from a loss model and was experiencing anticipatory grief from both career and relationship. The counselor attempted to reframe the career change into a "growth" perspective by which new skills would be developed and their relationship would take on new meaning. With Roger present, Lionel made the commitment to himself to attempt the career change and to discuss with Roger any concerns he had.

Summary

When making career decisions, many factors are considered. One issue is how well a particular career will allow a person to express his or her identity. Although a person's identity is composed of many different parts, sexual orientation is one element that gays and lesbians may give different importance to, depending on their definitions of orientation and their stage of sexual orientation identity.

In the four cases, each client gave a different meaning to his or her orientation. Initially, Martha was operating from the perspective that her sexual orientation was primarily "sexual" in nature and that she would define herself as lesbian when she had a sexual relationship with a woman. Russell, however, included in his definition his political and philosophical statements. For Sandy, her orientation created a support system, but for Lionel his orientation offered a monogamous relationship. Coupled with these definitions are the particular stages of gay or lesbian identity each is in. Martha is beginning to explore options of fitting her sexual orientation into her identity. Russell, Sandy, and Lionel have integrated sexual orientation more fully, yet each experiences its impact on the decision-making process differently.

Therefore, when working with gay or lesbian clients, the counselor should not assume all are the same, based on sexual orientation. Potter and Darty (1981) contended that lesbians are an extremely heterogeneous group in personality characteristics. In addition, the counselor also needs to be cautious not to place too much emphasis on sexual orientation. Brown (1975) reported that many counselors do place too great an importance on this factor when working with gays and lesbians. There needs to be a balance between recognizing sexual orientation as a factor and overemphasizing its impact. Two important sources of information in the career planning process that can be utilized by the counselor have been identified: (1) accepting the client's sexual orientation from the client's own frame of reference and (2) identifying the stage of identity formation in which the client finds him- or herself.

References

Amatea, E. S. (1975). Contributions of career development theories. In R. C. Reardon & H. D. Burck (Eds.), *Facilitating career development* (pp. 17–33). Springfield, IL: Thomas.

Brown, D. A. (1975). Career counseling for the homosexual. In R. C. Reardon & H. D. Burck (Eds.), *Facilitating career development* (pp. 234–247). Springfield, IL: Thomas.

Hetherington, C., Hillerbrand, E., & Etringer, B. D. (1989). Career counseling with gay men: Issues and recommendations for research. *Journal of Counseling and Development, 67*(8), 452–454.

Hetherington, C., & Orzek, A. (1989). Career counseling and life planning with lesbian women. *Journal of Counseling and Development, 68*(1), 52–57.

Holland, J. L. (1973). *Making vocational choices.* Englewood Cliffs, NJ: Prentice-Hall.

Lew, M. (1988). *Victims no longer: Men recovering from incest and other sexual child abuse.* New York: Harper & Row.

Potter, D. J., & Darty, T. E. (1981). Social work and the invisible minority: An exploration of lesbianism. *Social Work, 26,* 187–192.

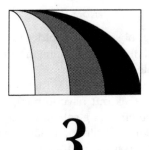

3

Counseling and Psychotherapy With Midlife and Older Lesbians

Barbara E. Sang, PhD

It has only been in the last decade or so that the lesbian community has turned its attention to documenting the experiences of midlife and old lesbian women (Adelman, 1986; Almvig, 1982; Berger, 1982; Copper, 1988; Friend, 1987; Kehoe, 1986, 1988; Kirkpatrick, 1989; Macdonald & Rich, 1984; Raphael & Robinson, 1984; Woodman, 1987). We currently have more information on old lesbians (over the age of 65) than we do on midlife lesbians (roughly ages 35 to 60). There is a growing body of literature on affirmative psychotherapy for lesbians (Coleman, 1987; Gonsiorek, 1982; Riddle & Sang, 1978; Sang, 1977; Stein & Cohen, 1986); however, there is little that deals specifically with counseling and psychotherapy[1] of the midlife and older lesbian population. This chapter is intended to fill that gap.

There is a small body of literature that addresses clinical issues and psychotherapy with older heterosexual women, but as Sands and Richardson (1986) point out, here too, this age group has been given scant

---

[1]The terms *counseling* and *psychotherapy* are used interchangeably in this chapter.

attention. Steuer (1982) observes that older heterosexual women who deviate from the social norm by not being married or by being childless are even more invisible.

Traditional heterosexual women who are currently midlife and older today are reported to seek out psychotherapy to deal with conflicts that center around the changing role of women in our society (Junge & Mays, 1985; Sheinkin & Golden, 1985). What these women were taught would bring them fulfillment has been challenged by contemporary women. Women who are not working feel guilty about not being out there, and those who do work feel guilty about being away from home. These women are also struggling to find their identity separate from husband and children and to assert their independence and autonomy. According to McGrath (1990), symptoms of post-traumatic-stress disorder are not uncommon among women in the middle age range because definitions of femininity and aging are rapidly changing. Psychotherapy involves helping this group of women find new ways to grow and realize themselves.

These midlife concerns are not likely to be relevant to older lesbians. Because midlife and old lesbians as a group have not conformed to traditional female roles, the problems that they bring to psychotherapy may be an outgrowth of their alternative lifestyle. Therefore, it is important that counselors and psychotherapists working with older lesbians be familiar with the lesbians' unique experience.

Based on my own experience as a midlife woman and on the experiences of my midlife and old women friends, colleagues, and clients, important areas that are relevant to older lesbians include:

- *Social factors*. Older lesbians grew up at a time when they had to hide their sexual orientation and were less accessible to one another. For some this has resulted in internalized homophobia and limited social networks. A large percentage of midlife lesbians were found to be hiding their lesbianism from most, if not all, of their family members, straight friends, and co-workers (Bradford & Ryan, 1991). This means that midlife lesbians are forced to hide their real selves, which is certain to produce stress and make for distortion in the way they relate.
- *Economic conditions*. Midlife lesbians are reported to have significantly low incomes relative to their level of education and experience (Bradford & Ryan, 1991; Hayes, 1991). Economic concerns are a big issue. Because most lesbians are self-supporting (Sang, 1990, 1991), they may have special retirement needs. Lesbians, who have worked

all their adult lives, may as they get older choose to work in a different way, change careers, or work fewer hours.

- *Child rearing*. Children are affected by parents' deviation from the norm, particularly at adolescence. This will be discussed further in a later section.
- *Roles*. One of the major issues for midlife women that I found in my study of 110 mostly White lesbian professional women between the ages of 40 and 59 (Sang, 1991) is the struggle to balance the various aspects of their lives, that is, work, relationships, personal interests, child care, aging parents, community, and spirituality.

The case histories in the next sections are intended to give the counselor or therapist a feeling for a few select issues that older lesbians bring to psychotherapy. Some of these issues are the result of the oppression of gays and lesbians in our society, whereas others have to do with the development of women who have not conformed to the traditional female role. There may be an interaction between the two. The way in which these issues are manifested for a particular individual depends on her own internal dynamics as well as other life circumstances. Women of color, minority lesbians, and disabled lesbians may also experience midlife and old age differently. Each individual needs help in arriving at her own meaningful solution. Lesbians who come to psychotherapy at midlife are likely to have already had some counseling in the past for emotional distress or relationship problems (Bradford & Ryan, 1991).

Midlife as a Time of Change

The midlife period, roughly ages 35 to 60, has been found to be a time of change (Downing, 1987; Levinson, 1978; Neugarten, 1968; Nichols, 1986; Rubin, 1979). The way in which these changes manifest themselves may be different for lesbians than for traditional heterosexual women and men. My own midlife study (Sang, 1991) suggested that both work and relationships have been an integral part of a lesbian's experience, unlike that of traditional heterosexual women and men who, at midlife, are first getting in touch with a neglected part of themselves, that is, work or relationships. Midlife changes, whether intentionally made or beyond one's control, can be freeing and conducive to creativity and growth (Sang, 1991, in press).

Counselors and therapists working with midlife and old lesbians must be aware of preconceived notions and biases about this age group and not assume that all older women are the same. Lesbians are less likely to be bothered by physical changes of aging (Posin, 1991) and are less likely to have difficulty managing if their long-term relationship breaks up. What midlife lesbians may need help with is the integrating of and the balancing of the various aspects of their lives.

Although the following case history is not unique to the lesbian midlife experience, it is included here because it deals with one of the most frequent issues that midlife lesbians bring to psychotherapy: the reprioritizing of their values, goals, and activities. As previously indicated, lesbians as a group have a long work history. By midlife there is often a need to make changes in job or career. Because lesbians tend to have many roles and involvements, this is also a time to let go of some and spend more time on others.

Case History: Donna

Donna, a college professor who had just celebrated her 40th birthday, came to psychotherapy because she felt confused, angry, trapped, and overwhelmed. She felt she had spent all of her adult years in a profession she didn't like because it gave her financial security. Turning "the magic number 40" made her realize that she wanted to make some changes—"to really live a little"—but she didn't know how. Although Donna shared a house with her partner Elayne, her salary was needed to make ends meet. Donna feared taking risks, and yet she felt stifled. She was tired of academic politics and longed to be out on her own; she was tired of the pressure to publish that took time away from her relationships and other interests. Like many lesbians of her age group, Donna is in a highly responsible position that is time consuming and leaves little room for the personal self (Hall & Gregory, 1991; Sang, 1982).

Donna needed a safe place to explore her needs and options. Her partner, friends, and family couldn't understand why she would want to leave her job at the height of her success. Psychotherapy gave Donna a chance to review her life in a nonjudgmental atmosphere, to see where she had been and where she might want to go. As an adolescent Donna spent many satisfying hours writing short stories, but as an English professor, all she did was read the writings of others. In the course of psychotherapy she began doing creative writing again and to feel more whole and in touch with her authentic self. With the help of psychotherapy, she also began to realize that much of what she did was what she "should" do or what looked good rather than being in touch with her own needs.

As Donna gained more confidence in herself, she was ready to explore other job options that might be more appropriate for her at this time in her life. She took a sabbatical and began freelancing as a travel writer. It was possible to make a living from it without spending most of her time on job-related work. For the first time in years Donna and Elayne felt closer because there was time to be together. With less stress and pressure, Donna was also easier to get along with—less argumentative and more loving.

Coming Out at Midlife and Old Age

A midlife or old woman can seek out professional help to deal with her newly discovered feelings toward women or may, in the course of therapy, get in touch with such feelings. It is important for counselors to be aware that coming out as a lesbian is not restricted to earlier periods of development (Charbonneau & Lander, 1991). Sexual orientation is complex: One can have had same-sex attraction or sexual experience in childhood, adolescence, the 20s and 30s, and not label oneself *lesbian* until midlife or older. Then there are those women who knew they were lesbians when they were younger but who did not act on it until midlife or old age. Some women report no history of attraction to women until midlife or older (Sang, 1991). In an otherwise excellent article entitled "Lesbians: A different middle age?" Kirkpatrick (1989) questioned whether such "behavioral change (coming out) represents a healthy effort to integrate a valuable but previously abandoned part of the self or represents the loss of ego integration and a retreat to a more limited and more infantile relationship" (p. 138). Would we raise this question if a woman went from a lesbian to a heterosexual orientation? Clearly, this kind of thinking comes from an underlying assumption that lesbianism is an immature and less healthy form of sexual development than heterosexuality. McGrath (1990) reported that many women in the middle are starving for intimacy, especially after living with traditional men most of their adult lives. These women describe finding intimacy with women at levels and depths they have never before imagined or experienced. And yet, she has found that this choice of alternative lifestyle is often problematic for some therapists.

There are certainly many advantages to coming out at midlife, one of which is the shortage of eligible men. Some of the problems that women may face in coming out at midlife are loss of economic support, fear of loss of support from family and friends, getting adjusted to another culture with its own customs, and possibly a limited opportunity to meet other lesbians of their age.

Case History: Lynn

Lynn is a 52-year-old biochemist, originally from a small town in the Midwest, who had been in a heterosexual marriage for 26 years. The couple was childless. For most of the marriage Lynn's relationship with her husband had been a platonic one. They shared a considerable number of interests and had a mutual respect for one another that enabled the relationship to satisfy both partners over the years. Each considered the other their "best friend." Lynn was attending adult education classes in French at the local high school in preparation for a trip to Europe with her husband. She became friendly with a woman her own age, and after class they often went out for coffee. Lynn found herself looking forward to these meetings. After about 3 months, Lynn realized she felt physically attracted to her classmate; she didn't know what to do about these feelings or what they meant. Lynn sought out psychotherapy because she felt confused about what was happening to her. She felt anxious and was unable to sleep or concentrate at work.

Psychotherapy enabled Lynn to sort out her feelings of sexual attraction for another woman. Why now? Was she really a lesbian all along and didn't know it? She began to explore why she had not been sexual throughout most of her marriage. Lynn also had to face the negative feelings she had about lesbianism: having had a religious, Catholic upbringing, she was taught that homosexuality was sick and sinful. She wondered if there was something wrong with her. During this period of questioning and exploration, the therapist suggested that Lynn do some reading on the subject.

Lynn had never had a sexual experience with her own sex or had sexual fantasies about women. Her attraction to Anna seemed to come out of nowhere, and yet she felt as if she had found the missing piece in her life. For the first time she felt sexual. With the support and understanding she was getting in therapy, Lynn was able to allow herself to be sexual with Anna. A close relationship was developing between the two women that was satisfying on many levels.

There reached a point in Lynn's therapy in which she felt depressed and angry at herself for having wasted so much of her life being non-sexual. She came to understand how she got to this point and was able to let go of the self-blame.

For several months Lynn agonized over Jim, her husband, and whether or not to tell him about Anna. She felt considerable guilt and tried to get the therapist to make her give up the relationship with Anna. In this way she would not have to deal with Jim's hurt and anger. At some level Lynn also appeared to be testing the therapist to see if she (the therapist) really believed that it was all right to relate sexually to women. This was brought out into the open and discussed. Lynn spent many sessions dealing with the conflict over her need to be true to herself and her fear of hurting her husband. If their relationship had been a stormy or painful one, it would have made separation easier. Anna was tired of their clandestine meetings and the limited time they could spend together. She began putting pressure on Lynn to make a choice. Lynn eventually left her husband to be in a relationship with Anna. As a result of coming out she lost a few close friends who were put off by her lesbianism, but she also began to build a new social life for herself.

Midlife and Older Lesbians and Their Adolescent and Adult Children

Women who are in midlife are likely to have children who are in adolescence or are approaching it. As Kirkpatrick (1989) pointed out, women of this age are burdened with the fear that their children will turn against them because of their sexual orientation. Not only are adolescents dealing with their own sexuality, but they are also under considerable pressure from peers to conform. The mother who comes out as a lesbian at midlife may be in the process of working out her own sexual identity and may be particularly vulnerable to rejection. In describing her own difficulties with her adolescent children when she came out at 40, Rothschild (1991) pointed out how they were mirroring her own inner conflicts. She was also forced to realize that her children had to go through a similar coming out process to their friends and that they also feared being stigmatized or rejected.

It is important for counselors and therapists to allow each client to work at her own pace; however, it is also important to bear in mind that the fear that coming out to one's children will lead to a loss of their love overshadows the potential for a positive outcome (Sowle, 1989). Not only must therapists and counselors be aware of the client's internalized negative stereotypes about lesbian mothers, they must also be alert to gender stereotyping: A male child needs a male role model for "appropriate" sex role identification. If a male child does not develop into a male that society considers masculine enough, this is blamed on the mother's lesbianism. Sowle (1989) cautioned that acceptance of the concept of male role modeling creates guilt in lesbian mothers and may force them to make choices that are not in the best interests of their sons.

I recently saw a lesbian for therapy who was a grandmother. Although her own children were ashamed of her lesbianism and thought her to be disturbed, her grandchildren, ages 10, 15, and 19, thought her to be "cool." They tended to feel more comfortable disclosing their own secrets to her than to their old-fashioned mothers.

Case History: Amanda

Amanda, a 46-year-old Black lesbian woman, entered psychotherapy for depression related to interpersonal difficulties on her job. As therapy progressed it became clear that one of the major sources of conflict in her life was her relationship to her two adolescent children: a daughter age 17 and a son age 13. Amanda had divorced her husband when the children were small and had set up a household with Kim, a Black lesbian a few years younger than herself who was childless. Although the couple slept in the same bed and had always been openly affectionate in front of the children, the nature of their relationship was never acknowledged openly.

The family was close and did things together on weekends. Both Amanda and Kim acted as disciplinarians, and one or the other attended on open school day. When the daughter, Paulette, turned 13 she began staying away from home for long periods of time and no longer brought friends home as she had in the past. On the rare occasions she was home, she stomped around in her high-heeled shoes, miniskirts, and overly made-up face as if to mock Amanda and Kim who dressed more casually. Paulette also became verbally abusive to Kim and stopped confiding in her. Kim felt it was time they came out to the children; however, Amanda was fearful that in doing so, Paulette would reject them. Kim tried to take matters into her own hands by insisting that Paulette be more responsible about time and not be disrespectful to her. Amanda felt threatened by this and felt that Kim was trying to usurp her position as the "real mother." As time went on, Kim could not deal with the hostility that was being directed at her from both daughter and mother and threatened to leave unless things changed.

In therapy Amanda explored her feelings about not being accepted by her daughter and her reluctance to be open with her about her lifestyle. She was afraid that by labeling their relationship she would push Paulette away even further. She also worried that if her daughter knew she was a lesbian, she would somehow become confused about *her* sexual identity. Amanda confessed that she felt guilty that her son was living with two women and that therefore she was not providing him with a proper male role model. Because George was a sensitive adolescent who preferred reading books to playing sports, she felt that she had failed him. Amanda's concerns are common ones and are a reflection of some of the negative stereotypes and myths about lesbians that exist in our culture. It is often helpful for the lesbian mother to be exposed to an alternate point of view either through current reading material or a lesbian mother's support group.

In exploring coming out to her children in therapy, Amanda was forced to face her own negative feelings about being a lesbian—that it was "sick" and not as "good" as being heterosexual. Amanda became aware of the fact that she turned on Kim because she despised the lesbian part of herself. She came to realize that by not coming out to her children she was in danger of alienating them. After exploring her options, one of which was to have the whole family meet with the therapist, she decided to speak to each of her children privately. Paulette did in fact admit to being ashamed of her mother and didn't want her friends to see that she came from a "crazy" home. She continued to act out her anger; however, now Amanda was in a better position to confront her behavior. Paulette eventually became more open to learning about her mother's lifestyle. Over time, mother and daughter became closer than they had ever been. The son was also having difficulties with his mother's lesbianism, which he did not know how to bring up and which he could not handle. He was being teased by his peers for having two mothers and for being a "sissy." By coming out to him, Amanda was able to validate his feelings and, at the same time, help him to cope with the situation.

By taking a risk and coming out to her children, Amanda not only improved her relationship with them but also gained the confidence to take risks and to be more open at work. Her relationship to her partner Kim improved, and in general, she was less depressed and more in control of her life.

Relationships and Social Supports

Current research on midlife and old lesbians indicates that, on the whole, older lesbians are not as isolated, lonely, and depressed a population as we might have predicted (Almvig, 1982; Berger, 1982,

1984; Friend, 1987; Raphael & Robinson, 1984; Woodman, 1987). According to Adelman (1988), lesbians have unique and creative ways to deal with aging, just as they cope creatively with other aspects of life. Based on her sample of 50 lesbians over the age of 65, Kehoe's (1986) data suggested that the lesbian is a survivor, a balanced personality, coping with aging in a satisfactory manner. Nevertheless, the need for companionship and for finding a partner can be a problem for many lesbians. Friendships are an important source of well-being for this population, more so than family. Older lesbians with high self-esteem tended to have weak sibling ties and strong friendship ties (Raphael & Robinson, 1984).

Although as a result of the women's and gay movements, lesbians now have more ways to connect with other lesbians, not all older lesbians avail themselves of this opportunity. In the studies cited, only about half of each sample were affiliated with any lesbian and gay organization. Reasons for not participating included being closeted, homophobia, not being a joiner, or finding the participants to be younger and ageist. Most older lesbians prefer to be with their own age cohort. Thus, for some older lesbian women, isolation and loneliness can be an issue. Isolation can also be a function of geographical location, physical limitations, and the personality of the individual.

When counseling a person who complains of loneliness, it can be useful to determine how much is due to reality factors, for example, unavailability of appropriate places to socialize, and how much is a function of homophobia, fear of rejection, or a life history of limited social skills. It can be therapeutic for counselors to provide clients with resources for the older lesbian or encourage them to find their own. Some lesbians may need assistance in working through their negative feelings about aging. As Siegel and Sonderegger (1990) have aptly said, "Helping a woman to love herself as an old woman, and to acknowledge the pain and anger that sexist/ageist oppression has produced in her is a delicate task, requiring patience and compassion" (p. 180). Other clients may need help with their personal problems that get in the way of their relating to others.

Case History: Miriam

Miriam, a 68-year-old Jewish retired lesbian professional who has been gay all her adult life, entered psychotherapy for intense loneliness. She was in the process of recovering from a cancer operation and had come to the conclusion that the only way she was going to continue living was if she had a significant other. Miriam was determined to find that special someone. Because most of her close friends had died and she was no longer on speaking terms with others, Miriam was socially isolated. She had a few heterosexual friends but only saw them on rare occasions. Her three brothers proved difficult to relate to because they were unable to accept her lesbian lifestyle.

Upon the suggestion of the therapist, Miriam joined a peer group sponsored by the local gay and lesbian senior organization. There she met Roz, another Jewish woman a few years older than herself. Miriam was radiant and hopeful about their future together; however, after a few months things began to go down hill. Miriam continually criticized Roz for not dressing stylishly, for not having enough intellectual interests, for liking people Miriam could never respect. The relationship broke up within 6 months. Miriam was equally critical of herself as well as the therapist. She insisted on rephrasing what the therapist said because she knew how to say it better.

Miriam continued to attend the older lesbian peer group and complained about how bored she was because the women did not share her interests. She finally left. Just because one is an older lesbian does not necessarily mean that one will automatically have something in common with other older lesbians. In Miriam's case, however, it did appear that her isolation was in part related to her critical judgments and hostility. The therapist actively confronted Miriam with the way in which she alienated herself from others, using the client and therapist interaction as an example.

Over the course of therapy Miriam felt less pressured about having a life partner. She took more pleasure in decorating her apartment and in doing water colors, a lifelong interest that she never had had time for. Because places to meet older lesbians were limited and she did want to make friends, Miriam had to be open to other possibilities. Each time a new option was mentioned, she found something wrong with it. Once again, out of desperation, Miriam reluctantly attended an older women's group that was predominantly heterosexual. Having fewer expectations of these women, and with the help of therapy, she was able to relate in a less critical and demanding manner. Over time Miriam developed a small network of friends with whom she spoke on the phone, went to concerts, and participated in small dinner parties.

Conclusion

In summary, several cases are presented here that illustrate some reoccurring issues that midlife and old lesbians bring to therapy. Some of the struggles that these older lesbians experience are a function of their unique position as self-identified women in a society in which females are the "other." For some lesbian women their problems can be related to the social oppression of women, lesbians, and older individuals. Not only are older lesbians dealing with such familiar women's issues as taking risks and pleasing others, they are also dealing with the need to create their own family, homophobia in the community, and their own internalized negative stereotypes of being old and lesbian. And finally, each individual brings her own personal dynamics to each of these areas. Counselors and therapists can be more helpful if they are aware of the complexities of the lives of older lesbians and the interplay among the different levels of their experience.

References

Adelman, M. (1986). *Long time passing: Lives of older lesbians*. Boston: Alyson.

Adelman, M. (1988). Quieting our fears: Lesbians and aging. *Outlook: National Lesbian and Gay Quarterly, 1,* 78–81.

Almvig, C. (1982). *The invisible minority: Aging and lesbians*. New York: Utica College of Syracuse University.

Berger, R. (1982). The unseen minority: Older gays and lesbians. *Social Work, 27,* 236–242.

Berger, R. (1984). Realities of gay and lesbian aging. *Social Work, 29,* 57–62.

Bradford, J., & Ryan, C. (1991). Who we are: Health concerns of middle-aged lesbians. In B. Sang, J. Warshow, & A. Smith (Eds.), *Lesbians at midlife: The creative transition* (pp. 147–163). San Francisco: Spinster.

Charbonneau, C., & Lander, P. (1991). Redefining sexuality: Women becoming lesbian in midlife. In B. Sang, J. Warshow, & A. Smith (Eds.), *Lesbians at midlife: The creative transition,* (pp. 35–43). San Francisco: Spinster.

Coleman, E. (Ed.). (1987). *Psychotherapy with homosexual men and women: Integrated identity approaches for clinical practice*. New York: Haworth.

Copper, B. (1988). *Over the hill: Reflections on ageism between women*. Freedom, CA: Crossing Press.

Downing, C. (1987). *Journey through menopause: A personal rite of passage*. New York: Crossroad.

Friend, R. (1987). The individual and social psychology of aging: Clinical implications for lesbians and gay men. *Journal of Homosexuality, 14,* 307–331.

Gonsiorek, J. (Ed.). (1982). *Homosexuality and psychotherapy*. New York: Haworth.

Hall, M., & Gregory, A. (1991). Subtle balances: Love and work in lesbian relationships. In B. Sang, J. Warshow, & A. Smith (Eds.), *Lesbians at midlife: The creative transition* (pp. 122–133). San Francisco: Spinster.

Hayes, S. (1991). Financial planning for retirement. In B. Sang, J. Warshow, & A. Smith (Eds.), *Lesbians at midlife: The creative transition* (pp. 245–257). San Francisco: Spinster.

Junge, M., & Mays, V. (1985). Women in their 40s: A group portrait and implications for psychotherapy. *Women and Therapy, 4,* 3–19.

Kehoe, M. (1986). Lesbians over 65: A triply invisible minority. *Journal of Homosexuality, 12,* 139–152.

Kehoe, M. (1988). *Lesbians over 60 speak for themselves.* New York: Harrington
Park.

Kirkpatrick, M. (1989). Lesbians: A different middle-age? In J. Oldham & R.
Liebert (Eds.), *New psychoanalytic perspectives: The middle years* (pp. 135–
148). New Haven, CT: Yale University Press.

Levinson, D. (1978). *The seasons of a man's life.* New York: Knopf.

Macdonald, B., & Rich, C. (1984). *Look me in the eye: Old women, aging, and
ageism.* San Francisco: Spinster/ Aunt Lute.

McGrath, E. (1990, August). *New treatment strategies for women in the middle.*
Paper presented at the annual convention of the American Psychological
Association, Boston.

Neugarten, B. (1968). *Middle-aged and aging.* Chicago: University of Chicago
Press.

Nichols, M. (1986). *Turning 40 in the 80s: Personal crisis, time for change.* New
York: Norton.

Posin, R. (1991). Ripening. In B. Sang, J. Warshow, & A. Smith (Eds.), *Lesbians
at midlife: The creative transition* (pp. 143–146) San Francisco: Spinster.

Raphael, S., & Robinson, M. (1984). The older lesbian: Love relationships and
friendship patterns. In T. Darty & S. Potter (Eds.), *Women-identified women*
(pp. 67–82). Palo Alto, CA: Mayfield.

Riddle, D., & Sang, B. (1978). Psychotherapy with lesbians. *Journal of Social
Issues, 34,* 84–100.

Rothschild, M. (1991). Life as improvisation. In B. Sang, J. Warshow, & A. Smith
(Eds.), *Lesbians at midlife: The creative transition,* (pp. 91–107). San Francisco: Spinster.

Rubin, L. (1979). *Women of a certain age: The midlife search for self.* New York:
Harper & Row.

Sands, R., & Richardson, V. (1986). Clinical practice with women in their middle
years. *Social Work, 31,* 36–42.

Sang, B. (1977). Psychotherapy with lesbians. Some observations and tentative
generalizations. In E. Rawlings & D. Carter (Eds.), *Psychotherapy for women:
Treatment towards equality* (pp. 266–275). Springfield, IL: Thomas.

Sang, B. (1982, August). *The impact of the women's movement on lesbian relationships.* Paper presented at the annual convention of the American
Psychological Association, Washington, DC.

Sang, B. (1990). Reflections of midlife lesbians on their adolescence. In E.
Rosenthal (Ed.), *Women, aging, and ageism* (pp. 111–117). New York: Harrington Park.

Sang, B. (1991). Moving towards balance and integration. In B. Sang, J. Warshow,
& A. Smith (Eds.), *Lesbians at midlife: The creative transition* (pp. 206–
214). San Francisco: Spinster.

Sang, B. (In press). Midlife as a creative time for lesbians. In G. Vida (Ed.), *Our
right to love.* New York: Penguin Books.

Sheinkin, L., & Golden, G. (1985). Therapy with women in the later stages of
life: A symbolic quest. *Women and Therapy, 4,* 83–92.

Siegel, R., & Sonderegger, T. (1990). Ethical considerations in feminist psychotherapy with women over 60. In H. Lerman & N. Porter (Eds.), *Feminist ethics in psychotherapy* (pp. 176–184). New York: Springer.

Sowle, J. (1989). *The web of motherhood: The psychology of lesbian-feminist mothers.* Unpublished doctoral dissertation, Union Graduate School, Cincinnati, OH.

Stein, T., & Cohen, C. (1986). *Contemporary perspective on psychotherapy with lesbians and gay men.* New York: Plenum.

Steuer, J. (1982). Psychotherapy with older women: Ageism and sexism in traditional practice [Special issue: Psychotherapy in later life]. *Psychotherapy Theory Research and Practice, 19,* 429–436.

Woodman, N. (1987, September). *Lesbian women in their midyears: Issues and implications for practice.* Paper presented at the health/mental health conference of the National Association of Social Workers, New Orleans.

4

Eros, the Aging Years: Counseling Older Gay Men

Fernando J. Gutiérrez, EdD

The stereotype of older gay men depicts them as lonely, depressed, oversexed, effeminate, and living a life without support of family and friends. This stereotype has been challenged by Adelman (1990), Friend (1990), and Kimmel (1978). The purpose of this chapter is to examine the issues of maladjustment with which some older and aging gay men, men 40 and over, are confronted. Two case studies highlight how a counselor might work with each client to further growth and adjustment to the gay golden years. Four developmental processes are examined: (1) individual identity development issues (Erikson, 1980), (2) difficulties in passing through the stages of Levinson's (1978) life cycle in single older gay men, (3) discrepancies in life-cycle stages within the couple relationship, and (4) discrepancies in stages of relationships in an older gay couple (McWhirter & Mattison, 1984).

Adult development and aging is one of the newer branches of the counseling field. Interest in adult development and aging in gay male culture emerged in the late 1970s (Kelly, 1977; Kimmel, 1978, 1979/ 1980). As in any other area related to gay and lesbian issues, the focus of the work has centered around demystifying stereotypes and documenting the reality of the gay and lesbian experience. Lee (1990a) suggested that:

> It would be more helpful for gay gerontology to admit that even the happiest senior sometimes fights loneliness, sometimes looks in the mirror and longs for lost beauty, is sometimes rejected by the young crowd at a bar, and sometimes wishes that sexual adventure were as easy as it once was. (p. xiv)

This warning is applicable to heterosexual seniors as well.

In order to understand the problems of maladjustment in older gay men, we must place these problems in the context of the mainstream homophobic and ageist beliefs of our society.

Homophobia and Ageism

It is evident in the literature (Adelman, 1990; Berger, 1982; Friend, 1990; Kimmel, 1978) that the problems of adjustment in aging gay men revolve around the management of stigmatization for being gay as well as for being old. Relevant contributors to the problem of maladjustment include ageism, the value orientation of time perspective, the socialization of gay men in an ageist and heterosexist culture, and noninclusive institutional policies. Ageism, the prejudice against someone because of age, and heterosexism are prevalent in our society. Recently, a retirement home in San Francisco allowed an outside heterosexual aging group to hold a support group in its lounge while denying the same courtesy to a gay aging group.

In their discussion of value orientations, Kluckhohn and Strodtbeck (1961) identified the value orientation of time perspective. Cultures vary in the value placed on time. For example, in Asian cultures, a strong value is placed upon knowledge of the past, acknowledgement of the contributions by elders, and the resulting respect accorded those elders. Some cultures, for example, the Latino culture, have a present time orientation and place emphasis on here-and-now interactions with family and friends (Levine & Padilla, 1980). Other cultures, like American society, have a future time orientation; therefore, the national personality—the collective personality of the culture that predominates—is one which is impatient with the pace of life in its hurry to get to the future. Society in the United States is not willing to slow down to accommodate the slowing down of its older people; it segregates the elderly and removes them from family by way of the retirement home, from the corporate world by way of early retirement. In doing so, American society is being deprived of the benefits of the participation of older people because of its ageist beliefs that the elderly are unproductive, overly dependent, asexual, unattractive, and senile (Friend, 1990).

Gay men have been socialized in a heterosexist and ageist culture; therefore, many internalize the value orientations of the mainstream culture. Kimmel (1978) stated that:

> The importance of a youthful appearance and one's status as a "sex object" can stigmatize older gay men—both in the eyes of younger gay men and in the eyes of the older man's own eyes ... it tends to segregate the gay male world into the young and the old so that effective links across these gay generations are less frequent than in the heterosexual world. (p. 128)

Berger (1982) pointed out that the problems faced by older gay men do not originate from their attitudes but from institutional policies, social service agencies' neglect, medical oversight, and legal discrimination. An example, given by Berger, is misdiagnosis with regard to sexually transmitted diseases because physicians assume that older gay men are sexually inactive. Thus physicians are often not able to recognize the presenting symptoms as those of a sexually transmitted disease.

Ageist biases are reflected in the research methodology of even the well-intentioned researcher. For example, Steinman (1990) conducted a study of the social exchange between older and younger gay male partners. The problem with Steinman's hypothesis was in the definition of the exchange benefits. Older men's exchange benefits were identified "to be heavily weighted in the direction of extrinsic resources such as material possessions, money, and services" (p. 181), whereas the benefits contributed by young men were weighted "in the direction of intrinsic attributes such as physical attractiveness, sexual appeal ...." Here Steinman expressed a bias that an older person's contribution is *external*, whereas physical attractiveness, a superficial and external quality, is labeled as an *intrinsic* attribute when in fact it is extrinsic; therefore, it becomes an equal exchange of extrinsic values by both the older and younger partner. The older man's contribution is not being perceived as coming from the intrinsic qualities of intellect, talent, expertise, maturity, and caring that allowed him to obtain the material possessions in the first place. The implication here is that the older man had only material things to offer the young person while the young person had more "personal" qualities to offer the older man, i.e., a good-looking body. The question for a relationship based on only extrinsic types of exchange becomes, What will happen when the money runs out or when the young man grows up and begins to age? The Steinman study failed to control for the intrinsic qualities of both the younger and the older participants in the study.

This practice of extrinsic exchanges is addressed in the following case study focused on Jack, a retired college professor engaged in transitory relationships with young men. The case illustrates how a counselor can assist the client in examining his intrinsic qualities, which can become the vehicle for finding more satisfying relationships and providing the client with an internalized sense of self-esteem.

Jack

Jack, a single 66-year-old gay White male, presented himself in counseling because of depression. He retired from his position as a college professor last year and was having difficulty adjusting to his retirement. Jack was very successful in his profession. He had many close friends and was active in professional organizations. At the age of 66, Jack was physically attractive and had the presence of an older movie star with class and style.

When Jack retired, his world began to crumble. Some of his closest friends began to die. Jack missed his students, particularly because he was proud of having assisted in their growth. Jack never formed a close relationship with a significant other. He grew up in a time when being gay was dangerous to his profession, were he discovered, so he coped by immersing himself in his profession and engaging in transitory relationships. Now that he is older, these relationships have become less meaningful for him and more difficult to find.

Jack had also met with his accountant to develop a budget for his retirement, and his accountant informed him that he needed to cut back on his spending. Jack commented that this was going to affect his relationships because he was used to providing monetary support to younger men who were destitute as a way of exchanging benefits for sex.

Jack's adaptational style was typical of the undisclosed gays of his time. One did not disclose one's sexual orientation, and achievement became a way of coping with the perceived stigma of being gay (Adelman, 1990). Note that this coping style fits with the value orientation of *doing* vs. *being* (Kluckhohn & Strodtbeck, 1961) inherent in the White culture. In a culture with a doing value orientation, one's sense of self-worth is obtained through one's accomplishments; whereas in a culture where the being value orientation predominates, one's self-worth is obtained through who one is, not through what one does.

Since doing is more valued in American culture and the being of gays is shamed, an unbalanced coping style favoring the doing side creates stress among minorities in this culture. In order to compensate for the lack of validation for being gay, or a minority, a person may attempt to obtain his or her self-esteem only from doing. This means that in order to maintain self-esteem, a person must constantly be achieving. To complicate matters, when gays and lesbians or other minorities are not allowed to participate in the system because of who they are, not only are they being devalued for who they are, but they are also not allowed to achieve or accomplish anything in order to obtain a sense of being valued. This explains stress-related problems among minority cultures such as high blood pressure, alcoholism, and drug abuse.

Now that Jack was entering his last phase of his life cycle, Integrity vs. Despair (Erikson, 1980), he felt integrity as to his intellectual accomplishments but despair as to his perceived failure in forming a close partner relationship. Jack's feelings are consistent with Berger's (1982) finding that gay men are more likely to report life satisfaction when they are happily coupled.

The counselor assisted Jack in his grieving process around the loss of his job through retirement and the loss of his friends. It was obvious that Jack obtained much of his identity through his professional accomplishments, and when he separated from that, a large void was created in his life. The counselor also assisted Jack in reconstructing a positive and affirmative sense of self, a coping response utilized by well-adjusted gays (Friend, 1990).

The counselor explored some of Jack's interests. As the counselor worked with Jack in processing Jack's past, the counselor became aware of the richness of Jack's information regarding the history of gay culture from Jack's experience in living during the pre-Stonewall era. The counselor encouraged Jack to spend some of his new-found free time in documenting this history for the younger generation to appreciate. This gave Jack a new sense of purpose and a sense of respect, value, and integrity.

Jack also needed to work on his perception of himself as a sexual and feeling being. He needed to explore his values as to what he was looking for in a relationship. In the past, Jack had status by his association with young gay men; however, these relationships left him unsatisfied emotionally because the young men repeatedly abandoned him and moved out of his life.

By reconstructing a positive and affirmative sense of self, that is, by taking stock in his intrinsic qualities, such as his caring, seriousness, stability, and fun-loving attributes, and accepting what he looked like physically, Jack was able to achieve integrity in his life. He also began to look at relationships as something to please him, not as something to please others, so that, in turn, others could reward him with approval.

The issue of pleasing himself as opposed to pleasing others was an important one for Jack to examine. Jack's satisfaction in doing for others and helping his students grow was a coping style for him as a gay person. Internalized homophobia caused Jack to feel that in order to be liked, he had to earn the approval of others by doing for them. He learned to be "other" oriented and self-denying. Now at the age of 66, Jack is in Levinson's (1978) life-cycle stage of Late Adulthood. The task at this stage is to find a balance between involvement with self and involvement with society. In this stage, Spencer (1982) stated, the person is experiencing more fully the process of dying but also the possibility of choosing more freely his or her remaining mode of living. According to Spencer, it is a time of acknowledging one's human contradictions, creativity, and destructiveness. Once Jack reconstructed this area of his life, he began to seek relationships with younger men who were closer to his developmental stage and found these relationships more satisfying.

Older Gay Men in Relationships

Older men in relationships have issues to work on as well as older single gay men. McWhirter and Mattison (1984) found that gay male relationships in which one member of the couple was 10 years older than the other were the most stable relationships. McWhirter and Mattison identified six developmental stages through which gay male couples pass as they maintain a relationship:

1. Blending (year 1)
2. Nesting (years 2-3)
3. Maintaining (years 4-5)
4. Building (years 6-10)
5. Releasing (years 11-20)
6. Renewing (year 20 +)

Because of age differences or differences in experiences due to prior participation in other relationships, each member of a couple can be experiencing these developmental stages at a different rate. This difference in rate creates a stage discrepancy in which one partner experiences characteristics of a stage sooner than the other (Mattison & McWhirter, 1987), thus forcing the other partner into a stage for which he might not be ready and creating stress for him.

Lee (1990b) pointed out that as a couple ages together, they are both changing. Neither of them is the same person today that they were when they first met. As a gay couple ages, especially if there are large age discrepancies, there will also be discrepancies among the individual's developmental stages (Levinson, 1978). These discrepancies may become sources of problems in some couples, needing outside intervention to resolve, whereas other couples might be able to negotiate the discrepancies and adjust on their own.

Levinson identified nine stages in a man's life cycle:

1. Early Adult Transition (age 17-22)
2. Entering the Adult World (age 22-28)
3. Age 30 Transition (age 28-32)
4. Settling Down (age 32-39)
5. Midlife Transition (age 39-45)
6. Entering Middle Adulthood (age 45-50)
7. Age 50 Transition (age 50-55)
8. Late Middle Adulthood (age 55-60)
9. Late Adulthood (age 60-65)

Developmental stage discrepancies because of age differences were evident in the relationship of Shawn and Jason, an aging gay couple who have been together for 12 years. Their relationship had been going well, but in the last year some difficulties surfaced for which they sought counseling.

Shawn and Jason

Shawn and Jason are 42 and 52 years old, respectively. When they met, Jason was working as an engineer for a Fortune 500 company in the city, and Shawn was in a terminal graduate program in sociology. Developmentally, Jason, then 40, was in the Midlife Transition stage (age 39-45) according to Levinson's (1978) schema. Shawn, then 30, was at the beginning of the Age 30 Transition (age 28-32).

At the time they met, Jason and Shawn seemed to be at compatible stages. They were both in transitional life-cycle stages in which they had to evaluate the stages that they had just gone through and make changes in their lives. Their meeting provided them with a feeling of successful attachment to a significant other. The fact that Jason was older provided Shawn a sense of security as he was entering a stormy period in his development. The Age 30 Transition stage tends to be difficult for many men. Jason had already gone through this period and could support Shawn in the process, and Shawn provided Jason with the sense of adventure that Jason had missed in his prior stages.

Both men successfully navigated through the first four developmental stages as a couple, through the Building stage (McWhirter & Mattison, 1984), as well as through their life-cycle stages (Levinson, 1978).

During the 11th year of their relationship, Shawn began to experience some discomfort in the relationship. This year coincides with the beginning of the fifth stage of McWhirter and Mattison's (1984) couple stages: the Releasing stage. The prior stage, the Building stage, is a stage where couples collaborate, increase productivity, establish independence while establishing dependability on each other. In the Releasing stage, the tasks are to build trust, merge money and possessions, constrict (i.e., withdraw from each other in a healthy way), and take each other for granted. While in the Building stage, Shawn and Jason had to work together. Now, in the Releasing stage, they had to learn to separate.

Shawn felt Jason's withdrawal and began to fear that something was wrong in the relationship. This coincided with the couple getting a pet. Some of the attention was getting diverted toward the pet, and because the pet slept in the bedroom with the couple, the frequency of sex diminished.

Within Levinson's schema, Shawn, now 41, was in the Midlife Transition stage (age 39-45) and Jason, now 50, was at the end of the Middle Adulthood stage (age 45-50). The task for Shawn in the Midlife Transition stage was to evaluate the early stages. In this evaluation, Shawn felt that he wanted to go further in his career. Herein was the problem: Shawn and Jason were at different developmental levels as well as in different relationship levels. Shawn was still in the Building stage of McWhirter and Mattison's schema, as well as in Levinson's midlife niche-building stage. In his relationship to Jason, Shawn was being pushed into McWhirter and Mattison's Releasing stage at a time when he was not developmentally finished creating his niche. Jason's task at this point, in Middle Adulthood, was to make choices and give them meaning and commitment. But it is hard to commit to the choices when your partner is on a career move, especially when he wants to make a geographic move that causes your commitments to be uprooted.

Shawn was offered a faculty position out of state. He had declined two prior offers because Jason was not willing to move to the particular geographical area. This new offer was in an area that Shawn knew Jason liked. Shawn presented the opportunity to Jason, and Shawn perceived Jason as unwilling to compromise. This created a crisis in the relationship.

Shawn was feeling guilty because he felt responsible for uprooting Jason in their second year into their relationship so that Shawn could take a job across the United States. This move was beneficial for both Shawn and Jason because Jason received a 30% salary increase, and shortly after Jason left his company, the company folded and Jason would have lost his job. Shawn felt that after 9 years of stability in the same location, and after he had sacrificed two other faculty positions in order not to create a disruption in Jason's career, it was Jason's turn to make some sacrifices. This scenario is familiar to couples who are in dual careers. For Jason, however, being gay complicated matters. Most heterosexual partners can explain relocation to their prospective employers in the new location by stating the facts that their partner was transferred or was making a career advancement and that they simply were following their partner. A gay partner may have difficulty explaining this to a prospective employer.

Jason felt anxiety about being put in the position of interviewing for a job and having to lie. He is "out" professionally at his present job because his boss is also gay, but the new boss and the new company might not be so understanding. Also, Jason was at a point in his career where he was making a high salary, and it may be difficult for him to make a lateral move to a new company. This meant a possible salary cut for Jason. The couple was at an impasse. Shawn, in frustration, told Jason that if Jason did not want to move with him, he might have to go on without him. Jason agreed to go with Shawn to the new city to explore the area and the possible market for Jason's career move.

The couple decided to seek counseling at this point. In counseling, the couple was able to review their relationship (Lee, 1990b). According to Lee, couples need to review where they have come from, how they are functioning at the present, and where they are headed in the relationship. The fact that Jason was willing to go with Shawn to explore the possibilities gave Shawn a sense of trust that Jason was not going to abandon him. Because they had been constricting, that is, moving away from each other in a healthy way, Shawn was feeling threatened. This reassurance allowed Shawn to relax more about where their relationship was headed.

The counselor was also able to reassure the couple that what was happening in their relationship was normal, thus taking away the fear that there was something pathological in their relationship. It was simply a matter of managing the stage discrepancies in the relationship and the developmental framework of the couple so that the relationship could continue flourishing while the couple could give each other room to operate within their developmental stages.

At this point, the counselor helped Shawn to explore his career options. The fact that Jason was willing to consider moving also let Shawn feel that Jason was being flexible. The relationship did not feel rigid and stuck anymore. Shawn decided to get retraining in his career so that he could make a career advancement without having to move out of state. This fit Shawn's developmental stage (Midlife Transition), and Jason could also continue establishing his roots in his developmental stage (Middle Adulthood).

Shawn and Jason model a couple's ability to put themselves in the other person's shoes and to look at things from the partner's perspective (Lee, 1990b). Lee stated that real talk is defined as "talk about the fundamental contractual relationships between the partners: the obligations which make a relationship's future more predictable and thus give it the stability essential if gay couples are to survive into happy old age together" (p. 147). Shawn and Jason were able to acknowledge their obligation to each other while considering their career transitions.

In counseling, the couple was also able to resolve the issue around the frequency of sex. Jason, at 51, was experiencing performance issues. He found that it took him longer to obtain an erection, and his interest in sex had waned somewhat. Jason also had some issues with sexuality. He came from a family in which sex was not seen as positive, so Jason carried many injunctions regarding sex and his sexual orientation. He was able to explore these issues in counseling and was able to enjoy sex with Shawn. Again, the counselor was able to normalize the experience of sexual functioning for Jason as something to which older men need to adjust (Kimmel, 1979/1980).

Shawn and Jason also learned that their experience with the pet was similar to a heterosexual couple's experience when they have a newborn. Sexual activity between the partners decreases when the newborn arrives (Bennets, 1990). Shawn and Jason learned to put the pet outside the bedroom when they wanted to engage in love-making.

Lee (1990b) talked about the process of the review of the relationship as serving the same function that a scrapbook or slide collection serves. Ironically, Shawn experienced this accidentally one day. In the process of exploring their relationship, Shawn was looking through their photo album as well as Jason's family photo album. This helped Shawn review the positive moments in his and Jason's relationship and created a renewal of their relationship.

Relationship reviews make the concept of "making memories" discussed in chapter 19 by Gutiérrez and Perlstein important. The couple is creating markers in their relationship that help to validate it in a world that does little to acknowledge these beautiful and thriving relationships that can last into old age.

Conclusion

As we have seen in the case of Jack and the case of Shawn and Jason, counselors need to view maturing gay men from a developmental rather than a clinical perspective. Instead of looking for pathology and evidence of the negative stereotypes of older gay men, counselors need to focus on at least four distinct developmental areas: (1) individual development, as in the case of Jack, who was dealing with the final identity development stage of Integrity vs. Despair; (2) difficulties in successful passage through the stages of the life cycle, also seen in Jack's case; (3) relationship stage discrepancies that can affect a couple's functioning; and (4) life-cycle discrepancies in the couple.

Adjustment for older gay men can be achieved by reconstructing a positive and affirmative sense of self in response to homophobia and ageism (Friend, 1990). As counselors, we need to look at our own internalized heterosexism, ageism, and homophobia so that we can free ourselves from our fears and become better able to assist aging gay men in achieving integrity in their final stages of adult development.

References

Adelman, M. (1990). Stigma, gay lifestyles, and adjustment to aging: A study of later life gay men and lesbians. *Journal of Homosexuality, 20*(3/4), 7–32.

Bennets, L. (1990). Sex after the baby. *Parents, 65*, 53–56.

Berger, R. (1982). The unseen minority: Older gays and lesbians. *Social Work,* 27(3), 236–244.

Erikson, E. (1980). *Identity and the life cycle.* New York: Norton.

Friend, R. (1990). Lesbian and gay people: A theory of successful aging. *Journal of Homosexuality, 20*(3/4), 77–87.

Kelly, J. (1977). The aging male homosexual: Myth and reality. *Gerontologist, 17,* 328–332.

Kimmel, D. (1978). Adult development and aging: A gay perspective. *Journal of Social Issues, 34*(3), 113–130.

Kimmel, D. (1979/1980). Life-history interviews of aging gay men. *International Journal of Aging and Human Development, 10*(3), 239–248.

Kluckhohn, F., & Strodbeck, F. (1961). *Variation in value orientation.* Evanston, IL: Row, Peterson.

Lee, J. (1990a). Foreword. *Journal of Homosexuality, 20*(3/4), xii–xix.

Lee, J. (1990b). Can we talk? Can we really talk? Communications as a key factor in the maturing homosexual couple. *Journal of Homosexuality, 20*(3/4), 143–155.

Levine, E., & Padilla, A. (1980). *Crossing cultures in therapy: Pluralistic counseling for the Hispanic.* Monterey, CA: Brooks/Cole.

Levinson, D. (1978). *The seasons of a man's life.* New York: Knopf.

Mattison, A., & McWhirter, D. (1987). Stage discrepancy in male couples. *Journal of Homosexuality, 14*(1/2), 89–100.

McWhirter, D., & Mattison, A. (1984). *Male couples: A study of how relationships develop.* Englewood Cliffs, NJ: Prentice-Hall.

Spencer, A. (1982). *Seasons: Women's search for self through life's stages.* New York: Paulist Press.

Steinman, R. (1990). Social exchanges between older and younger gay male partners. *Journal of Homosexuality, 20*(3/4), 179–206.

Section II
Marriage and Family Counseling

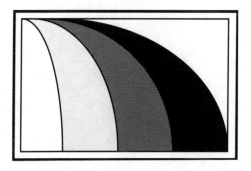

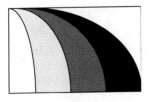

5

Counseling Lesbian Couples: Sexism, Heterosexism, and Homophobia

Bianca Cody Murphy, EdD

Lesbian couples are different from heterosexual couples. Although lesbian couples come to therapy with many of the same issues as their heterosexual counterparts, the issues and relationships with which they are struggling are often complicated by being lesbian in the dominant heterosexual culture. All lesbian couples are subject to heterosexism—homophobia, and sexism (the socialization of women into specific sex roles that are then devalued).

Lesbian couples are different from gay male couples. Although in both the partners are of the same gender, homophobia, heterosexism, and sexism affect male and female couples differently. The partners in a lesbian couple are doubly devalued and oppressed: as women in

The author wishes to acknowledge that discussions with colleagues Priscilla Ellis, Sarah Greenberg, Lin Reicher, and Sallyann Roth were helpful in the preparation of this chapter. The author also wishes to express her appreciation to the lesbian couples who shared their stories and gave her permission to share them with others.

a male-dominated, misogynist (woman-hating) society and as homosexuals in a heterosexually dominated, homophobic society. Furthermore, men and women are socialized differently, and therefore, gay
male and lesbian couples often handle the stresses of living in a heterosexual culture in different gender-related ways.

Lesbian couples are different from each other. Although heterosexism, homophobia, and sexism affect the dynamics of all lesbian relationships, it is important to recognize that the impact is mediated by
age, class, and race or ethnicity as well as by the unique dynamics of
each individual couple.

The counselor working with lesbian couples must be vigilant to the
ways that being lesbian in the dominant culture are reflected in presenting problems and relationship dynamics. She or he must attend
to the impact of heterosexism, homophobia, and sexism on the individuals in the couple, the relationship between the partners, the
interactions between the couple and other social systems, and, perhaps most importantly, on the relationship between counselor and
couple.

The following is a composite case study of a White middle-class,
able-bodied, lesbian couple with whom I worked several years ago.
The material presented highlights the prevalence and power of heterosexism, homophobia, and sexism on the lesbian couple and the
unique issues that they raise. However, it must not be assumed that
these are the only salient experiences of the couple's therapy.

Case Study

Eileen and Jackie were a lesbian couple who had been living
together for 3 years at the time that they made their first
appointment to see me. Eileen was a 31-year-old teacher and
Jackie, 30, was a self-employed painter. Both were White. Eileen came from an Irish Catholic, middle-class background
and Jackie from an Italian Catholic, working-class background. They lived in an apartment in a working-class part
of Boston that would be described as middle class.

They were referred to me by friends of theirs who had
worked with me in couples therapy 3 years previously. Eileen
and Jackie wanted to see a lesbian therapist, and they knew
before calling me that I was an openly identified lesbian
therapist.

Lesbian clients frequently ask to see lesbian-identified or lesbian-sensitive counselors. Many lesbian couples feel untrusting of counselors who they fear may pathologize their relationships. This fear is not unfounded. Numerous studies have shown that mental health professionals suffer from heterosexual bias and homophobia, and that stereotyping by clinicians influences information processing about gay men and lesbian women (Casas, Brady, & Ponterotto, 1983; Committee on Lesbian and Gay Concerns, 1990; Glenn & Russell, 1986; Graham, Rawlings, Halpern, & Hermes 1984; Wisniewski & Toomey, 1987). Despite official statements about the importance of sensitivity to sexual orientation, gay and lesbian issues are rarely discussed in graduate training programs or in the field (Burhke, 1989; Carlson, 1985; Dulaney & Kelly, 1982; Thompson & Fishburn, 1977).

Although it may be helpful, having a lesbian identity does not necessarily make the counselor free of heterosexual bias and homophobia, nor does it assure knowledge concerning the pervasive influence of sexism, heterosexism, and homophobia on lesbian couples. It is important that the counselor, whether lesbian, gay, bisexual, or heterosexual, be trained in issues specific to lesbian experience within the dominant society (Murphy, in press). All counselors need to have supervision to guard against the effects of sexism, homophobia, and heterosexism in their work (see chapter 21 for a discussion of supervision issues). In addition, the lesbian counselor must protect against overidentification with clients who share her sexual orientation.

Finally, the couple counselor who works with lesbian clients must be lesbian affirmative. It is not enough for the counselor working with lesbian couples to accept their lifestyle passively. She or he must be able to affirm actively the validity of their relationships and recognize both the specific challenges and strengths of lesbian couples.

The Presenting Problem

When Eileen called to set up the interview, she mentioned that she and Jackie were starting to have fights about "the silliest things," and although they felt secure in their relationship, they hoped that counseling would prevent things from getting worse. During our initial meeting, Jackie began by affirming her commitment to the couple. She stated emphatically that they were not there to break up. In fact, they had just decided to buy a house together. However, they found themselves irritable with each other and concerned that "things not get out of hand."

As they began to talk about their immediate concerns, it became clear that their negotiation skills were being tested. They began seeing each other 3½ years ago, and Jackie moved into Eileen's apartment after they had been dating for 6 months. Following what they described as a "blissful honeymoon period," they began to confront all those little domestic issues that most couples face: What is the correct way to fold towels— in half or in thirds? Should the shower curtain be left open or closed? And Eileen complained that Jackie never put the cap on the toothpaste. They felt that they had been through a rough spot in the beginning of their relationship and had found ways to resolve their problems. But now there was a dramatic escalation in the kinds of things to be negotiated. They had to decide in what neighborhood they wanted to live, whether they wanted a condominium or a house.

As they talked about this, they mentioned that they came from different family backgrounds. Eileen didn't want to be just like her parents with a two-car garage and a house in the suburbs. She wanted a condominium in the city. Jackie's parents lived in an apartment in a working-class part of the city. She longed for a garden, a big country kitchen, a den, and a finished basement for her painting supplies.

They were both quite discouraged. They thought that they were a couple who had a lot in common, and now they wondered whether they had anything in common at all.

The first task when working with any couple is both to refine and expand the presenting problem by attempting to understand it in a multiplicity of contexts that include the individual, the couple, and the family of origin as well as the larger sociopolitical context (Roth & Murphy, 1986). When working with lesbian couples, that includes understanding their presenting problem in the context of their lesbianism.

In the first session I included a question about what it meant for them to be lesbian women seeking to make these decisions. I was asking an open probe, not necessarily focusing on any specific issues. Eileen said she wanted to live in the city because she felt it would be "safer." She wanted to live in Jamaica Plain, a part of Boston that was known for its lesbian community. Jackie said that she did not want to be "ghetto-ized."

Lesbian women may often express fears about their physical safety. The concern for physical safety is realistic in a patriarchial society in which women are routinely assaulted by men. There is a 25% chance that a woman in this country will be a victim of rape in her lifetime and a 50% chance that she will be subjected to some sexually coercive act (DeVasto et al., 1984; Mims & Chang, 1984; Russell & Howell, 1983). Added to this, lesbian women are also subject to antigay violence (see chapter 14 for a discussion of therapy with victims of antigay violence). Herek (1989) noted that "In recent surveys, as many as 92% of lesbians and gay men report that they had been the targets of antigay verbal abuse and threats, and as many as 24% report physical attacks because of their sexual orientation" (p. 948). Lesbian women are victims of violence both as women in a sexist society and as lesbians in a homophobic culture.

Assessment

Part of assessment is understanding the couple within the contexts of their family of origin. I usually have each member of the couple do a genogram. With lesbian couples, it is useful to ask each partner to put on the genogram who knows about their lesbianism.

> Eileen said that she was not out to her parents but that she had told her only sibling, her married sister who was 2 years younger than she. Eileen said that she frequently brought Jackie home to her parents' house with her but that they pretended that they were roommates. Jackie was not out to her parents or either of her siblings, an older brother and younger sister.

The overwhelming majority of people in this country perceive lesbianism as sick, immoral, or criminal ("Gallop poll," 1982; "Newsweek poll," 1983). In a large national survey conducted by the Roper Center, 73% of the respondents said that "sexual relations between two adults of the same sex are always wrong" (Davis & Smith, 1984). Therefore, to be a lesbian woman in our culture is to be a victim of stigma and discrimination. It is no wonder that Jackie and Eileen, like a large majority of lesbian women, have chosen to hide their lesbianism from members of their family.

The decision not to disclose their lesbianism and the nature of their relationship can lead to awkward and inauthentic communication with family members. Many closeted lesbian women report that they feel a need to keep a distance from family members and feel isolated from meaningful contacts (Murphy, 1989). What closeness there is is perceived as a pseudo-closeness because the lesbian is hiding a large part of her emotional life. Family members may pick up this distance and respond in kind, resulting in a sense of mutual isolation and withdrawal (Murphy, 1989).

A woman's decision to buy a house or any major piece of property can be perceived as breaking the norms of female socialization. Even today, despite the advances of the Women's Movement, many women are expected to be economically dependent on men: They are expected to live in their father's home until they move into their husband's home. Although it is more common today than it was 20 years ago, many people perceive an unmarried woman's decision to own her own home as gender inappropriate.

> I questioned Eileen and Jackie about how their families understood their decision to buy a house together. Eileen reported that her mother had asked her what would happen to the house if Jackie decided to get married. Eileen added that her maternal grandmother said that she had been saying novenas that Eileen would have someone to share her life with and she was delighted that it was Jackie, whom she had met at many family functions. Eileen commented that her grandmother would be quite upset if she knew how much of her life Jackie shared. Eileen said that she was thinking that she would eventually want to come out to her family. She felt that she would feel uncomfortable having her parents visit the new house if they did not know the "truth" about her relationship with Jackie. Jackie reported that she would be the first member of her family to own a house and that her parents and siblings were very excited by the prospect. She was very clear that she did not want her family to know about her lesbianism.

Decisions about disclosing sexual orientation to families have an impact on the members of the lesbian couple as well as on the relationship between the lesbian and the rest of her family (Murphy, 1989). Each of the partners may make what feels to be a personal decision about coming out to parents. But there are consequences that impact on the couple. One particularly difficult situation is when the partners, like Jackie and Eileen, are at different stages of coming out to family. Often the woman who is more out feels that her partner's decision not to disclose her relationship reflects a lack of commitment to the couple. The counselor should help each woman in the couple explore the meanings that she gives to decisions about disclosure to family and encourage partners to acknowledge and respect the individual differences in family history that may result in different timetables for the coming out process. The counselor may provide the couple with resources on the coming out process that are written for both lesbians and their families (Borhek, 1983; Fairchild & Haywood, 1979; P-FLAG, 1984).

> While discussing the genogram, we began to talk about how decisions were made in their families of origin. For each of them, although in different ways, this was often along gender lines. In Jackie's family, her mother was in charge of things in the house: She decided on wallpaper, picked out the furniture, and Jackie's father paid for it. He handled family finances and made all the big decisions, such as where to live. In Eileen's family, her mother and father made all decisions together.

The models of intimate relationships in our society are heterosexual couples. Those are the couples we see on TV, read about in books, and discuss in advice columns. The members of these couples assume roles in relation to each other that are frequently based on sex roles. The gay or lesbian couple, composed of two members of the same gender, cannot resort to sex roles as a way of deciding how to handle issues in their couple. Brown (1989) suggested that gay men and lesbian women must be normatively creative, that is, they must create new norms that are not based on sex roles. Although this may be a liberating experience, it can also be difficult and lead to confusion and conflict between the members of the couple as they struggle to define a relationship pattern for themselves without readily available models.

Counselors sometimes ask which partner is in the "male" role. This is an example of heterosexual bias. Although, like all couples, lesbian partners may relate to each other in patterned ways, it is inaccurate for the counselor to overlay heterosexual sex roles on the lesbian couple. Studies of lesbian couples show that the butch/femme pattern is extremely rare (Cardell, Finn, & Marecek, 1981). Lesbian couples are more likely to have a relationship pattern that is based on role flexibility and equality. Lesbian couples in which both partners are socialized as women to be nuturant, caretaking, and relationship oriented are more likely to emphasize the importance of power equality, intimacy, closeness, and communication in their couple relationships (Eldridge & Gilbert, 1990; Peplau, Cochran, Rook, & Padesky, 1978). And not surprisingly, what they value in relationships is more similiar to heterosexual women than gay men (Peplau, 1981; Peplau & Gordon, 1982).

Couple History

With all couples, I take a relationship history. This was Eileen's first long-term relationship, and Jackie was the first partner with whom she had lived. Jackie had been married to a man for 2 years at age 18. She had also lived with a woman partner for 3 years from ages 22 to 25.

Most lesbian women have been in previous heterosexual relationships with men. Peplau et al. (1978) found that 95% of their sample had dated men, and others have found that one-quarter to one-third of lesbian women have been married to men (Bell & Weinberg, 1978; Blumstein & Schwartz, 1983). Many lesbian women report that these relationships were satisfying. The counselor should not assume that women are lesbian because they have had poor, or no, relationships with men. Lesbian identity is different from sexual behavior. Lesbian women may have had sexual relationships with men yet feel clearly lesbian identified; some women may have only had sex with women yet feel bisexual. It is important that the counselor be familiar with the literature of lesbian identity development (see Cass, 1979; Elliott, 1985; Sophie, 1988; Troiden, 1988).

Although not the case with Eileen and Jackie, some members of lesbian couples express concern when they have sexual fantasies about men. They worry that these fantasies mean that they are not real lesbians, that is, that they may be heterosexual or bisexual. It is quite difficult for a lesbian client to raise this issue, particularly with her partner. And it can be a delicate issue for the heterosexual therapist to address (Roth, 1989).

I also asked them about their couple history. How did they meet? When do they mark themselves as a couple? How do they define their relationship? When is their anniversary? And I asked them what the anniversary is a celebration of: the first time they met, their first date, their first sexual experience together? As we talked about their relationship, it became clear that buying a house represented a new level of commitment for both Eileen and Jackie, as it often does for couples. In addition, for them, as for many lesbian couples, the legal tie of buying a house together would be the first legal sanction of their couplehood.

The dominant culture disqualifies lesbian relationships, outlaws lesbian sexuality, treats lesbianism as invisible, and denies lesbian women the legal, religious, and social sanctions of their couple relationships. Lesbian partners can be prevented from visiting each other in the intensive care unit of a hospital because they are not considered immediate family; they can be denied the opportunity to provide health insurance for each other; or when one partner dies, the survivor may be evicted from an apartment they both have shared for 20 years. Because of the lack of societal recognition of their couple, lesbian women often seek ways of validating their couplehood, for example, by filing a power of attorney document with the county clerk. Seeing a couples therapist or buying a house together often provides the first institutional recognition of the relationship.

As part of their couple history, I asked them about their sexual relationship. They reported that they had had sex almost every day when they first got together, but by the time they moved in together they were having sex only once or twice a week. Currently they said it had been almost a month since they were sexual. Because I was a lesbian therapist who they knew had worked with lesbian couples in the past, Jackie and Eileen asked if their amount of sexual activity was normal.

Counselors often feel uncomfortable talking about sex. This may be particularly true for the heterosexual counselor working with lesbian clients. For their part, the members of a lesbian couple may feel uncomfortable talking about sexual issues with a therapist who they may feel is not knowledgeable about common lesbian sexual practices. The term *having sex* is usually used to describe heterosexual intercourse. Defining what is meant by lesbian *sexual contact* can be unclear. Lesbian women often have a "your turn, my turn" sexual pattern. If only one person's genitals are contacted, is that having sex? What about nongenital touch, caressing and kissing?

The counselor must feel comfortable talking explicitly about lesbian sex and should be familiar with information about common sexual practices and sex therapy for lesbian couples (see Loulan, 1984, 1986; Sisley & Harris, 1977).

Ongoing Therapy

Each of the members of the couple began to talk about what it meant to buy a house together. Eileen said that she felt as if they were getting married and that this was why she wanted her family to know of the nature of the relationship. She wanted her parents to stop thinking of her as a single woman. Jackie said that she too felt as if they were making a deeper commitment to each other and that she was quite clear that her parents would be highly disapproving and possibly even totally rejecting of her if she told them of her lesbianism.

Eileen began to talk about what it meant to her to be in a lesbian relationship with Jackie. Although she had lived with Jackie for 3 years, she felt that the decision to buy a house was a further commitment not only to Jackie but also to a lesbian lifestyle. We began to explore what were, for Eileen, the losses that being in a lesbian relationship in a heterosexist culture entailed. Eileen recognized that being in a lesbian relationship meant a loss of status and power. Jackie had a hard time hearing that Eileen was sad that she was giving up things that she would have had if she were heterosexual and married a man. Jackie began to be scared that Eileen would leave her.

For her part, Jackie felt quite clear that she was a lesbian and felt a sense of celebration of finally being able to have a relationship that validated her experience of herself. Eileen was grieving and expressing her ambivalence. Jackie was celebrating and feeling validated.

As lesbian women feel increasing commitment to the couple relationship, they frequently feel pressure to accept more fully their own identities as lesbian. When one partner in the couple is moving more slowly through the process of establishing a lesbian identity, sharing that identity with others, and deepening her commitment to the couple relationship, the partner who is moving faster may feel denied or rejected. At the same time, the partner who is moving more slowly may feel threatened with exposure (Roth & Murphy, 1986).

Furthermore, the lesbian woman frequently notices the discrepancy between the ways in which her relationship is validated and supported by the larger society, especially family, and the recognition and celebration of heterosexual couples. One or both of the partners may note with sadnesss and resentment the things that they did not get at the time of their coupling: a shower, a wedding, and presents. Although lesbian couples frequently reject these rituals, they often need permission to grieve over the loss of overt signs of familial and societal support of their relationship.

> We continued meeting weekly and worked on a variety of issues. About 4 months into therapy, Jackie and Eileen found a small house in a part of the city with a large lesbian community. They decided to put in a bid on the house. Jackie worried that they would not be able to get a mortgage. There was a salary differential between them. Jackie was self-employed and didn't earn as much as Eileen. As we talked about the meaning of this to them, it raised questions about how they saw themselves as a couple and how they planned on handling money. Until now they had maintained separate bank accounts, each contributing equally for rent and household expenses. Eileen had assumed that they would now pool their money as her parents did. Jackie, who earned less, felt that they should keep things equally divided so that it would be clear that she paid her half of all expenses. She wondered if she and Eileen were heterosexual if she would have felt as uneasy about their salary differential. She expressed her anger that the bank would be more willing to give them a loan as a married couple based on their joint income than as two "single" women buying the house together.

Lesbian partners, like heterosexual partners, often experience discrepancies in their earning potential (Blumstein & Schwartz, 1983). In heterosexual couples, the partner with more earning potential is often the man, and sex-role socialization prepares the members in the heterosexual couple for this discrepancy. Many lesbian partners have a feminist perspective and value both equality and autonomy (Eldridge, 1988). This can make the arrangement of finances a delicate topic (Roth, 1989).

Jackie and Eileen talked about who to use for a lawyer in buying the house as well as in drawing up the wills that they wanted to make. They had originally wanted to use a lawyer who was a childhood friend of Jackie's, but Eileen said she was afraid that the lawyer wouldn't know about how to protect them as lesbians. I asked them if they knew where they could find lesbian-sensitive lawyers. They found a lesbian lawyer who shared with them a self-help book on contracts for gay and lesbian couples.

It is important that the counselor be aware of the variety of support systems for lesbian couples that are available in the community. These may include legal and financial resources, activist organizations, lesbian couple support groups, and lesbian professional women's groups as well as newspapers.

Two weeks later, Jackie and Eileen went to the lawyer's office to sign their wills and the power of attorney documents. Jackie reported that she was surprised at the feelings that were evoked in her. She felt as if she and Eileen had just gotten married and that no one knew of this significant event in their lives. Eileen called a friend who came over with champagne to celebrate. Both Jackie and Eileen were surprised about how important and momentous that step seemed.

As already noted, the dominant culture provides few legal sanctions or public rituals for lesbian relationships. If the couple does not think about the changing status of their relationship, they may be surprised at what becomes for them a marker event. The couples therapist working with lesbian couples should encourage the members of the lesbian couple to anticipate and, if they desire, to plan rituals and celebrations to mark changes in their couple relationship (Berzon, 1988).

After signing the purchase and sale on the house, Jackie and Eileen felt the pressures to disclose their lesbian relationship become more intense. As they started telling people about the house, friends and colleagues began asking questions. How many bedrooms does it have? Will you have a roommate? Let's see the floor plans. Who is going to have the master bedroom? They were treated as single women who were buying a house together.

Jackie and Eileen began to discuss how they wanted to handle things when friends or co-workers with whom they were not out came to the house. Did they want to give people a tour of the house? Should they leave the bedroom doors open or closed? What would they say about who slept where? Should Jackie put her things in one of the bedrooms so that people wouldn't know they were sleeping in the same room?

Jackie and Eileen had to decide what degree of privacy and openness they wanted with the various people in their lives. They decided that they would have three house parties. One would be for heterosexual friends, and they would keep the bedroom doors closed. They felt comfortable being nondisclosing, yet not misleading them. With Jackie's family, they decided that they would deliberately lie, at least for the time being, calling one bedroom Jackie's and another Eileen's. Eileen decided that she wanted to come out to her family before she and Jackie moved in together. Finally, they decided that they wanted to have a third house-warming party with their gay and lesbian friends and those heterosexual people to whom they were out. For that event, they sent invitations asking people to come to celebrate their new home and their commitment to each other.

Counselors need to help clients explore the multiple contexts within which their decision to disclose or to conceal their lesbianism will reverberate. Lesbian couples who feel a need to hide their relationship often experience unknowing invasion of their couple boundaries by friends and family. The lesbian woman in a closeted couple is frequently invited to weddings, Bar Mitzvahs, and family picnics without her "roommate." Furthermore, the partners of the closeted lesbian couple may isolate themselves from others in order to keep the secret.

In addition, both partners in the lesbian couple have been socialized as women in a patriarchial society. They have been taught to place the needs of others before their own, to experience others' needs as their own, to inhibit expressions of anger, and to define themselves in terms of relationships (Chodorow, 1978; Gilligan, 1982; Miller, 1976). Chodorow (1978) argued that because women are able to mother, daughters, who share the same biological sex, do not differentiate from their mothers as completely as sons. Women, it is argued, have a stronger ability for intimacy and empathy but may have more difficulties with differentiation and separation.

The combination of the denial, invalidation, and invasion of couple boundaries by the larger heterosexual environment and female socialization with its emphasis on the importance of relationships may contribute to merger, fusion, and and other problems in distance regulation for lesbian couples (Burch, 1982; Krestan & Bepko, 1980).

Society's disapproving and sometimes hostile reaction to a woman's lesbianism can lead to internalized homophobia, that is, to the acceptance and internalization of society's negative attitudes about the lesbian self. Lesbian women may be particularly prone to internalized homophobia because women are taught that their self-concept depends on the view others have of them (Gilligan, 1982). Although there may be negative consequences to disclosing one's lesbianism, it is often this internalized homophobia that prevents clients from sharing the nature of their couple relationships with others (Murphy, 1989; Sophie, 1987). Counselors need to help their clients question homophobic assumptions that they may have internalized. Finally, the counselor can provide specific help and preparation to each member of the couple when one partner or both desires to come out to others. The counselor might use role playing to explore such issues as how different people might be told and how the lesbian can respond to their reactions. The counselor needs also to focus on how the decision to come out to specified others will affect both partners in the relationship.

In summary: Couples counseling requires that the therapist work on many interacting levels simultaneously. Jackie, Eileen, and I focused on a number of issues during our work together. For the purposes of this paper, I have highlighted those ways in which issues specific to their lesbianism and the attendant heterosexism, homophobia, and sexism appeared and reappeared in our work.

The Responsible Counselor

Not taking political stands is impossible. If we do not speak out against public policy that we know to be bad for mental health, we are in fact supporting such policy. (Sholtz, 1990, p. 11)

In addition to being trained as a couples therapist, the individual working with lesbian couples must take action to oppose heterosexism, homophobia, and sexism. Such activism can take place in a variety of arenas. First, the counselor must be lesbian affirmative. If lesbian, gay, or bisexual, she or he should be willing to be so identified. Second, she or he must be educated about issues that are specific to lesbian couples. Roth (1989) has offered a thorough and lucid description of these issues for therapists. Third, the counselor, regardless of sexual orientation, must explore the ways that her or his own heterosexism, homophobia and sexism affect the dynamics of the therapeutic relationship. Fourth, she or he should work within his or her professional organizations to insure that students and clinicians receive training and supervision on lesbian issues. Finally, the counselor who works with lesbian couples has an ethical responsiblity to take political action in the larger society to oppose the heterosexism, homophobia, and sexism of the dominant culture.

References

Bell, A. P., & Weinberg, M. S. (1978). *Homosexualities: A study of diversity among men and women*. New York: Simon & Schuster.

Berzon, B. (1988). *Permanent partners: Building gay and lesbian relationships that last*. New York: Dutton.

Blumstein, P., & Schwartz, P. (1983). *American couples: Money, work, and sex*. New York: Pocket Books.

Borhek, M. (1983). *Coming out to parents: A two-way survival guide for lesbians and their parents*. New York: Pilgrim.

Brown, L. (1989). New voices, new vision: Toward a lesbian/gay paradigm for psychology. *Psychology of Women Quarterly, 13*, 445–458.

Buhrke, R. A. (1989). Female student perspectives on training in lesbian and gay issues. *The Counseling Psychologist, 17*, 629–636.

Burch, B. (1982). Psychological merger in lesbian couples: A joint ego psychological and systems approach. *Family Therapy, 9*, 201–208.

Cardell, M., Finn, S., & Marecek, J. (1981). Sex-role identity, sex role behavior, and satisfaction in heterosexual, lesbian, and gay male couples. *Psychology of Women Quarterly, 5*, 488–495.

Carlson, H. (1985, August). *Employment issues for researchers on lesbian and gay issues*. Paper presented at the annual convention of the American Psychological Association, Los Angeles, CA.

Casas, J. M., Brady, S., & Ponterotto, J. G. (1983). Sexual preference biases in counseling: An information processing approach. *Journal of Counseling Psychology, 30*(2), 139–145.

Cass, V. (1979). Homosexual identity formation: A theoretical model. *Journal of Homosexuality, 4*, 219–236.

Chodorow, N. (1978). *The reproduction of mothering: Psychoanalysis and the sociology of gender*. Berkeley: University of California Press.

Committee on Lesbian and Gay Concerns. (1990). *Final report of the task force on bias in psychotherapy with lesbians and gay men*. Washington, DC: American Psychological Association.

Davis, J. A., & Smith, T. (1984). *General social surveys 1972–1983: Cumulative data*. New Haven, CT: Yale University, Roper Center for Public Opinion Research.

DeVasto, P., Kaufman, A., Rosner, L., Jackson, R., Christy, J., Pearson, S., & Burgett, T. (1984). The prevalence of sexually stressful events among females in the general population. *Archives of Sexual Behavior, 13*, 59–67.

Dulaney, D. D., & Kelly, J. (1982). Improving services to gay and lesbian clients. *Social Work, 27*(2), 178–183.

Eldridge, N. S. (1988). Correlates of relationship satisfaction and role conflict in dual career lesbian couples. *Dissertation Abstracts International, 48*, 3142B.

Eldridge, N. S., & Gilbert, L. A. (1990). Correlates of relationship satisfaction in lesbian couples. *Psychology of Women Quarterly, 14*, 43–62.

Elliott, P. (1985). Theory and research on lesbian identity formation. *International Journal of Women's Studies, 8*(1), 64–71.

Fairchild, B., & Haywood, N. (1979). *Now that you know: What every parent should know about homosexuality.* New York: Harcourt Brace Jovanovich.

Gallop poll on attitudes about gays. (1982, November 9). *San Francisco Chronicle*, p. 7.

Gilligan, C. (1982). *In a different voice: Psychological theory and women's development.* Cambridge, MA: Harvard University Press.

Glenn, A. A., & Russell, R. K. (1986). Heterosexual bias among counselor trainees. *Counselor Education and Supervision, 25*(3), 222–229.

Graham, D. L., Rawlings, E. I., Halpern, H. S., & Hermes, J. (1984). Therapists' needs for training in counseling lesbians and gay men. *Professional Psychology: Research and Practice, 15*, 482–496.

Herek, G. (1989). Hate crimes against lesbians and gay men. *American Psychologist, 44*, 948–955.

Krestan, J., & Bepko, C. (1980). The problem of fusion in the lesbian relationship. *Family Process, 19*, 277–289.

Loulan, J. (1984). *Lesbian sex.* San Francisco: Spinsters.

Loulan, J. (1986). *Lesbian passion.* San Francisco: Spinsters.

Miller, J. B. (1976). *Toward a new psychology of women.* Boston: Beacon Press.

Mims, F., & Chang, A. (1984). Unwanted sexual experiences of young women. *Psychosocial Nursing, 22*, 7–14.

Murphy, B. C. (1989). Lesbian couples and their parents. *Journal of Counseling and Development, 68*(1), 46-51.

Murphy, B. C. (In press). The education of mental health professionals about gay and lesbian issues. *Journal of Homosexuality.*

Newsweek poll on homosexuality. (1983, August 8). *Newsweek*, p. 33.

Peplau, L. A. (1981). What homosexuals want in relationships. *Psychology Today, 15*, 28–38.

Peplau, Cochran, Rook, & Padesky. (1978). Loving women: Attachment and autonomy in lesbian relationships. *Journal of Social Issues, 34*, 7–27.

Peplau, L. A., & Gordon, S. L. (1982). The intimate relationships of lesbians and gay men. In E. R. Allgeier & M. B. McCormick (Eds.), *Gender roles and sexual behavior* (pp. 226–244). Palo Alto, CA: Mayfield.

P-FLAG (Parents and Friends of Lesbians and Gays). (1984). *Coming out to your parents.* Available from P-FLAG, PO Box 24565, Los Angeles, CA 90024.

Roth, S. (1989). Psychotherapy with lesbian couples: Individual issues, female socialization and the social context. In M. McGoldrick, C. Anderson, &

F. Walsh (Eds.), *Women in families: A framework for family therapy* (pp. 286–307). New York: Norton.

Roth, S., & Murphy, B. C. (1986). Therapeutic work with lesbian clients: A systemic therapy view. In M. Ault-Riche (Ed.), *Women and family therapy* (pp. 78–89). Rockville, MD: Aspen.

Russell, D., & Howell, N. (1983). The prevalence of rape in the United States revisited. *Signs, 8,* 688–695.

Sholtz, D. (1990, August). *The politics of being apolitical.* Paper presented at the annual meeting of the Association of Lesbian and Gay Psychologists, Boston.

Sisley, E., & Harris, B. (1977). *The joy of lesbian sex.* New York: Simon & Schuster.

Sophie, J. (1987). Internalized homophobia and lesbian identity. *Journal of Homosexuality, 14*(1/2), 53–65.

Thompson G. H., & Fishburn, W. R. (1977). Attitudes toward homosexuality among graduate counseling students. *Counselor Education and Supervision, 17,* 121–130.

Troiden, R. R. (1988). *Gay and lesbian identity: A sociological analysis.* New York: General Hall.

Wisniewski, J. J., & Toomey, B. G. (1987). Are social workers homophobic? *Social Work, 32*(5), 454–455.

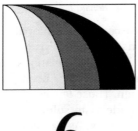

6

Therapy With the Male Couple

Ronald L. Hawkins, PhD

Many gay men who are trying to develop a primary relationship find themselves frustrated. They borrow relationship patterns from their heterosexual families, they observe relationship patterns through the media, they imitate relationship patterns that their friends use, and they invent patterns of their own. Some patterns work, some do not (Berzon, 1988). It is a trial-and-error process, and that is frustrating.

The frustration occurs as gay male couples struggle to find ways that both members of the couple enjoy and that provide a strong enough sense of commitment and security to be satisfying. This might be said of many couples, but gay men encounter particular environmental pressures that make this process especially painful and risky.

As gay couples begin a relationship, they may become increasingly aware of the lack of positive role models for two men (Clark, 1977). There are many reasons for this lack. In general, the American heterosexual culture does not promote but instead actually actively discourages images of men relating intimately, particularly sexually or romantically to each other (Malyon, 1982). Moreover, gay male couples generally develop with little societal support to help them in an atmosphere that is usually oppressive and pessimistic about gay lifestyle development. This lack of support and open antagonism reduce their chances of survival as a couple. Additionally, within their own sub-culture there are reasons for a lack of visible positive role models. Gay men may have few visible couple relationships in their social circle, especially if each of the partners has been predominantly socializing with other single gay men. Those few couples that are visible may not necessarily have found adequate solutions to the problems that the new couples are experiencing. As gay couples mature, they tend to socialize with other couples and remove themselves from the social scene in which the newer couples might meet them. The new couples may find themselves feeling stranded and isolated, thereby repeating some of the isolation they experienced growing up gay in a hetero-sexually biased family and culture. The couples that may have been together for some time may also isolate, particularly when they are experiencing relationship difficulties. They may choose to isolate be-cause it is a familiar coping mechanism from childhood, having been developed to hide their gay feelings. However isolation develops, it reduces their chance of resolving whatever problems they have.

Besides the lack of role models, two other major social processes interfere with and disrupt intimacy development in gay men. First, male socialization in the heterosexual culture tends to discourage the development of intimacy skills. The boy is taught to be primarily in-dependent, success oriented, and silent about emotion. Competition is taught to the boy as a fact of life that must be used when relating to most people. This training results in several characteristics: more aggressive behavior, a learned need for independence rather than re-lationship, an achievement orientation to everyday life, object-oriented sexuality rather than person-oriented sexuality, and competitive ways of relating (Witkin-Lanoil, 1986). As has been mentioned so often in connection with changing sex-role issues in this culture, male social-ization leaves men ill-equipped to deal with relationships (Goldberg, 1977). When two men then try to build a relationship, the problem is compounded because both are lacking in the interpersonal skills needed.

Homophobia, the second major inhibiting social process, further distorts the development of intimacy. The homophobia modeled by adults and peers affects the gay boy's development of identity. The gay boy usually grows up believing no one else is like him. If he does see socially visible gay men, they are often ridiculed or labeled as bad in some way, and thereby he believes he is bad. Most gay boys then learn through indirect but powerful messages that having sexual feel-ings toward someone of the same sex is an anathema. This usually results in feelings of shame about same-sex attractions, denial of sexual feelings, avoidance of sexual feelings, hate of self and other gay men, envy of heterosexuals, and a distorted negative body image. As the gay boy learns what others think of same-sex attractions, he learns to hate himself, and this is commonly called *internalized homophobia*. Many of these feelings are difficult to tolerate for long, and so the gay boy has to learn defenses against these feelings.

Internalized homophobia is often defended against through compulsive self-training in societally approved male practices: denial of feelings in general, except for sexual and aggressive ones; self-image and sexual feelings that are object oriented and not oriented toward emotion or intimacy; quests for power or illusions of power that are used to bolster self-esteem. These practices reinforce the male socialization and complicate further the possibility of forming and developing a relationship.

With all of these deterrents, the possibility of gay men finding and developing satisfying relationships may seem discouraging. However, many mental health professionals who work with gay men are heartened when they see the couple learning and growing despite the hurdles they must overcome. Many gay men feel understood when someone does validate just how hard the path is, but they may also need to know that it does not mean they have to give up. Many gay men have great inner strength that they developed while living in emotional isolation. With only a little encouragement from a therapist, gay men often put their inner strength into working through their relationship's conflicts.

Many kinds of conflict within the gay male relationship result from the previously mentioned socialization processes (Green, 1980; Malyon, 1982). Typical areas of conflict and frequent presenting problems include sexual difficulties, financial problems (either external or between one another), job or career problems, anger, violence, extrarelationship affairs, jealousies, and competitiveness. These presenting problems reflect the areas that men are traditionally taught as more permissible for men to develop: sex, aggression, achievement, and competitiveness. But without training in how to deal with their feelings and, even more basically, in how to recognize an area of emotional conflict, they frequently do not present themselves with some of the problems that actually trouble them the most. The helping professional then has to keep an ear open for the deeper, usually shame-laden, problem areas that the couple may not recognize or may be avoiding.

Underneath the presenting problems, certain syndromes frequently exist that are not identified by the client. These include one or both members being an adult child of alcoholic parents, abusing alcohol or other substances, surviving physical and sexual abuse either as a child or as an adult, and having one or more compulsive syndromes—sexual, spending, eating, or abusive and neglectful relationships. Obviously the early training for men to not talk about their feelings further complicates the identification of these syndromes and adds to the secrecy and denial so prevalent in their symptomatology. The clinician needs to be assertive in pursuing and exploring these possibilities and needs to be alert for denial as a frequent defense.

The professional must attempt an assessment of the general level of functioning of each individual within any couple—whether same sex or heterosexual: If either or both are functioning on a normal, neurotic, narcissistic/borderline, or psychotic level, how one treats the couple is drastically affected. The very nature of gay men's development in hostile environments, which results in internal and external isolation and the possible splitting off of their affectional and sexual feelings, leads some to develop defenses that are narcissistic (need for self-validation or validation from others) or borderline (splitting and acting out), as is generally true for persons developing in hostile, unsupportive environments whether same sex or heterosexual. But this does not necessarily mean that they have narcissistic or borderline personality disorders.

For example, an abused child may act out in aggressive or sexual ways and may tend to split off feelings and to behave in an inconsistent, radically contrasting manner (borderline defenses) or may need much validation (narcissistic defense or need). But to label the child as simply having a narcissistic or a borderline personality is likely to draw erroneous attention to intrapsychic causes and deny environmental responsibility. In addition, the abused child may drop these defenses if placed in a healthier environment. This latter situation indicates what Gonsiorek (1982), in discussing diagnosis and treatment of gay and lesbian clients, described as a personality overlay that has been developed to cope with a hostile environment, rather than a true personality disorder. In treating these clients, it may be helpful to tell them that they have grown up in a hostile environment and now need to learn to recognize and develop healthy, nonhomophobic, supportive interpersonal environments for themselves.

If the clinician notices narcissistic or borderline defenses, he or she must evaluate whether these defenses stem from early deprivations having nothing to do with the individual's sexual orientation and, therefore, constitute independent narcissistic or borderline issues, or whether these defenses relate more to a way of coping with sexual orientation in an unsupportive environment and, therefore, may be more amenable to change, particularly if a good relationship develops. This can be a difficult task, and consultation with a knowledgeable and nonhomophobic clinician may help to make such a determination. Moreover, the therapist must try to evaluate not only whether the environmental failure was early or late in development, and chronic or acute, but also the severity of the damage. Under the right circumstances, even late damage can be severe. Exploration in treatment may be required before these issues can be determined. The information from such evaluations and explorations helps the clinician determine how resistant or pliable the defenses are and what is needed to support their modification. Once a diagnostic evaluation and treatment contract have been concluded, the professional has a variety of treatment options available. Treatment possibilities frequently helpful in working with the gay male couple include education and information, role modeling of good communication and relationship skills in the treatment relationship, helping the couple to recognize and find healthy support for their developing relationship, exploration of deeper issues (dynamics and transference), containment (structuring sessions and possibly home environment to foster positive interpersonal processes and limit negative ones), and desensitization to and working through of shame reactions. Some of these are described in the cases presented in the following section.

Case Presentations

Three gay male couples illustrate some of the possible problems that may be presented by such couples and some of the ways to work with them.

Don and Phil

The first couple, Don and Phil had been together 2 years when they came for help. The principal presenting problem, which they both identified, was the lack of sexual relations for the last 6 months. Following the first 6 months in the relationship, they both noticed a decline in sexual interest between them, and each felt this was somewhat mutual and in contrast to an intense interest in the first months. The following year their sexual activity had declined steadily until they were having no sexual contact at all. Both feared that this meant that their relationship was doomed to end. Both feared this loss, but they were prepared to meet it, if need be, rather than continuing with things as they were. Additionally, Phil had discovered before their relationship began that he was HIV positive and had told this to Don before their relationship ever became sexual. Don was and continues to be HIV negative.

In the first session with their therapist, Don and Phil could express little more than their discouragement, their lack of sexual activity with each other, and their fear that the relationship would end. Although they were talkative, they were inhibited in speaking about themselves and their emotions. For example, in taking a sexual history from each of them, the therapist noted that they were uncomfortable in expressing what they sexually enjoyed. He also noted that there were differences in their sexual desires that were present long before this relationship began. Don preferred cuddling and oral sex, both insertive and receptive, and appeared to like sex with a much higher frequency than Phil. Phil tended to like to separate being sexual from times of being affectionate. His sexual interests were in insertive anal sex and mutual masturbation. However, they both were strongly attracted to each other and remained so. They had never talked about their sexual likes and dislikes, but they remembered how dissatisfied they were even a month or so after they had met when their differences in sexual interests became apparent. Don became more concerned at that point about whether he really wanted to get involved with Phil because Phil was HIV positive; nevertheless, Don very much enjoyed spending time with Phil. Phil had recognized Don's fears, and Phil wondered if he wanted to get involved with someone who was HIV negative. Phil feared that he might be abandoned by Don at some point if Don were to become more fearful.

As the therapist asked about their life histories, Phil told of being severely ridiculed in high school for being presumed gay, and both Don and Phil had never directly talked to their parents about being gay although they were invited to family gatherings together. These facts indicated that they both very likely felt ashamed of their homosexuality and relationship and therefore were struggling with internalized homophobia.

Intimacy was difficult for both of them. They noted in the first interview that many of the things discussed had never been shared between them, and that it was difficult for them to discuss these issues. However, they both showed excitement at talking about themselves and asked to come back to work on their relationship. In preparation for starting treatment, the therapist openly solicited their commitment to the relationship and the therapy and asked if they felt they were willing to cooperate in order to develop the relationship. Both felt willing. Their negotiation of their finances to pay for the therapy and their compromises in order to arrange a time indicated to the therapist that they indeed had some ability to cooperate (Reece, 1987).

The second session began with their reporting that after the first interview they had both spontaneously reached out to hug each other after they left and that it felt awkward. Exploration of their feelings about this occurrence got off to a slow start, but eventually they were able to describe their fears of being open with each other either affectionately or emotionally. Both were aware of a sense of embarrassment if they did not feel immediately validated by the other. Any hesitation or awkwardness was a sign to them that their feelings or needs were inappropriate (shameful). When the therapist asked whether they would feel comfortable hugging in his presence, they both quickly said no. In asking this, the therapist began eliciting the shaming transference that was an accumulation of direct and indirect messages from parents, teachers, media, friends, and strangers from their past who indicated that their affectional and sexual feelings for other men were bad. In the first few sessions the therapist simply encouraged them to express how they felt about various aspects of their lives and relationship. Occasionally he asked what they felt at that very moment. If this drew a blank, he sometimes asked more specifically how they felt when the other said this or that or when the therapist had responded thus. Sometimes the therapist also shared his perceptions or feelings about the moment as a way of modeling intimate communication. In doing this, the therapist helped Don and Phil to develop their awareness of the feelings in the here and now and their ability to communicate these awarenesses.

Feelings of embarrassment occurred often for both Don and Phil, indicating how much they had previously learned to be ashamed of their feelings, particularly their sexual and affectional feelings. In one session Phil recounted many of his high school experiences of being ridiculed about his homosexuality. For many years he had endured the taunts and criticisms of his peers. He had not been sexual with men or women until his first year at college when a male acquaintance approached him in a sexual manner. Phil had become enraged and forcefully knocked the man away from him. He immediately ran away from the man and was obsessed for days with killing him. Although he had never carried his feelings into action, he had feared since this incident that he might hurt someone and still feared his anger as a result. When Phil expressed this, Don spoke up that he now realized why Phil pulled away when they began any argument. Don said he had previously assumed that it was because Phil did not care enough to work things out, and Don had resented it. Now he realized that Phil was afraid. Phil also recognized how ashamed he had been of his sexuality to have become so enraged.

In the next few sessions, Phil traced some of the earlier roots of his fear of anger. Neither Don nor Phil had given any history of overt physical, sexual or chemical abuse in their families, but Phil's parents could be very hostile and emotionally cruel to each other. He had taken on the role of mediating conflict between his parents and between two of his brothers. He feared that if he were the one to get angry no one would be there to help him mediate his anger, and the previously mentioned incident had further proved to him that he could lose control of his anger.

During the same sessions, Don realized that his parents had rigidly directed him, had rarely praised him, and had never shown any real interest in his own wishes, and that because of these experiences he had come to expect no one would ever care about most of his feelings. So Phil's withdrawal during arguments and their decline in their sexual activity fulfilled his expectations. As they talked more openly in the sessions, both realized the many misunderstandings that had occurred. They became more comfortable in being angry with each other, expressing it outside the therapy sessions as well as during the sessions, and eventually they found they could resolve most conflicts at home. Sex could then more comfortably be discussed because some of the dynamics and misunderstandings had already been worked out in their handling of conflict in general.

At this time the therapist came back to the sexual desire discrepancies that he had discovered in their sexual histories. Don and Phil had enough communication skills and comfort with being in conflict at this point to talk about their sexual differences. The therapist gave them assignments, which were not focused on achieving sexual satisfaction but rather on discovering their sexual desire differences. This was suggested to desensitize them to being sexual with each other again. The therapist asked how they felt about safer sex practices, and both Don and Phil agreed that they felt comfortable following safer sex guidelines and that they both felt it was important to do so.

Talking about what they were feeling during their home assignments at these home sessions and beginning and ending these assignments with mutually satisfying activities, such as massaging, helped them contain their anxieties long enough to learn about each other sexually. Both had to face some loss—not all their sexual desires could be met. But with some acceptance they could return to regular and satisfying sexual activities because they could compromise on some differences, each enjoying certain activities more than others. Importantly, when the therapist asked, they reported no significant fears about health or HIV infection between them. Some possible activities were eliminated from their repertoire (e.g., Phil had never liked receptive anal intercourse, and neither Don nor Phil were going to take the health risks associated with unsafe sexual practices though they liked some of those activities), but both were satisfied with their new-found sex life, especially within the greater intimacy of their relationship. The therapy concluded with Phil and Don enjoying regular sexual activity, and they now had the skills to talk about and to resolve conflicts as they occurred.

Bruce and Jim

The second couple, Bruce and Jim, came seeking professional help after they had had what they called "the big blow up." They were not sure why all of a sudden they had become so angry with each other that they were both ready to end the relationship. Actually, once they calmed down, and by the time they reached the therapist's office, neither Bruce nor Jim felt he wanted to end it, but both were concerned over what had happened and knew that something needed to change. They described themselves as having argued frequently throughout their 13-year relationship, and the arguing had never seemed a great problem. Both of them came from families that were openly expressive of conflict and anger. Neither family was physically abusive, nor had Bruce and Jim ever become physically violent. Both of them thought that their anger was healthy because it resembled what they had seen expressed within their families of origin.

Initially the therapist was puzzled about what might have led to their anger escalating suddenly after many years. They seemed very loving and were openly affectionate with each other within the session. He did note after several sessions, however, that they sometimes entered into a teasing banter that resembled the kind of teasing that some men engage in in a locker room. The banter was often in the form of "sexual put-downs." When asked about this, they tried to push it aside as harmless and unimportant. As the therapist persisted in exploring it, he discovered that the men in Bruce's family frequently engaged each other in this manner and that Jim, who had no relationship of depth with his father as a child, had envied other boys who did tease with their fathers, brothers, or other boys. It represented a closeness to Jim that he had not had. But neither seemed to realize that this banter also expressed hostility.

About this time Bruce and Jim mentioned that Jim had changed jobs about 6 months before they had their big blow up and that he was now earning significantly more money than Bruce. Some of their teasing involved references to Jim paying for things. The therapist felt that at the bottom of this joking there might be some self-esteem injury, and he continued to lead them back to exploring the banter. Eventually Bruce admitted that he had felt himself to be a less worthy "man" now that Jim was earning more. He had even thought, at first, that perhaps Jim would leave him now.

Jim was shocked by Bruce's feelings, but after some prodding by the therapist, he discussed his feelings about the change. Jim slowly came to realize that he had felt unworthy as a partner to Bruce for many years before this change. Even though he was then earning about the same as Bruce, Jim had felt he was different and pitied by Bruce, although Bruce never did anything that Jim could think of to indicate this. When the therapist asked if Jim had ever felt this way before, Jim had to think. Then he clearly recalled how he felt with the men in his family. His brothers and father shared many activities from fishing and sports to, in later years, talking about business, their achievements and financial concerns. Jim had always felt left out and had assumed early on that it was because he was gay and, therefore, not as much of a man as his brothers and father. Jim realized that he had felt grateful to Bruce for accepting him in the early years of their relationship, but after his financial increase, he was aware of being proud of his success and wanting recognition from Bruce. He had not received this recognition and remembered being "insulted" by Bruce's "failure" to praise him. Jim paused when he said this and realized that he had always wanted that recognition from the men in his family. He wanted what he had seen the men in his family offer each other—validation of a sense of power and self-worth through recognition of their achievements (a part of their male socialization training that reinforced these narrow ways of finding a sense of self-worth).

These insights combined to allow a loving intimacy to develop between Bruce and Jim in the sessions. In the next few sessions, watery eyes were a frequent indication that their internal barriers were coming down. They exchanged many loving comments, and though they had some difficulty accepting such love, both voiced their desire to hear more and demonstrated their interest in not moving away from this developing intimacy.

After a few more sessions, the intimacy seemed to fade and some of the banter returned, albeit in a softer vein. The therapist pointed this out, and Bruce and Jim began recounting various incidents and comments between them that had hurt and angered them. The incidents often involved struggles for some form of power--decision-making power, power over resources (often money), or the power to validate one another. Often one or both of them wanted to be expressly recognized for something that was attached to their self-esteem. The next few months in treatment were spent in elucidating these issues. Bruce and Jim continued to struggle with what each has come to recognize as their vulnerability to the injury of their self-esteem. Both have learned that what the men in their respective families shared was far from ideal. The bravado expressed by the men covered a great deal of pain, and the men's sense of self-hate was bandied about among them and often projected onto the women in their families. Both Bruce and Jim, having secretly known about their own same-sex feelings, had felt sure that they deserved all the self-loathing that they unconsciously sensed in their fathers, brothers, and other male friends simply and utterly because they were gay.

Bruce and Jim are learning to recognize the injuries that commonly occur between them and are learning to let each other know what they need to help in the healing process. Frustration and anger follow at times when their needs cannot be met, but overall they are much more aware of feeling the enormous wealth of caring they have between them. Both have also established deeper relationships with certain family members who are open to discussing their feelings.

Bob and Allen

The third couple represents some of the most frequent problems encountered by therapists treating couples—whether heterosexual or homosexual (Bader & Pearson, 1988). These are the hostile, dependent couples, who often come wanting an immediate remedy for their problems but exhibit entrenched, hateful relating and scarcely any sort of positive interaction. These couples are difficult to treat, but because of the frequency with which many therapists encounter them, it seems important to address how gay male couples with such issues may present themselves and be treated.

Bob and Allen came for treatment and began arguing as they sat down. Bob mentioned the difficulty parking, and Allen pointed out that Bob was exaggerating and that if Bob had followed his advice there would not have been a parking problem. Bob withdrew in a pout. As the interview progressed the therapist learned that they were deeply estranged as a couple and actually had little communication. What they did have were angry, hostile arguments. The anger was mounting, and the therapist felt there was a possibility of incipient violence based on a history of violence in each of their families and on the recent escalation of anger between them. The therapist chose to be very directive of the initial interview because it was immediately obvious how intransigently hostile they were to each other. The therapist insisted on taking individual family histories and informed them that if they could not control their hostilities toward each other, they would have to come back for separate sessions. They calmed down, were able to complete sketchy histories, and actually added some information for each other that was helpful. The histories revealed that both had had verbally hostile and physically abusive parents, and that neither Bob or Allen had ever confronted their abusive parents with the abuse while their parents were alive. (Three of their four parents were dead.) Because the abuse began at an early age and continued throughout their childhoods, the therapist suspected that their hostilities were the symptoms of borderline/narcissistic issues that developed out of their families' dysfunctions and were not so related to their sexual orientation. This also indicated that their behavioral patterns would be harder to change. Their histories revealed that their sexual relationship had become sporadic during the last several years of their 8-year relationship and was now permeated with episodes of angry, hostile withdrawal as well as with teasing and taunting.

The therapist decided that the foremost issue should be containment of their hostility, so that the possibility of more positive forms of relating could develop. The therapist interrupted their hostilities in order to establish a contract to do just that. The therapist pointed out that their habitual, hostile acting out was their most serious problem, and that the first priority had to be working to eliminate their hostile interactions. They both agreed, but within the next few sessions, it became obvious how difficult this was for both of them. During these sessions the therapist asked them to negotiate rules for relating to each other that were more respectful and to which each felt that they could agree. The therapist was clear with them that unless they could come up with such agreements the therapy would have to end. The therapist understood that unless this could be done, the therapy would only be supporting and colluding with their hostile, dependent relating.

At the end of the first month of once-per-week sessions, they had developed rules for communicating. They could only maintain this more positive communication within the sessions if the therapist frequently interrupted to remind them of their agreements, but they returned to their hateful relating at home during the first few months. The therapy was contracted in 3-month segments with no threats of separation allowed until the end of each 3-month segment. At that time either partner could decide to stop the work and the therapy would end. This was helpful to contain their use of threats of separation to perpetuate the hostility. Slowly, they learned to referee themselves at home, and after 6 months they frequently returned to praise themselves for how they handled a particular situation that once would have inevitably become a battle.

As less time was needed during the sessions to negotiate and contain their hostility, memories from their childhoods returned that have helped them understand and empathize with each other. Both have come to recognize that they have reacted to their partner as if to their parents; both have identified that finding friends outside their families at an early age was a salvation. Their friendships prevented the abuses at home from further destroying the possibility of their healthy development. Bob developed a gay relationship at age 14, and Allen had a circle of gay friends, though no romantic or sexual encounter until college. The need for a strong bond outside the family from an early age had reinforced their holding onto their relationship no matter how bad it became. As they discussed the abuses in their families of origin and remembered tortures at the hands of their parents, they developed a mutual identification that has allowed them to feel closer to and more accepting of each other. Much more work must be done, but Bob and Allen are developing a relationship that demonstrates caring and now only rarely repeats the abuses of the past. They still need to work through their separation from their internalized parents and to develop more fully a sense of themselves as having more needs than just for a relationship in which to escape from a dysfunctional family. For the present they are providing themselves with a much healthier relationship than before and an environment in which each can heal and come to find a better life.

Conclusion

Besides involving all the usual clinical principles of working with couples, working with the gay male couple requires a balance of helping the individuals see how their socialization as men in a homophobic and sexist society has affected their feelings about themselves and each other, pointing out how they may perpetuate the abuses wrought upon them within their current relationships, and assisting them in finding healthier relationship patterns. Although not every couple can develop a healthy relationship, most can overcome the barriers placed between them by society and by themselves. Others can be helped to let go of a relationship that does not work well and further helped to find and develop new and healthier relationships.

References

Bader, E., & Pearson, P. (1988). *In quest of the mythical mate: A developmental approach to diagnosis and treatment in couples therapy.* New York: Brunner/Mazel.

Berzon, B. (1988). *Permanent partners: Building gay and lesbian relationships that last.* New York: Dutton.

Clark, D. (1977). *Loving someone gay.* New York: New American Library.

Goldberg, H. (1977). *The hazards of being male.* New York: Signet Books.

Gonsiorek, J. (1982). The use of diagnostic concepts in working with gay and lesbian populations. In J. Gonsiorek (Ed.), *Homosexuality and psychotherapy: A practitioner's handbook of affirmative models* (pp. 9–20). New York: Haworth.

Green, R. (1980). Patterns of sexual identity in childhood: Relationship to subsequent sexual partner preference. In J. Marmor (Ed.), *Homosexual behavior: A modern reappraisal* (pp. 255–266). New York: Basic Books.

Malyon, A. (1982). Psychotherapeutic implications of internalized homophobia in gay men. In J. Gonsiorek (Ed.), *Homosexuality and psychotherapy: A practitioner's handbook of affirmative models* (pp. 59–69). New York: Haworth Press.

Reece, R. (1987). Causes and treatment of sexual desire discrepancies in male couples. *Journal of Homosexuality, 14,* 157–172.

Witkin-Lanoil, G. (1986). *The male stress syndrome: How to recognize it and live with it.* New York: New Market Press.

7

Challenges Facing Gay and Lesbian Families

Jane Ariel, PhD
Sarah M. Stearns, PhD

The challenges facing gay and lesbian families are captured in an anecdote that could be titled "Even in San Francisco, Even in 1990." *San Francisco Chronicle* columnist Herb Caen mocked the theme selected for the 1990 Gay Pride Parade, "The Future is Ours," and when confronted about his comments, he explained in his defense that he was merely observing the obvious: Gays and lesbians don't have children (Caen, 1990). Indeed, it is a popular assumption that gayness is a state of compulsory childlessness, either because propagation is clearly impossible in a same-sex relationship or because a gay or lesbian parent, previously in a heterosexual marriage, is unlikely to receive the legal status or spousal cooperation necessary to continue in a primary parent role. This assumption also may be reinforced by the stereotypic impression that gays and lesbians lead self-focused lives in which there is neither the room nor the desire for children. Alternatively, gays or lesbians may be condemned for their interest in children on the assumption that they have pathological motives and want to recruit them into a "deviant" lifestyle or to molest them (Gurman, 1982).

Although it may have been true as recently as 20 years ago that choosing a gay or lesbian life style largely excluded the choice to bear and raise children, the current reality is that there exist multiple options that allow gays and lesbians the opportunity to form families and to parent. That this reality exists with such invisibility and absence of cultural validation and support is a reflection of broader issues of homophobia in our society. We cannot address the clinical issues that arise in gay or lesbian families without also looking at the social context and the developmental issues that are unique in the life cycle of these families.

Social and Historical Context

The progress within the gay parenting movement would be impossible to imagine without reference to the contemporary gay liberation movement that originated with the Stonewall riots of 1969 (Adams, 1987). The new-found visibility of the gay and lesbian community brought into the open the numbers of gay and lesbian parents who had elected to conceal their identity in order to avoid discrimination or rejection. In addition, insistence upon gay and lesbian rights brought attention to parents who were divorcing and coming out and to their struggle to retain custody and visitation rights in relation to their children. Historically, legal opinion substantially reflected popular prejudice by questioning the competence of gay and lesbian parents and projecting undesirable outcomes for children raised in a gay and lesbian environment (Harvard Law Review, 1990). Homophobic concerns were also apparent in studies pursued by researchers who looked for evidence that children were being negatively impacted by exposure to homosexuality (Hodges, 1986; Waters & Dimock, 1983).

The early and mid-1970s were a time of mounting legal challenge initiated by lesbians (e.g., the formation of the Lesbian Mothers' Legal Defense Fund to protect the custody rights of divorcing lesbians) and the appearance of art and literature seeking to answer questions about parental inadequacy from outside as well as inside the community (Kirkpatrick, Smith, & Roy, 1981). By the end of the decade, levels of awareness and available resources had dramatically increased, especially in communities with a strong gay and lesbian presence: Public workshops were offered to lesbians considering parenthood, and both single and coupled lesbians gained access to information and the technology of alternative insemination by donor (AID) (Noble, 1987). The 1980s then witnessed increasing recognition for the expanding number of gay and lesbian families. A recent *Newsweek* article (Seligman, 1990) estimated that there were more than 2 million lesbian mothers and gay fathers, and as many as 10,000 lesbians may have borne children (Gottman, 1990). In general, there was a broadening of pathways to the formation of alternative families, including adoption and foster parenting (Ricketts & Achtenberg, 1990) and the development of varied community resources to serve this population.

During this period, some progress was made in dealing with the misinformation and irrational fears that are components of homophobia. Substantial data have been collected that directly address the issues targeted by legal concerns. A comprehensive review of existing research (Patterson, 1990) has highlighted three domains in which the impact of lesbian and gay parenting has been examined:

- *Sexual identity*. Studies looked for evidence of disturbances in gender identity or sex-role behaviors and in sexual orientation.
- *Level of personal adjustment*. Studies examined personality development using variables of self-esteem, self-concept, or moral judgment and looked for the presence of psychological disorders.
- *Effect on social relationships*. Studies sought to identify elements of stigmatization, teasing, or isolation by peers, primary relationship dysfunction, and the longer term impact of life in a same-sex household (i.e., the possible influence of being cut off from important models).

The outcomes of these studies clearly and completely indicated no evidence of harmful effects. Patterson, author of the review, concluded that gay and lesbian families could serve as vehicles to force us to rethink traditional biases that implicitly suggest a narrow framework for healthy development. Long-term comparative studies still need to be undertaken to clarify the impact of alternative parenting situations, but Patterson suggested future research should be guided by positive inquiry about the strengths and values of diverse family configurations.

Even in this period of growth for the gay and lesbian parenting movement, many issues and obstacles remain. Parenthood, starting with the initial stages of conception, brings gays and lesbians into heightened contact with mainstream society. Dealing with the medical system, Lamaze classes, child care, the school system, and the child's peers and their families all bring up the issue of when and how to inform others of one's uncommon family structure. For this reason, many people report that coming out issues reemerge in a deeper way when they decide to parent. There is the renewed risk of rejection by others who may have been willing to accept a homosexual relationship between two consenting adults but who feel entitled to their prejudice when a child is brought into "that situation." Finally, relationships with extended families are often challenged when the presence of a child more clearly demarcates a new family unit, and continued support and involvement across the generations cannot be assumed.

Issues facing gay and lesbian parents may have serious consequences. One of them is the lack of legal status defining partners' relationships to each other and to the child, which can be crucial in the event of separation, medical emergency, and death. Such was the case of Sharon Kowalski who, in 1985, was seriously injured and hospitalized. Her lesbian lover was allowed neither contact nor say in medical decisions because Sharon's parents were appointed Sharon's guardians, and they did not accept the lesbian relationship (Thompson & Andrzejewski, 1988). In addition, there are routine issues such as filling out forms whose questions might not apply. These circumstances are unavoidable reminders of the marginal position of gays and lesbians in society, circumstances that continuously dictate that they take responsibility to educate others and advocate on behalf of their children.

On this frontier, there are no guidelines based on tradition or expertise and no official sanction from society. There is an absence of models, of affirmative points of reference, even of a language that adequately names the participants or communicates the experience. Internalized oppression often emerges due to the deeply ingrained paradigm describing a "normal" family. This may lead to the internal invalidation of one's relationships and one's capacity to parent, especially in a hostile world. Conversely, it may set up personal expectations to perform as superparents in order to defend against the over-attribution of problems to one's homosexual orientation (Bigner & Bozett, 1990). In the absence of historical precedents, gay and lesbian families rely heavily on the sharing of their common experiences. As one lesbian parent described it, hearing about other peoples' situations helped her "find her way along" and not feel so different or alone.

For counselors working with gay and lesbian families, it is important to remember the legacy of secrecy and fear of losing close, familial relationships that is an integral part of the fabric of the gay and lesbian experience. Similarly, it is important to remain sensitive to the continuing impact of ignorance and institutional oppression.

Configurations of Gay and Lesbian Families

A gay or lesbian family is a family in which two generations are present and one of the primary caretakers is gay or lesbian. Many various combinations of events can lead to the formation of a gay or lesbian family. One gay or lesbian family configuration occurs when children are born to a heterosexual relationship in which one parent (or both) subsequently comes out as homosexual and maintains at least partial custody of the children. In this situation, there may be a same-sex partner who forms a stepparent relationship with the child(ren), and if the new partner has children, there is the possibility of stepsibling relationships in a blended family. A second configuration involves a gay or lesbian couple who decide to have a child together in a co-parenting relationship and either conceive or adopt to this end. A variation on this may occur when, within a committed gay and lesbian relationship, one of the partners wants very much to parent and the other is ambivalent or in opposition. A third configuration occurs when a single person decides to have or adopt a child. A fourth configuration is when a child is born to other-sex gay or lesbian parents (or one gay or lesbian parent and one heterosexual parent) who decide to co-parent but are not in primary relationship to each other.

Each of these configurations shares general issues as part of its normative life cycle. These general issues and the issues specific to each familial configuration are discussed in the following sections. Clinical examples are used for illustration throughout. It should be noted that, given the nature of our practices and the fact that gay men are less likely to retain primary custody of children, there is more case material drawn from lesbian clients. It is also important to remember that case material has been selected from a clinical population and does not represent universal descriptions of experience within the general gay and lesbian community.

General Issues for Gay and Lesbian Families

Many issues common to the usual nuclear family also come up in gay and lesbian families, such as differences in parenting styles, differential involvement of extended family, problematic children, and allocation of family time and resources. Some general issues, however, pertain particularly to gay and lesbian families and may emerge in counseling. These issues, which include choosing parenthood, the roles and obligations of parents, role differentiation and gender differences, and the desire to parent, are presented here to assist people working with this population toward increased sensitivity and awareness.

Choosing Parenthood

The first issue concerns the decision about whether to have children, considering particularly the prejudicial attitude of most of the world and the often complicated process of conception. The decision of how to conceive carries with it questions regarding the anonymity of the other biological contributor and his or her degree of involvement. The choice of a donor can occur within a range of options: intentional casual sexual contact, the selection of an anonymous sperm donor, or the choice of a known donor (e.g., a helpful friend, a partner's family member) who may be interested in participating in a relationship with the child as a support person or a primary parent. This last option can be a cause for concern. In one case, a lesbian partner expressed in therapy that if they chose an involved father, she would feel like the "third" parent—a role that would not match the level of commitment and responsibility she envisioned for herself in raising a child.

In another case, a single lesbian came for counseling when her intention to be inseminated by a gay friend backfired after 5 years of preparation. She found herself in the position of having to reconsider all of the choices that had gone into the now abandoned plan. Her disappointment about the loss of the arrangement made her hesitant to look for another known donor, and yet she was still attached to the idea of having personal knowledge of the other biological contributor. She wanted her child to have the option of a relationship with its father. The counseling allowed her to explore her many mixed feelings about selecting a donor (including grieving for the lost donor) and to weigh anew the options in light of her own and the future child's needs.

As people consider these choices, they are likely to be faced with the need to negotiate and define for themselves the nonbiological parent's role. Unlike a stepparent who comes into an already determined situation, this gay or lesbian co-parent has elected to participate fully in the birth of a child and yet has no legal rights. At this writing, fewer than 20 couples have succeeded in petitioning for the nonbiological parent to adopt the child. In states in which there is no legal mandate prohibiting homosexual adoptive or foster parents, gays and lesbians still must find a judge who is sympathetic to their case and a social worker who will advocate for the fitness of their home. This is an arduous process involving the whim of the court and the social service system (Schetky & Benedek, 1985).

Some lesbian couples prefer the legal security and role clarity of a noninvolved donor that can enhance their sense of primacy as co-mothers. Similarly, gay men may choose adoption or the use of a surrogate mother to create a clear boundary around their family. In contrast, some couples prioritize the availability of a fathering or mothering figure because they wish their child to have full knowledge of his or her origin as well as the experience of an other-sex role model. As mentioned before, there are few precedents to guide people in their decision.

Roles and Obligations of Parents

A second issue is how to determine both the rights and obligations of parent to child in the absence of blood relationships. Is the nonbiological partner in a negotiable position regarding his or her parenting role, especially in regard to any on-going role should the relationship break up? This can become very complex: When gay and lesbian relationships end, there can be a network of multiple ex-partners (and perhaps their extended families), who may feel entitled to sustain meaningful relationships with the child and could be hurt if the biological parent uses legal custody as the grounds to sever the ex-partner contacts. Conversely, other ex-lovers may think nothing of breaking the bond with the child and feel no obligation to parent, leaving the partner and child without his or her support.

Given the absence of a legal framework, negotiation of clear contracts becomes very important prior to any crisis in which hostility or hurt feelings may interfere with a clear resolution of each partner's ongoing role in relation to the child. A counselor needs to be aware that the uncertainty surrounding these commitments can contribute additional stressors in the family and add to the confusion and pain of the children.

In one case, a couple came into therapy to receive help in resolving issues around the complexity of postbreakup relationships. Jeannie had a son, Tony, from her earlier relationship and had been continuing to share co-parenting responsibilities with her first ex-partner, Jan. Jeannie and Bev, Jeannie's current partner, then decided to have a child together, with Bev as the biological mother and a close friend, Steve, as the biological father. When Annie was born, she was cared for by Bev and Jeannie (primarily by Bev who became a stay-at-home mom for both kids), had regular contact with Steve, and had an active sibling relationship with Tony, which at times brought her into contact with Jan and her new lover.

Bev and Jeannie's breakup was sudden and involved many hurt and angry feelings. Their orginal contract had clearly committed Jeannie to a primary parenting role, but it was difficult for Bev to support an arrangement where 2-year-old Annie would be shuttling back and forth between Bev's new home, Steve's home, and Jeannie's home with her new lover. Further complications arose around providing on-going contact for Bev with Tony and Tony with Annie, and around the degree of involvement that Jeannie's new lover would have with the children.

The therapy consisted of providing a consistent framework in which different aspects of the relationship and the separation could be discussed with a third person to help avoid disruptive emotional explosions. It was particularly important to confront ways in which the children were being used as instruments of battle. In subtle ways, access to the children had been denied by one or the other of the partners, and there had been an increasing lack of consideration concerning visitation arrangements. It also became clear that one parent sometimes influenced a child negatively concerning the other parent when she was feeling hurt or angry. This was an important insight that helped the behavior to become more conscious.

The therapist participated in clarifying all specific agreements to facilitate the continuation of the separation process. This included financial and property divisions as well as decisions concerning the children's welfare. Each of the partners was encouraged to say what she needed and wanted as the separation became more resolved, such as how new partners might be involved in parenting or how much communication each wanted with the other.

When unresolved anger and pain disturbed the process, the partners were encouraged to look at some of their own individual issues and at the way they interacted as well as at the expectations they had had of the relationship. They agreed that it would be important, when emotions cooled down, to come back together in therapy to explore further why their dream of creating a family together had failed, so that, with a deeper understanding of themselves, they could continue to be effective co-parents and perhaps friends at some time in the future.

Role Differentiation and Gender Differences

Role differentiation is another issue facing the gay and lesbian family. Within same-gender relationships, both individuals have been socialized to develop certain skills and neglect others. Therefore, the evolution of role complementarity is less organic and has to be more deliberate. In lesbian relationships, both women may most easily experience themselves in the maternal, nurturing role, so issues of overparenting may arise. As one lesbian described her household, she reported frequently hearing in stereo, "Don't forget to wear your jacket" or "Do you need to go to the bathroom?"

Further, issues of direct competition can frequently emerge because both women desire gratification from the role of primary parent. Partners can experience jealousy and hurt, for example, when their child's affectional preferences shift over time. A lesbian couple came into therapy when the biological mother was feeling extremely anxious over the fact that her 3-year-old son was showing distinct preference for her partner. The tension dissolved when the couple began to understand that each parent can contribute significantly to the child's development by providing different experiences that can be appropriate at different times and in different circumstances. In this case, the nonbiological partner's calmness and willingness to sit quietly attracted the child during a certain stage of his exploratory play.

Competition can also be felt when one partner, for one reason or another, becomes more involved in a specific aspect of the child's life. This can happen in the child care setting or the school when a teacher may talk more to one parent. It can happen through contact with one of the extended families if it is more giving than the other or more attentive to the blood-related partner.

Another effect of training for certain roles is felt in the material sphere. Neither woman may be prepared to assume primary financial responsibility for the family, in part because of women's reduced earning power relative to men's (U.S. Department of Labor, 1981) and ambivalence about assuming the role of provider. Limited financial resources can cause much strain in the couple's relationship, and often the two women find it difficult to know whether and how to share the resources.

A couple who was co-parenting came in for mediation after the primary relationship ended. The biological mother said she was very angry at her partner because she had been "supporting" her and the child for several years. Although this had been their agreement, she was now insisting that her partner pay her back, even though their earning capacities were significantly different. Both because of unresolved conflicts in the relationship and the lack of models and precedents for dealing with financial issues, this couple was very confused about their obligations and rights. The therapy helped the couple to examine their embedded expectations around money and roles and to address separately the practical and emotional consequences of breaking up.

The issues for men as co-parents that arise as a result of gender socialization appear to be somewhat different. For example, one issue for men can involve learning to assess their feelings of resentment or alienation when faced with women who are accustomed to being in charge in situations requiring child care, or who may inadvertently invalidate men in the role of caregivers. This can happen, for example, when men are excluded from parenting circles, such as at day care or at the playground, because it is assumed that they are *not* in a primary parent role. One gay father told of numerous occasions at the supermarket or in the park in which comments were made that implied that he was just standing in until the child's mother was available. His feelings of being personally slighted as well as his own self-doubts could be addressed when the counselor labeled them as gender-related biases and provided support for him to insist on having the space to parent in his own way and to ask for recognition of his role.

In the absence of a social environment that embraces the nurturing role of fathers, gay parents frequently have to struggle to oppose the stereotypic roles assigned males in parenting. For example, there can be greater pressure on men than on women to accept the long work hours or the frequent travel often required for professional advancement. Because men may lose more stature in the workplace when family commitments take precedence and because employers are less likely to affirm their primary parenting role, they may need support and validation for insisting on the prioritization of their parenting responsibilities. However, recent research shows that given the struggle that gay fathers often have endured to be able to create their own families, they are already highly motivated to take care of their children (Bigner & Bozett, 1990; Bigner & Jacobsen, 1989).

Desire to Parent

Another issue that can cause severe problems is a discrepancy in the desire to parent. This may come up whether a couple's relationship preexists the birth of the child or whether the partner joins the family afterwards, believing that she or he can remain separate from parenting responsiblities. For some women, accepting a lesbian identity may have included resolving to relinquish the option of parenting, and there can be resentment when the decision needs to be reevaluated.

Susan and Amanda came to therapy because they seemed to be constantly fighting over Susan's two young children. Amanda was constantly annoyed at their behavior and blamed them for the fact that she did not have more time with Susan. Susan felt torn between her lover and her children, guilty when she felt forced to choose between them and resentful that Amanda was not invested in mothering. In the course of therapy, it emerged that Amanda had never been interested in parenting but was very dependent and attached to Susan and wanted to stay with her. Susan became aware that she was frightened of her children's reactions to her lesbianism and therefore held herself back from showing affection openly to Amanda, sometimes even excluding her from family functions. Over time, the couple learned to make compromises and deal with each other directly rather than through resentment about the children, but the issues around homophobia and dependency often kept them distant.

Specific Issues in Different Gay and Lesbian Family Configurations

The Gay or Lesbian Blended Family

A common situation leading to a gay or lesbian blended family occurs when a heterosexual marriage breaks up and one of the parents owns his or her gayness, retaining at least partial and often full custody of the children. (Other kinds of blended families occur when two gays or lesbians each with children come together.) Because of the varied needs and reactions of different people involved, and the divisive effects of homophobia, many questions arise: How much information is to be given to whom? If there is a new gay or lesbian partner, what should his or her parenting role be? How should the different extended families be handled? How much should the children know? How should children of different ages be treated and how might they be affected differently?

Good communication is essential. This is particularly true between the two biological parents and their children. In the case in which the wife has become involved with another woman (a usual case scenario), the husband's cooperation and support can be very important for the children's adjustment. In the cases in which the ex-husband is angry and hostile, the children often feel confused about what alliances and attitudes are appropriate.

Sandra and Jean were a couple who had been together for 5 years. Jean had three children under 12 from a previous marriage. When the couple came into therapy, there was a lot of fighting around what seemed like Jean's lack of commitment to the relationship. Various tensions had grown up around the children, who, in Sandra's estimation, seemed omnipresent in their relationship. The couple could not find a way to talk rationally with each other.

In therapy Jean admitted that she was still ambivalent about her lesbianism and had not told her children that Sandra was her lover, even though the two women had been living together for 3 years. Her own internalized oppression as well as the fact that the children's father was homophobic and hostile to the relationship kept her silent. When she did tell her children, her older son began to act out by becoming anorexic. This forced the family to confront each other more directly and make clearer boundaries for the children around the adults' needs and everyone's familial tasks. As each of the partners became more conscious of her own issues in therapy, such as fear of intimacy, abandonment, and anger, the relationship was able to move toward more trust and open communication. Although these problems still cause some tension, the children have come to accept the lesbian relationship so that the family can act as a more loving unit. Jean has become less fearful and ashamed of her lesbianism while learning to avoid destructive conflicts with her ex-husband, who is now at least periodically willing to talk about the issues, particularly as they concern his children.

As in blended, heterosexual families, the stepparent often receives a great deal of the anger, resentment, and disappointment felt by the children about their parents' separation. When the apparent reason for the separation is a gay or lesbian relationship, this resentment can become even stronger. If the children are older and have to worry about their peers' reaction, the anger can lead to disruptive behavior. If the father is not present in the children's life after the separation, the mother's partner can receive much of the intense emotion surrounding that issue. The children may well feel that their mother is choosing her happiness over theirs (they did not choose to live in a gay or lesbian family or be different in the world). Although the lesbian parent needs to be sensitive to the child's feelings, it is also important she be clear about her own right to enjoy the kind of relationship she wants. This boundary helps the child to accept the situation, without internalized homophobia adding further confusion for either generation.

Issues of adjustment for the blended family depend on the age of the children involved (Whiteside, 1989). Very young children can simply have the benefit of two mothers or two fathers who often make a wonderful parenting team. Children think it is the most normal thing to have "two mommies/daddies" and create primary bonds with both parents. These children can have more confusing experiences as they grow up and realize through contact with peers that they are different, but the strong family feeling that has been created usually helps them move through whatever social and perceptual difficulties they might encounter.

In our experience, if children are older when their parents split up, their concern about what their friends think and about their parents' life choices manifests itself more. Particularly in adolescence these problems can become of grave concern. The teenager is struggling with his or her identity and place in the world. Generally, she or he is very worried about impressions within the peer group and has difficulty deciding whether it is viable to come out as the child of gays or lesbians. Often she or he feels inhibited about inviting friends into the home. She or he may also be struggling with issues of sexual identity and expressiveness and perhaps about sexual orientation. Several lesbian families came into therapy concerning their adolescent sons. In one family the 14-year-old son said to his mother, "If you don't like men, why do you say you love me?" Or in another case, the child asked his mother why he couldn't be present at the various gatherings she attended. She tried to explain to him that there were places that women wanted to be alone, but it was hard for him to understand.

Girls have similar and different problems. They also worry about peer reactions. One girl in a lesbian family explained in therapy how many of the jokes the other kids made were around "faggots" or "dykes" and how that was one of the most insulting things to say. She said she did not have the nerve to come out about her mother, but that she felt very isolated and as if her family was invisible. Young women are often concerned about their own sexual orientation because they are closely identified with their mother. They want to be part of the dominant culture, but they also want to be a part of their family. Some girls in treatment have expressed that they actually experience their mother's lesbianism as a rejection of males and of their own heterosexual desires. They may feel unjustly judged or scrutinized in their selection of boy friends and in their exploration of sexual behavior. These concerns should be articulated by both mother and daughter, so that respective values and clear boundaries can be clarified as necessary. Again, there are no right or wrong answers to these issues, but communication and sharing about them remains a vital priority.

Same-Sex Co-Parents

Relationships between gay or lesbian partners who choose to form a discreet family unit are affected independently of whether they succeed in acquiring a child. The process begins when a couple considers parenthood and must begin dealing with their own and others' reactions to the prospect. Some conflict between the partners may arise if there are different levels of interest in child rearing. At the beginning of their relationship, one lesbian couple came to counseling because one of them was thinking constantly about having a child. The other felt that their relationship was too young to be ready for this. There was continual conflict over the issue. As underlying dynamics were revealed, it became clear that the partner wanting the child was very scared of being abandoned and was choosing somewhat unconsciously to resolve the issue by having a child who would never leave her. The other woman, who had felt invisible most of her life, accused her partner of not "seeing" her enough because she was too focused on the idea of the baby. Eventually the relationship ended because of unmet individual needs and strong differences around the desire to create a family together.

As with any couple who must make deliberate efforts to conceive, the focus on issues of fertility (Harkness, 1987), the logistics of insemination, and the emotional roller coaster of waiting each month for the results of the pregnancy test can intrude on a couple's life and cause strain in their relationship. For example, many couples report that their intial attempts at insemination are orchestrated with romantic intimate contact, but as time passes, inseminations become more mechanical, are experienced as more intrusive, and can create predictable periods of tension between the partners, both at times of ovulation and menstruation. Any difficulties with the pregnancy or the event of a miscarriage can feel even more traumatic, given the effort with which the pregnancy was achieved.

Preparation for childbirth requires partners to take special steps to insure that the nonbiological parent has the right to make decisions during labor and delivery. This is just the first experience the couple has in terms of the power differential between a biological and a nonbiological parent. The role of the nonbiological parent must be negotiated in terms of her or his authority as a parent, her or his degree of child care responsibilities, and her or his identification as equal parent or support person. Often, partners who choose a more limited role report being surprised at the fierceness of their opinions about child-rearing decisions or at the degree of resentment they feel at being left out of daily arrangements. Nonbiological parents also frequently express pain at the invisibility they experience when most institutions do not recognize or acknowedge them and when their role is unclear even within their own community. One man reported feeling painfully discounted when a long-time friend, who was well aware of his co-father status, inquired when he would be "baby-sitting the child."

The Gay or Lesbian Single Parent

When a single gay or lesbian person decides to parent, she or he faces many of the same issues that any single parent does. Because of homophobia, however, there is a question of whether the extended family will accept her or his child as part of the family and give her or him the support often so sorely needed. On the other hand, because the lesbian and gay community is more accustomed to creating its own family-like support system, she or he might have an easier time finding people to help her or him raise the child in a consistent fashion. There are many stories of lesbian and gay parents who have friends who commit to a certain weekly period of time that they will spend with the child.

Jaime, a 28-year-old bisexual woman, became pregnant just as she was beginning to date Debra. Both women were unsure of the seriousness of their relationship, so when Jaime decided to have the child, she spoke with a number of her friends who were willing to provide a support network for her as a single parent. Two different couples committed themselves to take her son 1 day a week. Debra agreed to care for the boy one night a week, as long as they were living separately. The relationship between Jaime and Debra remained uncommitted and later transitioned into a friendship. All three "support families" made Jaime's life as a single parent more manageable.

Lesbian and Gay Co-Parents

Another scenario of co-parenting occurs when two adults who are not in primary relationship to each other come together for the sole purpose of having a child. Very often, each individual has experienced a long history of searching for a viable intimate relationship or for an appropriate partner with whom to parent. It can be a great relief to find someone whose desire and timing are the same. Sometimes, however, potential co-parents enter into agreements without thinking through their consequences or without appreciating the complexity of the co-parenting relationship.

Although two co-parents may not have the emotional baggage that often accumulates in a primary intimate relationship, they also do not have the benefit of a history of sharing daily responsibilities and resolving conflicts that helps couples develop the skills needed for the complex decision making involved in parenting. In the case of a gay couple contracting with a lesbian couple, there are questions of who will bear the child and who will be the donor. What will be the nature of the involvement of the two parents and their two partners? What are the financial commitments? Concomitantly, what are the long-term emotional commitments to the child, especially if the adults do not get along? Will the co-partners live together? Or if they live separately, how much time will the child spend at each house? During the child's infancy, what arrangements will be made to provide the consistent presence of each adult that is needed for the bonding process? And what effect will daily or weekly separations have on the child's development?

In one case, a heterosexual man and a lesbian who had been friends for a long time sought therapy when the woman was pregnant. For the most part, they had been able to find creative solutions to difficult questions. The key to their success was their mutual desire for a child, their cooperative attitude, and an established friendship that could weather the inevitable conflicts and tensions. They came to therapy to make sure that their communication process was effective and that they were thinking things through in a conscious manner. The therapy brought to light issues concerning assumptions about parenting that each individual brought from his or her family of origin, and subsequent discussion focused on their possible influences. The therapy also clarified spoken and unspoken expectations. Ways to maintain open and frequent communication throughout all aspects of the process were discussed as well as how support systems could be developed for each of the parents.

In another case involving two lesbians, the arrangements were difficult because the adults' relationship was fairly new and centered primarily around the desire to have a child. Jealousy, resentment, and unclear goals kept them from being able to make viable decisions together. After a period of time, the woman who was going to carry the first child broke off the co-parenting relationship, creating very hard feelings.

Even when contracts between co-parenting couples clearly state everyone's intentions and responsibilities, it is impossible to anticipate adequately all the issues. For example, one lesbian couple and the gay father came into therapy to discuss the lesbians' objections to the gay partner's wish to take the child to his parents' church service. The counseling sessions ended up focusing more generally on the tensions and loss of trust that had occurred during the first year of co-parenting. All parties were grateful that the bottom line in their agreement was to use mediation or therapy to try to sustain a healthy relationship. Unfortunately, there are also cases in which bitterness and injustice can ensue as a result of the numerous decisions faced and the lack of control each person feels when accommodating everyone's different parental wishes.

Summary

General issues concerning gay and lesbian families as well as issues concerning some specific family configurations are discussed in this chapter. It is our hope that counselors working with such families will be more informed about the possible concerns and problems their clients are facing. There are no clear answers to many of the questions raised, but there is a significant beginning to the discussion among researchers, clinicians, and family members. More experience and knowledge can lead to understanding the most effective way to work with gay and lesbian families and can help to establish social, legal, and personal traditions that can inform and give guidelines to life within the home and in the world outside.

References

Adams, B. D. (1987). *The rise of the gay and lesbian movement*. Boston: Twayne.

Bigner, J., & Bozett, F. (1990). Parenting by gay fathers. In F.W. Bozett & M. B. Sussman (Eds.), *Homosexuality and family relations* (pp 155–175). New York: Harrington Park.

Bigner, J., & Jacobsen, R. (1989). The value of children for gay versus nongay fathers. *Journal of Homosexuality, 18*, 163–172.

Caen, H. (1990, June 13 & 14). Herb Caen's column. *San Francisco Chronicle*.

Gottman, J. S. (1990). Children of gay and lesbian parents. In F.W. Bozett & M. B. Sussman (Eds.), *Homosexuality and family relations* (pp. 177–196). New York: Harrington Park.

Gurman, A. (1982). *Questions and answers in the practice of family therapy* (Vol. 2, pp. 225–229). New York: Brunner/Mazel.

Harkness, C. (1987). *The infertility book*. San Francisco: Volcano.

Harvard Law Review. (1990). *Sexual orientation and the law*. Cambridge, MA: Harvard University Press.

Hodges, W. (1986). Evaluation of homosexual parents. In W. Hodges (Ed.), *Interventions for children of divorce* (pp. 137–138). New York: Wiley.

Kirkpatrick, M., Smith, C., & Roy, R. (1981). Lesbian mothers and their children: A comprehensive survey. *American Journal of Orthopsychiatry, 51*, 85–100.

Noble, E. (1987). *Having your baby by donor insemination*. Boston: Houghton Mifflin.

Patterson, C. (1990). *Children of gay and lesbian parents*. Unpublished manuscript, University of Virginia, Charlottesville.

Ricketts, W., & Achtenberg, R. (1990). Adoption and foster parenting for lesbians and gay men: Creating new traditions in family. In F.W. Bozett & M. B. Sussman (Eds.), *Homosexuality and family relations* (pp. 83–118). New York: Harrington Park.

Schetky, D. H., & Benedek, E. P. (Eds.). (1985). *Emerging issues in child psychiatry and the law* (pp. 115–125). New York: Brunner/Mazel.

Seligman, J. (1990, Winter/Spring). Variations on a theme. *Newsweek* (Special edition: The 21st Century Family), pp. 38–46.

Thompson, K., & Andrzejewski, J. (1988). *Why can't Sharon Kowalski come home?* San Francisco: Spinsters/Aunt Lute.

U. S. Department of Labor, Bureau of Labor Statistics. (1981). *Employment in perspective; Working women* (Report No. 653). Washington, DC: U. S. Government Printing Office.

Waters, B., & Dimock, J. (1983). A Review of research relevant to the custody and access disputes. *Australian and New Zealand Journal of Psychiatry, 17*, 181–189.

Whiteside, M. F. (1989). Remarried systems. In L. Combrinck-Graham (Ed.), *Children in family context: Perspectives and treatment* (pp. 135–160). New York: Guilford Press.

Section III
Diverse Populations

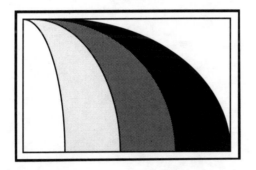

8

Cultural Considerations in Counseling Asian American Lesbians and Gay Men

Connie S. Chan, PhD

For all lesbians and gay men, there is a developmental process through which an individual accepts and affirms an integrated identity as a lesbian or gay man. Vivienne Cass (1979) first described the six-part developmental sequence in which an individual moves from the initial stages of identity confusion and identity conflict to acceptance, affirmation, and then identity pride and identity synthesis (see Introduction). For ethnic minority lesbians and gay men there is the additional task of developing an ethnic minority identity and integrating it with a lesbian or gay identity. This task, described in a minority identity model by Atkinson, Morten, and Sue (1979), requires a five-stage process similar to the developmental process of lesbian and gay identity development.

For Asian American lesbians and gay men, there are some culture-specific and gender-specific psychological and social issues in accepting and affirming a lesbian or gay identity. Because the traditional Asian cultures tend to be more homophobic and less accepting of differences in behavior and identity, Asian Americans frequently feel caught between two conflicting cultural values, between Asian and western influences. Because lesbian and gay Asian Americans challenge deeply held cultural assumptions of male and female roles, they may have more difficulty integrating their lesbian and gay identities with the demands of family and community to conform to traditional role behaviors. As counselors and clinicians we need to be aware of these cultural issues. Yet we must also be careful not to stereotype behaviors based upon our own limited generalizations of Asian cultural values and customs. (In this chapter the term *Asian* refers to East Asians and covers the Chinese, Japanese, Korean, and Southeast Asian cultures.) Such generalizations about Asian cultural issues are only broad-stroke guidelines: Certainly each clinician needs to confirm the validity of and, as necessary, modify the information presented in this chapter to fit each of his or her clients.

Note that although an understanding of and familiarity with cultural issues are important in counseling members of any ethnic minority group, these provide only background information. Specific factors within the context of each individual client's situation must also be considered. For example:

1. Is the client an immigrant or American born?
2. What ethnic group does the client belong to?
3. What are the specific cultural values of this group, of the client's family, of the client?
4. How strongly does the client follow traditional customs?
5. What is the client's socioeconomic status?
6. What is the client's level of bilingualism?

In the sections that follow, general issues concerning the role of family, separation and individuation, sexuality, and invisibility within the community are discussed in the context of counseling and psychotherapy with lesbian and gay Asian Americans. Individual cases illustrate the issues.

The Role of the Family

In traditional Asian culture, identifying oneself as being lesbian or gay is perceived as a rejection of the primary roles for women and men—being a wife and mother and being a father and carrying on the family line through procreation of heirs. Unlike western cultures in which individuation and establishment of oneself as an individual with one's own relationship and family is the goal, in Asian cultures an individual's primary responsibility is to one's parents and family of origin. The traditional Asian cultural norm is to have marriages arranged by families with little input from sons or daughters. Because the purpose of the marriage is to continue the family line in the most desirable way for the families, the individual desires of the bride and groom are considered to be irrelevant.

Within this context of the importance of family roles, if a daughter or son is lesbian or gay, the child is seen as not only rejecting the traditional social role as a wife-mother or husband-father, but even worse, as also rejecting the importance of family and Asian cultural values. Any overt acknowledgement of being lesbian or gay is perceived as bringing great shame upon the family. To be openly lesbian and gay within the Asian community, or even within one's extended family, may be perceived both as a child's rejection of the family and as a failure of the parents in their role of perpetuating cultural values and the family line.

For many lesbian and gay Asian Americans, disclosing their lesbian or gay identities to their families, especially to their parents, is the most difficult task of their coming out process. Chan's (1989) study of 35 Asian American lesbians and gay men revealed that only 26% had come out to their parents, although they self-reported being out for a mean of 6.2 years. However, 77% had come out to other family members, and 97% were out to their friends. In Wooden's study of 13 Japanese American gay men, only half of the respondents were open with their families about their gay identity (Wooden, Kawasaki, & Mayeda, 1983). In comparison, 72% of a general population of 848 lesbian and gay respondents to an *Outlook* magazine survey reported that they were out to all of their siblings, 76% to their mother and 59% to their father. These data support two of the most common themes described by counselors of Asian American lesbians and gay men: the fear of rejection from their families for being lesbian or gay and the expectation of a complete lack of understanding from parents.

Henry

Henry is a 31-year-old Chinese American man who says he "discovered" that he was gay when he was 21. He became socially and sexually active and was generally satisfied with his social and professional life. The one aspect of his life that was not fulfilling was his relationship with his parents and his extended family. Although he had been close to his family until his early 20s, he found himself being more and more distant as he withheld information about his own personal life. He longed to tell his family about his friends, his lover, and about his life, but he was afraid that they would never understand how positive he felt about being gay and that they would reject him. Unable to imagine another choice, Henry resigned himself to being distant from his family. Saddened that he could not fully share in his family's experiences, Henry frequently felt the pain of isolation when he was with his relatives. He might have continued in this way for years had his mother not been diagnosed with a form of terminal cancer. Her fondest wish was to see her only son Henry married, and she begged him to grant her this one last wish. This was the precipitating event that brought Henry into psychotherapy. During his first sessions, he described feeling as if he was stuck in a no-win situation: He felt that if he told his mother the truth, he would disappoint her so greatly that she would feel that she had failed, and that if he continued the pretense and married a woman, he would not only be living a lie but would also not be able to have any self-respect.

As a counselor, my work with Henry focused upon separating out his own personal issues within the broader cultural context. While affirming that the cultural issues played an important role in his inability to be honest with his family, we also examined his own fear of rejection by his parents, his need to meet their standards for approval, and his reluctance to confront them in any way. Henry began to understand that he did not know how to be an adult individual with his own needs and yet still be part of the family. He needed to affirm that being gay and being proud of the person he is did not necessarily mean that he would never be accepted by his family.

Henry sought me out as a therapist who is both Asian American and openly gay because he wanted someone who understood and had perhaps experienced similar cultural conflicts. In the initial sessions, we dealt with his internalized homophobia: Henry knew intellectually that being gay was okay, but he still felt ashamed of being gay and, thus, different. Henry recognized that he needed support and also wanted to find out how other Asian Americans had dealt with their families. He asked me, as his counselor, to share with him how I had come to affirm myself as an Asian lesbian. In addition to sharing my own experiences with Henry, I encouraged him to seek out other lesbians and gay men by joining an Asian lesbian and gay organization, attending a coming out support group for gay men focusing on similar issues, and reading stories and books about the experiences of both Asian and non-Asian lesbians and gay men. With this support and exposure to new role models, Henry felt less isolated and much more accepting of himself as a gay Asian man.

The next step in his counseling was to help him prepare to come out to his family. Whenever he talked about telling his family, Henry became very nervous and visibly agitated. Several sessions were devoted to anxiety-reduction techniques and role playing how he would tell his mother and his siblings about being gay. During these role plays, it was useful to switch roles with Henry experiencing, and thus anticipating, the different reactions of his mother and siblings as well as acknowledging his own reactions.

After he came out to his family, Henry needed a great deal of support to work with their shock and nonacceptance. We focused upon the process of educating them and supporting Henry in being patient with the long process of his family's understanding and acceptance of his being gay. Henry rejected the possibility of family therapy because he felt his family would have been too uncomfortable to confront difficult personal issues in front of a stranger, the counselor. Work in our sessions sometimes meant bringing in his family in a figurative sense.

In counseling, Henry worked on separating out his feelings of guilt for choosing a life he wanted for himself instead of what his family wanted for him. As his counselor, I needed to give him permission as an independent adult individual to have needs of his own that were different from his family's. Henry began to accept and then affirm his right to be who he is: a gay man. He was able to achieve a balance between his own needs and his family's demands. The result was that Henry actually became more available to his mother and his siblings, both emotionally and temporally. As he worked out these issues in therapy, Henry began to feel more sure of himself and the ways in which he could share more openly his own life with his family. It was a long process, but Henry eventually developed a closer relationship with his family.

The issues involved in coming out to family may be universal ones, but an understanding of the cultural background in Henry's situation was necessary to separate out his individual issues from broader cultural issues.

Separation and Individuation for Asian American Lesbians

The task of separation and individuation can be more difficult for Asian American lesbians than in western culture because of the traditional Asian cultural perception that an unmarried woman, regardless of her age, is still part of her family of origin until she is married. In many Asian families, fathers consider themselves to be responsible for their unmarried daughter's welfare. The daughter's role is to submit to her parents' authority; she is not considered to have an identity separate from her parents until she is married. Asian American lesbians, because they are not married in the traditional sense, are rarely considered to have separated from their families, regardless of financial or professional status. Because individuation is desired within American culture, many Asian American lesbians report that it is necessary for them not only to come out to their parents so that they will not have false expectations of their getting married but also to demonstrate that they are capable of taking responsibility for themselves. Other Asian American lesbians report that they attempt to establish the legitimacy of a lesbian relationship as proof of their independence; however, this relationship is rarely acknowledged by the family.

Cathy

Cathy, 35, is a Korean American lesbian who is struggling to become a separate individual from her parents and family. She came out when she was 26 but did not disclose her lesbian identity to members of her family until this past year. Cathy and her lover have owned a home together for 6 years; she is a professionally and financially successful businesswoman. Although her parents were distressed to find out that Cathy is a lesbian in a committed relationship with another woman, they continued to treat her in the same way, as if she were an unmarried daughter, inviting her (and not her lover) to family gatherings. In fact, her father encouraged Cathy to consider the idea of getting married to an immigrant Korean friend of the family's, implying that since she wasn't interested in men, she might as well go through an arranged marriage to meet her family's needs and perhaps have children. When Cathy expressed her anger that her father would even suggest such a marriage and again described her relationship with her partner-lover as a marriage, her father seemed genuinely surprised. He insisted that she could continue her relationship with her lover "on the side as well" because then she would be on her own (and no longer part of her parents' immediate family) if she were married.

The issues that emerged in therapy concerned the conflicting cultural expectations and roles that Cathy and her parents each held. By trying to impose a heterosexual marriage upon Cathy, her parents were trying to hide the family "shame" of having an unmarried daughter. As Cathy discussed these problems in counseling, it became clear that there was little direct communication of each individual's perpective. Instead, there was a great deal of unspoken resentment while attempting to avoid conflict. What had been avoided was direct confrontation of the fact that Cathy, although still part of the family, was now a separate responsible adult who had established a long-term primary relationship on her own. The work in treatment focused upon helping Cathy to initiate open discussion with her parents about their expectations of her as a daughter as well as to share with them her own expectations. When these expectations were not compatible, Cathy negotiated with her parents, agreeing to meet some needs but also requiring her parents to acknowledge her individual needs. As one example, Cathy agreed to attend large family functions without her lover but would bring her to smaller gatherings when only immediate family was present.

There were many conflicts around Korean, American, and family cultural values in Cathy's case, and some of these conflicts remained unresolved when she terminated treatment. However, the avenue of communication was opened between Cathy and her parents, and she had some ability to confront difficult issues because she established herself as a lesbian with a primary relationship and as an independent individual. Although the task of separation and individuation from their families of origin may be harder for all unmarried Asian American women, this process can be even more difficult for Asian American lesbians who have the added burden of not having their relationships acknowledged or their identities as lesbians accepted by the family.

Sexuality

Coming out as a lesbian or gay man includes a declaration of a new identity, and this identity is by definition perceived to be a sexual identity. Because sexuality (along with death) is one of the taboo subjects in Asian cultures, and rarely if ever discussed, coming out requires bringing the subject of sex, sexual orientation, and sexuality into the open. Asian American lesbians and gay men have reported that family and friends frequently have as much difficulty with acknowledging that their sons or daughters are sexually active in any way as with acknowledging that they are lesbian or gay. To declare that one is a lesbian or gay man clearly focuses upon one's sexuality and implies that one is sexually active. For some Asian American lesbians and gay men, the issue of being lesbian and gay may be avoided while family and friends are busy focusing upon their being sexually active. As in many cultures, sexual activity outside of marriage is forbidden for women; in this age of AIDS, sexual activity of any kind with other men is considered dangerous for men. Thus, family and friends may choose to focus upon confronting the more "concrete" subject of sexual activity and expend energy in condemning sexual activity and the expression of one's sexuality. In this way, the even more unapproachable topic of being lesbian or gay may be avoided or ignored.

Sachiko

Sachiko, 32, is a Japanese American lesbian who came out to her family shortly after becoming sexually active. Refusing to accept or even discuss her identity as a lesbian, her parents were extremely upset that she was sexually active in any way and declared that she would never be fit to become married or to be a real part of the family again. No matter how she tried to explain her sexual orientation or identity as a lesbian to her parents, they refused to acknowledge that Sachiko was anything but a sexually active unmarried woman. By affirming her own identity, Sachiko was perceived by her parents as having willingly brought considerable shame upon her family. The family forbade her to disclose her lesbian identity to others. Sachiko, however, refused to remain closeted. This refusal brought about a complete rejection by her parents, which was extremely painful for Sachiko. In the therapy process, we worked upon maintaining Sachiko's self-esteem and dignity and upon bolstering her support from other sources, including her involvement with an Asian lesbian and gay organization. This support organization played a large role in Sachiko's life, and she found great comfort in knowing that other lesbians and gay men from similar cultural backgrounds had also experienced—and survived—rejection by their parents.

While encouraging Sachiko to maintain some relationship with her parents, I focused upon the importance of going through a grieving process for the loss of her parents' approval and support and also for the loss of the benefits associated with playing the daughter role. I felt that a direct acknowledgement and grieving of the losses were necessary in the process of resolving her feelings of anger and sadness. Sachiko continued in counseling until she felt she had accepted the losses and was ready to move on in her life as an openly gay Asian woman.

Invisibility Within the Community

Lesbian and gay Asian Americans, like other lesbian and gay members of ethnic minority groups, may be considered to have a double minority (and triple minority for lesbians who are part of the women's community) status because of membership in both the Asian American and lesbian and gay communities. Asian American lesbians and gay men report feeling marginalized or unrecognized in both communities. They express a desire to feel complete by being supported for both parts of what they are: Asian American and lesbian or gay (Chan, 1989). Yet this support seems to be lacking from both communities, as 77% of a sample of 35 Asian American lesbians and gay men reported that they felt it was harder to come out to other Asian Americans because of the high risk of rejection and stigmatization. There are also comparatively higher costs of being rejected by your own ethnic community, which is frequently one's main source of support against racism and provides a sense of belonging in a different culture. To risk losing this support is sometimes too high a price to pay for some individuals who may be openly lesbian or gay in all other facets of their lives but remain closeted within their own ethnic communities. As one Asian American lesbian wrote, "I feel most comfortable when both parts of myself—my lesbian and my Asian selves—are accepted and valued" (Chan, 1989, p. 18).

Conclusions

As counselors and clinicians, we know that denying any important aspect of one's identity exacts its own toll in feelings of isolation, shame, and fear. As we work with Asian American lesbians and gay men, we need to develop new models of working toward a gay-affirmative and culturally affirmative perspective that assists our clients in integrating both aspects of their lesbian or gay and Asian American identities. Within the mainstream gay and lesbian community, greater awareness and inclusivity of cultural differences and diversity will enrich a community frequently unaware that it is dominated by a White majority cultural perspective.

References

Atkinson, D. R., Morten, G., & Sue, D. W. (1979). *Counseling American minorities*. Dubuque, IA: Brown.

Cass, V. C. (1979). Homosexuality identity formation: A theoretical model. *Journal of Homosexuality, 4,* 219–235.

Chan, C. S. (1989). Issues of identity development among Asian American lesbians and gay men. *Journal of Counseling & Development, 68,* 16–20.

Wooden, W. S., Kawasaki, H., & Mayeda, R. (1983). Lifestyles and identity maintenance among gay Japanese-American males. *Alternative Lifestyles, 5,* 236–243.

9

Counseling Latino Gays and Latina Lesbians

Eduardo S. Morales, PhD

The Case of Juan

It is a typical day and time for your next appointment. A slender man is in the waiting room and introduces himself in English with a slight Spanish accent as Juan, a 26-year-old from Nicaragua. He is undocumented and lives with a roommate in the city. He describes his symptoms as wanting to be alone, feeling restless, not sleeping well, not remembering things, and fighting with his roommate. He describes the fights as having many arguments with occasional hitting. He feels it is getting worse, and his roommate has asked him to move out. He does not have a place to stay nor the monetary resources to rent an apartment of his own. He does not know many people and has few friends. He knows of some cousins and an aunt who live in the area, but he does not know them very well. He has never been in therapy and was recommended by a friend to see someone.

As the session continues he discloses that he has had sex with men but feels he is attracted to women. He reveals he has some high school education, is currently employed as a bus boy in a restaurant, and has been living with his friend for 3 years. When asked if this is his *amante* (lover), he says that his friend calls him that, but he does not see himself as gay. He met his friend at a neighborhood bar one night, and they saw each other for 4 to 5 months before deciding to share an apartment together. His White-Anglo friend works at the phone company, was born and raised in the city, and speaks some Spanish. Juan says he has had two other relationships with men that were of similar duration, but this time things were different. During his teens he recalls dating a girl in Nicaragua, and he feels he is bisexual and not homosexual. Juan has been feeling alone and would like to return to his country but is fearful of not being able to return to the United States. He has never seen a therapist but understands that he needs to talk with someone.

Many therapists find themselves faced with clinical issues of multiple dimensions, as in the case of Juan. To be effective one must integrate the various clinical aspects and clinical interventions in order to design an approach appropriate for the clinical issues at hand. With Juan some of the presenting concerns include a deteriorating relationship with his "roommate" and an immediate need for housing; limited social support and monetary resources; lack of support to facilitate change; sexual orientation issues; an undocumented status; cross-cultural, bilingual, and assimilation issues; high risk for AIDS and the lack of safer sex practices; and his first encounter with counseling. Each presenting concern is a separate challenge, and the combination of a few of these concerns is a substantial clinical challenge for even the more seasoned therapist, particularly in light of the limited literature available to guide the clinician and to lend some understanding of the multiple interactive aspects.

The case of Juan can be said to be unprecedented in the literature but commonplace in urban centers in the United States. Most clinicians have never had training and supervision in these types of cases. Consequently, many clinicians find themselves in situations in which they are forced to integrate various parts of their clinical training and generate creative approaches and perspectives. Many of the necessary clinical perspectives on multicultural populations have only recently been included in the literature and become available in some clinical trainings. Yet a multicultural perspective becomes more critical to clinicians as the population in the United States changes and as many urban centers typically have many multilingual and multicultural communities. The purposes of this chapter are to examine the psychosocial and cultural issues commonly faced by Latino gays and Latina lesbians and to generate clinical perspectives and strategies for counseling.

Psychosocial Factors

The life of a Latino gay and a Latina lesbian in the United States often means a life that is lived within three communities: the gay and lesbian community, the Latino and Latina community, and the predominantly White heterosexual mainstream society. Each community has its set of norms, values, and beliefs, some of which are fundamentally in opposition to each other. Some choose to keep each community separate, and others vary the degree to which they integrate the communities and lifestyles. Each community offers important aspects supporting lifestyles and identities. The gay and lesbian community offers support in the expression of one's sexual orientation identity, the Latino and Latina community offers emotional and familial bonding as well as cultural identity, and the mainstream society offers a national and international identity as well as a mainstream culture and multidimensional social system.

Although there are reasons for associating with each of the three communities, there are negative consequences for maintaining such associations (Carballo-Diéguez, 1989; Espín, 1987; Morales, 1990). The Latino and Latina community has homophobic and negative attitudes toward gays and lesbians in general. The gay and lesbian community is a reflection of the mainstream White community and mirrors the racist attitudes toward Latino men and Latina women through discrimination and prejudice. The mainstream White heterosexual community embraces the homophobic and negative attitudes toward gays and lesbians as well as the racist attitudes and practices toward Latino men and Latina women. The Latino gays and Latina lesbians find themselves weighing the options and managing the tensions and conflicts that arise as a result of the multiple interactions (de Monteflores, 1986).

Other psychosocial factors come into play that further differentiate various values and beliefs. One of these is socioeconomic class, which plays a significant role in the development of cultural values and within social networks. In the United States, Latinos and Latinas are proportionately overrepresented in the lower socioeconomic groups in the United States; they may, however, have value systems that are associated with other socioeconomic classes. For instance, some Latinos and Latinas were raised in middle or upper middle class families, with corresponding values and status, but in the United States they are in a lower economic status because lack of English, discrimination, or misinterpretation of educational background by licensing boards has restricted their opportunities. For these people, values associated with working class and poverty groups are not applicable. Thus, determination of socioeconomic status should be made by value system rather than by actual economic status. In addition, it is important to distinguish between values and beliefs that are a function of socioeconomic class and those that are a function of the culture. Because an individual is reluctant to associate with the activities of the *barrio*—that is, the Latino and Latina ghetto—it does not mean necessarily that he or she is in conflict with his or her cultural identity as a Latino or Latina. The reluctance may instead be associated with a different socioeconomic class.

The use of different languages play a significant role in modes of communication and in perceptions and views of life. A commonality among Latinos and Latinas is their use of Spanish despite their different nationalities and cultural backgrounds (Carballo-Diéguez, 1989). Language is a part of culture, and translation from one language to another often loses the essence of the message. Variations in Spanish can be found across nations. Through casual conversations Latinos and Latinas often learn of these variations from each other. Language may also be a good indication of the level of acculturation and affinity to one culture over another. The determination of the frequency of an individual's use of Spanish and of the persons with whom he or she speaks in English versus Spanish can be an invaluable tool in the assessment of assimilation and acculturation.

Many Latinos and Latinas have the opportunity to visit their homelands and find such visits rejuvenating and reaffirming of their identity and sense of self. The visits are often described as healing and as a relief from the stresses of the discrimination and prejudice experienced in the United States. Some families send their children to their country of origin to stay with family members so they, too, can experience the culture firsthand and develop a stronger sense of self as part of their development.

The sex role stereotyping of Latinos and Latinas is often misunderstood in the literature and is further confused when applied to Latino gays and Latina lesbians. As in most cultures, Latinos and Latinas have traditional value systems, and the sex role expectations are similar to those of other cultures with the rigid assignment of sex roles leading to sexism. Because homosexuality is a nontraditional lifestyle, it is expected that negative attitudes will prevail in the Latino cultures. As Latino gays and Latina lesbians develop their sexual orientation, the gender role models parallel those of the socially accepted heterosexual models. Hence, individuals assume certain sex roles as do heterosexuals, except that both gender roles can be found among gays as well as lesbians rather than being sex specific. Some Latino gays and Latina lesbians may identify more with effeminate characteristics, usually termed as *fem*, *loca* (outrageous), or *drag queen*, and others may identify with masculine characteristics usually referred to as *butch* and *machito*.

The influence of socioeconomic class and acculturation in the United States plays an important role in how Latino gay men and Latina lesbians socialize. Certain studies have found that gay men in other countries mimic gender roles within their social networks (Carrier, 1976, 1977, 1989). Some gay men present themselves as more masculine, others as more feminine. The rigid gender roles are carried into relationships in a similar form as in heterosexual coupling. Cross dressing can be a way to amplify these lifestyles as well as a way of entertainment for certain Latinos. Latina lesbians may have similar characteristics and dynamics, commonly referred to as *butch* and *fem*.

Variations seem to occur as a function of sexual orientation identity. The more the person is gay or lesbian identified, the more varied the sex roles. The more heterosexually or bisexually identified, the more the traditional same-sex gender roles are preferred. This seems to be a function of the negative attitudes that Latino and Latina cultures have toward gays and lesbians combined with the traditional heterosexual expectation that children will live at home, get married, and continue the family with their own children (Carballo-Diéguez, 1989; Carrier, 1976, 1977, 1989; Espín, 1987). In large urban areas in Latino countries, or in other cultures or environments in which gay and lesbian lifestyles are more accepted, such sex role stereotyping may be less apparent and less applicable. The interaction of gender role playing and sexual orientation identity is a significant factor in the socialization and psychosocial development of Latino gays and Latina lesbians.

Latino Cultures: Commonalties and Cross-Cultural Factors

Latinos and Latinas represent a wide variety of nations and races of people and are characterized as multicultural and multiracial. They have no common culture, belong to no one group. A Puerto Rican therapist working with a Mexican client is more likely doing psychotherapy in a cross-cultural context rather than in a same-cultural context. Additionally, such a dyad can vary by race with the therapist being of one race, for example, Black or mulatto (mixed race), and the client being of another, for example, White or Indian. Therefore, cross-cultural and biracial or multiracial aspects need to be considered in a manner that incorporates the culturally specific relevance of race within each culture. Attributes given to one race by Puerto Ricans can be radically different or even opposed to those given by Mexicans or Argentinians.

Despite the basic cultural differences among Latinos and Latinas, commonalties, which include language and certain value systems, also exist. Several writers have identified cultural constructs that represent values commonly shared among Latinos and Latinas (Bernal, 1982; Falicov, 1982; Garcia-Preto, 1982). These constructs include *familismo, machismo, simpatía, personalismo, respeto,* and *saludos.*

- *Familismo* refers to the importance of the family as the primary social unit and source of support. Frequently, the extended family is intimately and actively involved. The godparents of the children tend to function as co-parents, *compadre* or *comadre,* and are considered as part of the family, as a brother or sister of the parents.
- *Machismo* refers to the responsibility of the man to provide, protect, and defend his family. It is his loyalty and sense of responsibility to his family, friends, and community that makes him a man and is reflected in his *machismo.* This is entirely different from the Anglo view of *macho* as a sexist, male chauvinist.
- *Simpatía* refers to the sense of empathy and the importance of "smooth relations" and social politeness. Confrontation and persistent behaviors are viewed as offensive. It is common that the Latino or Latina listener appears to agree with messages, with no intention of following advice, in order to avoid disagreement and confrontation.
- *Personalismo* refers to a preference of Latinos and Latinas for having personal relationships with others in their social group. In developing these relationships a sense of trust and cooperation develops. Because health workers have established this special rapport, Latinos and Latinas commonly relate to the health provider as to a member of their family.
- *Respeto* refers to the need for respect, especially for authority figures. *Respeto* requires that the person be treated with dignity and respect.

This is especially true in the differential treatment of older citizens through the use of *Don* or *Doña* when addressing them.

- *Saludos* refers to the importance of greeting others, of touching, of expressing affection. The proper ways of addressing others, introducing people to each other, and using social protocol when meeting others are included in *saludos*.

These cultural constructs provide a general conceptual framework that is useful in therapy. These value systems may be the basis of some common ground between client and therapist that multicultural counseling can build upon in the process of therapy. For Latino gays and Latina lesbians, these cultural values set the tone for their socialization and bonding with their family, friends, and community. How their sexual orientations are incorporated may be conceptualized in terms of an identity formation process as they live in the United States as a minority within a minority.

Sexual Identity Formation

How do Latino gay men and Latina lesbians develop a healthy perspective and a positive integration of these multiple identities? First, they must come to grips with their sexual orientation. As they do so, they tend to feel strained by the tensions of living in three different societies simultaneously. Many refer to this as a "schizy" period in which they are living three lives, and this can be a very anxious time. As the awareness of multiple identities becomes clearer and more differentiated, the process of change toward a positive and integrated identity begins. Morales (1983) presented a process that centers around five different states reflective of cognitive and lifestyle changes. This model proposes different states rather than stages. It is possible that persons may experience several states or parts of states at the same time, unlike a stage model in which resolution of one stage leads to another.

State 1: Denial of Conflicts

During this state the person tends to minimize the validity and reality of the discrimination they experience as an ethnic person, and through the use of denial they believe they are treated the same as others. They feel their personal lifestyle and sexual orientation have limited consequences in their life. They may identify themselves as gay, lesbian, or bisexual. An idealistic and utopian philosophy of life tends to dominate their perception of reality and their ability to predict how others see them. Problems focus on having few supportive friends, being perceived as easily manipulated by the dominant sources of power, and tending to attract White lovers with the central focus of attraction being race or ethnicity. The focus of therapy centers around developing a more accurate picture of how the environmental stressors affect their functioning and how their multiple identities can be assets in their personality and lifestyle.

State 2: Bisexual Versus Gay or Lesbian

The preference for some is to identify themselves as bisexual rather than as gay or lesbian. They sense that they are neither exclusively heterosexual nor exclusively homosexual. Examining their sexual lifestyles may reveal, however, that there is no difference between those who identify themselves as gay or lesbian and those who identify themselves bisexual. Some may view this as a conflict in sexual identity formation, but ethnic minorities distinguish a difference in two ways: (1) their conceptualization and perception of sexuality and (2) their perception of the gay and lesbian community as an extension of the White racist society. Some may view sexuality more generally and conceive of sexuality as sexual feelings for someone regardless of sex. A person who expresses sexual feelings, even though he or she may lead an exclusively gay or lesbian lifestyle, may thus be perceived as having a bisexual identity. Assuming a bisexual identity may also be a way to avoid being labeled and categorized.

Another way sexuality may be viewed is by perceiving the gay and lesbian community as White, as not inclusive of people of color, and thereby as racist. Latinos and Latinas may feel the challenges of being racial and ethnic minority persons as extraordinary both in the mainstream society and in the White gay and lesbian community. As a result, they prefer to be more identified with their Latino and Latina community and to be referred to as bisexual rather than gay or lesbian. The perception of a Latino gay and Latina lesbian community may not be realistic for them. The focus of therapy may be to explore the sense of hopelessness and depression resulting from the continued feelings of conflict. Imagining a Latino gay and Latina lesbian community that is supportive of the lifestyle without prejudice may highlight the yearning and need for a supportive community and is a useful technique to illustrate this dynamic.

State 3: Conflicts in Allegiances

The awareness of being both Latino or Latina and gay or lesbian can provoke uneasiness. Many choose to live the different parts of their lives independently. For others, anxiety about mixing the different parts of their lives, about taking sides, about betraying either the Latino and Latina or the gay and lesbian communities becomes a major concern. Families emphasize the importance of sticking together as Latinos and Latinas in order to deal with the mainstream society; the gay and lesbian community points to the common struggles of gays and lesbians as a way to emphasize the need for unity across cultures and nationalities. The focus of therapy centers around prioritizing these allegiances rather than around choosing sides in order to reduce the conflict. Examining the supportive aspects of each community tends to shift the conflict from a monocultural perspective into a multicultural dimension in which their lives can be viewed as containing multiple identities.

State 4: Establishing Priorities in Allegiance

A primary identification to the Latino and Latina community prevails in this state. Feelings of resentment and frustration concerning the lack of integration among the communities become a central issue. There are feelings of anger and rage stemming from experiences of rejection by the gay and lesbian community because of their ethnicity. These feelings and personal history encourage a primary identification with their Latino and Latina community. Separating White gay friends from ethnic friends and developing relationships with persons who have similar community allegiances are common characteristics. Therapy can focus on an examination of their anger and rage and on the development of a proactive rather than a reactive or victim perspective in their relationships and allegiances. An example of a proactive, affirmative attitude is the reluctance of the individual to be referred to as an ethnic minority. The term *minority* has an oppressive connotation. The client's preference turns to *Latino* or *Latina*. An additional strategy in therapy should be the enhancement of support systems through the formation of support networks with affirmative Latino gays and Latina lesbians and with other supportive persons.

State 5: Integrating the Various Communities

For Latino gays or Latina lesbians, the need to integrate their lifestyle and develop a multicultural perspective becomes a major concern.

Optimizing the use of social and support groups becomes more important. Adjusting to the reality of limited options becomes a source of anxiety, facilitating feelings of isolation and alienation. The pressure to be the bridge or go between for the Latino and Latina community and for the gay and lesbian community presents a constant challenge to the issues of allegiance and may result in feeling misunderstood. For the career-oriented gay or lesbian Latino or Latina, anxiety feelings are heightened when integration issues are presented. For these persons, coming out means running the risk of losing career opportunities that are already limited by their visible minority status (see the case of David in chapter 20). The focus of therapy centers around reassuring them that they are aware of the various dynamics and can better predict outcomes and consequences. By building confidence in their judgment in assessing others and expanding their support system to include persons with similar multicultural perspectives, anxiety and tension around these issues can be alleviated.

Gays and lesbians who are born and raised abroad and then move to the United States do not seem to have the problem of allegiance to their Latino and Latina community. They tend to express a strong sense of identification with their country of origin. Both foreign-born and U.S.-born Latinos and Latinas agree that they feel like a minority within a minority in the United States, however. Their minority status as Latinos or Latinas is visible: They can not hide being Latino or Latina. Their minority status as gays or lesbians is invisible and relative to their disclosure, to their being out of the closet. Consequently, their lives are ones of constant conflict management and mediation as they attempt to separate negative attitudes relative to being Latino or Latina versus being gay or lesbian and to decide how and when to respond, when to choose their battles.

Clinical Strategies for the Case of Juan

One of the important aspects of Juan is his relative inexperience with psychotherapy and his multiple immediate needs. Once rapport is established it is important for the therapist to identify these multiple immediate needs and together with the client decide on the ranking of priorities. The clinical strategy requires a result-oriented, practical approach in which concrete problems are resolved during the initial part of the counseling sessions and issues that are more long-term are gradually incorporated as the sessions progress. This approach demonstrates to Juan that the therapist is able to understand his needs, is able to act and be helpful, which increases the likelihood that Juan will continue the counseling sessions. Some of Juan's immediate needs require referral information and a social work intervention rather than insight-oriented counseling.

The potential for domestic violence can be alleviated through suggesting a temporary separation and making a housing referral. This should be done immediately, perhaps during the session, as a way to demonstrate concern and responsiveness. Juan's monetary concerns can also be handled through an appropriate referral, for example, for general assistance together with a job finder's referral. Providing an appointment for a counseling session within 24 to 48 hours and a phone number for him to a call any time between sessions will also acknowledge his emotional distress and reassure him of your support. Once his immediate needs are met, Juan may be better able to benefit from insight-oriented conseling. In addition, couples counseling can be offered as a way to provide some conflict resolution in the relationship. If both parties are agreeable, then mediation may be the best course of action, allowing the other issues to be deferred for individual counseling.

Juan's psychosocial issues center around State 2, Bisexual Versus Gay or Lesbian, of the Morales model. His identity as a bisexual is inconsistent with his exclusively homosexual lifestyle. He may be unable to come to grips with "speaking the unspeakable," that is, with his homosexuality and the contradictions in his lifestyle in relation to a bisexual identity. Consequently, he may also be in State 1, Denial of Conflicts, as evidenced by his negative attitudes toward homosexuals, by what is commonly referred to as internalized homophobia. This may interfere with the couples counseling and support the need for individual counseling. In this case, the clinical strategy will be to work with Juan's ambivalence in coming out to himself and in feeling supported for his gay sexual orientation. Additionally, it is important to note the strengths in his personality that enable him to manage such a difficult contradiction in his life. This serves to empower the individual and help change the perception of life as one of adversities to the perception of life as one of challenges that can be managed. Counselors must not forget to acknowledge the struggles amid such conflicts and the strengths involved for survival. Once the inner conflicts are identified, the relationship issues around Juan's sense of self and his gay identity can be reexamined. The relationship issues may mirror his inner struggles, lending support to the clinical processes identified. Through such a process a sense of integration will emerge and overcome the feelings of fragmentation and contradiction noted earlier.

The Case of Maria

Maria, a 32-year-old Puerto Rican woman, began the session with "I don't know where to begin." She has been progressively more anxious and nervous as a result of the various stresses in her life. She is unable to maintain her performance level at work and finds herself getting more irritated and angry with people in general and taking it out on her lover of 5 years. She was born and raised in Puerto Rico. Her family moved to a major metropolitan area on the East Coast, and because they were poor and had limited resources, they were forced to live in a high-crime ghetto. Understandably, her parents were very protective of her, and at times overbearing. In the family are three children, all of whom graduated from high school and are now living independently. Maria continued with her studies, graduated from law school, and is currently working in a large, highly respected law firm. The pressure and expectations to perform on the job combined with the generally covert negative attitudes in the office about professional women and minorities have been a source of stress for her.

Maria proceeded to reminisce about her past. At age 7 she recalled feeling different from her friends. As a teenager she realized she was strongly attracted to other women. She came out while in college and had several lesbian relationships before meeting Leslie, her current partner of 5 years. She described the relationship as sweet and sour. On the one hand, Leslie is warm, caring, and very supportive; but on the other hand, she is pressuring her to be more active in the lesbian community and the feminist movement.

Leslie is from Ohio, from a middle class White family, and has been very active in lesbian and gay community affairs. She has been able to be out in her career as a health professional. Maria's sense of social responsibility is compromised by the consequences of coming out in her profession. Although her partner has encouraged her, Maria feels some resentment at the people pressuring her to make choices. She recalled her involvement in lesbian and gay groups in the past and how torn she felt about choosing between the lesbian and gay community and the Puerto Rican community. Either way she felt she had much to lose; yet she felt obligated to choose.

The pressure and stress has reached a point at which Maria suspects that someone in her office saw her at a lesbian bar, thereby discovering her sexual orientation. Maria feels the grapevine gossip in the office will threaten her job and career. She is currently under consideration for promotion, has received excellent job performance ratings, and has been widely praised for her work. She feels angry that the results of her hard work may dissipate because of this issue. She expressed feelings of anger toward Leslie for not fully understanding what she is going through. Maria is beginning to believe that if her lover were Latina, these relationship issues would be better understood. Perhaps there is some reason and truth to "sticking to your own kind." She came to counseling because she had been in therapy before and found the sessions helpful.

Clinical Strategies for the Case of Maria

In contrast to Juan, Maria's experience in therapy allows for a different approach toward counseling. Her history suggests a person who has much determination, ambition, and broad-based experiences in life. Through her inner and familial resources, she was able to change her socioeconomic and educational level dramatically and maintain a commitment to social issues and to her own personal growth.

The preferred counseling approach is an insight-oriented perspective involving an in-depth examination of her personality processes. In relation to her sexual identity concerns, one can see that Maria is faced with several challenges that seem to center around State 4 of the Morales model, Establishing Priorities of Allegiance. It appears that Maria has been maintaining at State 3, Conflicts of Allegiance, until the recent challenges and conflicts created an imbalance and dissonance. Her frustration and anger force her to set priorities in her allegiances. She may also elect to reinforce her integrated identity as a Latina lesbian and assert her identity accordingly. This would place her in State 5, Integrating the Various Communities, in which she must learn how to incorporate a multicultural perspective and to manage the conflicts that arise among those who are less integrated. These issues need to be incorporated into the overall clinical assessment of her personality characteristics in order to enhance an integrated counseling strategy.

Incorporating Community and Social Support

For both Juan and Maria there is a central need for integration and cohesion in their lives. For Juan, State 2, Bisexual Versus Gay or Lesbian

Identity, seems to explain his issues of sexual orientation in addition to the acculturation and assimilation issues, whereas for Maria the other later states seem to apply. The support systems from their Latino and Latina background can be further enhanced through the cultural values centered around the family. Reinforcing their sense of who is family for them and how they can be supported according to their culturally based expectations may provide a sense of psychosocial support. Depending on the appropriateness of each case, coming out to the family may be a way to further develop a sense of integration. Exploring the availability of and contact with organizations, coming out groups, support groups, and other support systems for Latino gays and Latina lesbians will enhance the identity process.

Social support and community resources vary by geographical region and urban centers. Many counselors may feel helpless amid the lack of resources available to such clients. Keeping abreast of events, conferences, and gatherings of such groups on a local and national level can be a way to provide some alternatives to clients. Many individuals find ways to attend such events, and others appreciate the information and may eventually seek out more information. Books and articles are useful in providing a sense of identity and support.

The issues of Latino gays and Latina lesbians will continue to evolve as the community becomes more developed. There are various Latino gay and Latina lesbian organizations at local, state, and national levels that have been formed to advocate for the needs of their community. It is important that counselors keep abreast of the issues and developments in the community for Latino gays and Latina lesbians. The skills of a therapist can be instrumental in alleviating these stress-related problems. The role of the therapist is to facilitate change by encouraging the development of a positive identity within a multicultural context so that individuals can approach and reach their potential and maximize their skills and talents.

References

Bernal, G. (1982). Cuban families. In M. McGoldrick, J. Pearce, & J. Giordano (Eds.), *Ethnicity and family therapy*. New York: Guilford Press.

de Monteflores, C. (1986). Notes on the management of difference. In T. S. Stein & C. J. Cohen (Eds.), *Contemporary perspectives on psychotherapy with lesbians and gay men* (pp. 73–101). New York: Plenum.

Carballo-Diéguez, A. (1989). Hispanic culture, gay male culture, and AIDS: Counseling implications. *Journal of Counseling & Development, 68,* 26–30.

Carrier, J. (1976). Family attitudes and Mexican male homosexuality. *Urban Life, 5*(3), 359–375.

Carrier, J. (1977). "Sex-role preference" as an explanatory variable in gay behavior. *Archives of Sexual Behavior, 6*(1), 53–65.

Carrier, J. (1989). Sexual behavior and spread of AIDS in Mexico. *Medical Anthropology, 10,* 129–142.

Espín, O. (1987). Issues of identity in the psychology of Latina lesbians. In Boston Lesbian Psychologies Collective (Eds.), *Lesbian psychologies: Explanations and challenges.* Urbana, IL: University of Illinois Press.

Falicov, C. J. (1982). Mexican families. In M. McGoldrick, J. Pearce, & J. Giordano (Eds.), *Ethnicity and family therapy.* New York: Guilford Press.

Garcia-Preto, N. (1982). Puerto Rican families. In M. McGoldrick, J. Pearce, & J. Giordano (Eds.), *Ethnicity and family therapy.* New York: Guilford Press.

Morales, E. (1983). *Third world gays and lesbians: A process of multiple identities.* Paper presented at the 91st national convention of the American Psychological Association, Anaheim, CA.

Morales, E. (1990). Ethnic minority families and minority gays and lesbians. In F. Bozett & M. Sussman (Eds.), *Homosexuality and family relations.* New York: Haworth.

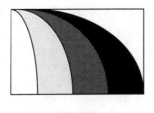

10

Gay, Lesbian, and African American: Managing the Integration of Identities

Fernando J. Gutiérrez, EdD
Sari H. Dworkin, PhD

The purpose of this chapter is to provide a brief look at the issues faced by African American lesbians and gay men and to discuss appropriate counseling interventions that can facilitate their growth and development within the context of the different worlds in which they operate. Loiacano (1989) pointed out that several theorists (Cass, 1979; Minton & McDonald, 1984) have conceptualized the process of gay identity development as a series of linear stage models (see the Terminology section in this book's Introduction on the coming out process). Loiacano also pointed out that research exists outlining differences between men and women in the process of developing a gay or lesbian identity (Faderman, 1984; Groves & Ventura, 1983; Schultz & de Monteflores, 1978).

Recently, several authors have explored the gay and lesbian identity issues of African Americans (Cornwell, 1979; De Marco, 1983; Icard,

The authors wish to thank Darryl Loiacano for his editorial comments on this chapter.

1986; Loiacano, 1988, 1989). Loiacano's (1988) study pointed out three major themes influencing the adjustment of African American gays and lesbians: (1) searching for validation in the gay and lesbian community, (2) searching for validation in the African American community, and (3) integrating these identities.

Often, validation in the gay and lesbian community requires African Americans and other minorities to deny their race and culture, in whole or in part, and to blend in, culturally, to the White gay and lesbian cultures or risk ostracism (Lorde, 1984). Loiacano (1989) cited De Marco's (1983) and Icard's (1986) work, noting that discrimination in admission to bars, in advertising, and in employment are just as relevant and present in the gay and lesbian community as in the mainstream White society, despite the gay and lesbian community's firsthand experience with sensitivities to oppression and sexism. This discrimination theme is also captured in Riggs' (1989) film, *Tongues Untied.* The resulting oppression by the White gay and lesbian culture forces African American lesbians and gay men to go back to their African American communities for support (Icard, 1986; Johnson, 1981). In doing so, however, gay and lesbian African Americans encounter the homophobic attitudes within the African American community (Riggs, 1989). According to Riggs, many African American gay and lesbian people perceive themselves as African American first and gay or lesbian second; therefore, the need for support from the African American community becomes more important to them.

This perceived lack of support both from the White gay and lesbian cultures and from the heterosexual African American cultures affects gay identity development (Icard, 1986) as well as racial identity development (Parham, 1989) because a positive identity depends upon interpersonal relationships with others, in this case those who are also gay or lesbian and African American (Icard, 1986).

Loiacano (1989) suggested the following questions for counselors to consider in their work with gay or lesbian African American clients:

1. What is the client's perception of support for his or her dual identity in the community?
2. Are there local groups in the client's community organized specifically for the needs of African American gay men and lesbians in which racial and sexual minorities can receive validation?
3. What are the client's personal issues in his or her journey toward gay and lesbian and racial identity development? What messages

has the client received in this regard from his or her respective reference groups?

4. What are the counselor's assumptions and the client's assumptions regarding the expression of one's homosexuality and degree of coming out? What might be realistic in a White context might not be realistic in an African American context or vice versa.
5. What African American gay men or lesbian women might be identified as contacts for the client or as examples of how to negotiate his or her identities in the respective communities?
6. What are the client's preferences for a counselor? Gay or lesbian, African American, or both?

We want to add a further question:

7. What are the counselor's assumptions regarding racial identity development?

These questions will be relevant as we discuss two cases in which an African American gay man, Charles, and a lesbian African American woman, Linda, deal with their issues in counseling. Charles was seen by a Latino gay counselor; Linda was seen by a White lesbian counselor.

Charles

Charles is a 23-year-old African American man who works as a retail clerk in a major department store in a large western city. He is out as a gay man to his family, and he is out at work. He grew up in a predominantly African American community in the Southeast where he had to deal with prejudicial attitudes of neighbors and classmates toward gays. As he is attempting to immerse himself into the gay world, he is encountering prejudice because of his race. He is feeling disconnected from the African American world as well as from the White gay world. Charles came to counseling because of depression, feelings of isolation, and problems with intimacy.

Charles had gone to three therapists prior to choosing a Latino counselor. Two of these counselors were White heterosexual women, and the third counselor was a gay African American man. There were no other African American therapists in the area. The Latino counselor had been recommended by a co-worker. Charles saw the change in his co-worker after seeing the Latino counselor, so Charles decided to attempt to work with him.

Course of Therapy

Charles' choice of an identified gay Latino counselor is significant. Charles wanted to work with a counselor who was sensitive to gay issues as well as ethnic minority issues, but he did not feel comfortable going to a gay-identified African American counselor. When Charles arrived in the Latino counselor's office, he began to look around the walls of the waiting room, where the counselor had his diplomas, license, and certificates of inclusion into several honorary societies. The counselor observed Charles looking at these items when he went to greet Charles. Charles was startled when he saw the Latino counselor. The co-worker had not mentioned to Charles that the Latino counselor was Caucasian. The counselor noted Charles' reaction but did not address it at that point.

The counselor asked Charles what had brought him to the session. Charles mentioned his prior work with the three therapists. He dismissed the first two therapists because they were White, stating that they could not understand where he "was coming from." He also dismissed the African American counselor because, by Charles' own admission, Charles felt internalized oppression and perceived the African American counselor as not competent because of his race. This internalized racism was also discussed by Valdés, Barón, and Ponce (1987) in their work with Latino clients.

The counselor pondered with Charles what reasons Charles might use to discredit him as a counselor, and at this point, the counselor brought up his "Whiteness." The counselor also pointed out to Charles that he was the fourth therapist that Charles had seen and that a pattern was emerging: Charles tended to withdraw from the intimacy that he might begin to feel with a therapist. The counselor assured Charles that despite his Caucasian appearance, the counselor was ethnically identified. Charles felt reassured at this point, and a fruitful discussion centered around his fear of rejection by the therapist once the therapist began to get to know Charles. Charles also expressed shame in seeing the African American gay therapist because Charles did not have a clear racial identity developed and was embarrassed to admit this to the African American therapist, who strongly identified with his ethnic group. He was afraid that the counselor would impose his values on the client and that he might not "measure up" to the counselor's expectations for Charles' behavior as an African American gay male. A counselor who is ethnically identified but racially and culturally different gave Charles a feeling of distance that allowed him the freedom to explore his identity.

Charles' defense was to create distance from people. Feeling always different from his African American, White, and heterosexual counterparts, Charles learned to relate to people from a distance. A counselor who is not sensitive to the defenses that minority clients employ to adapt might not have seen this distancing as an issue for Charles and would not have been able to address Charles' choice of counselor as a therapeutic issue for Charles. This situation underscores the need for cross-cultural and sexual orientation training in counselor education programs.

Charles' identity issues are addressed by Parham (1989), who stated that:

> ... as long as Black people are subjected to racist and oppressive conditions in this society, and are confronted with the question of how much to compromise their Blackness in order to successfully assimilate, they (Blacks) will continue to need therapeutic assistance in struggling with issues of self-determination ... wherein an individual strives to become comfortable with the recognition that he or she is a worthwhile human being regardless of valuation or validation from Whites. (p. 217)

This statement is also certainly applicable to gays, lesbians, and bisexuals.

Charles' situation can be viewed using Gutiérrez' (1985) theoretical model of bicultural personality development. This model, shown in Table 1, incorporates Erikson's identity development model and several other sociological and anthropological models of acculturation/assimilation, including Atkinson, Morten, and Sue's (1983) model of minority identity development.

Column I in the table depicts Erikson's stages. Column II depicts the stages of disequilibrium that ethnic minorities or gays and lesbians can experience in their transition from a heterosexually imposed identity to a gay or lesbian identity. These stages of disequilibrium, according to Gutiérrez (1985), represent natural identity crises that individuals must resolve as they begin to experience cultural changes. Column III depicts the stages of acculturation/assimilation that lead to bicultural personality formation.

Table 1
Stages of Bicultural Personality Development

	I Psychological Stages	II Stages of Disequilibrium	III Stages of Acculturation/ Assimilation
1.	Trust vs. Mistrust	Lack of Knowledge of Host Culture	Culture Shock vs. Conformity
2.	Autonomy vs. Shame and Doubt	Sense of Nationalism for Native Country	Alienation vs. Role Accommodation
3.	Initiative vs. Guilt	Assimilation	Marginality vs. Role Accommodation
4.	Industry vs. Inferiority	Militancy	Immigrant Group Appreciation vs. Host Group Appreciation
5.	Identity vs. Identity Diffusion	Introspection	Rejection of Host Culture vs. Bicultural Sense of Peoplehood
6.	Intimacy vs. Isolation	Selective Appreciation	Self-Hatred vs. Bicultural Adjustment
7.	Generativity vs. Self-Absorption		
8.	Integrity vs. Despair		

The stages, numbered 1 through 8, are sequenced in the order in which they first appear; however, interactions among the stages do not necessarily occur in just one direction. A person may have experienced some of the stages in one culture earlier, and when exposed to another culture, he or she may go back to an earlier stage in order to incorporate this new information into the earlier developmental stage (for a detailed explanation see Gutiérrez, 1985).

According to Gutiérrez' model, Charles is in the Identity vs. Identity Diffusion stage (Stage 5, column I) (Erikson, 1980). Charles reports that despite the fact that he grew up in an African American community, his mother raised him to become White identified. As a result, Charles has not been able to develop a solid African American identity. He borrows from both cultures in a tentative manner and is afraid to solidify these cultural ways into his personality for fear of rejection by the various groups. He also borrows from the heterosexual culture as well as from the gay culture, again in a tentative manner, not allowing himself to identify with either culture.

Charles is experiencing various stages of disequilibrium (in column II). He lacks knowledge of the host gay culture as well as African American gay culture. He mistrusts his knowledge and identification of his African American culture due to the fact that his mother has unconsciously discouraged his identification with his "native" or African American culture in her attempt to have him assimilate and become successful in a White-dominated world. Charles' attempt at assimilation is creating stress at this time because of his fear of rejection by all the groups to which he is attempting to relate; therefore, he is feeling marginal as he attempts to accommodate the roles required of him from all his reference groups (as shown in Stage 3, column III). This feeling of marginality and fear of rejection are creating his sense of isolation and fear of intimacy.

Now that Charles' situation has been mapped out based on the stages of the bicultural personality development model, the goal of therapy is to assist Charles in solidifying his identity as an African American and gay person so that he will be able to move onto the next stage, Intimacy vs. Isolation (Stage 6, column I). In doing so, Charles will move from a feeling of marginality to a feeling of militancy (Stage 4, column II) and pride toward his African American and gay identities. This sense of pride will give him the strength to choose who he is within his reference groups, without fearing rejection by these groups.

The role of the therapist, in Charles' presenting complaint, is to accept Charles' perceptions of his world rather than challenge them at this point. Acceptance of his world creates a feeling of safety and understanding for Charles, which allows him to trust that the counselor understands his world view and will let Charles move at his own pace, not at the pace of the counselor's agenda. Because Charles is feeling marginal and is not perceiving support from either his African-American community or his White-dominated gay community, this support must now come from the counselor. The counselor must spend time listening to Charles' assumptions about his racial identity and gayness in order to understand how Charles is interpreting his world. This will give the counselor the clues as to what is working for Charles in his life and what is not.

The counselor can then reinforce what is working for Charles so that Charles can feel a sense of competence and a sense of identity. For example, the counselor can engage Charles in a conversation about what he likes or does not like about his racial and sexual identity. This will allow Charles the opportunity to explore both of his identities so that he can own what he likes about each of them, and thus, his identities will begin to take shape (Stage 5, column I). It also will teach Charles to evaluate these identities for himself rather than through his counselor's eyes, or the eyes of the White gay world or the heterosexual African American community.

As Charles begins to define these identities for himself and to receive support from the counselor for these identities, Charles may be ready to test these perceptions of his sense of self with members of the same racial and sexual communities. This will be Charles' attempt to assimilate and to move to the next stage, racial/gay group appreciation vs. rejection of the groups (Stage 4, column III).

During this stage, Charles may need support from the counselor in managing his self-perceptions as opposed to the group perceptions, which can often appear militant in stance. Charles may not be feeling the same passions for some of the issues the communities are confronting. Afraid that he may not be accepted by his communities, Charles may be tempted to retreat to the marginal stage (Stage 3, column III).

Throughout this process, Charles will be trying to work through his personal identity while immersing himself into the groups to which he belongs, with decreasing fear that his identity will be engulfed by the group identities. This identity resolution process is difficult for a typical White adolescent in a heterosexual White society. One can well imagine attempting to navigate this process while taking the variables of two other major groups into consideration in a hostile environment.

At this point, the support needed for this resolution to take place cannot be contained in the one-on-one counselor client relationship.

A counselor must be knowledgeable of the resources in the gay community as well as the resources in the African American community that Charles can plug into in order to work through and receive validation for his emerging identity. If there is a counseling group for gay African Americans in the community, the client may be referred to the group as a next step in the therapy. Before referring Charles to a predominantly White gay and lesbian group in which the client is the only African American, the counselor should screen the facilitator for his or her knowledge and sensitivity of African American culture and issues. Otherwise the referral could backfire if Charles experiences insensitivity from the other group members and/or the facilitator.

As Charles learns not to be threatened by the communities that are his source of support, he will learn from other gay African American men what his options are. The counselor as a role model is important here; therefore, a counselor working with a client like Charles may need to be more self-disclosing. The counselor shared with Charles some of the parallels of his own identity development as a Latino gay man. A counselor can highlight the fact to Charles that there is more than one group identity within the racial gay minority group, just as there is more than one group identity in the White culture, allowing him to choose from among the variety within each group to develop a more personal identity. The counselor thus can give Charles permission to express his own identity within a gay or African American group.

It is important for Charles to connect how his difficulties with intimacy and feeling of connectedness with others stem from his identity diffusion. Once Charles begins to commit to himself and define who he is, he will be able to solidify his identity, drop the defenses that protect his sense of self, and allow another person to approach without fearing engulfment. Solidifying his identity will allow Charles to remain consistent when approaching someone or when approached by someone or a group. As Charles' identity becomes stronger, it can withstand the challenges to his world view that others will make.

Charles' process has obviously been encapsulated because of space limitations: As O'Bear and Reynolds (1985) pointed out, this process can take years. A counselor can facilitate this process and show Charles that it is a process. Once Charles learns how to work with the process, the counselor can begin to slowly detach from Charles so that he can be on his own and tap into the natural support systems in his life. This process is further illustrated in the case of Linda.

Linda

Linda is a 22-year-old African American lesbian currently in a relationship with a Caucasian woman of the same age. They are both majoring in psychology at a large university in a small, conservative midwestern city. Linda came to the therapist because she knew the therapist was lesbian. In fact, they had seen each other at some community events, although they had never met.

Linda's presenting complaint included feelings of mild anxiety and mild depression. Linda was at a loss to explain what was happening. School was going well, her relationship of a year was going well; she had a nice circle of friends and participated in events in the women's community. It was true that she did not particularly like the city because it was small, too hot in the summer, and too cold in the winter; however, the living arrangements were temporary. Both she and her lover expected to move to a larger city as soon as they both completed their studies, probably to San Francisco.

Linda grew up in Los Angeles, the youngest of two children. Her parents were both professionals. Her father was an attorney, and her mother was a high school teacher. Her brother was 25 years old, attending UCLA Law School, and soon to be married to an African American woman. The family lived in a primarily White, middle-class suburban neighborhood. As Linda was growing up, most of the family friends were Caucasian, but Linda remembers attending family gatherings every year in Mississippi and learning about her African American heritage. Her brother rebelled against the family he perceived as "oreo" (Black on the outside and White on the inside).

In recent years, her parents were also identifying more with the African American community in Los Angeles. Linda always felt different and recognized her same-sex attraction in high school. In fact, the reason she was attending college in this city, much to her parents' dismay, was that she followed her high school sweetheart there. That relationship did not last long, but Linda decided to stay here for a number of reasons. A major reason was that she was not out as a lesbian to her family and actually felt more free to be herself in this distant community. The lesbian activism in this conservative city amazed her, and she felt she could be herself here. Her lesbian identity was her primary identity. Linda was comfortable with her lesbian identity and appeared to be in the Identity Acceptance stage of the Cass (1979) model (see Introduction).

Course of Therapy

One of the first things the therapist discussed with Linda was how comfortable she felt working with a White therapist. According to Linda, it was of primary importance that the therapist was a lesbian. The therapists's race did not matter. In fact, she felt more comfortable with White people than with African American people. According to Cushman (1990), individuals who differ from the White characteristics valued by society may nevertheless grow up valuing these characteristics.

African American lesbians go through at least two identity developmental processes: ethnic identity development and lesbian identity development. The five-stage model of minority identity development (Atkinson et al., 1983) proposes the following stages: Conformity, Dissonance, Resistance and Immersion, Introspection, and Synergetic Articulation and Awareness. In terms of her racial identity, Linda appeared to be in the Conformity stage, in which the dominant group and values are preferred.

Linda's eyes welled with tears when she stated that she felt more comfortable with White people; the therapist asked what the pain was for her. The pain had to do with shame about being different and with feeling that she did not belong anywhere. Her family of origin, and especially her extended family, held the traditional values of marriage and family as important to women.

The oldest brother, whom Linda respected, had made statements about homosexuality being a product of White culture. African Americans tend to deny the existence of gayness and lesbianism in their culture by "blaming" its existence on the White culture; however, homosexuality exists in almost every culture. This belief in the African American culture creates a feeling of shame among African Americans who are gay or lesbian. As a result, the lesbian community was the only place where Linda felt she belonged, but even here she felt different because there were few lesbians of color, although she never realized this mattered. Now she began to question whether or not the lesbian community was really a safe place.

Linda was becoming cognizant of racist attitudes within the lesbian community. The therapist validated the hurt and anger this beginning awareness was causing, especially within the one community originally thought to be safe. This validation of the loss felt after breaking through the denial of the oppressive attitudes is considered to be especially important when working with African American gay men or lesbians (Gock, 1990).

Linda was aware of these oppressive attitudes in the African American world regarding homosexuality, so she defended by creating a haven for herself in the lesbian world. As she worked through her identity issues, she began to be aware of the dynamics of rejection within the lesbian community as well. This questioning of the lesbian community resulted from her enrollment in a women's studies class focusing on women's literature. The readings included works by lesbians of color, and class discussions included issues of multiple oppressions such as racism and anti-Semitism within the lesbian community.

Suddenly, or so it felt to her, Linda's African American identity began to take on more importance. This class served as the impetus for Linda to see that she often struggled between the pride she felt when she was with her extended family and her brother began asserting his identity and the pain she felt at her parents' lack of identification with her African American heritage. This struggle continued when her acceptance of her lesbian identity separated her from her family and caused her to entrench herself into the White Lesbian community, where she felt support for one of her identities.

Now Linda was confused about where she belonged, which of her identities was most important, and if there was any way to integrate it all. She also, hesitantly, wondered what impact this might have on her relationship with her White lover. As an adjunct to therapy, the therapist suggested that Linda might join the support group for lesbians of color, a critical experience in which lesbians are dealing with the integration of both their lesbian and ethnic identities. Linda was unaware of this group's existence because she had little contact with the few lesbians of color within the community.

Attending this group was anxiety provoking at first because Linda was afraid she would not even fit in here, but the group proved to be beneficial. It was a safe place to explore issues of identity, pain from racism in the lesbian community, and pain from homophobia in ethnic communities.

Linda and her lover came to some sessions together and began exploring the impact of Linda's new-found sense of pride about her racial identity on their relationship. Some problems had begun to arise as Linda became more vocal about her identification of racist incidents to her lover, Sue. This was causing anxiety for Sue as she began to recognize the racism in her White culture. Sue felt her culture was under attack, and she felt lumped into the "oppressor" group.

Feeling the need to defend against this unwanted identification, Sue accused Linda of being sensitive to things which never seemed to matter before, the implication being that the issues did not exist and Linda was perceiving these incidents inaccurately. Linda felt unsupported and was often irritable. In spite of the fact that Linda's African American identity was not clear to her as a factor before, Linda felt different from the White ideal and had constructed armor to protect herself from racist onslaughts, a process discussed by Clunis and Green (1988). This armor was now cracking as she felt the lack of support from Sue.

Sue was fearful that racial differences might prove insurmountable and would destroy the relationship, which was very important to her. The relationship was loving and strong, with good communication skills; however, Sue needed to learn to let Linda have her anger and not feel threatened by it. Sue agreed to join a group that was exploring racism and anti-Semitism within the lesbian community. In this group, Sue learned exactly what it meant to have White privilege.

Sue and Linda agreed to begin socializing with some of the other interracial lesbian couples. The therapist validated that this was a difficult time for their relationship and reinforced their ability to listen and accept each other's feelings. The therapist helped them to set some ground rules about how they would deal with racist issues, Linda's occasional feelings of resentment about Sue's White privilege, and Sue's insecurity regarding Linda's anger, as suggested by Clunis and Green (1988). There was no doubt that the nature of their relationship was changing significantly.

Another issue explored in therapy was Linda's coming out to her family. This was important to her as it was getting more difficult to hide in spite of the distance between them. Linda wanted her family to accept her and her lover. Linda's perception was that in her family of origin her brother would have the hardest time with her lesbian identity.

The therapist gave Linda reading material about families' reactions to a child who is gay or lesbian. Linda remarked how deficient the reading material was in dealing with ethnic issues. We explored the similarities between her coming out process and her family's grief process in acknowledging her lesbianism: the denial (no, it's her exposure to White culture), anger (how could she betray our African American heritage—from her brother), bargaining, (she'll grow out of it), depression (this is hopeless), and acceptance (she's our daughter and we have to understand who she is and love her because of who she is).

Role plays were used in which Linda could practice sharing her new-found sense of African American pride with her family, especially by telephone with her brother. Linda felt that she and her brother would become closer, but at the same time Linda's anxiety increased because of the possibility of rejection. Linda came out to her family, and they did not reject her. There were some harsh words (particularly with her brother, and this had more to do with the fact that her lover was White than that Linda was a lesbian), lots of tears, and eventual reconciliation.

The family did demand that Linda not come out to her extended family in Mississippi and not bring Sue to extended family gatherings. Linda accepted this, although she shared with me that eventually she would like to start bringing Sue as a "friend." She doubted that she would ever come out to the extended family because their support was too important to her. Linda hoped this would not become an issue for Sue who seemed to be out to everyone.

Therapy ended when Linda and her lover Sue felt that the support groups were doing more good than the therapy sessions. Linda was still attending the lesbian of color support group; and Sue was attending the racism and anti-Semitism group. They also attended the group for interracial lesbian and gay couples. An integration of Linda's identities was developing. The therapist left the door open for Linda to return if she needed to, and the therapist also gave her the name of a female African American, nonlesbian psychologist in the city to contact to deal with her African American identity more in depth.

Conclusion

Identity development is an important theme in the adjustment of African Americans to their homosexuality. Managing the environment of the client is essential in facilitating the support needed for African Americans to integrate their racial identity with their sexual orientation.

As we saw in Charles' case, he was accepting of his sexual orientation, to the point that he was out to his family and employer; however, his adjustment went in a direction that disconnected him from the White heterosexual and gay worlds as well as the African American community.

In Linda's case, she chose to identify with the White lesbian world, which seemed safer than the African American world, initially.

As Charles and Linda progressed through their stages of minority identity development, the counselors assisted them in the process through self-disclosure, validation, and management of identity diffusion by allowing the clients to define who they were, without feeling rejection or fear of engulfment. Accepting the client's world view and assisting them in testing the reality of that world view is also an important process in the counseling. Loiacano's (1989) questions become important for counselors to examine as they engage in this process with their clients.

In Linda's case, the counselor worked not only with Linda but also with her lover, Sue, so that Sue could examine her assumptions of Linda's culture and perceptions. This way the burden was not on Linda to adapt to Sue's culture, but for both of them to learn to understand each other's differences as well as similarities.

Knowledge of the resources in the community to deal with both sexual orientation and racial identity is essential for counselors to be effective.

Finally, recognizing that within a group there are cultural differences can be freeing for clients. Such recognition allows clients to choose the characteristics of the culture to which they relate and allows them room for individual identity.

References

Atkinson, D., Morten, G., & Sue, D. (1983). *Counseling American minorities.* Dubuque, IA: Brown.

Cass, V. C. (1979). Homosexual identity formation: A theoretical model. *Journal of Homosexuality, 4,* 219–235.

Clunis, D., & Green, G. (1988). *Lesbian couples.* Seattle, WA: Seal Press.

Cornwell, A. (1979). Three for the price of one: Notes from a gay Black feminist. In K. Jay & A. Young (Eds.), *Lavender culture: The perceptive voices of outspoken lesbians and gay men* (pp. 466–476). New York: Jove.

Cushman, P. W. (1990). Case II: Black gay male from psychiatry. *Journal of Gay and Lesbian Psychotherapy, 1,* 6–9.

De Marco, J. (1983). Gay racism. In M. J. Smith (Ed.), *Black men/White men: A gay anthology* (pp. 108–118). San Francisco: Gay Sunshine Press.

Erikson, E. (1980). *Identity and the life cycle.* New York: Norton.

Faderman, L. (1984). The "new gay" lesbians. *Journal of Homosexuality, 10,* 85–95.

Groves, P., & Ventura, L. (1983). The lesbian coming out process: Therapeutic considerations. *The Personnel and Guidance Journal, 62,* 146–149.

Gock, T. (1990). Case II: Black gay male from psychology. *Journal of Gay and Lesbian Psychotherapy, 1,* 9–12.

Gutiérrez, F. (1985). Bicultural personality development: A process model. In E. García & R. Padilla (Eds.), *Advances in bilingual education research* (pp. 96–124). Tucson: University of Arizona Press.

Icard, L. (1986). Black gay men and conflicting social identities: Sexual orientation vs. racial identity. In J. Grinton & M. Valentich (Eds.), *Social work practice in sexual problems* [Special issue, *Journal of Social Work & Human Sexuality,* 4(1/2) 83–93]. New York: Haworth.

Johnson, J. (1981). *Influence of assimilation on the psychological adjustment of Black homosexual men.* Unpublished doctoral dissertation, California School of Professional Psychology, Berkeley.

Loiacano, D. (1988). *Gay identity acquisition and the Black American experience: Journeys of pride and pain.* Unpublished master's thesis, University of Pennsylvania School of Social Work, Philadelphia.

Loiacano, D. (1989). Gay identity issues among Black Americans: Racism, homophobia, and the need for validation. *Journal of Counseling & Development, 68,* 21–25.

Lorde, A. (1984). *Sister outsider.* Trumansburg, NY: Crossing Press.

Minton, H., & McDonald, G. (1984). Homosexual identity formation as a developmental process. *Journal of Homosexuality, 9,* 91–104.

O'Bear, K., & Reynolds, A. (1985). *Opening doors to understanding and acceptance: A facilitator's guide for presenting workshops on lesbian and gay issues.* Manual presented at the American College Personnel Association convention, Boston.

Parham, T. (1989). Cycles of psychological nigrescence. *The Counseling Psychologist, 17,* 187–226.

Riggs, M. (1989). *Tongues untied.* New York: P.V.O.

Schultz, S., & de Monteflores, C. (1978). Coming out: Similarities and differences for lesbians and gay men. *Journal of Social Issues, 34,* 59–72.

Valdés, L., Barón, A., & Ponce, F. (1987). Counseling Hispanic men. In M. Scher, M. Stevens, G. Good, & G. Eichenfield (Eds.), *Handbook of counseling and psychotherapy with men* (pp. 203–217). Newbury Park, CA: Sage.

11

Psychotherapy With Physically Disabled Lesbians

Ricki Boden, LCSW, MFCC

Psychotherapy relevant to lesbians with physical disabilities[1] must include (1) awareness of the societal context confronting disabled lesbians as members of a minority group and (2) an understanding of

---

[1] I began my involvement in disability work, politically and as a therapist in 1977. I have used many terms over the years, e.g., *physically challenged, differently abled*, etc. After much soul searching and many hours of consultation with other colleagues with disabilities I have decided to continue to use the term *disabled*. I feel the other terms, although well intentioned, are euphemistic and avoid the real issue. Those of us with disabilities really do have limitations caused by physical conditions that require us to seek accommodation and access in order to function at our fullest potential. Almost all people with disabilities would take a pill without hesitation to make their disability go away. I would never take a pill to make me straight. I have no desire to be heterosexual; I do desire to be able-bodied. The route to self-affirmation and acceptance, in that sense, is different than the route to lesbian and gay pride. For me, *physically challenged* or *differently abled* do not capture the seriousness and depth of our pain and struggle. A friend of mine who is visibly disabled described her daily struggle as being "center stage but invisible"—stared at but avoided. I want to be appreciated, and appreciate myself, for what I really deal with. From that I derive pride and self-esteem.

the experience of difference. When difference is experienced as a defect, it results in shame, self-loathing, and fear of exposure. These shame-based feelings become the central themes that color self-organization. When the feeling of defect is due to a physical difference or disability, shame surrounding the perceived defect—which can be conscious or unconscious—may become a focal point for shame related to other areas of vulnerability.

This chapter focuses on psychotherapy with lesbians who have birth and childhood-onset physical disabilities. Selected aspects of two cases are presented that demonstrate the psychological impact of lifelong disabilities. In addition to shame, which is a pervasive dynamic in both cases, several common clinical themes are described. It is important to note that each client specifically sought services in a lesbian-and gay-identified clinic from a lesbian- and disabled-identified therapist. Self-psychology, with its emphasis on subjective experience, provides this chapter's framework for an understanding of difference and the revelation of shame.

Although I focus on depth psychotherapy, I do not mean to imply that all lesbians with physical disabilities require long-term treatment. Physical disability itself is not determinant of psychological dysfunction (Blumberg, Lewis, & Susman, 1984; Drotar, Crawford, & Bush, 1984; Offer, Ostrow, & Howard, 1984). Many disabled clients benefit from supportive, short-term counseling, particularly if they are newly diagnosed or when an adjustment to a new level of functioning is required by a progression of symptoms of lifelong disability. If these events occur during an on-going depth psychotherapy, a temporary change of therapeutic focus and style is often necessary. Disability issues will become foreground and crisis or problem-solving-oriented interventions may be most appropriate.

Depth psychotherapy is helpful for those disabled clients who have personality structures that are particularly vulnerable to low self-esteem and who have difficulty regulating their affective states. This may prevent them from benefiting from brief problem-focused treatment. Clients with childhood-onset disabilities may also benefit from psychotherapy because a subjective sense of difference or defectiveness in any arena is inextricably interwoven with feelings about their disability. Lesbians must grapple with a sense of difference from a predominantly heterosexual culture. This feeling of difference, especially if it is experienced as defectiveness, is likely to restimulate earlier feelings of defectiveness related to disability that may bring previously unavailable affects about a childhood disability into awareness. Additionally, psychotherapy focused on disability issues can provide an avenue to examine other areas of early childhood trauma, including incest and abuse. The reverse may also occur, in which the exploration of incest, abuse, and other shame-inducing trauma can lead to the revelation of shame about a physical disability.

Creating a "Disabled Lesbian Assumption"

People with physical disabilities and chronic illness live in a world where the values, ideals, and goals of the dominant culture are based on what I refer to as an "able-bodied assumption"—a world in which physical limitations are seen as the exception, viewed as problematic, and often judged perjoratively. In an environment with a "disabled assumption" physical differences are the norm. The assumption is that all situations require some modification both for physical access and for effective communication. In the psychotherapeutic setting, it is assumed that the psychotherapist is familiar with the clinical issues of disability therapy and is aware of any countertransference regarding disabilities that might interfere with the treatment (Boden, 1988).

Lesbians with physical disabilities not only live in an able-bodied world in which they experience a sense of difference but must also negotiate a world that has a heterosexual assumption. In this world, heterosexuality is the norm and is culturally reinforced. De Monteflores (1986) presented an insightful description of the management of difference by ethnic and sexual minorities as they struggle to live in a society that devalues them. Like ethnic minority gays, disabled lesbians are twice removed—at a minimum—from the dominant cultural ideal, which makes it particularly difficult to develop self-esteem and maintain a firm and cohesive identity.

A "disabled lesbian assumption" creates an environment in which being a lesbian and being disabled is normative. Barriers to understanding and communication are reduced when one feels surrounded by shared values, goals, and ideals. The client can feel fully welcomed. She does not have to hide her lesbianism in order to discuss her disability concerns, nor does she have to minimize her disability in order to discuss her lesbian issues. Creating a disabled lesbian assumption in psychotherapy is a challenging task. But as we all know, there is no such thing as value-free therapy. If we do not expand our thinking about psychotherapy to include issues relevant to lesbians with physical disabilities then we are simply promulgating a heterosexual able-bodied assumption that does not facilitate the building of an effective therapeutic alliance. In particular, a therapy environment that does not embrace difference will impede the exposure of difference, revelation of shame, and therefore the healing process itself.

Self-Psychology

Self-psychology defines psychopathology, or self-disorders, as a function of derailed self-development due to disruptions in the necessary attunement from the caregiving environment (Kohut, 1977). Kohut (1984) described three needs of the developing self: (1) the mirroring self-object function—the need to be recognized, affirmed, and admired; (2) the idealizing self-object functions—the need to merge with and be part of an omnipotent, idealized other; and (3) the alter ego or twinship self-object functions—the need to feel the same as others and to be part of a larger community, part of humankind. Self-psychology's transference conceptualizations provide a useful understanding of self-esteem vulnerabilites, defects of the self, and shame. These three needs of the developing self as applied to physically disabled lesbian clients contribute to a useful framework for therapy.

A prominent feature of self-psychologically informed psychotherapy is the therapist's understanding of the client through empathic immersion in the client's subjective experience. The client's current experience is then explained (interpreted) by the therapist in the context of both present and early childhood self-object needs (Ornstein & Ornstein, 1985). Self-psychology focuses on the impact of disruptions in the therapy relationship, which are considered "empathic failures." Working through these ruptures leads to the building of self-structure and therefore to increased self-cohesion and self-esteem. This framework provides a uniquely receptive psychotherapy environment in which difference experienced as defect is more likely to be revealed, understood, and, hopefully, transformed.

Shame: The Hidden Thread

Shame is a thread running through the self-structure of people with childhood-onset physical disabilities or chronic illness. A physical disability produces vulnerability to lowered self-esteem and affective dysregulation. A difference, or defect, of the body-self affects the most primitive levels of self-organization. A responsive environment modulates the potentially destructive impact of difference. A nonresponsive or damaging surrounding increases this feeling of defectiveness. This sense of defectiveness is central to the experience of shame.

A lesbian with an early-onset disability, already high risk to be shame-prone, must now deal with yet another difference as sexual identity develops. Often seen as defective by the heterosexual world, she may experience her new self-awareness as another shame-inducing flaw.

The experience of shame leads to the desire to hide and cover over a flawed, loathsome, and defective self. In social shame, a person hides to get distance from a viewing other who is experienced as sharing the view of the person as defective. Humiliation, the most intense form of interpersonal shame, involves an external or internalized humiliator (Morrison, 1989). Women are socialized to be more attuned to relational nuances and therefore are at high risk for this form of shame (Boden, Hunt, & Kassoff, 1987). Shame can also result from the perception of one's own defectiveness or when needed self-object responses are disrupted. Hiding is common in these instances as well because the experience of shame is too overwhelming to tolerate.

Nonempathic, nonresponsive interpretations rupture the self-object (transference) relationship and can bring hidden shame into the foreground of therapy. For clients who have been continually exposed to a nonresponsive or inappropriately responsive milieu, the need for support and validation itself can elicit shame (Morrison, 1989). We can identify ruptures in mirroring, idealizing, or alter ego self-object transferences and notice the resulting overstimulations, fragmentation, or depletion that ensues. At these junctures there is an opportunity to address underlying shame. Clients with a more developed and cohesive self-structure can experience shame and express feelings associated with shame directly. Shame in clients with self-esteem vulnerabilities is more hidden, experienced as devastating, and is less likely to be revealed in psychotherapy.

I find it more reflective of the empathic vantage point in psychotherapy to think of the use of defense and resistance as "hiding" behaviors, that is, they are conscious and unconscious attempts to get distance from the therapist or the painful affect of shame itself. Clients can hide by denying attachment to the therapy or the therapist. Needs themselves may be denied. Clients who appear stylized or inauthentic in sessions may be hiding shame by avoiding potentially overexposing contact. Shame may be a hidden precipitant of depression and rage (Morrison, 1989), disavowed affect, and dissociative states. Confusion and difficulty in knowing what one feels are often also rooted in shame.

Shame is an often neglected affect in the psychological literature and in the psychotherapy setting. Exploration of the underlying threads of shame in the complex fabric of a person's experiential world deepens and enriches the psychotherapeutic process.

Clinical Themes in Psychotherapy With Disabled Lesbians

Common themes in psychotherapy with lesbians with childhood-onset disabilities are described in this section. The severity of one's symptoms is directly correlated with the level of self-disorder. It is important to remember that physical disability itself is not the determinant of self-pathology (Zeltzer, Kellerman, Ellenberg, Dath, & Rigler, 1980). The interaction of constitutional factors and the responsiveness of the self-object environment serve to determine the degree of self-esteem vulnerability we see in our clients.

Abandonment. Children with disabilities typically spend time undergoing medical procedures and hospitalizations. Abandonment is experienced as the actual physical absence of parental figures, as the disruptions in emotional ties with significant figures who provide needed self-object functions. These ruptures provide fertile ground for the development of shame-proneness. Coming out as a lesbian may lead to parental and societal abandonment that restimulates earlier wounds.

Inclusion/exclusion. Disabled children often are excluded from many activities of their peers, particularly during adolescence, which heightens sensitivity to this issue. The desire to be included, which is often experienced as not wanting to be different, may unduly affect life decisions. Lesbians who have been abandoned and excluded by their families of origin need to develop support networks and families of choice. Group psychotherapy with other disabled lesbians provides the needed alter ego self-object functions of sameness and peer bonding that diminish the sense of difference and defect and allow shame to surface and be worked through.

Anger. Lesbians with birth-onset disabilities may have repressed, denied, or disavowed much of their anger, which I have observed to be an effective survival strategy for the disabled child who must maintain ties to her caretakers. The angry child is at higher risk for abandonment. Current research shows us that disabled children are more likely to be physically and sexually abused than their able-bodied peers (Courtois, 1988). It is important to note that rage is a disintegration product of a collapsing self-structure. Rage and anger that are used to hide intolerable shame need to be differentiated from healthy anger.

The discovery and expression of healthy anger is an important therapeutic goal.

Self-knowing. Disruptions in self-knowing occur when the client is unable to identify feeling states. Confusion, disorganization, and fragmentation result in severe cases. Although the origins of this disruption may be understood in terms of unmet mirroring needs related to physical disability, it can generalize to other areas of self-knowledge. Healthy self-development requires a nurturing parental environment that is attuned to the unfolding needs of the infant. The child's grandiose exhibitionistic self requires affirmation of its uniqueness and assertion. The child is then able to move forward in life, fueled by healthy grandiosity and pulled by goals and ideals. The experience of "not being seen" (Schavrien, 1989) leads to the inability to see one's self. The recognition and development of lesbian identity may parallel early experiences of confusion and "not knowing" or may function reparatively as a source of affirming self-knowledge that can aid in the healing of old wounds.

Specialness. Entitlement, with its accompanying demands for special treatment and rage at disappointments, is the most overt form of this clinical theme. Feelings of entitlement underlie fiercely dependent, passive, and manipulative behaviors and impair one's capacity for empathy. Legitimate "special" physical needs may not be addressed directly, but instead unrealistic emotional demands are expressed. It is important to understand that these behaviors function as protection against feared misunderstanding, rejection, and disappointment. The underlying experience as special, different, and set apart from others generates shame. Mirroring deficits and distortions prevents needed modulation of the grandiose exhibitionistic self, which leads to overstimulation and exposure of deficiency. This produces shame so intolerable that it must be securely hidden behind a screen of entitlement. Pride in lesbian identity is a means to positively embrace specialness and difference; as it reverberates through the self-organization, it can strengthen a structure weakened by specific unmet self-object needs.

Case Examples

Dana

Dana, a profoundly depressed 27-year-old White woman, contacted me periodically over a period of 5 years requesting information about the psychotherapy group for lesbians with physical disabilities and chronic illnesses that I facilitate. She finally "got up the nerve" to make an intake appointment, stating that she "felt abandoned" by her individual therapist who had become less available to her because of the therapist's family crisis. Dana has a history of severe learning disabilities, which were diagnosed in the third grade. She developed arthritis during her childhood and now suffers with chronic pain. She hoped that group therapy with other disabled lesbians would help her "accept" her disabilities. Dana feels comfortable with her lesbian identity. This was the only area of self-knowing she trusted. She came out during early adolescence and had a best friend who was also a lesbian. She participated in lesbian community events and received support from several older lesbians. Dana's lesbian identity is a cohesive source of self-knowledge and served as a bridge to beginning a psychotherapy that focused on disability.

Dana described her mother as absent, sometimes psychotic, and suicidal. Her idealized father both "mothered" and sexually abused her, which caused severe deficits and distortions in her mirroring line of development. Dana finds it difficult to trust in her own experience and often questions if she is really physically disabled and if she experienced incest. She expresses a deep conviction that she is defective and is overwhelmed by shame. This shameful defectiveness manifests itself both in a history of cutting and burning herself since age 7, and in chronic suicidal ideation. She is frequently confused, shows dissociative symptoms, is often fragmented, but is not psychotic.

Dana was reticent to take time in group therapy at first. When she eventually spoke, she said she wished to have the power to decide "not to be disabled anymore." After several sessions she came in saying she was afraid that she was "too heavy" for the group and that they would "kick her out." She seemed to respond well to the group's reassurances that this was the right group for her even if she did not yet know that herself. She asked for help knowing how "normal" people felt about things and how they took care of themselves.

Following are process notes that illustrate the pervasive dynamic of Dana's disturbance in self-knowing—a deficit in her mirroring line to self-development:

> Dana: I'm a fake and a liar. There's nothing really wrong with me, I can do things, walk up a hill, if I really want to.
> Therapist: When you do these things, like walk up a hill, how do you feel?

Dana: I don't feel anything, it's not a big deal. My hips and knees hurt a lot, the rest of the day is hard.

Therapist: Hard?

Dana: I hurt a lot.

Therapist: It seems that you often have to decide how much pain is worth it to you to do physical things, yet you have voices inside saying you're a fake. That must be so confusing, to know you hurt, that there's something wrong, but to think you're lying at the same time.

[Dana has great difficulty sorting out her own experience and did not receive help with this when growing up. Rather than rush in to reassure her that she is indeed disabled, I focused on her difficulty "knowing" her own experience.]

Dana: (Crying) I just don't know, maybe everyone is like this. Do people wake up hurting in the morning?

Therapist: Most people don't unless they have something physically wrong with them.

Dana: Do you think something is wrong with me?

Therapist: Yes, I do. You have arthritis which causes you differing amounts of pain at different times.

[I felt it was important to respond directly to Dana's question at this time. She was asking for help to clarify her own self-experience. Many people with childhood-onset disabilities have trouble knowing what is normal. What is normal for Dana, that is, chronic pain, is unusual for others. It was important to include my understanding of the fluctuations in her pain level. She is confused by the fluctuations, often using them to invalidate her own experience.]

Dana: Do you think I'm crazy?

Therapist: What do you mean?

Dana: That I'm a liar, a fake.

Therapist: No, I can see that you are hurting right now. I understand how hard it is for you to believe yourself. So here you are hurting, not believing yourself, and I can see how that makes you feel crazy.

Dana: It does, it really does.

[Dana is very fearful of being "crazy" like her psychotic mother. Her fear is compounded by having a learning disability— "There's something wrong with my brain"—that was denied in her family. At age 12 Dana was hospitalized for 6 months in an attempt to diagnose her developmental delays. Many tests were performed, and exploratory brain surgery was discussed and then ruled out after a psychiatrist intervened. She was then moved to a psychiatric unit, and family therapy was recommended, which her father refused to attend. Her mother slashed her wrists after his refusal. Her father's insistence that there was nothing wrong with Dana left her confused. She has maintained a connection with the psychiatrist and uses the memory of the hospitalization to anchor her perceptions: "At least I know I was really in the hospital." This hospital stay became a family secret, which left Dana laden with shame and believing she had to hide the fact that there was something wrong with her. The one event that helped her organize and understand her experience was colored with shame and confusion. In the above intervention I try to convey my understanding of her feeling "crazy."]

Nine months later, Dana asked the group if she could bring in a card her father had sent her and a tape recording of a family dinner scene when she was 10 years old. She blushed profusely. The group members said yes. She said she just wanted "to show us." I did not inquire further, wanting to support her willingness to expose more of herself and not induce a shame reaction, which I knew would lead to self-loathing and withdrawal. In the next session Dana haltingly read us the card, which on the surface sounded warm and chatty. It included a reference to a specific page in a religious pamphlet that her father had also sent. The most striking paragraph in the pamphlet referred to preoccupation with hypochondria as a way to avoid the correct religious path and seemed to reveal Dana's father's opinion of her. The room fell silent. Dana sat very still with a pleading look in her eyes. Outbursts from group members followed, expressing outrage at her father's implication that Dana was a hypochondriac. Group members expressed how invalidating and wounding this was.

Then Dana played the tape. At first it sounded like an ordinary, happy family dinner time. And then her father began to direct the conversation to a specific topic using a friendly and warm tone of voice. He asked 10-year-old Dana a question to which she responded in an animated way. Without any change in voice tone he repeatedly reasked the question, refocusing it slightly, waiting for the right answer. What followed was an interaction in which Dana's voice became increasingly lowered and monotonal. She sounded profoundly depressed at the end of the exchange when she finally made the "correct" response. The other siblings were silent, which was quite a contrast to the boisterous chatter at the tape's beginning. The image of Dana, utterly defeated and publicly humiliated, crystalized. The tape then proceeded as if nothing strange had happened, the father warm and friendly, the siblings chatty; but nothing more was heard of Dana's voice.

Dana said, "See, it's a nice happy family, it sounds good, doesn't it?" A group member asked Dana what she thought about the tape. Dana said she didn't know, it sounded "regular." The group member said that what she (the group member) thought about the tape wasn't important, but Dana's feelings were. Dana stared at the ground, unresponsive. I intervened saying to the group member that Dana was confused by the tape and had trouble knowing how she felt about it. I said she played the tape for us so we could help her understand how she felt about it. I then asked Dana if it would be helpful for me to share some of my observations and reactions to the tape with her. She appeared to be struggling to release herself from a suffocating burden as she slowly looked up and nodded. I told her that I was struck with how nice everything sounded on the surface for most of the tape. I shared with her how painful it was to witness how her father coerced her into saying exactly what he wanted her to say. I noticed how she resisted at first before finally capitulating. I noted how "crazy making" this must feel, things looking so good on the surface and feeling so horrible inside. She said it was like that a lot and that it made it hard for her to know what was real. Other group members, following my lead, gave her their impressions of the tape. I closed the group saying I was very glad Dana had brought in the letter and the tape and encouraged others to bring in things that they needed help understanding. Dana was quite alert and animated at group's end. I added that sometimes things are so hidden in families and in ourselves that the only way to figure them out is to get help from someone else.

Dana's need for a mirroring self-object experience was mobilized in group therapy. A dysfunctional family milieu made it impossible for

Dana to get the responses she needed. Struggling with the low self-esteem often seen in children with learning disabilities (Palombo, 1979) and the onset of a painful disability had overwhelmed her. She knew that she was "special." She had attended special classes in school. She was a medical conundrum. From ages 14 to 21 she lived in a residential facility. The incestuous attentions from her father furthered this special message. Her own authentic expression was ignored and suppressed. Although out to her family, her lesbianism was never addressed. Her preoccupation with being different quickly became a preoccupation with being defective and loathsome. Group psychotherapy with other disabled lesbians and with a lesbian therapist who is also disabled provides Dana with an opportunity to develop a new relationship to her feelings of difference and specialness. Although specific lesbian issues are not being addressed in the therapy at this point, Dana's experience of a lesbian assumption in the group therapy mileu was a critical transference element. The alter ego experience of being with other lesbians who were different, as she is, combined with the twin-ship experience with me, created a solid therapeutic container within which she could allow her mirroring self-object needs to unfold. Additionally, early experiences with affirmation of her lesbian identity by her best friend and by the lesbian community left her with a sense of hope for responsiveness by lesbians. She is beginning to step out from behind a curtain of shame and reveal previously hidden feelings. She is now asking for the attention and help she did not receive for her disability in her childhood. Although therapy with Dana will require much longer treatment, we can see the beginning of increasing self-esteem and cohesion as she benefits from an optimally responsive therapeutic environment.

Jan

Jan is a 50-year-old White woman with multiple disabilities, several of which had a childhood onset. During the intake assessment she minimized a long history of depression and elaborated on how well she was functioning. She reported having difficulty coping with her visual impairment, which occurred 4 years ago. She said she felt comfortable with her other disabilities, which were lifelong. She is in a wheelchair, paraplegic, and hearing impaired. Jan joined a group for lesbians with physical disabilities, which she stayed in for 4 months. In the group she played a caretaking role and found it difficult to focus on her own feelings and needs. She began individual therapy with me after her second group session, which she requested because she feared being overwhelmed by stressors in her life. In the first session, Jan told me how happy she was to work with a therapist, who like her, was visually impaired. She spoke of her difficulties with attendant care, a new apartment, and other stressors and began to cry. I said it sounded as if she was dealing with a great many difficult things all at the same time. She agreed and said it felt like too much for her. I asked if she was concerned about becoming depressed again, and she responded with relief at being able to talk about it. She said that her vision loss was making life so much harder, and it was not easy before. Sobbing, she said she felt she had never really dealt with her lifelong disabilities, and it was all coming up now; she feared being overwhelmed and unable to cope.

Two sessions later Jan decided to drop out of school. She felt unable to ask for the accommodation that her hearing loss, now complicated by her inability to compensate by visual cues, necessitated. She felt guilty about this decision and then told me of her older sister, her most supportive family member, who always pushed her to be "strong and like everyone else."

Recognizing and asserting her own needs felt weakening to Jan. Having a need meant she was not like everyone but was different and disabled, which caused Jan to feel diminished and depleted. Her sister frequently told her that she felt embrassed by her being in a wheelchair and felt it was important that Jan be exceptionally well groomed because she thought people stared at her. This was complicated by Jan's having recently told her sister that she was a lesbian, at which point her sister's concern with Jan looking normal expanded to include Jan not looking gay as well as not looking disabled. I commented on the dilemma Jan was in; that by taking care of herself, protecting herself, she risked losing her sister's approval and perhaps her sister's help as well. She sobbed and spoke more of her childhood isolation, her dependence on her depressed, "crazy mother." She told me that her father abandoned the family soon after her birth. Jan's mother and siblings told her it was because her disability was just too much for him to handle. This had made it particularly difficult for her to tell her sister that she was a lesbian, fearing abandonment and withdrawal of the promise of help in medical emergencies. At the end of the session she thanked me, saying that she felt she could take in more of what I said to her this week.

Therapy appeared to be going very well: Jan was receptive to my interventions and told me repeatedly that she liked the therapy. She was a type of client I usually enjoy working with. I felt a kinship with her in several ways: I am visually impaired as was she; we were both mothers of adult daughters; and we were both lesbians. Yet I felt some strain in my ability to immerse myself empathically in her experience. I considered that perhaps her issues were "too close to home," but after consultation I realized that her style of communication felt stylized and inauthentic to me, as though she was performing. I also noted her frequent use of my name in sessions, which felt jarring. It was much too early in the therapy to address her inauthenticity as it would have been too exposing and shame-inducing.

Jan developed a pattern during the next several months of therapy of first addressing a daily life difficulty with her disability and then quickly breaking down in tears. She would then tell me of painful past events in her life in which boundary problems with physicians and other therapists were a prominent theme. At this time she told me she felt confused about her sexual identity as a lesbian, saying that she hated labels and that she didn't know what her sexual orientation was. She said she felt confused and overwhelmed in all areas of her life. Jan told me she had never cried so much in therapy before and didn't cry outside of our sessions. She said she felt she could be less controlled in therapy. I asked her what she meant by this, and she said that she felt free to say what was bothering her and felt I could help her sort her feelings out. The idealizing transference that ran throughout the therapy was foreground.

At this time she decided to drop out of group therapy for two reasons. She said it was a group for lesbians, and she felt she was probably bisexual. She wanted to continue to explore issues from the past and felt the group plus individual therapy was too emotionally overwhelming for her. She was not interested in spending much time examining her sexual identity issues, stating that she did not want to be in a lover relationship at that point, as it was difficult for her to focus on herself while relating intimately to another. I knew that Jan's fears of abandonment made it difficult for her to recognize and assert her own needs in an intimate relationship, choosing to please her partners instead. I explained that knowing more about her own feelings, in this case her sexuality, could be helpful to her. When I explored how she felt about her own sense of herself as a lesbian or a bisexual, she remained uninterested. Her only worry was that her sexual orientation confusion would prohibit her receiving services at the clinic and from me. She was relieved and surprised that I would continue working with her even though she was feeling something she feared I would not approve of. I decided not to pursue her sexual identity confusion at this point because the foreground therapeutic issue was her fear of abandonment. I wanted her to experience that I could tolerate her confusion—confusion being a necessary step in moving towards authenticity—and that I would not abandon her.

After 6 months of therapy, Jan began one session by telling me that she had noticed her depression lessened after she had taken the risk to tell a friend directly how she felt about a disturbing interchange they had. She spoke of how difficult it was for her to do this in any relationship. A series of sessions followed in which she reported similar exchanges. I listened and encouraged her to tell me what the experience was like for her. She said it scared her, and she was afraid the other person would not like her and would end their relationship. I noted how she had to hide her feelings growing up and that in order to keep her ties with her caretakers—her mother, the doctors—she had to be very good, polite, and what they wanted her to be. I commented that it must have felt very dangerous when she felt other kinds of feelings, like anger or impatience. She sobbed saying she "never knew how her mother would react" or if the "doctors would be mad." She said she felt so exposed in the hospital—she had 30 surgeries and was hospitalized most of the time from ages 10 to 15—and hated her body, which would "never be perfect."

In the ninth month of therapy Jan began a session saying that she had noticed how "phoney" she sounded when she was not saying what she really felt. She could almost watch herself speaking, and she said it seemed so "staged." I asked if she felt this happened in therapy too. She said more at the beginning. I said I had noticed that change too and said it seemed that she needed to protect herself from too much exposure and that this was a survival strategy that kept her safe. She said she did not want to do it anymore. I offered that maybe now she was more able to talk about the ways in which she felt different and damaged, rather than have to hide her pain. In the following months Jan began to reveal the painful feelings of shame and humiliation she had experienced growing up with her disabilities. Although she had spent time on historical material previously, at this time her focus was on her sense of difference and defectiveness. Deep feelings of body shame emerged and were inextricably interwoven with shame at having any needs at all. It was at this time that Jan began to express long buried anger towards her family and the medical establishment.

As Jan's authenticity increased, she began to talk more honestly of her conflicts around her sexual orientation. She had related to men most of her adult life, never marrying, but having a series of affairs. She said she always picked older, successful men who she felt would make her appear "legitimate," which to Jan meant not different and "like everyone else." She spoke of the male doctors she had idealized growing up, and her childhood hospitalizations, as the only times she had felt safe and cared for. She came out in her 40s, told her sister and her daughter, even though she feared their rejection. Her family did not desert her but preferred she did not talk of her lesbianism with them and she complied with their request. Jan spoke of the stresses of being both a disabled woman and a lesbian, her fears of being excluded by society, and her longing to simply "fit in." She felt she was more willing now to be honest about her conflicts regarding her sexual orientation and wanted to take time to sort through her feelings.

We terminated therapy after 18 months as mandated by clinic policy. Jan was feeling little depression and was more natural and intimate in her relationships with others. Shame was a less controlling factor in her life decisions. Jan was able to ask for more of the physical accommodations she needed, and although undecided about her sexual orientation, she felt she was now able to continue exploring this issue in an honest and authentic manner. Fears of abandonment and denied and repressed anger emerged as prominent clinical themes. Jan's inauthenticity was the way she hid, protecting herself from overexposure and resulting depletion and depression. An acute disability concern served as the entry point into shame-related issues of the past. Jan developed an idealizing self-object transference through which she was able to contain her fears of being overwhelmed and depleted so that she could begin to reveal deeply hidden, shame-laden experiences, including confusion regarding her sexual orientation. Choosing a therapist who Jan perceived as "like her" set the frame of twinship in which her idealizing self-object needs could unfold so that she could continue her heretofore derailed self-development. Without being silenced by shame, Jan could now directly express her feelings of being different in the context of a responsive and affirming therapeutic relationship. Self-esteem and self-acceptance can grow in this fertile soil.

Common Themes

The case examples of Dana and Jan have several themes in common. Both Dana and Jan presented with depression and would have benefited from a psychotherapy that focused on their affective disturbance alone. Depression is a common presenting problem in women and can mask underlying emotional disturbances. Attention to the shame underlying the depression led to the unfolding of self-object needs about feelings of defectiveness related to their lifelong disabilities. Both women found it very difficult to identify and express their anger. Jan feared abandonment and exclusion. Dana, unable to maintain her own perceptions, turned her anger inward, which led to self-mutilating behaviors.

Differences in the cases are important to note. Jan "hid" behind a staged, inauthentic social veneer, whereas Dana was stuck in a quagmire of confusion and "not knowing." Dana, whose reality had been systematically distorted, desparately needed recognition and affirmation of her own perceptions and intentions. As a result, mirroring self-object needs predominated in the transference. Jan's need for idealizing self-object experiences was the foreground transference theme. Her years of hospitalizations and medical treatment by idealized health care workers were her primary source of help and attention. She continued to look to idealized others to help her soothe and contain her feelings. Self-psychology provided a theoretical and developmental understanding of these selected aspects of the transference as they unfolded.

Conclusion

When working with any minority group, the psychotherapist needs to be aware of the societal context confronting her or his client, her- or himself, and the therapy itself (Dworkin & Gutiérrez, 1989). Self-psychology's emphasis on protracted immersion in the client's subjective world provides the opportunity for an in-depth understanding of the experience of minority group members, which by definition of their minority status deviates from majority group assumptions. Therefore, it is imperative that psychotherapy with disabled lesbians be highly attuned to difference—difference stemming from being disabled in an able-bodied society and difference stemming from being a lesbian in a heterosexual culture. Without this attunement, feelings of defectiveness, self-loathing, and associated shame will stay hidden. Psychotherapy under such conditions will be limited in its scope. The grieving of losses will remain incomplete, which will thwart progress toward honest appreciation of individual uniqueness. When difference is welcomed and understood, shame-laden material can be revealed and worked through, leading to increases in self-esteem and the blossoming of full potential.

References

Blumberg, B., Lewis, J., & Susman, E. (1984). Adolescence: A time of transition. In M. G. Eisenberg, L. C. Sutkin, & M. A. Jansen (Eds.), *Chronic illness and disability throughout the life span* (pp. 133–149). New York: Springer.

Boden, R. (1988). Countertransference responses to lesbians with physical disabilities and chronic illnesses. In M. Shernoff & W. Scott (Eds.), *The sourcebook on lesbian and gay health care* (pp. 119–122). Washington, DC: National Lesbian and Gay Health Foundation.

Boden, R., Hunt, P., & Kassoff, E. (1987, March). *The centrality of shame in the psychology of women*. Paper presented at the Association of Women in Psychology Conference, Denver, CO.

Courtois, C. A. (1988). *Healing the incest wound*. New York: Norton.

de Monteflores, C. (1986). Notes on the management of difference. In T. S. Stein & C. J. Cohen (Eds.), *Contemporary perspectives on psychotherapy with lesbians and gay men* (pp. 73–101). New York: Plenum.

Drotar, D., Crawford, P., & Bush, M. (1984). The family context of childhood chronic illness: Implications for psychosocial intervention. In M. G. Eisenberg, L. C,. Sutkin, & M. A. Jansen (Eds.), *Chronic illness and disability throughout the life span* (pp. 123–129). New York: Springer.

Dworkin, S., & Gutiérrez, F. (1989). Counselors be aware: Clients come in every size, shape, color, and sexual orientation. *Journal of Counseling & Development, 68*(1), 6–8.

Kohut, H. (1977). *Restoration of the self*. New York: International Universities Press.

Kohut, H. (1984). *How does analysis cure?* Chicago: University of Chicago Press.

Morrison, A. P. (1989). *Shame: The underside of narcissism*. New Jersey: Analytic Press.

Offer, D., Ostrov, E., & Howard, K. (1984). Body image, self-perception, and chronic illness in adolescence. In R. W. Blum (Ed.), *Chronic illness and disabilities in childhood and adolescence* (pp. 59–73). Florida: Grune & Stratton.

Ornstein, A., & Ornstein, P. (1985). Clinical understanding and explaining: The empathic vantage point. In A. Goldberg (Ed.), *Progress in self-psychology* (Vol. 1, pp. 43–61). New York: Guilford Press.

Palombo, J. (1979). Perceptual deficits and self-esteem in adolescence. *Clinical Social Work Journal, 7*(1), 34–61.

Schavrien, J. E. (1989). The rage, healing, and daemonic death of Oedipus: A self in relation theory. *The Journal of Transpersonal Psychology, 21*(2), 149–176.

Zeltzer, L., Kellerman, J., Ellenberg, L., Dath, J., & Rigler, D. (1980). Psychologic effects of illness in adolescence. II. Impact of illness in adolescence: Crucial issues and coping styles. *The Journal of Pediatrics, 97*, 132–138.

12

Bisexuality: A Counseling Perspective

Timothy J. Wolf, PhD

Approaches to counseling individuals and couples who present concerns about bisexual feelings, fantasies, or behaviors have been contaminated with myths and misconceptions that have been questioned only recently with valid and reliable research. Bisexuality has been continually attacked as a nonentity, a transitional stage from heterosexuality to homosexuality or vice-versa, and as a denial of one's homosexuality (Klein, 1978). For a certain number of persons these factors may apply. Yet higher percentages of men and women report bisexual behavior than exclusively homosexual behavior (Kinsey, Pomeroy, & Martin, 1948; Kinsey, Pomeroy, Martin, & Gebhard, 1953). This chapter examines the misconceptions and conceptions of bisexuality as they relate to counseling individuals or couples concerned with their own or their partners' bisexual feelings or behavior.

Research on Bisexuality

Recent research no longer describes sexual orientation in terms of a dichotomy of heterosexual and homosexual behavior and feeling (Klein & Wolf, 1985). Sexual orientation can be viewed multidimensionally as sexual behavior, sexual attraction, sexual fantasy, social preference, emotional preference, lifestyle, and self-identification. Sexual orientation is a continuum that ranges from exclusively heterosexual to exclusively homosexual; and when changing over time, bisexuality takes on a more understandable framework (Klein, Sepekoff, & Wolf, 1985). The Klein Sexual Orientation Grid (Klein, 1980) (see Figure 1) provides an understandable model of sexual orientation as a multidimensional dynamic process.

Within this model, a wide range of social-sexual-bisexual behaviors and feelings may be described. For example, some persons may have an exclusively heterosexual emotional preference and have sexual behavior with both men and women. Other persons whose sexual behavior is exclusively heterosexual may have homosexual attractions and fantasies. Still other men and women may have both heterosexual and homosexual behavior, fantasies, attractions, and social and emotional preferences that change periodically throughout adulthood.

Bell, Weinberg, and Hammersmith (1981) attempted to explain this variability when they reported "exclusive homosexuality tends to emerge from a deep-seated predisposition, while bisexuality is more subject to influence of social and sexual learning" (p. 201). Most bisexual persons begin adulthood eroticizing heterosexually and identifying heterosexually, and later in adulthood discover homosexual interests (Bell et al., 1981; Bode, 1976; Klein, 1978; Zinik, 1983). Bisexual persons also report erotic fantasy differently from heterosexual or homosexual persons. As might be expected, bisexual persons report high levels of both heterosexual and homosexual fantasy whereas heterosexual persons report more heterosexual fantasy and homosexual persons report more homosexual fantasy (Saliba, 1982; Storms, 1978, 1980; Zinik, 1983). Many bisexual persons maintain their erotic response patterns over time and have identified as bisexual for much of their adult lives. Rubenstein (1982) found that bisexual persons scored higher on measures of self-esteem the longer they had identified as bisexual. Bisexuality tends to be more problematic for men than for women ("Playboy," 1983), partly because of more rigid male sex-role expectations. Both bisexual men and women report more emotional satisfaction from their relationships with women (Saliba, 1982). Several research studies (Harris, 1977; Markus, 1981; Twichell, 1974) have reported bisexual groups showed no differences from heterosexual and homosexual groups on several standard measures of psychological adjustment. Weinberg and Williams (1974) stated that bisexual individuals did not report greater psychological difficulties, with the exception of feeling more guilt and anxiety over their homosexual behavior.

Figure 1

Klein Sexual Orientation Grid

1	2	3	4	5	6	7
Hetero-sexual persons only	Hetero-sexual persons mostly	Hetero-sexual persons somewhat more	Hetero-sexual/homo-sexual equally	Homo-sexual persons somewhat more	Homo-sexual persons mostly	Homo-sexual persons only

Please fill in the following blanks with a number from the above choices which most appropriately describes your response:

My sexual attraction is to: Present _____
                                                                  Past   _____
    Ideal   _____

My sexual behavior is with: Present _____
Past _____
Ideal _____

My sexual fantasies involve: Present _____
Past _____
Ideal _____

My emotional preference is for: Present _____
Past _____
Ideal _____

My social preference is for: Present _____
Past _____
Ideal _____

My self-identification is with: Present _____
Past _____
Ideal _____

My lifestyle involves: Present _____
Past _____
Ideal _____

Note. This figure is from "Are You Sure You're Heterosexual? Or Homosexual? Or Even Bisexual?" by F. Klein. © December 1982, *Forum Magazine*, pp. 41–45. Reprinted by permission.

Because of its inherent complexity, both psychologically and socially, bisexuality may initially be experienced as a source of confusion and conflict. Over time, however, the bisexual person may reach a balance in which seemingly "opposite" erotic interests are synthesized and positively integrated into the self-identity. This may be achieved when the bisexual person experiences bisexuality within a model of flexibility rather than a model of conflict (Zinik, 1985).

All men and women will experience their bisexual feelings and behaviors in different manners. In some cases they will be dealing with bisexuality as a transitory stage of adult sexual development, in other cases as a fixed identity and lifestyle. To this extent it is less advantageous to label the feelings as heterosexual, homosexual, or bisexual, but rather to provide the counselee with an informed intervention in acknowledgement of his or her feelings. Many persons who enter therapy are fixated in behavior patterns that mirror the label they have chosen. Once these persons acknowledge alternative ways of thinking and acting that are unique to their needs, the label becomes less important and restricting. An example of this was a 25-year-old male who complained of restricted emotional response. His idea of his gay lifestyle excluded relationships with women. When he was able to include close social relationships with women in his lifestyle, he was able to meet more of his emotional needs. Most persons will label their sexual identification accurately (Klein, Sepekoff, & Wolf, 1985) once they have received the necessary counseling intervention.

An Intervention Model

Within a counseling perspective the bisexual person who seeks assistance may be experiencing confusion and anxiety because of his or her internalized dichotomous model of sexual orientation. He or she may also be suffering from the lack of social validation of the model of bisexuality. Within this framework, the counselor must be aware of his or her own homosexual or heterosexual prejudices, examine his or her internalized model of sexual orientation and identity, and be knowledgeable of the psychosocial support available in the community. Lourea (1985) effectively adapted the PLISSIT behavioral intervention model (Annon, 1974) in his counseling with bisexual persons. This model of permission, limited information, specific suggestions, and intensive therapy follows graduated steps of necessary intervention.

Permission. Few bisexual persons are given permission either by the heterosexual or homosexual communities or their families to explore their bisexual interests (Lourea, 1985). Social stigma and interpersonal rigidity further stop most persons who have bisexual attractions from acting on these feelings. Some bisexual persons who are given permission to fantasize about, or to relate sexually to both men and women, do not require further counseling intervention. Others will need counseling intervention. The object of this permission intervention is to give persons more flexibility in regard to their choices. This is also an important time to educate persons seeking counseling in regard to their sexual orientation about safer sex practices. For those persons who have or plan to act sexually on their feelings, education on safer sex practices can reduce anxiety and protect them from life-risk behaviors.

Limited information. Other persons move to the intervention level of limited information in which they are given lists of books, addresses of organizations of bisexual persons, fact sheets, or educational materials on bisexuality, or ways in which they might meet other bisexual persons. Many men and women who are given permission and limited information are able to resolve their initial confusion and conflict about their sexual identity. This also applies to persons for whom bisexuality is a transitory phenomenon on route to a heterosexual or homosexual adjustment. Until the steps of permission and limited information are taken, it is usually difficult for the therapist to predict or for the person in therapy to sort out the direction of sexual feelings and behaviors. At this time some persons cognitively begin to validate their bisexual feelings and behaviors, and the nonacceptance of heterosexual or homosexual preference becomes irrelevant. The freedom to explore bisexual attractions, fantasies, and behaviors in an informationally validated and supported context allows most persons to establish a sexual identity that is less confused by latent, transitional, or closeted feelings. Giving limited information begins to free persons from the psychosocial prejudices they have been carrying. A bibliography of relevant educational materials regarding bisexuality is included at the end of this chapter.

Specific suggestions. The third step in the PLISSIT model requires the counselor to make specific suggestions. These suggestions may include guidelines about how and when or when not to disclose bisexual feelings or behaviors to family and friends. They may also include how to deal with bisexual feelings and behaviors within a relationship. Many bisexual persons are married and require extensive assistance in negotiating a workable framework that may allow them to continue to feel or act on their bisexuality within their marriage. Finally, all bisexual persons need other persons who can give them support and encouragement. Specific suggestions may help bisexual persons to build a support network that will provide the validation for their feelings and behaviors. These suggestions are developed in light of a person's resources and experiences and are presented as alternatives rather than given as advice.

Intensive therapy. The fourth step in the PLISSIT model applies to a limited number of persons who require intensive therapy. For some individuals and couples, permission, limited information, and specific suggestions do not constitute a degree of intervention that allows the couple or individual to function successfully. In these cases in which individual or relationship pathology interferes, intensive therapy is necessary. In these cases difficulties with sexual orientation coincide with problems with relationships, substance abuse, compulsive sexual behaviors, severe marital discord, or other personality, mood, or thought disorders.

Case Study 1: Permission

John was a 23-year-old male who danced for a professional company. He had identified as homosexual early in adolescence and appeared well adjusted in his homosexual relationships. Recently he had been seeking more companionship with women and, in this process, was having sexual attractions and fantasies. His complaint concerned confusion regarding his heterosexual attraction and the negative reactions from his male friends.

In the single session with John, he was told in many ways that his heterosexual attraction was a valid part of his sexual identity and that his emotional needs certainly included relationships with women. It was emphasized that his heterosexual and homosexual attractions could exist together, although one of these choices may predominate at any given time—not necessarily because of the sexual object choice but most likely because of the personality involved. He was told, for example, "It is fine to fantasize about both men and women," "Erotic feelings about men and women are proper to entertain, and one always has a choice of acting or not acting on those feelings," and "You may love men and women in different ways."

John was introduced to a neurolinguistic timeline, a therapeutic technique whereby a person establishes a physical timeline in a room that matches his or her perception of time and space (Andreas & Andreas, 1987). He was able to find a time period on his timeline in childhood and adolescence when he shared a close emotional relationship with a sister. In this time regression, John was able to reexperience the intense bond he had then with his sister, which had apparently formed a link to his heterosexual attachment needs.

In this short process John was able to give himself permission to enjoy both his heterosexual and homosexual attractions. Although his predominant erotic attractions and lifestyle remained homosexual, he also began to enjoy sexual and emotional relationships with women.

Case Study 2: Limited Information

Most persons who enter therapy with questions regarding their bisexual feelings and behaviors need information as well as permission. It is not unusual for persons with bisexual concerns never to have talked to anyone about this, never to have known a person with similar feelings, and never to have read about bisexuality.

Fran was a 45-year-old mother of two older children who was recently divorced. The divorce appeared to have little to do with her emerging issues of sexuality. Recently she found herself attracted to a long-time female friend. She had not acted on these feelings for many personal reasons but wanted more information about her homoerotic feelings and how she might gently begin to act on these feelings.

Fran was relieved to find out that many women without a history of homosexual feelings or behaviors experience fulfilling homosexual relationships in their 30s, 40s, and 50s (Dixon, 1985). This also relieved her anxiety and guilt from the misperception that "latent homosexuality" may have interfered with her marriage and child rearing.

Fran was directed to some literature on female bisexuality and began to attend a bisexual group for women. In a short time she established a homosexual relationship with a woman with whom she now lives. Although she continues to maintain relationships with men, she finds her sexual and emotional relationships with women currently more satisfying.

Case Study 3: Specific Suggestions

Permission and limited information sometimes provide an adequate counseling intervention. For other bisexual persons more specific suggestions or guidelines regarding issues of their bisexuality are necessary. These suggestions most frequently revolve around issues of coming out and finding a support network.

Phillip was a 35-year-old single accountant with a history of heterosexual relationships. In the previous year, however, he had frequent homosexual masturbatory fantasies and was confused about how to deal with these feelings. His difficulties were confounded by his perceived loss of family support should he disclose his feelings. He was also anxious about how the accidental disclosure of his feelings would affect his impending promotion to partner in his firm.

When Phillip was more comfortable with his conceptualization of his bisexual feelings through his access to bisexual literature, and after he had given himself permission to have these feelings, specific suggestions allowed Phillip to begin a slow step-by-step coming out with his feelings and behaviors.

Phillip's initial task was to form friendship relationships with a group of men in a gay athletic organization. Second, he successfully found one member of his family to whom he could disclose his new feelings. Third, he was able to find another gay man in his firm. From this man he learned how to compartmentalize his homosexual feelings and experiences in ways that did not jeopardize his position at work. This was also accomplished by his introduction to a social circle that was separate from his work.

During the 6-month period in which Phillip saw this counselor twice monthly and later once monthly, he was able successfully and confidently to explore his bisexual feelings. Phillip continued to rely on his female partners sexually and emotionally.

Case Study 4: Intensive Therapy

A very limited number of persons who seek counseling for their bisexual feelings and behaviors require intensive therapy. Some persons may use a bisexual label to mask a strong internalized homophobia and may benefit from therapy to resolve homophobic issues. For others, dealing with bisexual feelings and behaviors may intensify other pathological issues, such as anxiety, depression, or personality disorders, and certainly may complicate existing relationships. At this point it is important for the counselor to use his or her diagnostic abilities to differentiate what problems may be due to sexual orientation confusion and what problems may be due to inadequate communication skills, unresolved family relationships, unmet independent or dependent needs, or mood, thought, or personality disorders (Gonsiorek, 1982). Issues of sexual orientation may often be secondary to one or more of these issues.

John and Mary had been married for 10 years and had two young children. John had been having covert homosexual liaisons throughout his marriage and within the last year had become romantically involved for the first time with another man. Mary had recently learned about John's lover by accidentally discovering a trip they had taken together. Mary was upset and confused about the future of her marriage, the prospect of living alone, and the effect of recent events on their children. John presented himself to this counselor confused about his sexuality and suicidally depressed over the demands of wife and lover and the future of his marriage and family.

The first task of the counselor in this situation was to diffuse a snowballing pattern of dissolution of the marriage due to anxiety, depression, confusion, and misinformation. John began to take an antidepressive medication to lower his anxiety and depression. He was later able firmly to set temporary limits regarding the demands of his lover and to focus on the issues of his marriage. Mary was able to confront the grief she was feeling about the loss of her marriage as it was originally perceived. She found counseling support with another counselor, who worked closely with this counselor, and began to read information regarding homosexuality, bisexuality, and mixed-orientation marriages. Mary (and John) found the book *When Husbands Come Out of the Closet* (Gochros, 1989) especially helpful in the initial period of this crisis. This book focuses on the experiences of women in mixed-orientation marriages and provides helpful advice. Whereas there are many books written for men, few books address these issues from a woman's perspective.

John and Mary also began to face issues of coming out. Neither had gay friends nor knew of couples like themselves. John had only known gay men in the context of anonymous sexual contacts. John and Mary began to attend a couples support group specifically designed for couples in which the husband was gay or bisexual (Wolf, 1988). The group met at one of the couples' home where the wives and husbands had time together and time apart. Mary found the support of the women in this group especially helpful in understanding John's homoerotic feelings and behaviors. At this time Mary began to understand that John's feelings were not a matter of his choice and that denying those feelings could result in psychological difficulties. She was also able to learn that his homoerotic behaviors were a matter of choice that affected her role in the marriage. John and Mary were also able to disclose to a limited number of friends. Building a sensitivity with one another regarding John's bisexuality was an important part of rebuilding trust in their relationship. Together they decided it was not necessary to disclose their current situation to parents.

John and Mary were able to agree that although John's feelings were not a matter of choice, his decision to act on those feelings was a matter of consequence in their marriage. Many therapy hours and hours at home were spent negotiating a relationship style that would allow John to express his homosexual feelings and behaviors. Eventually John and Mary decided on a 6-month trial plan. This plan included a night out for John each week to be spent with other men as long as safe-sex practices were observed. For the remainder of the week, John was to concentrate his time and attention on Mary and the children unless other arrangements were specifically negotiated. If the mutually decided upon plan was not working after 6 months, they agreed to file for a separation. During this period of negotiation, John and Mary continued to enjoy sexual activities. John reported an increase in sexual desire for both men and women during this period.

In the process of dealing with issues of sexuality, the couple was also able to deal with their dependent and codependent difficulties. Although there were no complaints of substance abuse, the dependent and codependent issues often found in addictive persons and their partners presented themselves. John began to realize how nonassertive he was about his needs and how he relied on Mary to run the household, care for the children, and protect him from the consequences of his extramarital behaviors. John began to take more responsibility to compartmentalize his homosexual behaviors and greater responsibility at home and with the children. Mary began to be less protective of John and learned to be more self-confident, seeking out the support, feedback, and encouragement of other women. Mary also began to build confidence in her ability to function independently at home, to ask for help from John and friends, and to be more successful professionally. In this process, psychodynamic issues for John and Mary were explored in light of their marital roles.

John and Mary were also able to deal with their feelings about their children. They mutually decided there was no need to tell the children about John's homoerotic feelings because the children were toddlers. A strategy of disclosure was planned when the children were able developmentally to understand their father's bisexuality in late adolescence. At the same time John and Mary discovered John's bisexuality would not determine sexual orientation for their girls, that children who are raised in bisexual or homosexual relationships are no more likely to be homosexual than if they were raised in a heterosexual relationship (Kirkpatrick, Roy, & Smith, 1981).

John and Mary chose to file for divorce after approximately a year of negotiating their lifestyle. John was able to acknowledge his bisexual feelings comfortably, but both partners were uncomfortable with an open marriage style in which John could express his bisexual behaviors. Mary was uncomfortable giving John the freedom to have extramarital experiences, and John wanted more freedom to explore a bisexual lifestyle. They remain close friends, live nearby, and share custody of their daughters. Although John and Mary chose to live separately, many couples negotiate a married relationship style that allows them to maintain their bisexual feelings and behaviors (Brownfain, 1985; Coleman, 1985; Dixon, 1985; Matteson, 1985; Wolf, 1985). For these couples, an intensive counseling intervention as described in this case history allows both persons the opportunity of independent growth and marital success. Or it may allow the dissolution process to proceed with the least sexual and emotional disruption.

Conclusion

For individuals and couples facing the complex issues of bisexual feelings and behaviors, integrating an appropriate identity and lifestyle is dependent to a large extent on relationship, peer, and professional support. Counselors must seriously examine their prejudices and theoretical ideas of sexual orientation before assisting others. Most concerns can be addressed with permission, limited information, and specific suggestions. A limited number of persons need intensive therapeutic intervention to integrate their bisexual feelings and behaviors with their identity and lifestyle.

References

Andreas, S., & Andreas, C. (1987). *Change your mind and keep the change.* Moab, UT: Real People.

Annon, J. S. (1974). *The behavioral treatment of sexual problems. Vol. 1: Brief therapy.* Honolulu: Enabling Systems.

Bell, A., Weinberg, M., & Hammersmith, S. D. (1981). *Sexual preference: Its development in men and women.* Bloomington: Indiana University Press.

Bode, J. (1976). *View from another closet: Exploring bisexuality in women.* New York: Hawthorn.

Brownfain, J. (1985). A study of the married bisexual male: Paradox and resolution. In F. Klein & T. Wolf (Eds.), *Bisexualities: Theory and research.* New York: Haworth.

Coleman, E. (1985). Integration of male bisexuality and marriage. In F. Klein & T. Wolf (Eds.), *Bisexualities: Theory and research.* New York: Haworth.

Dixon, J. (1985). Sexuality and relationship changes in married females following the commencement of bisexual activity. In F. Klein & T. Wolf (Eds.), *Bisexualities: Theory and research.* New York: Haworth.

Gochros, J. (1989). *When husbands come out of the closet.* New York: Haworth.

Gonsiorek, J. (1982). The use of diagnostic concepts in working with gay and lesbian populations. In J. Gonsiorek (Ed.), *A guide to therapy with gay and lesbian clients.* New York: Haworth.

Harris, D. A. (1977). *Social-psychological characteristics of ambisexuals.* Unpublished doctoral dissertation, University of Tennessee.

Kinsey, A., Pomeroy, W., & Martin, C. (1948). *Sexual behavior in the human male.* Philadelphia: Saunders.

Kinsey, A., Pomeroy, W., Martin, C., & Gebhard, P. (1953). *Sexual behavior in the human female.* Philadelphia: Saunders.

Kirkpatrick, M., Smith, A., & Roy, R. (1981). Lesbian mothers and their children: A comparative study. *American Journal of Orthopsychiatry, 51,* 545–551.

Klein, F. (1978). *The bisexual option.* New York: Arbor House.

Klein, F. (1980, December). Are you sure you're heterosexual? or homosexual? or even bisexual? *Forum Magazine,* pp. 41–45.

Klein, F., Sepekoff, B., & Wolf, T. (1985). Sexual orientation: A multivariable dynamic process. In F. Klein & T. Wolf (Eds.), *Bisexualities: Theory and research.* New York: Haworth.

Klein, F. & Wolf, T. (Eds.). (1985). *Bisexualities: Theory and research.* New York: Haworth.

Lourea, D. (1985). Psychosocial issues related to counseling bisexuals. In F. Klein & T. Wolf (Eds.), *Bisexualities: Theory and Research.* New York: Haworth.

Markus, E. (1981). An examination of psychological adjustment and sexual preference in the female (Doctoral dissertation, University of Missouri). *Dissertation Abstracts International, 41,* 4338-A.

Matteson, D. (1985). Bisexual men in marriage: Is a positive homosexual identity and stable marriage possible? In F. Klein & T. Wolf (Eds.), *Bisexualitites: Theory and research.* New York: Haworth.

Playboy readers sex survey. (1983, May). *Playboy Magazine,* pp. 126–128, 136, 210–220.

Rubenstein, M. (1982). *An in-depth study of bisexuality and its relation to self-esteem.* Unpublished doctoral dissertation, Institute for Advanced Study of Human Sexuality, San Francisco.

Saliba, P. (1982). Research project on sexual orientation. *The Bimonthly: Newsletter of the Bisexual Center of San Francisco, 6,* 3–6.

Storms, M. (1978). Sexual orientation and self-perception. In P. Pilner, K. R. Blanstein, I. M. Spigel, T. Alloway, & L. Krames (Eds.), *Advances in the study of communication and affect: Perception of emotion in self and others* (Vol. 5). New York: Plenum.

Storms, M. (1980). Theories of sexual orientation. *Journal of Personality and Social Psychology, 38,* 783–792.

Twichell, J. (1974). Sexual liberality and personality: A pilot study. In J. R. Smith & L. G. Smith (Eds.), *Beyond monogamy: Recent studies of sexual alternatives in marriage.* Baltimore: Johns Hopkins University Press.

Weinberg, M. S., & Williams, D. J. (1974). *Male homosexuals: Their problems and adaptations.* New York: Oxford.

Wolf, T. (1985). Marriages of bisexual or homosexual men. In F. Klein & T. Wolf (Eds.), *Bisexualities: Theory and research.* New York: Haworth.

Wolf, T. (1988). Group psychotherapy for bisexual men and their wives. In E. Coleman (Ed.), *Psychotherapy with homosexual men and women.* New York: Haworth.

Zinik, G. (1983). *The sexual orientation inventory.* Unpublished pilot study, University of California, Santa Barbara.

Zinik, G. (1985). Identity conflict or adaptive flexibility: Bisexuality reconsidered. In F. Klein & T. Wolf (Eds.), *Bisexualitites: Research and theory.* New York: Haworth.

Selected Bibliography

Geller, T. (1990). *Bisexuality: A reader and sourcebook.* Hadley, MA: Common Wealth.

Gochros, J. (1989). *When husbands come out of the closet.* New York: Haworth.

Kohn, B., & Mattusow, A. (1980). *Barry and Alice: Portrait of a bisexual marriage.* Englewood Cliffs, NJ: Prentice-Hall.

Malone, J. (1980). *Straight women/gay men: A special relationship.* New York: Dial Press.

Nanas, R., & Turley, M. (1979). *The new couple: Women and gay men.* New York: Seaview Books.

Section IV
Incidents of Violence

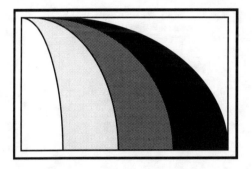

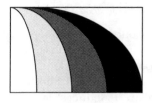

13

Gay and Bisexual Male Incest Survivors

Fernando J. Gutiérrez, EdD

Few data exist in the literature regarding gay and bisexual male incest survivors. What exists is mostly anecdotal (Halpern, 1987; Lew, 1988; Williams, 1988). Reasons for this include denial of the incidence among boys and adolescents as well as problems with memory retrieval.

Incest issues among gay and bisexual men differ from those of heterosexual men who have been assaulted by male perpetrators. Heterosexual male incest survivors are able to distance the sexual assault by the perpetrator in their sexual relationships because their sexual partners are women. In contrast, gay and bisexual men must overcome the negative feelings of same-sex sexual behavior in order to enjoy a normal sexual life with their same-sex partners.

Gay and bisexual men often misinterpret the origin of their sexual orientation as the result of the sexual assault and, therefore, carry much guilt and shame about their sexual orientation based on this

The author would like to acknowledge George Bilotta, PhD, psychologist in private practice in San Francisco, for his suggestions on issues presented in this chapter.

sexual assault. They are often unable to separate the two issues without assistance from a gay-affirmative counselor.

Williams (1988) reported the working definition of incest as "any contact by the adult with the child's body which leads to sexual excitement and orgasm" (p. 166). Incest is sexual behavior with a blood relation. The category of sexual abuse takes into consideration other acts that do not involve physical contact but that are considered sexual abuse. Examples are the exploitation of children by having them pose nude for the pornographic enjoyment of the adult or voyeurism by the adult while the child or the adolescent engages in sexual acts, such as masturbation, in front of the adult. (For a more extensive discussion, see Hunter, 1990, pp. 3–9.)

A problem in the interpretation of an incestual act is the assumption that the perpetrator is homosexual. Williams' (1988) analysis of the reported incidents reviewed suggested that the seduction of the sons by their fathers was motivated primarily by the desire to retaliate against their wives who cherished their sons, not by sexual attraction. In fact, incest is not a sexual act; as in the case of rape, it is an act of domination and power against the victim. The majority of perpetrators of incestual acts against young boys and adolescents are heterosexual men (Cambridge Graduate School of Psychology [CGSP]/AATBS, 1986; Lew, 1988). When the perpetrator uses his or her influence, power, or trust to obtain sexual gratification, this behavior becomes abusive. The perpetrator usually knows the child or adolescent.

A guideline used in determining when sexual abuse is taking place is when the perpetrator is about 5 years older than the victim (CGSP/AATBS, 1986). The perpetrator not only violates a minor's sexuality but also betrays the relationship. Relational boundaries dissolve; family loyalties are questioned; and the child or adolescent becomes confused. He or she feels unsafe and unsupported.

Issues

Three cases of intervention by counselors with men who have been survivors of incest or sexual abuse are presented in this section. In Carlos' case, the issue of memory retrieval is addressed. In the case of Sam, the issues of feeling responsible for the incest and abuse and misunderstood enjoyment are examined. And finally, In Jim's case, assisting the client in grieving the losses is discussed. Some alternative interpretations of the traditional psychoanalytic framework utilized to explain incestual behavior are presented. The section opens with discussion of issues of physical violence and closes with a discussion of treatment goals.

Physical violence often accompanies the adult's sexual assault. The adult forces his or her body onto or into the child or adolescent. Incest does not occur only with children or adolescents, however. Lew (1988) includes a statement from a client named Phillip, who was sexually molested by his father as an adolescent and then again as an adult: On one occasion, Phillip asked his father to meet with him after his mother's death. Phillip had graduated from medical school by this point. He and his dad sat in Phillip's VW Bug to talk. His father grabbed the back of Phillip's neck and twisted him downward toward his crotch. A struggle ensued, and Phillip's head banged on the steering wheel, smashing his lower and upper back teeth and causing a neck injury. Phillip described himself as 6'2" and his dad as 6'4".

Physical violence was also an issue in the case of Carlos.

Carlos: The Issue of Memory Retrieval

Carlos is a Mexican American in his late 20s. He came to counseling to explore dysfunctional family of origin issues. Carlos frequents public restrooms in parks and malls and seeks out anonymous and often noncontact sex, in which he and his sexual partner masturbate themselves in front of each other. Carlos feels guilty about this behavior because he has a supposedly monogamous relationship with his lover, Toni. Toni is an incest survivor who attends Incest Survivors Anonymous (ISA) meetings for gay men. One day he asked Carlos to accompany him to an ISA meeting. During the meeting, Carlos began to have a panic attack and to cry uncontrollably, which scared him.

The counselor had already suspected that Carlos had had an incestuous past because of the sexual acting out in the public rest rooms. This seems to be a common way for gay male incest and abuse survivors to act out the victimization from their past. The counselor began to explore possible incest incidents in Carlos' past. Carlos could not remember specific incidents from his childhood. As he explored his childhood, Carlos began to get in touch with his feelings. Whatever happened seems to have been preverbal. Carlos described a family in which his father abandoned the family when Carlos was 3. Carlos' mother then moved back to her parents' house, where the family lived in an in-law apartment connected to the house.

Carlos describes his relationship with his grandmother as extremely close, although anger comes out in discussing this closeness. Carlos feels as though he gave up his identity in order to please his grand-mother, who seemed to be a needy and demanding woman. Carlos did not remember much about his grandfather, but whenever he spoke about him, Carlos became aware of angry feelings, although he could not pinpoint the source of the anger. As we explored other possible sources of incest, Carlos kept coming back to angry feelings toward his grandfather. The counselor was careful not to press Carlos in this process of exploration. He assessed Carlos' level of comfort in exploring the issue.

Carlos came to a session one day and reported that he had gone to a Linda Rondstadt concert, *Canciones De Mi Padre* (Songs of My Father), the preceding weekend. While in line to enter the concert, Carlos began to cry. Some of the songs that Linda Rondstadt was going to sing were songs that his grandfather used to sing when Carlos was a child. Carlos also reported retrieving two images of his grandfather. One was an image of his grandfather sitting on the toilet, followed by an image of hairy testicles coming down toward Carlos' face. The other image was of Carlos' grandfather raising a cane as if about to strike someone with it; then the cane comes down, but Carlos wakes up before the cane makes contact.

As the earlier discussion of some of the dynamics of incestuous families indicated, Carlos' family fitted the description, with a grand-mother who was abnormally close to her grandchild and a grandfather who was resentful of this closeness and retaliated with physical as well as sexual violence. The scenario now needed to be validated.

Carlos vacillated from feeling as though he had been sexually mo-lested to thinking that this was all in his imagination and that he was making it all up. It was important for the counselor to provide support for the client during this period. The counselor pointed out to Carlos that, even though Carlos' images weren't clear yet, the fact that Carlos reacted on a feeling level so intensely was indicative that something traumatic had to have happened in his childhood with his grandfather. The counselor also shared the observation that Carlos' right arm in-flated like a balloon to more than twice its normal size and began to twitch uncontrollably when Carlos talked about these images, that perhaps this was a chemical reaction that pumped up Carlos' arm muscles to become ready for a defensive posture.

The counselor provided positive affirmations to Carlos for having been able to bring up the images that he did. Carlos became impatient that he could not produce images as fast as he wanted to, and some-times he projected that impatience onto the therapist for not helping him in the process. It is important for the therapist not to fall into this type of transference/countertransference trap. The counselor can feel pressured to push the client to remember incidents when the client is not ready to do so, causing the client to deepen his defenses against the memories or breaking through the defenses when the client is not ready and so causing a crisis.

The counselor voiced to Carlos that it would be Carlos who would bring up the memories when he was ready, that the counselor was there to support him when the memories did come up (Courtois, 1990). The counselor needed to let Carlos know that there is no set pace as to how this process takes place so that Carlos would desist in trying to force the issue. As Courtois (1990) suggested, the client's defenses are there for a reason. The counselor's role is not to betray those defenses but to support the client as the client navigates this painful process and brings down the shields when ready to do so. (For an elaboration of the remembering phase, see Bass & Davis, 1988.)

Sam: The Issues of Feeling Responsible and Misunderstood Enjoyment

Another issue that an incest survivor faces is the feeling of responsibility for the act. Adults seeking psychotherapy to face their childhood trauma of sexual abuse often interpret childhood events from an adult point of reference. Clients feel guilty for not having stopped the incidents or for enjoying part of the acts. No matter how old a victim is, a victim is not responsible for the abuse. As Bass and Davis (1988) discussed, one does not become assertive and powerful simply by leaving home. When someone with more power pressures another into a sexual relationship, that person is engaging in molestation.

Sam, a gay young professional in his early 20s, was in a relationship with his lover of 2 years. He went to a job interview out of state and stayed at the home of his potential boss, Harry, a married man with several children and an acquaintance of Sam's who knew that Sam was gay.

The night before the interview, Sam could hear Harry making passionate love to his wife in the room right above him. The next morning Sam was finishing his shower when Harry walked into the bathroom, while his wife was cooking breakfast downstairs, and began to fondle Sam's genitals. Sam felt confused for several reasons: One was that Sam was in a monogamous relationship with his lover, and until that point, he had been faithful to him. Sam was apprehensive during this trip because he was straining his relationship by looking for a job out of state. Getting the job would mean asking his lover to relocate with him—at a stage in their relationship when they were trying to evaluate whether they wanted to remain in the relationship or not (see McWhirter & Mattison, 1984).

A second reason was that Sam was afraid to set limits with Harry because the fate of his career future was about to be decided by Harry. As Harry was molesting Sam, he expressed to Sam that Sam was under no obligation to put out for Harry if Sam did not want to. In fact, Harry would see it as Sam prostituting himself if Sam accepted sexual advances from Harry just to get the job. Notice that Harry put the responsibility on Sam. The advances occurred right before the interview, when Harry was in a position of power. Harry then exonerated himself by creating guilt and shame in Sam and making him feel like a prostitute.

A third reason for confusion was that Sam liked the attention that he was getting from Harry. Harry was considerably older than Sam, and Sam had been accustomed to seducing older men.

For Sam, this was an adult reenactment of his adolescent relationship with his father, except that Sam began the sexual advances in that scenario. Sam grew up in an alcoholic family in which he was the child closest to his mother. Sexual boundaries were not clear in his family: Sam's parents were not sexual with each other; they slept in separate bedrooms; and Sam's father was known to have had several extramarital affairs. Sam's father resented Sam for setting limits in the family and made Sam feel ashamed for calling the police on several occasions when his father was battering his mother. Sam's mother had a pseudomarriage with Sam. Bradshaw (1990) referred to this as emotional incest. Sam's mother also behaved in sexually seductive ways with Sam. Sometimes she would change clothes in front of Sam, having nothing but her bra and girdle on, or she would ask Sam to zip up her dress. This made Sam feel uncomfortable.

Sam felt unloved by his father so, at the age of 13, Sam began exposing himself to his father, letting his father see his erect penis. His father did not object, so Sam decided to take it further and began disrobing completely in front of his father and masturbating in front of him, while pretending to be looking at a *Playboy* magazine. His father never said anything but stayed in the room and watched Sam until the act was completed. Then Sam went and took a shower. This became a weekly routine for Sam and his dad until Sam became 18.

At 13, Sam was also going through the confusion of realizing that he was gay. Living in an enmeshed family, that is, a family in which all the needs are met within the family and there is no support from outside sources, Sam was afraid to take his explorations outside of the family unit for fear of bringing more shame to the family if he were found out. Sam felt a great sense of power in being able to seduce his dad and have his dad pay attention to him. So when Harry volunteered to seduce him that way, Sam transferred his feelings toward his dad toward Harry. Sam ended up not taking that job after all. This was ·Sam's way of taking control of his past and learning to set limits. Sam confessed what happened to his lover, who was a forgiving person.

This was also a case of misunderstood enjoyment. Gay and bisexual men often blame themselves for enjoying the physical pleasure sometimes felt when having sex with the perpetrators, or they might blame themselves for having seduced the perpetrator. Summit (1983) stated that although an adolescent might be attractive, seductive, and even deliberately provocative, that adolescent has no equal power to say no to a significant other or to anticipate the consequences of such sexual involvement. Bass and Davis (1988) emphasized that it is incumbent upon the adult to set the limits, discuss the problem with the child or adolescent, and assist in obtaining professional help. Sam sought out this help and learned to develop self-esteem so that he did not have to buy his self-esteem through sexual favors.

In therapy, Sam also retrieved earlier images that indicated that sexual molestation had taken place in his early years. Through his therapist's support, Sam clarified what went on in his adolescence. By learning to see himself as a survivor rather than as a perpetrator, Sam was able to feel more comfortable in exploring the earlier childhood images. As the counselor reframed Sam's self-perception from perpetrator to survivor, he allowed Sam to learn when people are violating his boundaries so that Sam can learn to set limits.

After the incident with Harry, the job interviewer, Sam also developed some problems with his lover. Whenever his lover approached him sexually, Sam rejected him, causing confusion in his lover to the point that his lover stopped approaching Sam sexually. Then San complained that his lover was sexually disinterested in him. In counseling, Sam learned to connect approach and avoidance in sexual initiation with his own perception of power and vulnerability in the relationship. Sam learned to let his lover approach him sexually. As Sam got uncomfortable, he was able to repeat an affirmation for himself and say,

"This is not my perpetrator. He is the man who loves me, and I can relax and enjoy my sex with him."

Jim: The Issue of Mourning the Losses

In addition to mourning the loss of a healthy relationship with the perpetrator, the gay incest survivor must also mourn the loss of the unhealthy lover relationship that he feels with the perpetrator. As a gay person, the incest survivor may be perceiving the perpetrator as a lover.

Jim, a middle-aged man who just recently came out as a bisexual person, is an example. In the past, Jim was in counseling for incest issues with his older brother. His older brother seduced Jim when Jim was in his early teens. Jim had homosexual feelings, and because he was raised in a traditional Catholic household, he felt conflicted with his relationship with his brother. He enjoyed sex with him but at the same time felt guilty about the relationship.

The incest stopped when Jim's brother entered the military and told Jim that he did not want to continue doing those "queer" things anymore. This put down made Jim feel ashamed of his same-sex feelings and also made Jim feel responsible for having "instigated" the acts, event though it was actually his brother who began to molest Jim.

Jim finished his therapy regarding the incest, became a successful business executive, and then married a woman, with whom he shared a life for 20 years. Jim's same-sex feelings began to become stronger and stronger, so he began frequenting public restrooms. He was caught by an undercover police officer, and because of the charges against him, his wife found out about the incident and filed for divorce.

Jim made several attempts at forming loving relationships with other men without success. Even though he is bisexual, his preference for the dominant relationship was with men. He became depressed and sought counseling. He began to doubt if this preference toward men might not be a result of his incest issues and that maybe he should be pursuing dominant relationships with women instead.

The counselor was able to validate for Jim that incest happens to gays, lesbians, and bisexuals, just as it happens to heterosexuals, and that there is no cause and effect relationship between incidence of incest and sexual orientation. The counselor also validated for Jim that he could have a bisexual relationship, even though his dominant attraction was with a man, thus giving Jim permission to pursue a relationship with a man as the dominant relationship and still be able to satisfy his desire to be with women.

As Jim talked about his incestual past, he began to feel very sad. He could not understand why, because he felt that he had successfully dealt with the incest issues in his prior therapy. What Jim discovered was that he had not grieved the loss of his relationship with his brother as lover. Jim had been in love with his brother and shared many intimate and close sexual moments with him. All of a sudden, his brother stopped this relationship, and Jim felt abandoned. Jim had to let go of this image of his brother as lover. He had to reframe his feelings of closeness toward his brother, so that he could make room for other men in his life. This freed Jim, and he recently celebrated a Holy Union, which is a religious ceremony similar to a wedding, with his lover of 1 year.

For gay youth, dealing with issues of incest and sexual abuse can be more complicated than for heterosexual children. Summit (1983) has identified five stages of the child abuse accommodation syndrome: (1) secrecy; (2) helplessness; (3) entrapment and accommodation; (4) delayed, conflicted, and unconvincing disclosure; and (5) retraction. Many gay youth have difficulty breaking the secret because of fear that their homosexual feelings will be revealed if they do so, leading to a feeling of helplessness. Feeling trapped by their own sense of guilt and feeling that they are responsible for the abuse because they are gay, these youths begin to develop accommodation mechanisms, such as multiple personalities, altered states of consciousness, and such self-destructive behaviors as alcohol and sexual addictions, prostitution, and frequenting public restrooms, porno theaters, or peep show bookstores. Other accommodation mechanisms may include the development of sexual dysfunctions that interrupt sexual intimacy, such as inhibited ejaculatory functions, failure of penile erections, or premature ejaculations.

When an incest survivor has been sexually molested, the reaction may be delayed for a short period or for years; or the disclosure may have conflicting elements or sound unconvincing to the person hearing the recounting of the events. The survivor may even retract his statements for fear of not being believed because of shame, or guilt.

Many gays have had fantasies of what it might have been like to go to bed with one's father, brother, uncle. These fantasies are normal, as long as they remain fantasies and the individual moves on to sublimate this attraction with an available and suitable mate. In fact, incest experiences may prevent gay men from completing this phase of development and sublimating the attraction toward an available and suitable mate, other than one's family members.

Treatment Goals

Individual psychotherapy for gay incest survivors needs to focus on self-acceptance as a gay person, internalization of control in order to learn to set limits and boundaries, individuation and separation, intimacy, sexuality, detachment, and objectivity (CGSP/AATBS, 1986). Grief work around the losses needs to also be included in this list of issues.

According to CGSP/AATBS (1986), group psychotherapy goals should focus on self-confidence, trust, sexuality, social skills, coping skills, and limit setting. It is important that the context of the group be gay and bisexual oriented. A mixed group of heterosexual and gay incest survivors is contraindicated because heterosexual men must work through feelings about being perceived as gay or being angry at the perpetrator's assumed homosexuality. Gay men do not need to witness these shaming feelings about being gay, especially when these negative characteristics are being erroneously assigned exclusively to gay people.

Conclusion

From the discussion of three real cases of incest and sexual abuse, we can conclude that gay and bisexual men have unique needs for intervention by counselors. A counselor's knowledge of the issues and sensitivity to alternative interpretations of traditionally psychodynamic interpretations of incest and sexual abuse can assist clients in exploring these issues in a gay and bisexual affirming context. These alternative interpretations can provide a climate of safety for the client that will allow the client the atmosphere needed to facilitate the painful process of memory retrieval, reliving the shame, mourning the losses, and moving on to a more fulfilling gay and bisexual life.

References

Bass, E., & Davis, L. (1988). *The courage to heal: A guide for women survivors of child sexual abuse.* New York: Harper & Row.
Bradshaw, J. (1990). *Homecoming: Reclaiming and championing your inner child.* New York: Bantam Books.

Cambridge Graduate School of Psychology/AATBS. (1986). *Breaking the cycle: Assessment and treatment of child abuse and neglect*. Los Angeles: Cambridge Graduate School of Psychology.

Courtois, C. (1990). *The memory retrieval process in incest survivor therapy*. Paper presented in a symposium on techniques for treating survivors of incest at the annual convention of the American Psychological Association, Boston.

Halpern, J. (1987). Father-son incest, *Social Casework, 68*, 88–93.

Hunter, M. (1990). *Abused boys: The neglected victims of sexual abuse*. Lexington, MA: Lexington Books.

Lew, M. (1988). *Victims no longer: Men recovering from incest and other sexual child abuse*. New York: Harper & Row.

McWhirter, D., & Mattison, A. (1984). *The male couple: How relationships develop*. Englewood Cliffs, NJ: Prentice-Hall.

Summit, R. (1983). The child sexual abuse accommodation syndrome. *Child Abuse and Neglect, 7*, 177–193.

Williams, M. (1988). Father-son incest. *Clinical Social Work Journal, 16*, 165–179.

14

Psychotherapy Issues in Working With the Lesbian Incest Survivor

Elaine Brady, MFCC

Lesbian incest survivors struggle with many of the same adult symptomatology as their heterosexual counterparts and also experience certain advantages and disadvantages unique to their lifestyle. The therapist working with this population must be aware of these specific differences in order to treat the lesbian incest survivor effectively. Utilizing what little research has been done in this area, as well as my own clinical experience with this population, this chapter attempts to outline these differences and offers therapeutic approaches for their treatment.

Treatment issues specific to lesbian incest survivors addressed include (1) questioning the possible cause-and-effect nature of childhood molestation and later homosexual orientation, (2) dealing with societal and introjected homophobia, (3) compounding of survivor shame and guilt, (4) erotophobia, (5) xenophobia, (6) incest effects on sexuality, (7) alcoholism, and (8) dual-survivor relationships.

Homosexual Orientation: Free Choice or Symptom?

The mental health profession long defined homosexuality as an "illness" to be treated and "cured." Although this definition was removed from the American Psychological Association's *Diagnostic and Statistical Manual* in 1973, many people and even some therapists continue to ask, "What *causes* homosexuality?" In the case of the lesbian incest survivor, the question becomes, "Did the incest *cause* the homosexual orientation?" The underlying assumption here is that the adult's sexual orientation is an abnormal and unhealthy symptom of the incest that should be treated and cured.

Surveys have shown that from one-fifth to one-third of adult women were sexually molested as children (Herman, 1981). The incidence of homosexuality (both gay male and lesbian) in the general population is estimated at 10 to 15% (Fassinger, 1991). According to Herman (1981), we would then expect that 7.5% or less (separating out gay men from lesbians) of the total number of female incest survivors would be lesbian. Herman (sample size 40) found 5% of her study were lesbian and another 7% were bisexual. Van Buskirk and Cole (1983) (sample size 8) found 75% of their subjects had had female sexual partners. Maltz and Holman (1987) (sample size 35) found 33% of their subjects had had female sexual partners. Of these, about half felt strongly that the incest had no bearing on their sexual orientation, whereas the other half felt that it was related. In one survey of 1,566 lesbians, 38% reported they had experienced childhood sexual abuse (Loulan, 1987). Meiselman (1981) (sample size 23) found an incidence rate of 30% lesbianism among incest survivors. A nationwide survey of 225 lesbians by Grundlach (1977) found that a significantly higher proportion of these women reported childhood rape or molestation, compared with a matched group of heterosexual women.

Although these data do seem to indicate that a higher than normal percentage of incest survivors are lesbian, it is risky to draw conclusions given the various research issues involved (i.e., small sample size, random vs. therapeutic groups, and lack of clarity as to the meaning of *homosexual experience*). For example, some studies asked for any adult same-sex experiences rather than for stability of homosexual orientation. What can we say, then, regarding a cause-and-effect relationship between childhood molestation and later homosexual orientation? Obviously, the vast majority of incest survivors are heterosexual, and therefore a direct cause and effect between incest and adult homosexuality cannot be assumed.

When reviewing the statements of research participants, we find conflicting opinions regarding the issue of cause and effect. Maltz and Holman's study (1987) reported that half of their lesbian respondents did not believe the incest experience had affected their sexual orientation and that half did. The two lesbian incest survivors in Herman's study (1981, p. 104) "felt strongly that their incest experience had influenced their orientation" and "that in developing a lesbian identity, they had to some degree mastered their childhood traumas and achieved a healthier and more rewarding personal life than would otherwise have been possible."

Maltz and Holman (1987) speculate that their two groups of lesbian incest survivors represent (1) lesbians who also happen to be incest survivors (they would have been lesbian with or without the incest experience) and (2) basically heterosexual or bisexual women who were open to experimentation with female partners as part of their healing process (the incest *did* have an impact on their choice). There are many reasons why a heterosexual incest survivor might choose female partners. Some survivors may feel safer and more comfortable with females because their bodies lack many of the reminders of the abuse (e.g., penis, semen, body hair, low voice, body size). Female partners may be less pressuring than males for sexual contact and more understanding and supportive of the survivor's anxieties about sex.

In contrast to the idea that childhood molestation may cause later homosexuality, Herman (1981) suggested that it may, in fact, simply block a preexisting bisexual or homosexual orientation. The forced sexual contact with a male, coupled with the resultant anger at a mother who failed to protect, can block recognition of an attraction to women.

> I feel I would have been bisexual … but for the shit from my father. It made it impossible for me to relate to men sexually. I found myself in relations with men casting myself in the role of a sickie. As soon as I was with a man, I would become crazy and fall apart. I don't repeat that with a woman, or if I do, I can stop and control it. (Herman, 1981, p. 105)

> I think, for me, I didn't have any conscious awareness of being a lesbian until I had gotten through a lot of work on the incest. My feeling is that I was lesbian from the time I was born. (Maltz & Holman, 1987, p. 74)

Case 1: Homosexual Orientation—Free Choice or Symptom?

Composite case dialogues, of which this is the first, are utilized to illustrate the client issues and therapeutic interventions discussed here and in the following sections.

Client issue: Questioning of cause of orientation
Therapist's goal(s): Normalize orientation and deal with underlying issues of question.

   Client: You know, every time I break up with a lover I question whether I want to go back to men or not.
   Therapist: What do you think that's about?
   Client: Well, I kind of miss some things about being straight. Like I used to really enjoy sex with men, and it was nice being able to be public about the relationship, you know? Like just holding hands in public or kissing. Knowing my family would be more comfortable with a man. Sometimes I think my life might be easier if my dad hadn't done that [molestation] and I'd just stayed straight.
   Therapist: Are you saying you think the molestation made you gay and wishing it hadn't?
   Client: Well, I'm not really sure the molestation made me gay. I can remember playing doctor with both boys and girls when I was little. Even then I was real excited about being with another girl. Is that weird? Abnormal?
   Therapist: No, not really. Studies have shown that humans have a wide range of sexual behavior. Childhood sexual experimentation with other same-sex children is not an uncommon experience. But I'm hearing that you're questioning your current sexual orientation and wondering if it's really your choice or a reaction to your incest. If being gay was more accepted in our society, what do you think you would have done as a child, before your dad molested you?
   Client: That's easy. I would have continued to be with women *and* men. I would probably still have phased men out of my life though, cause that seemed more related to the incest, the bad marriages I had, and becoming more of a feminist.
   Therapist: Listening to yourself now, what do you think about the relationship between the incest and your current homosexuality? You might have been bisexual if it hadn't happened, but probably not heterosexual.
   Client: Well, now that I put it all together I'm pretty sure that's not why I'm gay. And even phasing men out of my life seems more the result of other things in my life than just dad. I guess it's just that I question my lifestyle when rela-

tionships don't work, and it's a little hard being in the minority and hiding all the time.

Therapist: OK. So let's work on why relationships don't work for you and how you can take care of yourself in a society that doesn't support your lifestyle.

Societal and Internalized Homophobia

The idea that a homosexual orientation can be a healthy and positive choice is reinforced in the recent literature that demonstrates that lesbians are less pathological than nonlesbian women (Freeman, 1971; Obersone & Sukoneck, 1976). Many specialists in the field urge that instead of buying into the lesbian incest survivor's identity confusion with active efforts to change orientation, we should instead focus on the underlying issues which generate concern (Bass & Davis, 1988; Starzecpyzel, 1987; Woititz, 1985). Key among these issues is that of introjected homophobia. Apuzzo (as cited in Nichols, 1987b) has suggested that incest may be perpetrated upon young tomboy girls (who are somewhat more likely to grow up to be lesbians, according to Bell, Weinberg, & Hammersmith, [1981]) as a way of punishing them and keeping them in line. This was true of at least one of my own clinical cases. Even if there is not such a direct connection between orientation and incest, it would be easy for the lesbian incest survivor to internalize homophoia in our homophobic society.

Therapy with the lesbian incest survivor needs to address the client's erotophobia (fear of or discomfort with one's own sexuality). Because lesbianism is a sexual identity, the client may not be comfortable with a self-identification that emphasizes a part of her with which she is uncomfortable. With no courtship rituals or wifely duty to hide behind, lesbian sex can be perceived as purely for sexual pleasure. The therapist needs to help the lesbian incest survivor struggling with this problem to recognize the broader context within which she chooses to be lesbian (e.g., the emotional, philosophical, and spiritual connection to women). Education is needed regarding the continuum of normal sexual behavior. Support and information may need to be given to connect the client with lesbian incest survivor support groups and other positive lesbian social resources. A reading list may be provided that addresses the issues of self-acceptance (e.g., Berzon, 1979; Loulan, 1984, 1987).

Introjected homophobia can add to the incest survivor's feelings of guilt and shame. She may expect and fear the public experiences of prejudice, which are overtly or covertly threatening to lesbians in this culture. It can also trigger negative feelings of hiding another secret.

Xenophobia: Compounding Guilt and Shame

Another underlying issue for the lesbian incest survivor uncomfortable with her sexual orientation may be that of xenophobia (discomfort with one's strangeness). Margolies, Becker, and Jackson-Brewer (1987) suggested that the lesbian's xenophobia is experienced as a fear of parental and social rejection based on differentness from perceived expectations. As an internal conflict it is grounded within the family. The fear of being unacceptable to one's family, the fear of rejection and expulsion, lead to powerful self-hate. Tampering with established patterns in one's family or society is often accompanied by shame, guilt, fear, and anxiety.

If the lesbian incest survivor chooses to pass as straight, to hide her homosexual identity, she adds to and perpetuates her already existent incest survivor guilt and shame. As Klausner and Hasselbring (1990, p. 142) suggested, "the cost of passing ... often includes feeling dishonest with family members and/or may result in distancing from our families to avoid being discovered .... when we conceal our true sexual orientation, we can only guess the degree of real acceptance by our families and friends."

Here the therapist is confronted with the dilemma of believing that breaking the silence (revealing the incest/confronting the molester) is necessary to the recovery and ego development of his or her client on the one hand and knowing his or her client faces a double danger of family rejection because of the client's homosexuality on the other. The most common family reaction to the incest survivor's breaking silence is one of initial shock and outrage followed by denial (Herman, 1981). Likewise, coming out or revealing the homosexual orientation to the family is most often met with negative reactions (Zitter, 1987). In many families, scapegoating of the lesbian occurs, either reinforcing her already existing role as the family scapegoat or shifting this role from another sibling to the lesbian (Zitter, 1987). Coming out as a lesbian compounds the risk of breaking silence about the incest secret. Here, the lesbian risks doubling the chances of family rejection as the mother and father react with denial of the incest and then, perhaps, accuse the daughter of trying to distract their upset over her lifestyle with a false attack on the father. Therapy can help the client (1) decide whether she wishes to break silence or come out to her family, (2) decide whether she wishes to break silence or come out in other settings, (3) build alternative, lesbian-affirming support resources, and (4) develop a positive self-identity regardless of whether she breaks silence or comes out.

Case 2: Erotophobia and Xenophobia

Client issue: Discomfort with sexuality
Therapist's goal(s): Address and process.

> *Client*: The same thing's happening again. It seems like about 6 months to a year into the relationship I just lose interest in sex. In the beginning there's all this great sex and then there's nothing.
>
> *Therapist*: You seem to think there's a pattern to your relationships. Tell me more about how they go.
>
> *Client*: I meet someone in a bar. I'll want to go home with them that night or real soon after meeting them. We become lovers and it's real hot. Pretty soon, within a couple of months, we'll move in together. From 1 to 2 years later, we break up. Within a couple of months I meet somebody new and it starts all over again. It's awful. I'm really tired of not being able to maintain a relationship.
>
> *Therapist*: Can you remember if something begins to change in your way of viewing the relationship after the first 6 months?
>
> *Client*: Hum, let me think about that. Well, it seems that after about 6 months I start to get uncomfortable with how much we make love. I mean, we've usually been living together for a couple of months by that time and it's getting exhausting [making love]. I get tired of having to deal with the questions every night of "Do I feel like making love?" "Does she want to make love?" Then, too, I start getting uncomfortable with not being able to have orgasms. Every time we make love I have to deal with it. Wondering if I'll be able to this time. Wondering if she'll get upset if I don't. More and more I just don't want to deal with it. I don't want her to start anything with me [lovemaking] and I don't want to approach her. I'd rather just not have to do it at all. It's nice to just be close and affectionate with one another.

Also, we're in a *relationship* now, we *live* together. After about 6 months it's like I come out of a fog. I start worrying about what the neighbors think, what my straight friends think, what strangers on the street think about us, what my *family* might suspect. I think everyone can take one look at us and know we're *lovers, lesbians*. I'd just die if my parents found out. I mean, that's just *all* they'd need. After all the trouble I've been anyway, then to find this out. They'd probably never talk to me again.

Therapist: It sounds like a lot starts to go on for you early in the relationship. It sounds like you have a lot of issues around being a sexual being and enjoying sex. Do you think anything else is going on around the way you feel about being a sexual person?

Client: Well, it does seem to get harder once I'm out of that intense, honeymoon stage of the relationship. It seems that once I'm sort of more in control of my passion it's harder for me to be comfortable with being sexual at all. I'd rather just forget about that part of me. Sometimes the memories and flashbacks [of the molestation] start up when the passion dies down and that makes me really uncomfortable. And, of course, not being able to climax makes me feel inadequate. I get real anxious that my lover will leave me if I can't perform even though I know that probably won't happen.

Therapist: I think all these things you're talking about are very closely tied together. I suspect that your childhood molestation has made you very uncomfortable with being sexual. Perhaps you don't want to be like your father, sexually inappropriate. You seem to focus on your relationship with women purely from the sexual side, which would feed into that discomfort. I think we need to do some work around the difference between love and sex and around the normality of homosexuality.

Case 3: Coming Out and Breaking the Silence

Client issue: Fear of rejection/abandonment
Therapist's goal(s): Support in development of positive self-identity, reduction of self-blame/guilt, assessment of ego strength in confronting parents, preparation for and processing of grief.

Therapist: How are you doing?

Client: Well, I'm alive, but I'm really depressed.

Therapist: What happened?

Client: It was pretty bad. I told them about being gay first, like we'd talked about. Mom just got kind of huffy and mumbled something about how I should see a doctor and quit seeing those women. But I told her I had seen a doctor and it was OK. I was gay, I was happier this way. She didn't say much after that. Dad said something about how I'd always been into "it" and this was just one more thing. It was really the hardest with him because I wasn't sure what he'd do. My fear was that he'd either get real mad or he'd get that look in his eye—thinking he knew what would cure me of that all right. But I remembered the role plays we did and I stuck with it. I told him that I felt that being gay was a lot healthier than all the screwing around I'd done when I was young.

Well, of course, he got all defensive and tried to minimize everything. I just kept saying that what he had done to me had deeply affected me and that I really needed to be able to talk about it. Mom kept fussing around in the kitchen and wouldn't deal with it. What it finally came down to was dad getting all righteous and saying he wouldn't hear about it or allow any of those women in his house. He sidetracked the whole incest issue with the gay issue. We kind of figured he'd do that, huh? I was pretty stressed out by the whole thing and really afraid of what dad might do, so I finally just said I didn't feel like either one of them was able to face the truth or accept me for who I really was. I told them I was going to stay away from them for a while and that maybe we could really talk someday, but that for now I didn't want to be around them. I went back to the motel and just cried and cried. Thank God Helen [female partner] was there for me.

Therapist: How do you feel about how they reacted?

Client: Confused. It was really good that you talked to me about the classic characteristics of the incestuous parents because it helped me see them a little more objectively. I mean, my mom is the classic emotionally distant, passive, nonaccepting mother and my dad the classic authoritarian, rageful, out-of-control abuser. It's really hard to get out of my tendency to blame myself for what happened and how I am [gay]. He's so powerful and scary, it's like I don't want to do or say anything that might provoke him. But I realized keeping these secrets was eating me up inside. Making me feel like the sick one because I was so afraid of how angry or disgusted they'd be if they knew. Isn't that crazy? After what dad did to me, that I'd still be so concerned about their rejection of *me*?

Therapist: No, fearing the rejection or emotional and physical abandonment of your parents is a pretty primal fear in all of us. For the adult survivor who actually experienced the emotional abandonment of one or both parents, it's especially strong. It takes a lot of strength to push through that fear and stand up for yourself anyway. That's why we worked so long getting you ready to confront them. You really needed to feel good about yourself and have a lot of support to deal with the possible loss of their love and acceptance, even though that love wasn't healthy to begin with.

Client: Yeah, I'm really glad we did all that work around the incest and that you helped me see it wasn't my fault. It really helped to go to the lesbian incest survivors group, too. To hear about how everybody else struggled with the same feelings and how some women had worked through their own issues around being gay. The professional lesbian group you told me about was really helpful, too. It was great meeting so many women who were self-confident and successful! It really made me feel it was OK to be gay. Your idea to adopt a surrogate family was a lifesaver. My "sister" was a big support through all this, and I feel that my new gay family will really be there for me in a way my own family was never able to. It's not so scary thinking about not having my mom and dad there.

Therapist: I'm glad those things were helpful to you. And I'm sure your friends will be there for you as you continue to work through your normal feelings of loss around your parents. Just as you and I will continue to work on your grieving for them and your lost childhood.

Lesbian Incest Survivor Sexuality

Herman (1981) reported that regardless of sexual object choice over half (55%) of the incest victims in her study complained of impairments in sexual enjoyment. Many of the informants reported that their pleasure in sex was minimal or even entirely absent. However, in her research with lesbians, Loulan (1987) found that most lesbians in her study with a history of sexual abuse had sex just as frequently and were as satisfied with their sex lives as lesbians with no history of sexual abuse. However, 16% of her respondents were not satisfied with their current sex life and offered such reasons as no sexual desire, fear of sex, incest background of self or partner, and self-hatred. This suggests that although many lesbian incest survivors lead satisfactory sex lives, some will still experience and need to be treated for sexual difficulties. My own clinical experience with this population has shown this to be true. Nichols (1987a) is a good resource for those desiring more specifics on sex therapy with lesbians.

Alcoholism

Possible alcoholism is a problem that may need special attention when working with the lesbian incest survivor. Herman's (1981) study of incest survivors revealed that 20% became alcoholic or drug dependent. Most described their drug abuse as ineffective attempts to cope with feelings of loneliness and depression. Loulan (1987) reported that of the lesbians who were currently addicted or who were in recovery, 49% reported childhood sexual abuse, with another 16% unsure (of childhood abuse), whereas those reporting no current or past chemical addiction had a 34% incidence of childhood sexual abuse, with another 10% unsure.

Alcohol abuse and alcoholism appear to be more of a problem for the lesbian population, in general, than for heterosexual women (Nicoloff & Stiglitz, 1987). Therefore, assessment of and treatment for alcohol and drug abuse in the lesbian incest survivor is warranted. Efforts need to be made to refer clients to recovery resources and nonalcohol-oriented social alternatives. While working with the recovering lesbian incest survivor, the therapist needs to be aware of the general issues that any recovering person might experience as well as the special problems she may face as a homosexual: issues of coming out in the treatment and 12-step program, onset or increase of flashbacks, intense feelings related to childhood abuse, sexual identity confusion, negative changes in sexual functioning during early recovery (i.e., first year), availability of nonalcoholic avenues for socializing, and availability of gay Alcoholics Anonymous and Narcotics Anonymous groups (Klausner & Hasselbring, 1990; Nicoloff & Stiglitz, 1987).

Elaine Brady

Dual-Survivor Relationships

If almost 40% of lesbians are incest survivors (Loulan, 1987), then the chances of two lesbian incest survivors becoming partners is high. When both members of a relationship are incest survivors, the relationship can be affected in complex ways. Depending on how far along each woman is in the healing process, they may be able to offer each other tremendous support, reassurance, and understanding. But they may also intensify each other's struggles, trigger memories and old patterns, and otherwise get entangled in painful dynamics (Bass & Davis, 1988). In dual-survivor relationships, there may be some element of competition: "I'm over that. Why don't you get over it?" Or "I can have sex, why can't you?" Often there's an unspoken battle: Whoever is in the most pain wins. If her partner had a worse experience than she did, your client may feel she doesn't deserve to get her own needs for nurturance and support met. The abuse can become the focus of the relationship: "We're so close because these awful things happened to us." This couple needs to remember the other things that brought them together, so the focus is not solely on this aspect of their relationship. Exploration of the couple's interactions around their incest issues is needed.

Case 4: Dual-Survivor Relationships

Client issue: Sexual and chemical addictions, sexual difficulties
Therapist's goal(s): Educate regarding adult survivor characteristics and symptoms, assess interplay of couple dynamics, assess for and confront addictions (see chapter 17), refer for couples therapy.

> *Therapist*: Now that you know more about the characteristics and symptoms of the adult survivor and you're more familiar with your own attitude and behavior difficulties, how do you think your relationship is affected by both of you being survivors?
>
> *Client*: Well, sex is real important to both of us. We're real intense around sex, it's a big part of our connection. Plus, we have a nonmonogamous relationship, so each of us gets to be with other people. I remember you told me some survivors are promiscuous.
>
> *Therapist*: Yes, that's right. Do you see this as a problem in your relationship?

Client: It might be. I know it's real hard for me to separate my feelings from the people I date. I usually become infatuated for a while and break some of our rules about being with other people. Lately, I've been thinking more and more about this one woman I've been seeing and feeling unhappy with Sandy [female partner]. But I think things would be worse if I couldn't be with other people sexually. I think I'd get bored with it like I have all the rest. Plus, I'd be stuck with the problem Sandy and I have around sex.

Therapist: It sounds like the affairs serve as a distractor from the problems of the relationship. Have you and Sandy talked about the sexual problem?

Client: Not really, she's real sensitive about it. It seems like something we can't talk about or change. She got upset because I was honest with her when she asked me if her weight gain made me less attracted to her. I said it did a little, and ever since she's more uptight about me making love to her. So I just don't push the issue, but I feel like she's not as open to me as she used to be. Maybe that's part of her incest survivor stuff?

Therapist: It could be. It seems you both have an extreme focus on sex, and that at least for Sandy, there's a strong connection between being sexually attractive and being loved. Maybe that's attached to a fear of abandonment.

Client: Hum, you know, as you said that it occurred to me that that's what goes on for me about needing to be non-monogamous. Right before I left home my dad started trying to control my seeing my boyfriend. He was always asking me where I'd been and actually following me! Then I was devastated when my husband left me later. I think part of what happens with my wanting to date other people when I'm in a relationship is that I don't want to ever give anyone the kind of power over me that my dad and husband had—both sexually and emotionally. Having other lovers around helps keep a little piece of me safe from my partner, and I'm not so vulnerable to only having my partner meet my sexual needs.

Therapist: That sounds like a really important thing to have realized about yourself. Are there any other ways you think you protect yourself in the relationship?

Client: Well, I'm not sure. Maybe how much we drink and smoke grass isn't good for us?

Therapist: How do you see this as creating problems?

Client: Well, every night we have drinks, and we figured out that we often have fights after drinking a bit. So we're trying to watch that, but I'm not real comfortable with how much we drink anyway. But I'm afraid to say anything. Sandy's so hung up on our doing everything together. Then, with the grass, it's great when we make love stoned, but then when we make love straight it's not as great, so I've gotten to where I don't really want to make love unless we're stoned. I don't think that's so good.

Therapist: No, it does sound like you two are drinking and using too much and that creates problems for the two of you. It sounds like problems in your relationship aren't getting dealt with either. I'm wondering if you two might benefit from some couples counseling to begin to look at some of these issues?

Client: You're probably right. Just from this talk I can see that there's stuff going on we'd better work on before it gets worse and there's probably more that will come out in the couples work.

Summary

This chapter has attempted to outline eight key issues in working with the lesbian incest survivor that are seen as distinct from the more general survivor issues that both lesbian and heterosexual women share. These key issues have been identified as (1) a questioning of the possible cause-and-effect nature of childhood molestation and later homosexual orientation, (2) dealing with societal and internalized homophobia, (3) compounding of survivor shame and guilt, (4) erotophobia, (5) xenophobia, (6) incest effects on sexuality, (7) alcoholism, and (8) dual-survivor relationships.

In working with the lesbian incest survivor, the therapist is urged to examine his or her own perceptions for possible homophobic beliefs and feelings and to evaluate his or her ability to work effectively with the lesbian client. Confused or negative beliefs and feelings toward a homosexual orientation might make it difficult for the therapist to work with the client's own struggles with identity confusion.

No clear cause-and-effect correlation appears to exist between childhood molestation and later homosexual orientation. The lesbian incest survivors who did believe the incest had affected their sexual orientation felt that it was a healthy and adaptive choice for them. In the case of identity confusion, efforts can be made to examine the underlying issues that generate the client's confusion and resolve these. These issues may include internalized homophobia, erotophobia, and xenophobia. Education on normal human sexual behavior and referral to lesbian-affirming resources may be helpful.

As a result of internalized homophobia, the therapist may need to help the client resolve the double guilt and shame of being both an incest survivor and a lesbian. This may be particularly important around such issues as coming out and breaking the silence with parents or others.

Although many lesbian incest survivors apparently have satisfactory sexual relations, sexual difficulties may need to be addressed and resolved. Here, again, the therapist may need to help the client resolve issues of internalized homophobia and erotophobia.

Because alcoholism appears to be higher among lesbian incest survivors than among their heterosexual counterparts, special care may need to be taken in assessing for and treating this problem. Awareness should be maintained on the special issues in recovery for the lesbian incest survivor: coming out in treatment and 12-step programs, intense feelings related to childhood abuse, sexual identity confusion, negative changes in sexuality during early recovery.

Dual-survivor relationships are a distinct possibility for the lesbian incest survivor, and the possible advantages and disadvantages of these were outlined. Exploration of the client's own dual-survivor relationship should be made to clarify its particular dynamics.

References

Bass, E., & Davis, L. (1988). *The courage to heal*. San Francisco: Harper & Row.
Bell, A., Weinberg, M., & Hammersmith S. (1981). *Sexual preference: Its development in men and women*. Bloomington: Indiana University Press.
Berzon, B. (1979). *Positively gay*. Los Angeles: Mediamix.
Fassinger, R. (1991). The hidden minority: Issues and challenges in working with lesbians and gays. *Counseling Psychologist, 19*, 157.
Freeman, M. (1971). *Homosexual and psychological functioning*. San Francisco: Brooks/Cole.
Grundlach, R. (1977). Sexual molestation and rape reported by homosexual and heterosexual women. *Journal of Homosexuality, 2*, 367–384.
Herman, J. (1981). *Father-daughter incest*. Cambridge, MA: Harvard University Press.
Klausner, M., & Hasselbring, B. (1990). *Aching for love*. San Francisco: Harper & Row.

Loulan, J. (1984). *Lesbian sex*. San Francisco: Spinsters/Aunt Lute.

Loulan, J. (1987). *Lesbian passion*. San Francisco: Spinsters/Aunt Lute.

Maltz, W., & Holman, B. (1987). *Incest and sexuality*. Lexington, MA: Lexington Books.

Margolies, L., Becker, M., & Jackson-Brewer, K. (1987). Internalized homophobia: Identifying and treating the oppressor within. In Boston Lesbian Psychologies Collective (Eds.), *Lesbian psychologies: Explorations and challenges* (pp. 229–241). Urbana, IL: University of Illinois Press.

Meiselman, K. (1981). *Incest*. San Francisco: Jossey-Bass.

Nichols, M. (1987a). Doing sex therapy with lesbians: Bending a heterosexual paradigm to fit a gay lifestyle. In Boston Lesbian Psychologies Collective (Eds.), *Lesbian psychologies: Explorations and challenges* (pp. 242–260). Urbana, IL: University of Illinois Press.

Nichols, M. (1987b). Lesbian sexuality: Issues and developing theory. In Boston Lesbian Psychologies Collective (Eds.), *Lesbian psychologies: Explorations and challenges* (pp. 97–125). Urbana, IL: University of Illinois Press.

Nichols, L., & Stiglitz, E. (1987). Lesbian alcoholism: Etiology, treatment, and recovery. In Boston Lesbian Psychologies Collective (Eds.), *Lesbian psychologies: Explorations and challenges* (pp. 283–293). Urbana, IL: University of Illinois Press.

Obersone, A., & Sukoneck, H. (1976). Psychological adjustment and lifestyle of single lesbians and single heterosexual women. *Psychology of Women Quarterly, 1*, 172–188.

Starzecpyzel, E. (1987). The Persephone complex: Incest dynamics and the lesbian preference. In Boston Lesbian Psychologies Collective (Eds.), *Lesbian psychologies: Explorations and challenges* (pp. 261–282). Urbana, IL: University of Illinois Press.

Van Buskirk, S., & Cole C. (1983). Characteristics of eight women seeking therapy for the effects of incest. *Psychotherapy: Theory, Research, and Practice, 20*, 503–514.

Woititz, J. (1985). *Struggle for intimacy*. Pompano Beach, FL: Health Communications.

Zitter, S. (1987). Coming out to mom: Theorectical aspects of the mother-daughter process. In Boston Lesbian Psychologies Collective (Eds.), *Lesbian psychologies: Explorations and challenges* (pp. 177–194). Urbana, IL: University of Illinois Press.

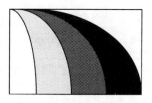

15

A Gay Male Survivor of Antigay Violence

Dee Bridgewater, PhD

Violence is a fact of life in America. An especially onerous form of violence extant in American society is the hate crime. Hate crimes are verbal and physical assaults motivated by the assailant's perception that the victim is a member of a minority group (Herek, 1989). Spurred by prejudice, hate crimes include verbal insults, taunts, or threats; spitting; kicking; punching; throwing objects; vandalism; arson; attacks with weapons; rape; and murder (Cerio, 1989; Comstock, 1989; D'Augelli, 1989; Herek, 1989). Hate crimes are particularly destructive: Not only do they harm the individual victim but they also violate the integrity and well-being of the minority group singled out for attack (Herek, 1989; National Gay and Lesbian Task Force [NGLTF], 1990).

Gays and lesbians have historically been a minority group in American society singled out for discrimination (Katz, 1976). Currently, this antigay bias is extant in the general population (Gallup, 1983; NGLTF, 1990), among college and university students (Cerio, 1989; D'Augelli, 1989), and the psychological profession (Morin, 1977; Rudolph, 1989; Walters, 1986). This bias, termed *homophobia* (Weinberg, 1972), has become institutionalized in America's public policy (Melton, 1989).

A virulent form of homophobia is the hate crime of antigay violence. Hate crimes perpetrated against gay men are especially prevalent (Herek, 1989) and violent (Wertheimer, 1987) in comparison to attacks against other stigmatized minority groups.

The purpose of this chapter is to examine the impact of hate crimes on gay men. The goal of the chapter is to give counselors practical information on how effectively to assess the negative impact of antigay violence on the gay male client, initiate appropriate therapeutic interventions that minimize the immediate effects of the assault, and aid the client in making a successful, long-term adjustment after the attack.

Owing to the prejudice that motivates antigay violence, the resulting trauma to the individual victim is destructive on several levels. The violent assault is an attack on both the individual's person and his identity as a gay man. Therefore, in addition to recovering from the physical and psychological trauma inherent in any violent assault, the gay male survivor must also cope with the trauma to his gayness (Herek, 1989; Wertheimer, 1987).

The task of achieving a positive gay identity is a long, arduous, and complex process in which the individual strives to overcome his internalized homophobia (Cass, 1979; Troiden, 1979, 1989). In rejecting popular negative attitudes toward homosexuality, the gay person becomes more accepting of himself and thus more capable of leading a happy life (Malyon 1981/1982; Miranda & Storms, 1989; Schmitt & Kurdek, 1987). A violent assault on an individual motivated by antigay prejudice can have a deleterious impact on the individual's striving to achieve a positive gay identification in a society he perceives as hostile to gays (Anderson, 1988; Comstock, 1989; Herek, 1989; Wertheimer, 1987).

Data garnered from diverse research studies indicate that antigay violence is prevalent throughout America and can occur at all social strata and in any social setting (Caldwell, 1988; Cerio, 1989; Comstock, 1989; D'Augelli, 1989; Lynch, 1987; NGLTF, 1990). Therefore, counselors who have the possibility of seeing gay male clients in their clinical practice have a potential of dealing with the issue of antigay violence.

Furthermore, the impact of antigay violence is not limited to gay men who are survivors. Gay men who have not been personally victimized may have friends, relatives, or long-time companions who are survivors of assaults. The concern of a gay male client for his victimized significant other could become an issue of clinical concern. In addition, a gay man who has not been victimized and who does not know any survivors of antigay violence may have been exposed to the reportage of antigay violence in the popular gay and nongay media. The knowledge one may be physically attacked due to one's sexual orientation could raise concerns that might become a clinical issue (Lynch, 1987). Furthermore, incidents have been filed reporting assaults on nongay men who were mistakenly perceived as gay by their assailants (Wertheimer, 1987). These nongay survivors of antigay assaults may all seek counseling; however, their unique issues are outside this chapter's focus.

A scenario of a gay man who has been subjected to an antigay assault is presented in the following case study. This case study is a synthesis of clients treated by the author over the last 10 years and encompasses the salient clinical issues and counseling dynamics of the gay male survivor. It is to be hoped that counselors dealing with clients more indirectly affected by antigay violence can extrapolate information pertinent to their clients from the material presented.

Steve

Steve is a 23-year-old White man who entered therapy reporting feelings of depression and anxiety. Currently married, Steve reported increasingly frequent fantasies of engaging in sex with men. These homoerotic longings were at odds with his heterosexual lifestyle and were causing him a great deal of dissonance and subsequent distress. Steve was reticent to explore his homosexual feelings. Because of the social stigma of being gay, Steve stated he would rather be straight. He was also fearful of AIDS and the risk of possible HIV infection from a homosexual lifestyle. Finally, Steve was anxious that if he discovered he was gay, it would disrupt his marriage and end the security of his established lifestyle.

Despite these fears, Steve stated that his urge to have sex with men was becoming increasingly intrusive and that it was "tearing him apart." He came to therapy to "sort things out."

In the first 2 months of counseling, Steve became more accepting of his homoerotic feelings in a pattern consistent with the developmental schemas proposed by Cass (1979; see Introduction) and Troiden (1979, 1989; see Chapter 1) for men establishing a positive gay identity. In the nonjudgemental atmosphere of therapy, Steve was able to explore more freely and acknowledge his same-sex attractions and to make the self-declaration that he was gay.

Subsequently, Steve took the risk of informing his wife of his sexual orientation and through the process of conjoint sessions conducted by another therapist made an amiable separation from his wife. Steve moved into an apartment of his own, and although he was anxious and lonely at times, he felt greatly relieved at no longer being clandestine in his interactions with gay men.

Steve started going to gay social gatherings with increasing regularity. He formed a social network of gay friends and with them ventured into bars and restaurants in the predominantly gay neighborhoods of the city. He was now desirous of dating men. I asked Steve about his knowledge of HIV infection. He stated that he already had made contact with a local AIDS organization for information. We spent time discussing safer sex practices and strategies that Steve could use to negotiate safer sex with potential sex partners.

One day, I received a call from Steve. He reported that on the previous night, he had been leaving a bar in a popular gay neighborhood and had been accosted by four youths in their late teens. They had shouted "faggot" and "queer" at Steve and had accused him and other "homos" of "trying to kill us all with AIDS." The four youths had surrounded Steve and started to punch him with their fists. They shoved Steve to the ground and started to kick him.

Other men in the area heard the commotion, ran to the scene, and started yelling at the men, ordering them to stop. Someone started blowing a whistle. Alarmed the youths fled in a car. One eyewitness recorded its license number as it sped away.

Steve was taken to a nearby hospital by ambulance and was examined in the emergency room. Although he had suffered bruises and lacerations over much of his body, there were no broken bones and no signs of internal injuries or a concussion. Steve had been held in the hospital overnight for observation and had been released that morning.

On the phone, I asked Steve if he was physically able to care for himself—get food, obtain any assistance he needed. He said that he was able to take care of his basic needs. I also asked if he had people around to offer emotional support. He said that he had decided to stay at a friend's apartment for a few days.

I then set up an appointment for Steve to come in later that day. This was in addition to our regularly scheduled session late in the week. These initial crisis intervention procedures are in keeping with suggestions proposed by Anderson (1988) and Bohn (1984) for male clients who are the victims of violent assault.

Steve arrived for the scheduled appointment with his face bruised and in obvious pain. He seemed calm as he matter-of-factly described the attack. I asked Steve how he felt, and he reported a numbness: "no feelings at all." Halfway through the hour, Steve started to cry. He stated that he did not know the reason for the tears.

Throughout this initial session, I spent most of the time listening. I invited Steve to express his feelings without trying to edit them. Near the end of the hour, Steve realized he was feeling a great shame. He felt that he had deserved to be attacked because he was gay. He felt that he wasn't a real man and that he had only himself to blame for being in a gay neighborhood in the first place. "The world hates gays and since I'm gay the world will always hate me. Getting beaten up is just part of it." This sense of despondent resignation, shame, self-recrimination, and self-attribution of guilt has been noted by counselors dealing with gay male assault victims (Bohn, 1984).

I reflected that Steve was feeling he was the guilty party, not the assailants. Then I tentatively introduced the idea that the assailants were "guilty" in the legal sense of the word. Steve was adamant that he was the one who was responsible. I made no further effort to offer an alternative view (at this time). I established that Steve was still staying with a friend and would not be alone that night. We agreed to meet the next day for a second, auxiliary meeting to our usual weekly session.

Steve entered this session depressed. Gay friends were telling him that he should report the incident to the police, but Steve was fearful that an official report would create a record of his gayness that could lead to a damaging public disclosure of his sexual orientation. He was still feeling physical pain from the attack as well as sadness. The pressure and criticism from people whom he wanted to be understanding and sympathetic was exacerbating his depression. We dealt immediately with the issue of his friends. In the session, we devised ways that Steve could make it clear to his friends that he needed some support. He didn't need to be put on the defensive.

I asked Steve to tell me how he was feeling as we talked about his friends. He said that he was aware of "a little anger." I asked at whom he was angry. Steve started lambasting himself. He was angry at himself for being gay, for coming out, and for going to gay social events. He stated that if he was still with his wife and not going out to gay places he never would have been attacked.

I asked Steve what his need was to keep focusing on himself as the guilty part in the assault. He stated that it was a pattern he had gotten used to—blaming himself, thinking he was the one who was wrong and thus deserving of attack. In boarding school he had been ridiculed and shoved around by schoolmates who called him a sissy. His two older brothers had chided him for not being more athletic. His father had been consistently critical of him for not being "more of a man." This criticism was particularly painful because Steve's father was his only surviving parent. Steve's mother had died in a boating accident when he was 10. This pattern of reacting to accumulative rejections with self-blame has been noted among gay clients by Colgan (1987).

I asked Steve if he had ever considered why his four assailants were in a neighborhood that was well known to be predominantly gay. Were they there to enjoy the social scene? It seems that they were there to attack gay people. I pointed out that researchers had stated that certain men in society try to assert their heterosexuality by attacking gay men (Herek, 1989; Morin & Garfinkle, 1978). The goal of these attacks is to humiliate the gay man and demonstrate their superiority (Bohn, 1984). To insure that the gay man has little chance of successfully defending himself, the attackers are usually armed and outnumber the gay man in a gang with an average number of four (Bohn, 1984).

Hearing this information, Steve stated that he was no longer depressed. He was furious. He realized how unfair the attack had been. It violated his basic right to be free from harm. Steve then began to relate the present anger he was experiencing to the anger he had felt toward people in his past. He recalled similar, long-forgotten angry feelings because of the schoolmates who had taunted him, because of his siblings, and because of his father. Steve and I continued to explore this repressed anger in on-going therapy.

Steve had repeatedly stated that if he had not been in a popular gay neighborhood, he would never have been attacked. I pointed out that survey results (Comstock, 1989; NGLTF, 1990) indicated the majority of attacks on gays did occur in popular gay neighborhoods; however, these results also demonstrated that a substantial number of attacks occur in nongay locales—public places, homes, schools (Comstock, 1989), and universities (Cerio, 1989; D'Augelli, 1989).

We discussed Steve's need to believe that if he had not been in a gay neighborhood he never would have been attacked. He realized that this belief gave him the notion that outside of gay neighborhoods he would be safe from the possibility of assault. The use of such fallacious beliefs by victims to control their anxiety levels has been noted by Janoff-Bulman (1989). Steve came to the realization that antigay assaults can occur anywhere, not just in gay neighborhoods. We then explored his anxieties and anger regarding this realization. Then we devised a plan of action. Steve took a self-defense course designed for gay men that offered him strategies for defending himself and tips on how to avoid future antigay attacks.

Steve also mentioned that if he had not been drinking he might have been better able to defend himself. This led to a discussion of Steve's recreational drug use and its impact on his life. (See chapter 17 on counseling chemically dependent gays and lesbians.)

Readers may note a pattern in my dealings with Steve after the assault. The goals of these cognitive interventions were to stabilize Steve's physical and psychological well-being immediately after the attack and to facilitate Steve in becoming more aware of his emotions, in better understanding the cause of these emotions, and in generating strategies for action(s) that would have a positive outcome.

After the assault, Steve went through the phases of numbness, despondency and self-blame, depression, and anger. This is a common pattern noted for the survivors of antigay assaults (Bohn, 1984; Colgan, 1987). I made no attempt to rush Steve through these phases. I listened patiently to the emotions he was expressing (anger at himself, depression). I then asked Steve to look at the way he was cognitively setting up the situation (self-attribution of blame). I further explored his reason for perceiving the situation in that particular way (a long-term pattern of self-blame). I then offered an alternative way of thinking (the assailants were responsible), providing supportive evidence for my viewpoint (data on the motives and modus of perpetrators).

This alternative viewpoint led to a greater realization of his emotions (anger at both contemporary and past assailants and anxiety regarding possible, future assaults). The realization of these uncomfortable emotions created the motivation to take action (process his anger in therapy and enroll in a self-defense class).

Such a pattern of interventions is in keeping with the cognitive therapy techniques delineated by Beck (1976). Due to the crisis nature of an antigay assault, cognitive techniques are often appropriate for the initial interventions with survivors. These techniques may be integrated with interventions used by therapists working in other modalitites, for example, psychodynamic psychotherapy.

In summary, immediately after an assault it is necessary for the counselor to assess the survivor's physical and emotional well-being and support network and to aid the survivor in becoming stabilized.

To then continue the work of assessing and processing the effects of the attack, the counselor needs to be aware of the dynamics of antigay assaults: their volume, modus, motivation. These data are essential so the counselor can better understand the dynamics of what is happening with his or her client. These data are also necessary so that the counselor can offer alternative, realistic viewpoints in the face of the client's possibly distorted perceptions. To become more aware of antigay violence, counselors are referred to the reference list at the end of this chapter and are encouraged to continue their research, gaining a practical knowledge of the area.

Assessing the impact an antigay assault has had on a gay male client's positive gay identity is vital. After the assault, Steve expressed anger at being gay and denounced himself for going to gay social settings. He also expressed a desire to go back to his wife and resume a heterosexual lifestyle. Earlier in therapy, Steve had come to the realization that he was gay in a process common to many gay men, examining the contradiction between a heterosexual lifestyle and homosexual desires (Coleman, 1987). As is the case with many gay men, Steve had repressed his homosexuality because of the homophobia he had experienced since he was a child (Cass, 1979; Stanley & Wolfe, 1980; Troiden, 1979, 1989). The trauma he had experienced from a physical assault *promoted by the assailants' perception he was gay* had caused Steve to revert to an earlier period in his gay identity development, a period when he wanted to deny his gayness. This periodic regression is a natural part of the coming out process when the individual is faced with homophobic challenges to his fledgling gay identity (McWhirter & Mattison, 1984; Troiden, 1989).

A tenet in gay affirmative psychotherapy is the therapist's objective neutrality vis-à-vis the client's choice of sexual orientation: Homosexuality and heterosexuality are viewed as equally valid (Malyon 1981/1982). Maintaining this objectivity, I listened attentively to Steve's anger at being gay and his desire to return to a heterosexual lifestyle. Following the cognitive therapeutic interventions outlined earlier, I asked Steve what was causing him to regret his decision to come out. Steve came to realize that he was anxious about the homophobia he would have to face living the life of a gay man. I acknowledged that his anxiety was realistic; society was homophobic. I then asked Steve how it would be to return to the heterosexual lifestyle he had been living. Steve remembered the terrible anxiety and depression he had experienced when he tried to deny being gay and how much freer he had been when he had accepted his gayness and had started to come out to people. These realizations strengthened Steve's re-solve to continue his arduous but fulfilling process of coming out.

He attended a survivor's support group in which he shared his experiences with other gay men who had been victimized. The group gave Steve emotional support and practical ways to deal with the aftermath of the attack, benefits noted for other survivors of antigay violence (Bohn, 1984). It should be pointed out that Steve was attacked solely for his sexual orientation. Some survivors of antigay assault are people of color. Assailants in these attacks may be motivated by racism as well as homophobia. Counselors need to be sensitive to the complex interplay of minority *identities* within the client who is gay and a person of color, assessing and treating the impact an assault has had on both the individual's gay identity and his ethnic minority identity. (For further discussion of ethnic minority issues vis-á-vis gays and lesbians, see chapters 8, 9, and 10.)

Steve decided to report the assault to the police; however, he had heard stories from gay friends about police abuse. I acknowledged the fact that there were documented cases of police harassment of gays (NGLTF, 1990). I volunteered to go with Steve to make the report, offering support, but this proved unnecessary.

Steve contacted an advocate in the legal department of the local gay and lesbian community services center who aided him in preparing the crime report. This advocate also went with Steve to the police station to file the report. Other advocates helped Steve track the case through the DA's office and offered Steve legal advice for the duration of the court proceeding that resulted in convictions of the assailants.

Steve also continued his work in therapy, dealing with his anger about the attack and the subsequent chain of associations to past angers he had held onto for years. He made the decision to come out to his father and brothers. This caused a period of disruption and separation from them that eventually led to a reuniting in which Steve felt more accepted and respected. He also started to deal with pre-viously unacknowledged anger he had for his mother who had "de-serted him" by dying.

Finally, Steve continued to bring in material dealing with his on-going coming out process. He had started to date "one special man," and they were considering moving in together. He also decided to volunteer for a local AIDS organization, working on their hotline. He had thought about working with victims of antigay violence through the local gay and lesbian community center, but he came to the de-cision that this work would be too upsetting for him.

Dee Bridgewater

Summary

It is vital that counselors understand the impact antigay assaults have on gay men who are their counselees. Counselors can be a valuable resource, aiding the survivor in dealing with the trauma inherent in any assault and facilitating the client in coping with the trauma the attack has inflicted on the client's gay identity.

In fulfilling this valuable resource role, the counselor could be called upon to serve as a *crisis counselor*, aiding the client in coping with the immediate physical and psychological trauma of the assault; a *social service advocate*, aiding the counselee in dealing with medical, law enforcement, judicial, and public service bureaucracies that can be hostile to gays (NGLTF, 1990; Wertheimer, 1987); and as an *on-going counselor*, facilitating the client in making a successful, long-term adjustment after the attack. Counselors can also serve as *public service advocates*, working at decreasing the incidents of antigay violence by offering workshops on homophobia to gay and nongay populations, lobbying for legislation that addresses antigay violence, and educating colleagues on the issue.

Additionally, counselors working in a gay-affirmative therapy mode (Malyon, 1981/1982) can play a vital role in aiding the gay male client who is in the process of acquiring a more positive gay identity by working through his internalized homophobia. The trauma of an antigay attack obviously has an impact on this process. Counselors can help the gay male client assess the assault's immediate damage and place its harmful effects in context with previous challenges encountered in the client's struggle to forge a viable gay identity.

Throughout this chapter I have used the terms *survivor* and *victim* to designate a gay male client who has been subjected to an antigay attack. An effective counselor can make a profound difference in the accuracy of these terms in describing such a client. By facilitating the gay man's recovery in his life and by aiding him in the continuing process of developing a more positive gay identity, the counselor can have a powerful impact in ensuring that the assaulted gay man is a survivor.

References

Anderson, C. L. (1988). Males as sexual assault victims: Multiple levels of trauma. *Journal of Homosexuality, 7,* 145–162.

Beck, A. T. (1976). *Cognitive therapy and the emotional disorders*. New York: International Press.

Bohn, T. R. (1984). *Homophobic violence: Implications for social work practice*. New York: Haworth.

Caldwell, J. (1988, August). *Organized hate crimes and antigay violence*. Paper presented at the annual meeting of the American Psychological Association, Atlanta, GA.

Cass, V. C. (1979). Homosexual identity formulation: A theoretical model. *Journal of Homosexuality, 4*, 219–236.

Cerio, N. G. (1989). Counseling victims and perpetrators of campus violence. *New Directions for Student Services, 47*, 53–63.

Colgan, P. (1987). Assessment of sexual orientation. *Journal of Homosexuality, 14*, 9–24.

Coleman, E. (1987). Victims of antigay/lesbian violence. *Journal of Interpersonal Violence, 4*, 101–106.

Comstock G. D. (1989). Victims of antigay/lesbian violence. *Journal of Interpersonal Violence, 4*, 101–106.

D'Augelli, A. R. (1989). Lesbian and gay men's experience of discrimination and harassment in a university community. *American Journal of Community Psychology, 17*, 317–321.

Gallup, G. H. (1983). *The Gallup poll*. Wilmington, DE: Scholarly Resources.

Herek, G. M. (1989). Hate crimes against lesbians and gay men: Issues for research and policy. *American Psychologist, 44*, 948–955.

Janoff-Bulman, R. (1989). The benefits of illusion, the threat of disillusionment, and the limitations of inaccuracy. *Journal of Social and Clinical Psychology, 8*, 158–175.

Katz, J. (1976). *Gay American history*. New York: Crowell.

Lynch, F. R. (1987). Nonghetto gays: A sociological study of suburban homosexuals. *Journal of Homosexuality, 13*, 13–42.

Malyon, A. K. (1981/1982). Psychotherapeutic implications of internalized homophobia in gay men. *Journal of Homosexuality, 7*, 59–69.

McWhirter, D., & Mattison, D. (1984). *The male couple: How relationships develop*. Englewood Cliffs, NJ: Prentice-Hall.

Melton, G. B. (1989). Public policy and private prejudice: Psychology and law on gay rights. *American Psychologist, 44*, 933–940.

Miranda, J., & Storms, M. (1989). Psychological adjustment of lesbians and gay men. *Journal of Counseling and Development, 68*, 41–45.

Morin, S. F., & Garfinkle, E. M. (1978). Male homophobia. *Journal of Social Issues, 34*, 29–47.

Morin, S. F. (1977). Heterosexual bias in psychological research on lesbianism and male homosexuality. *American Psychologist, 32*, 629–637.

National Gay and Lesbian Task Force. (1990). *Antigay violence, victimization, and defamation in 1989*. Washington, DC: Author. (Available from National Gay and Lesbian Task Force, 1517 U Street, N.W., Washington, DC 20009).

Rudolph, J. (1989). Effects of a workshop on mental health practitioners' attitudes toward homosexuality and counselor effectiveness. *Journal of Counseling and Development, 68*, 81–85.

Schmitt, J. P., & Kurdek, L. A. (1987). Personality correlates of positive identity and relationship involvement in gay men. *Journal of Homosexuality, 13,* 101–109.

Stanley, J. P., & Wolfe, S. J. (Eds.). (1980). *Coming out stories.* Watertown, ME: Persephone Press.

Troiden, R. R. (1979). Becoming homosexual: A model of gay identity acquisition. *Psychiatry, 42,* 362–373.

Troiden, R. R. (1989). The formation of homosexual identities. *Journal of Homosexuality, 17,* 43–73.

Walters, A. T. (1986). Heterosexual bias in psychological research on lesbianism and male homosexuality (1979–1983), utilizing the bibliographic and taxonomic system of Morin (1977). *Journal of Homosexuality, 13,* 35–56.

Wertheimer, D. (1987, August). *Community empowerment: Strategies for responding to homophobic violence.* Paper presented at the annual meeting of the American Psychological Association, New York.

Weinberg, G. (1972). *Society and the healthy homosexual.* Garden City, NY: Anchor.

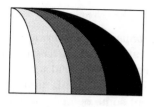

16

Same-Sex Domestic Violence

Ned Farley, MA, CMHC

Domestic violence is a critical topic in the mental health field today. However, the issue of domestic violence in the gay and lesbian community is still largely ignored (Hart, 1986; Walber, 1988).

This chapter focuses on exploration of same-sex domestic violence, particularly on how counselors and therapists can effectively recognize, intervene, and provide a therapeutic environment that will eliminate the destructive nature of battering in gay and lesbian relationships.

What Is Domestic Violence?

Domestic violence can be defined as an act of aggression, either psychological or physical, that is an attempt by the perpetrator to intimidate or harm another in an intimate relationship, out of a real or perceived frustration with a given situation (Farley, 1985). It is important to recognize that violence in a relationship is never an appropriate response. One of the myths—and one of the most common answers given by batterers when asked "Why?"—is "She or he made me do it!"

Domestic violence incorporates emotional, psychological, and physical abuse. This is commonly called the abuse spectrum (Walker, 1979,

1984). Often the terms *abuse* and *battering* are used interchangeably; this chapter, however, refers to abuse as emotional and psychological in nature, and battering as the physical acting out of aggression. There is no one pattern or course of events that is found in domestically violent relationships, but some or many of the behaviors included in the abuse spectrum are always a part of any abusive or battering situation.

A common myth around battering states that if the violence between partners is mild or infrequent, it need not be taken seriously (Farley, 1985). It is imperative to recognize that battering, even a one-time occurrence, is almost always preceded by a history of emotional and psychological abuse within the relationship. More specifically, the physical battering will most certainly escalate if the perpetrator (and the survivor) do not seek help. Abuse and battering never stop by themselves!

Working With the Perpetrator

Janice is a 32-year-old White lesbian. She was referred for treatment by the court system: She had thrown her partner through a window, and the police were called. During the intake process, Janice presented with issues of low self-esteem, depression, and fear that her relationship with her partner of 3 years is not working out. Janice reported insecure feelings because her partner recently got a job and is no longer dependent on Janice's income.

The partner is often late in coming home from work and appears (to Janice) to be more assertive. Lately they have been having arguments, mostly about "silly little things," but now Janice's partner stands up for herself. Janice wondered if this is a result of her partner being in therapy. "I don't know what's going on! She went to therapy to deal with all of *her* problems!" Janice stated that if her partner had not yelled back during their most recent fight, "none of this would have happened. It's not my fault that she made me angry. If she just realized how upset she made me, I wouldn't have to be so extreme. She asked for it!" Janice felt that her partner is "very lucky to have me .... I saved her from a rotten ex-lover ...." Janice also reports that her previous relationship ended for similar reasons, and after many fights. "They [her partners] just don't understand me!"

When looking at perpetrators, several questions come to mind. The first and foremost is why is she a batterer? From current research on heterosexual male batterers (Sonkin & Durphy, 1985; Star, 1983) and my own research on gay and lesbian batterers (Farley, 1985), it becomes clear that persons batter primarily because it gets an intended result: It stops the argument or situation from continuing. It is an effective means of control over another individual; and society, on the whole, has taught us that violence is a means to an end.

Research into the causes of battering behavior (Farley, 1985; Hauser, 1982; Marmon, 1978) point out that batterers come from homes where battering occurred. Such family histories are a major factor in domestic violence. Behaviors that are abusive become reinforced throughout childhood as an effective way of dealing with any confrontive situation. When parents act out their anger in violent ways, children are taught that anger and violence are synonymous. Fear is also a natural part of family dynamics, and it is automatically assumed that in order not to be abused, you cannot be angry. Another prevalent factor in these family histories is the lack of ability to express feelings of almost any kind (other than anger).

In gathering Janice's psychosocial history, the therapist discovered that her father physically abused her mother for several years before her mother left the marriage. Janice reported several memories of being sent to stay with relatives after particularly violent altercations between her parents. Her mother has since remarried. Her current husband has also been abusive. As previously stated, Janice has been abusive to partners in previous relationships. We also found that Janice had been in a heterosexual relationship in which she had been battered.

In continuing to gather information about Janice, the therapist discovered that her use of alcohol and marijuana has been problematic in the past. This needs to be monitored during treatment. If it appears to be abusive, referral for a more formal drug and alcohol assessment and treatment is appropriate (see chapter 17). This issue is not surprising. Addictive behaviors such as substance use, eating disorders, and sexual compulsivity are common in perpetrators of domestic violence (Sonkin & Durphy, 1985). With substance abuse already a high-risk problem in the gay and lesbian community, it becomes necessary to look carefully at the role addictive behaviors may be playing in same-sex battering. It is important to remember that use of drugs or alcohol is not the reason people batter; such use can, however, lower resistance to controlling the battering behavior.

Because of the clear battering behavior that Janice exhibits, as well as the domestic violence charges, it seems appropriate to place Janice in a group for lesbian batterers. Important to note here is that Janice most likely would not have sought out therapy on her own: She clearly stated that her partner is to blame for her behavior. Instead, Janice was arrested and court-ordered into treatment. Such intervention usually occurs when the violence has escalated enough to cause a severe outbreak, when one of the partners is physically injured or worse, and the police are called in. Even at this point, however, the police may not have been trained to perceive the situation as domestic violence, and the intervention may not occur.

If Janice had not been arrested, intervention is still possible through careful assessment. Counselors and therapists see clients enough to be able to notice the clues of domestic violence. Such signs can be easily overlooked, however, if the counselor or therapist does not know what to look for, or feels somehow inadequate to deal with the issue.

Signs to look for include:

1. A client discussing repeated fights. It is up to the counselor or therapist to explore whether or not these fights are verbal or physical.
2. Family histories that contain emotional, psychological, and physical abuse. (In Janice's history, she reported the abuse included slapping, punching, and threats of bodily harm. Her father once pulled out a gun and threatened the entire family.) Information about how the respective parents fought, and how she or he and previous partners fought is important to obtain. What kinds of things were said to each other? How were they said? Who owned responsibility for what? What other ways did they act out besides physically?
3. Couples seeking couples counseling in which one client appears intimidated or frightened by the other ... or remains quiet during the interview.
4. Physical signs of bruising or other injuries that seem to happen with frequency.
5. Reticence to discuss any of the above, if you mention them, or angry denial.

Although the signs and questions are fairly standard, the major problem with same-sex battering is that counselors and therapists, including a large percentage of gay and lesbian counselors and therapists, are ignorant about its existence. Often the service provider may not be gay- and lesbian-sensitive enough to even be aware that the client is in a relationship at all, much less an abusive one. It is important to remember that domestic violence is behavior that is out of control. Such behavior can kill, so it is always critical to intervene when necessary.

With perpetrators like Janice, therapy should focus first on stopping the battering behavior. Janice is in denial about her battering. She is unwilling to take responsibility for her actions. This is a common factor when working with any perpetrator. As a lesbian, other issues may (and probably are) also clouding the picture. For gay men and lesbians these additional issues may include externalized and internalized homophobia, the extent to which one or both partners are closeted, the individual acceptance of sexual orientation identity, heterosexualization (the extent to which gays and lesbians are impacted by sex-role stereotypes and societal "norms), and the lack of information and resources around this issue of same-sex domestic violence.

Counselors and therapists must also recognize differences between gay male couples and lesbian couples that impact battering. For gay men there is the issue of holding back from commitment in intimate relationships for fear of losing power and control (Berzon, 1988; Sonkin & Durphy, 1985). There is also world conditioning that accepts fighting between two men. Socialization issues include how our culture defines *masculinity* and thus how gay men may view competition and aggression within relationships.

For lesbians in intimate relationships, bonding can easily become fusion, with the struggle becoming one of individuation. Both partners can become so dependent upon one another that personal goals and personal space are often confused with relationship goals and expectations (Burch, 1982; Elise, 1986; Krestan & Bepke, 1980). Another issue for lesbians that will impact the larger battering issue is the belief that women are not (or cannot) be violent, thus denying the abuse and violence that they are seeing or experiencing.

In Janice's case, her denial of her behavior is more than likely impacted by many of these issues and requires the need to deal with other layers of denial. For example, by being a survivor of domestic violence in a heterosexual relationship, Janice has difficulty perceiving herself (as a woman) as being a perpetrator.

As stated earlier, Janice will be placed in a therapy group for lesbian batterers. If possible, group therapy is almost always the most appropriate modality for perpetrators. Group therapy is effective because it forces perpetrators to break through their denial and own responsibility for their behavior. It is much harder to remain in denial when others are dealing with the same issue, in the same room. Confrontation is an invaluable tool. Group therapy can help lessen the shame, guilt, and isolation by demonstrating the commonality of abuse (Purdy, & Nickle, 1981). With gay men and lesbians, the group format aids in confronting any denial regarding same-sex battering. It also provides a safe environment to explore the other issues mentioned above that may exacerbate their behavior.

Janice and her group will begin work with a psychoeducational model that includes learning about the cycle of violence: (1) tension building, (2) violent outbursts, and (3) repentance and forgiveness (or the "honeymoon" period) (Steinmetz, 1977). Each group member must learn how to identify the course and dynamics of the cycle in her personal relationship, how to separate out anger (the feeling) from violence (the behavior), and appropriate and healthy ways to express anger. Behavioral techniques include keeping anger logs and doing anger check-ins. Anger logs are usually presented during group. When Janice takes her turn, she will be able to tell the group about incidences of anger and violent outbursts and to begin to identify her own patterns of "up-talk"—the internal dialogue that occurs prior to an outburst. (As an incident unfolds, for example, Janice retrieves from her memory bits and pieces of other unrelated circumstances that caused her to feel angry or scared and that are now fueling whatever sparked this situation and causing the cycle to escalate.) She then will learn and practice "down-talk"—the internal dialogue that helps to neutralize the "up-talk" to a point that the anger can be expressed appropriately instead of acting it out. (Example: As Janice becomes more aware of her "up-talk," for example, she can use such phrases as "Calm down, take a nice deep breath," or "What is it that is really bothering me right now?") Anger control techniques and assertiveness training are also taught.

As Janice (and other group members) practice these techniques, their denial will slowly erode. Janice will be more able to utilize a walk around the block (a time-out) instead of escalating into violence. She will begin to see that often what she is angry about has little or nothing to do with the precipitating event. Group members will begin to support each other in their work and look at the personal and developmental issues that can lead to violent behavior. They will also increase their understanding of the place of violence in their lives and in our culture. At this point, because group members come from diverse ethnic and social backgrounds, cross-cultural issues need to be addressed. Sexism and homophobia also need to be looked at. For Janice, this will include recognition of her own continuing struggle with her sexual orientation.

By the time group members successfully break denial and stop the battering, it becomes important to begin addressing the historical significance that the family of origin plays in abusive behavior. This is the point at which intergenerational abuse is looked at, often using tools such as genograms and roleplaying. Janice needs to recognize those of her personality traits that have a direct connection to her own family of origin. These include her tendencies to be controlling, possessive, and insecure as well as her previously identified tendency to abuse substances. She also needs to begin to recognize how dependent she is on her partner. Other group members may share personality traits that include impulsivity, inability to deal with stress (or a low threshold for stress), few outside friends, compulsivity, difficulty in emotional closeness, difficulty in nonsexual intimacy, or vulnerability in many areas. These characteristics are common to perpetrators and often go hand in hand with the anger and denial already mentioned as well as mistrust and lack of motivation in intimate relationships (Farley, 1985; Sonkin & Durphy, 1985). Individual work outside of the group may be a helpful adjunct to the group work.

The course of this work is long term. Many treatment programs for domestic violence only last 12 to 24 weeks, often only touching on the behavioral interventions. In my own experience, a minimum of 6 months is needed just to break through the denial thoroughly, especially considering the additional layers of issues that compound this work with gay and lesbian perpetrators. Twelve or more months seem to be a realistic timeline.

Working With the Survivor

James is a 29-year-old gay Black man. His first request for treatment was for couples counseling for himself and his partner of 2 years. When it was established that his partner was being physically abusive to James, it was made clear that couples counseling was not to be offered, and it was suggested that his partner consider working in a gay men's batterers group.

In looking at James' case, one of the first issues to be considered is the decision not to offer couples counseling. The most important reason reflects the balance of power, which in battering relationships is often in the hands of the perpetrator. Seeing both partners together almost always results in the survivor not participating in the therapy and minimizing the abuse out of fear of reprisal (Farley, 1985; Sonkin & Durphy, 1985; Walber, 1988).

Further history taking revealed that James has been in two previous relationships: one lasted a few months, the other a little over 3 years.

Physical abuse occurred in both. His presenting problems at this time were to (1) keep his relationship together and (2) to find out what he was doing wrong that incited his lover to abuse him physically. He reported that the last time he had been hit, his lover apologized the next day and promised that it would never happen again. James believed that his partner truly loved him and meant what he said; however, it had happened again. Friends were suggesting that James leave the relationship, that he could "do better." James felt unsure and seemed afraid of the thought of leaving his partner.

Another important component of James' report is his reference to his partner's repentant behavior after an episode of battering. This is an example of how the cycle of violence works, specifically the repentance and forgiveness stage. In truth, James' partner most likely does love him, but battering is a learned behavior and love alone will not make it stop!

It is important to note that survivors are NEVER responsible for being battered. No one ever "asks" for this abuse. However, they do have a role in the dynamics of the relationship, often stemming from their own historical experience in a dysfunctional family. Research shows that survivors tend to come from families in which abuse was a common pattern (Farley, 1985; Star, 1983). The difference is that here the abuse is more often psychological in nature. In other words, survivors most often come from families that were psychologically abusive, whereas perpetrators usually come from families that were physically abusive.

In James' psychosocial history, he reported that his parents often argued, with his father then reverting to hostile silence. His mother often responded to this by resorting to covert behavior in order to "get even." She often spoke badly of her husband to the children and the neighbors. He remembered his grandparents yelling and demeaning each other. These episodes "would go on for days. None of us kids knew what to do, or how to respond. I always tried to get them to make up." This scenario fits with reports from other survivors about the inability to express emotions fully as well as reports about high percentages of substance abuse or other addictive behaviors.

James referred to himself as the "mediator" in his family of origin as well as the "pleaser" in his own relationships. This role of helper and rescuer," whose job is to make peace in the family and relationship, is not uncommon in survivors. Often their belief is that eventually the altercations will cease and the inappropriate behaviors will change. In adult intimate relationships, they often hope that with love and careful intervention, they can help their partner. As children, this mediation did not work, and the results were feelings of helplessness and hopelessness as well as low self-esteem. When these same attempts do not work in adult relationships, these feelings and low self-esteem are amplified.

In James' case, his history and current profile showed this low self-esteem. He also reported his fear of leaving this relationship, believing that he could not find a better one. It is important to note that such fear is often reality based, the result of very real threats of harm from a partner. Other survivor traits and behaviors are the inability to set limits, passive-aggressiveness, compulsivity, and utilization of emotional and psychological abuse as coping mechanisms within their relationships (Farley, 1985; Sonkin & Durphy, 1985).

As stated earlier, intervention usually does not occur unless the violence has escalated enough for a severe outbreak to happen. James was seeking couples counseling, not treatment for domestic violence. He felt that the violence was somehow his responsibility and therefore his problem. If a careful assessment by a trained professional had not caught the battering, intervention might not have occurred. This assessor had asked the right questions of James. The assessment included a clarification of what was meant by *fighting*, who did what to whom, the frequency and history of fighting in James' current and past relationships.

Based on his intake assessment, James was placed in a group for domestic violence survivors. Although individual therapy would be fine, group therapy offers a supportive environment not only for learning about the cycle of violence and its role in his relationship but also for getting support from other survivors in order to diminish the shame and isolation. As a gay Black man, James' social support system was limited. His family was not supportive, and he felt isolated in a mostly White gay community. Group therapy therefore helped to provide some support for him. The role of group is similar to that of the perpetrators' group in that survivors must also learn to understand how violence works in their lives. This group also helped James identify resources for remaining safe during any potentially violent confrontations, take responsibility for his safety, and begin the exploration of his own patterns of being emotionally and psychologically abusive within his relationships. James began to understand how fear has played into his reluctance to leave the relationship. He saw more clearly how his partner's threats of harm were really only a reflection of his partner's own fear and dependency and low self-esteem. James does not have a very lucrative job, and he is now realizing that this is (in part) in response to his partner's constant berating of his abilities. James now knows that his previous fear of financial instability is something he can handle. For other gay and lesbian survivors, the issues of AIDS, a smaller pool of potential partners, or the lack of support from family and friends may also add to the fear of leaving.

It is also important to be aware that love and violence often get mixed up in these relationships. When dealing with low self-esteem, attention of any sort becomes preferable to being ignored. This is learned at a very early age. When emotions are so difficult to express, it is possible that an act of aggression or violence is, in some situations, construed as attention and love (Miller, 1983).

Learning to identify the difference between anger and violence as well as learning anger control techniques are ways in which James became more empowered. Again, a focus on understanding the cultural and social issues that surround violence are part of this group. Cross-cultural issues such as the role anger and violence play in Black culture (particularly between men) helped James identify other ways his issues were impacted. James was also able to look at his isolation tendencies and his own internalized homophobia to see how these issues play into his relationship with his partner. James is becoming more assertive, reporting an increase in self-esteem. He no longer feels that it is his responsibility to control his partner's violence or anger. Rather, he now owns his anger and keeps himself safe from potentially abusive situations with anyone else in his life.

The group format also blends in a focus on the family of origin's dynamics that were talked about earlier. The intergenerational abuse dynamics are explored through role plays, genograms, and other techniques, thus enabling the survivors to make connections to their current life dysfunctional patterns as well as make changes in their own behavior.

Conclusion

It is important to stress that domestic violence, and battering in particular, is not the issue itself but rather a symptom of the much larger issue of intergenerational dysfunctional family systems.

Although anger is often a part of domestic violence, it is incorrect to assume that anger is the problem. Neither is battering the problem. In fact, many current programs that stress anger management and battering as the primary treatment components may wind up teaching batterers how to supress their anger and that anger is somehow wrong.

It is also important to stress that treating the survivors therapeutically is as important as treating the perpetrators. Supporting the victim role may be why survivors often go back into the same or another abusive relationship (Walker, 1977–1978). Survivors, too, need a place to explore and identify their strengths, increase their self-esteem, and ultimately remain out of such dysfunctional relationships in the future.

Remember that couples counseling is not an appropriate modality to explore these issues. The dynamics of abusive relationships preclude the feasibility of safe and appropriate intervention. However, if by the end of separate treatments, both partners still want to pursue a healthier relationship, couples counseling may be a perfect way to start them on the road to a truly intimate relational experience.

When working with a client who is either a perpetrator or a survivor of domestic violence, a clear understanding of and desire to work within this area is imperative. It is strongly recommended that counselors and therapists receive some formal domestic violence training as well as gay and lesbian sensitivity training. (The latter should include the issues of homophobia, relationship dynamics, and cultural and cross-cultural awareness.)

Same-sex domestic violence is still an ignored and unrecognized issue both within and outside the gay and lesbian community. Only with increased awareness, education, and a willingness to create appropriate treatment models will this problem be resolved.

References

Berzon, B. (1988). *Permanent partners: Building gay and lesbian relationships that last.* New York: Dutton.

Burch, B. (1982). A psychological merger in lesbian couples: A joint ego psychological and systems approach. *Family Therapy, 9*(3), 201-208.

Elise, D. (1986). Lesbian couples: The implication of sex differences in separation-individuation. *Psychotherapy, 23*(2), 305-310.

Farley, N. (1985). *Not a myth, a fact: An overview of same-sex domestic violence.* Unpublished master's thesis. Norwich University, Northfield, VT.

Hart, B. (1986). Lesbian battering: An examination. In K. Lobel, *Naming the violence: Speaking out about lesbian battering* (pp. 173–189). Seattle: Seal Press.

Hauser, W. J. (1982). *Relative resources: Familial power and spouse abuse.* Palo Alto, CA: R and E Research Association.

Krestan, J., & Bepko, C. (1980). The problem of fusion in the lesbian relationship. *Family Process, 19,* 277-281.

Marmon, J. (1978). Psychosocial roots of violence. In R. L. Sadoff (Ed.), *Violence and responsibility.* New York: SP Medical and Scientific Books, Spectrum.

Miller, A. (1983). *For your own good: Hidden cruelty in child rearing and the roots of violence.* New York: Hannum.

Purdy, F. S., & Nickle, N. (1981). *Practice principles for helping men who batter.* Olympia, WA: Authors.

Sonkin, D. J., & Durphy, M. D. (1985). *Learning to live without violence: A handbook for men* (rev. ed.). San Francisco: Volcano Press.

Star, B. (1983). *Helping the abuser.* Family Services Association of America.

Steinmetz, S. K. (1977). *The cycle of violence.* New York: Praeger.

Walber, E. (1988). Behind closed doors: Battering and abuse in the lesbian and gay community. In M. Shernoff & W. A. Scott (Eds.), *The sourcebook on lesbian and gay health care.* Washington, DC: National Lesbian and Gay Health Foundation.

Walker, L. E. (1977-1978). Battered women and learned helplessness. *Victimology,* pp. 525–534.

Walker, L. E. (1979). *The battered woman.* New York: Harper & Row.

Walker, L. E. (1984). *The battered woman syndrome.* New York: Springer.

Section V
Counseling Techniques

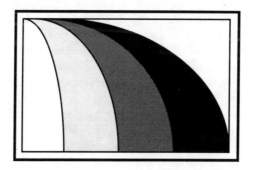

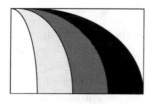

17

Counseling Chemically Dependent Lesbians and Gay Men

Barbara G. Faltz, RN, MS

Chemical dependency has been recognized as a problem in the lesbian and gay community for some time. Several authors stress its high prevalence (Lewis, Saghir, & Robins, 1982; Lohrenz, Connelly, Coyne, & Spare, 1978; Morales & Graves, 1983). Others discuss chemical dependency issues as part of a legacy of hidden lives. The institution of the gay bar has been historically the only social outlet for lesbian and gay men (Finnegan & McNally, 1987; Pohl, 1988; Ratner, 1988a). Delaney and Goldblum (1987) place the use of chemicals in a cultural context within the lesbian and gay community: "It is no secret that many gay men [and lesbians] have had an on-going affair with conscious-altering substances. . . . Using illicit drugs was but another small step for those who had already crossed the lines of sexual conformity" (p. 119).

Lesbians and gay men have often paid dearly for the embrace of drugs and alcohol with a diminished quality of life. They have lost their lives from suicide, automobile accidents, violence, and the medical complications of drug or alcohol abuse, including HIV disease.

Lesbians and gay men have suffered most from the conspiracy of silence and misinformation surrounding the subject of chemical abuse.

Therapists may incorrectly conclude that homosexuality is the cause of the chemical dependency. Conversely, they may assume that a lack of a positive lesbian or gay identity is the etiology of abuse. Often, lesbians and gay men have sought treatment for relationship difficulties, depression, anxiety, compulsive behavior, or phobias and have never been asked about, nor have they mentioned, their drug or alcohol use. This chapter outlines a way to evaluate substance abuse as a primary diagnosis, highlights various manifestations and consequences of addiction, presents three case histories, and offers basic guidelines for early intervention with lesbians and gay men who may have substance abuse or codependency problems.

Chemical Dependency Assessment

Therapists wishing to evaluate substance abuse disorders in their clients in a mental health or counseling setting can use the Form for Substance Abuse Assessment included here (Falz, 1988, 1989). As a method of introduction to this assessment, one can state that it is customary to discuss a client's alcohol and drug use as part of an initial evaluation of his or her situation and needs. An evaluation includes gathering information about all drugs used and the amount, frequency, and method of use. Listings of specific substances and key indicators of chemical dependency are included in the form to help the practitioner make such an assessment.

Another method of evaluation is to gather data from interviews and counseling sessions (Falz, 1988, 1989). Clues to problematic use of alcohol and other drugs include the presence of difficulties with social life, intimate relationships, employment, finances, and legal or other matters that are linked to alcohol or other drug use. Additionally, a client can experience loss of control of frequency or amount of use, preoccupation with drug(s) of choice or alcohol, and self-medication for anxiety. Often he or she drinks or uses while alone, has a rapid initial intake, and protects his or her supply by hoarding or hiding the drugs or alcohol. Tolerance to large quantities of alcohol or drugs usually develops, and a person can experience withdrawal symptoms when discontinuing use. Blackouts often occur when a client is alcohol dependent.

Assessments are most effective when they are made in the context of evaluating other life issues. Successful interventions are handled in a matter-of-fact nonjudgmental manner and are often done with a touch of humor. Clients may not only have their own problem with

Form for Substance Abuse Assessment

I. Use of Drugs and Alcohol (Review pattern, frequency, amount, method of use, and last use for each classification of drug):
1. Alcohol
2. Opiates (heroin, methadone)
3. Sedative hypnotics (barbiturates)
4. Stimulants (cocaine and amphetamines, amyl/butyl nitrites (poppers)
5. Hallucinogens (marijuana, LSD, PCP, MDMA [amphetamine/hallucinogen compound])
6. Antianxiety agents (benzodiazepines)
7. Prescribed psychoactive drugs

II. Indications of Substance Abuse
1. Consequences of use (presenting problems):
2. Loss of control of amount or frequency of use
3. Preoccupation with drug or alcohol use or related activities
4. Self-medication for emotional states such as anxiety or depression
5. Use of drugs or alcohol while alone
6. Rapid intake of alcohol or drugs
7. Protection or hoarding of supply of alcohol or drugs
8. Tolerance to increasing amounts of a drug or alcohol with the same level of intoxication
9. Presence of withdrawal symptoms
10. Blackouts with alcohol use

III. Impression

IV. Plan

substance abuse, but they may be also involved in an unhealthy pattern of codependency that needs to be evaluated.

Codependency

Codependency occurs when an individual's life is centered upon preventing another from using drugs or alcohol or in trying to stop or repair the calamities resulting from another's use. Codependency is often accompanied by other conditions and addictions such as compulsive spending or sexual activity, eating disorders, and anxiety disorders (Wegscheider-Cruse, 1985).

A codependent person may experience a loss of control because he or she is unable to leave the other person alone to live his or her life (Young, 1987). Often the codependent's self-esteem is based on the ability to be able to change the partner "through love" or manipulation. A codependent individual can be preoccupied with the other's problem to such a great extent that he or she experiences a profound sense of loss when no longer needed (Finnegan & McNally, 1987). And should the partner leave for another who is perhaps less nagging, the codependent partner may be devastated (Falz, 1988).

Codependent behavior patterns are learned in childhood while growing up in an alcoholic or drug-dependent household. Referral to Al-Anon meetings, specifically to adult children of alcoholics (ACA) groups, is urged for these clients. Therapy focused upon codependency issues can begin the process of recovery from the patterns and wounds of childhood that are reenacted and reopened in successive adult relationships. Because of the high incidence of substance abuse disorders in the lesbian and gay community, the clinical concern about codependency and related disorders is correspondingly large. Abuse and codependency disorders need to be identified, evaluated, or ruled out in the early phases of the therapeutic relationship.

If there is a dual problem of addiction and codependency, both need to be addressed in recovery. The primary addiction is usually the initial focus, but if codependency issues are not addressed, they may lead to relapse into chemical abuse. One client who was sober for 2 years related that he usually had increased craving to drink each time that he talked with his alcoholic father.

Considerations in Referring Lesbians and Gays for Treatment

When a client agrees to seek help for his or her chemical dependency, several options are available. First, it is important to decide if the problem is primarily drug, alcohol, or polydrug use: Many programs are more appropriate for one or another problem. It is also important to decide if the person can stay clean or sober long enough to be able to avail him- or herself of an outpatient clinic or if the impulse control or situation is such that the individual needs the safety of an inpatient treatment setting (Guilliani & Schnoll, 1985). In some cases, a detoxification program may be needed first: Detoxification programs are safe, monitored environments in which a client can withdraw from chemicals under supervision. In addition, medical intervention is sometimes necessary in order to insure a safe and comfortable withdrawal.

Another important concern is the client's comfort with programs that are specifically for lesbians and gays or for women only (Ratner, 1988b). This needs to be fully explored, and the therapist's personal biases need to be shelved in order to insure that the best program available is selected. For example, the therapist should not insist that a client come out in treatment or that he or she go to a gay- or lesbian-identified program: Some clients may be most comfortable revealing their sexual orientation, but for others it may be too anxiety producing. In early recovery, the first priority in treatment is the consideration of what actions will maximize the chances of the client staying clean and sober. As a client progresses in the recovery process, however, issues of self-acceptance in all areas of his or her life arise, including that of establishing a positive gay or lesbian identity (Finnegan & Cook, 1984).

If the client is a heroin addict, there is the choice of abstinence programs or of methadone maintenance programs. Methadone blocks many of the mind-altering effects of opiates. When used in appropriate doses, it prevents the physical withdrawal symptoms and the subjective feeling of "craving." It is effective, when used in conjunction with counseling programs. Methadone treatment is indicated if the habit is longstanding (over 2 years in duration), and detoxification and abstinence programs have not worked. Long-term residential treatment is also an alternative for this group and for others who have tried on numerous occasions to stay clean and sober but have relapsed.

In the early phases of treatment, individual psychotherapy and couples counseling on a regular basis is usually not indicated. The goal at this time is to treat the chemical dependency: Do not be sidetracked into other areas. After a period of at least 3 months of abstinence, other issues can slowly begin to be addressed. Chemically dependent clients who are also children or alcoholics or partners of alcoholics may particularly need to be sober for a while before risking their recovery by pursuing wounds from their family of origin. Partners of chemically dependent clients who are codependent should be referred to counseling individually, rather than as part of couples counseling, in order to begin their own healing process. Each client must be evaluated as an individual in order for the best treatment plan to be formulated.

Countertransference Issues

Working with lesbian and gay substance-abusing clients can trigger countertransference issues for the practitioner. If the therapist is lesbian or gay, it may be easier to minimize the alcohol and drug use of a lesbian or gay client whose pattern of use may be similar to that of the therapist or the therapist's partner or close friends. Idealization of clients can also occur. Statements that exemplify this include "She can't be a drug addict, she plays sports and is so politically active," or "He's not like a real addict, he really takes care of his body."

A counselor's negative stereotypes of lesbians and gays can also interfere with therapy. For example, one therapist reported that his client's difficulty with drugs was caused by his homosexuality and would disappear once he was "able to change his lifestyle." This therapist shifted the problem away from the chemical abuse to homosexuality.

When countertransference issues lead to a collusion between client and practitioner not to confront the substance abuse problem, the result can be a sentence of "death by denial." For example, a therapist recently told of a colleague who treated a gay man involved in a pattern of self-destructive compulsive sexual behavior. He discussed the need to use safe sex guidelines several times but never confronted the client's inability to follow them when intoxicated, which was every time he had sex. Killing with kindness, by benign neglect, from a fear of alienating a client, or from self-deception produces the same result.

Being aware of the countertransference issues for such emotionally charged subjects as substance abuse and homosexuality is essential. It also leads to the improvement of the quality of care that gay and lesbian clients receive from the helping professions.

Case History: Anna

Becoming familiar with specific issues pertaining to counseling lesbian and gay substance abusing clients is helpful. Anna's case history illustrates a client with multiple social barriers who exhibits manipulative behavior and codependency.

Anna is a 32-year-old Latina heroin addict. She has been treated in an outpatient treatment program of methadone maintenance for 2 years. She works as a cab driver in a company managed by her brother and has made some progress in staying free of illicit drugs consistently. Her use of heroin and cocaine has been reduced dramatically over the past year. Her partner, Cindy, is a 27-year-old Latina woman who still lives with her parents and has begun using intravenous heroin. Anna is afraid that if her brother finds out about the true nature of her relationship with Cindy, she could lose her job and be alienated from her family.

Anna has experienced increased cravings for heroin, has been requesting a higher dose of methadone, and has recently begun shooting speedballs, a combination of heroin and cocaine. She has been irregular in keeping scheduled appointments with her counselor and blames her relapse on Cindy's use. When Anna sees her counselor, she is often defensive, justifying her use and demanding higher doses of methadone. She argues against loss of privileges gained in treatment, such as take-home doses and reduced urine toxicology testing, and blames the counselor and medical staff when her special requests are denied, stating, "You'll make me use more drugs."

The counselor intervened by acknowledging the concerns Anna had about possible job loss and the pain of seeing her partner begin using. She helped Anna accept her inability to change Cindy's behavior. She pointed out the similarities of concern the staff had with Anna, whom they also cared about and who was using again. The counselor made it clear, however, that continued use had consequences that ultimately would result in termination from the program. Anna was held responsible for her own use by the staff. Her counselor presented her with a behavioral contract that included monitoring by urine toxicology, consistent attendance at weekly recovery support groups held at the clinic, and doubling the number of individual counseling sessions.

Slowly, the feelings around Cindy's use were exposed. Anna expressed guilt that somehow she had caused Cindy's use by introducing her to some friends who were still using. She expressed shame at not being able to stop Cindy by begging or nagging. Her shame about this issue tapped into previous shame about "being that way," illustrating that her own view of herself as a lesbian was negative. Her counselor's acceptance of Anna's lesbianism enabled her to be more open to discussing her fears and concerns about her sexual orientation.

The counselor encouraged expression of feelings at the same time that she helped Anna problem solve ways she could avoid further use.

One example of this was structuring her time by attending Narcotics Anonymous meetings and coming to the clinic daily for her dose, rather than having the privilege of coming three times a week and getting take-home doses. She also called other clients who were doing well for pep talks daily and at times when she felt shaky. The counselor's matter-of-fact acceptance of her lifestyle helped Anna be more trusting and able to be self-revealing of her concerns and fears.

Anna, who was additionally fearful of losing everything, began meeting the expectations of the behavioral contract and fulfilling other program requirements. Within 1 month, Anna broke off her ties with Cindy until Cindy sought treatment. Cindy later did request a 21-day detoxification at a local clinic.

This case history illustrates the need for a consistent and fair approach to chemically dependent clients. Clearly stated expectations from and limit setting by counselors are necessary, so that counselors can then be free to be compassionate with clients without compromising treatment goals. The client in this case was aware that she was an addict and was already in treatment. Often a client may seek treatment for other emotional difficulties but may deny the need for substance abuse treatment.

Case History: Jim

Jim's case history illustrates a client who had minimal understanding of his drug and alcohol abuse, who denied the extent of the consequences in his life resulting from his substance abuse, and whose motivation for treatment was consequently minimal. His case history also touches upon the issues of physical abuse and the difficulties in treating homeless gay youth.

Jim is a 16-year-old unemployed, homeless, White gay man who injects speed (amphetamines) in a binge pattern. He also drinks to ease withdrawal symptoms, consuming about a quart of vodka after 2- to 3-day binges. He admits to exchanging sex for drugs and occasionally "turning tricks." He states that he ran away from home when his family found out that he was gay and hoped to find help and a more supportive environment in a large urban center.

Unfortunately, when he arrived in this center, he was unable to get work, was homeless, and began earning money through prostitution. This was 2 years ago. Since then he has often exchanged sex with older men for a place to stay for a few days, and he began using when his "Johns" shared drugs with him. He has been using his money for drugs and has been unable to save for rent or other necessities. Jim's one close friend, who has tried to help him on occasion, has given up.

Additionally, Jim has been physically beaten by men he has had relationships with over the years. As a child, he was physically abused by his alcoholic father, and he has been physically and verbally abused by his peers and by a brother who guessed that Jim was gay at an early age. Jim candidly stated that he used to "blot out" disturbing feelings, such as underlying shame about being gay, and rage at the physical abuse he sustained by drinking and drug use. This also helped him gain a sense of power over his life.

Jim stated that he was seeking help for depression because life was so hard. He denied suicidal ideation or intent but felt that things were getting out of hand. Although his friend thought he had a drug problem, Jim blamed his numerous problems on bad luck and being "gay in the city." He felt that he could get by, that things weren't so bad yet. He felt that he needed to meet better men and sooner or later he will find someone who will help him and who is a person with whom he could have a decent relationship.

The counselor continued to meet with Jim and discuss his drug and alcohol use and ask about recent difficulties. When asked if he ever had sex with someone that he didn't want to or if he did so in a way that could endanger his health, Jim admitted to HIV sexual risk behavior. The counselor assessed chemical dependency using the format suggested in the Substance Abuse Assessment form included in this chapter. He shared the conclusion of alcohol and amphetamine dependency with the client, pointing to the mounting consequences of use and the continued use despite these problems. Jim seemed to begin to understand the relationship between the continued drug and alcohol use and his financial and social difficulties. He told the therapist that he might have a problem and that he could cut down on use or stop using altogether, now that he knew "what the score is." The counselor explored times that Jim has tried to stop previously and was unsuccessful. The counselor also discussed the options of total abstinence and of controlled use. Although the counselor did not think that it was still possible, the client stated that he could stop use and agreed to do so. He was unwilling to go for chemical dependency treatment at this time.

The counselor and Jim explored alternatives (if Jim should use again), such as attendance at Narcotics Anonymous and Alcoholics Anonymous meetings or enrollment in an outpatient chemical dependency treatment program that is understanding of gay issues. The counselor also helped Jim explore what it would take for him to consider his situation bad enough to seek chemical dependency treatment. Jim stated that it would be if he were beaten again by a partner or if he had to panhandle to get money for drugs. Additionally, the counselor reviewed HIV risk reduction behaviors and explored what Jim was willing to do to change HIV-related risk behavior.

The counselor did not see Jim for 1 month. Jim returned to the crisis center, with bruises, looking disheveled, stating "I need help!" He was willing to seek residential treatment because of the genuine understanding that his drinking and drug use were out of control and that he was unable to remain in the street environment and maintain sobriety. Jim stayed in a shelter for a few days while he was applying for admission to a long-term rehabilitation program and checked in each day with his counselor until admission.

This case history illustrates the need to approach denial of chemical dependency by highlighting clear connections between use and resulting problems. It also points out that this approach does not guarantee that a client will seek treatment. The additional issue of shame, often expressed in being in physically abusive relationships, may have contributed to delay in seeking treatment earlier (see chapter 16).

Often it is necessary for the therapist to help the client to define for him- or herself what consequences indicate a problem serious enough for treatment and what indicates that his or her substance use is out of control. For the client reluctant to accept his or her drug or alcohol problem, this latter approach can be helpful. If a client is chemically dependent, the addiction will probably progress to the point at which the identified consequences will result.

Case History: John

This case history involves a man who had accepted his own alcoholism and sought treatment. It raises the issues of professional codependency and treatment of chemical dependence for clients living with AIDS.

John is a 38-year-old gay man who drank up to a fifth of alcohol daily for 3 years prior to admission to the hospital for pneumocystic pneumonia, an AIDS diagnosis. He had numerous financial, relationship, and vocational problems as a result of his alcohol use and decided to go to a residential alcoholism treatment center for a 6-month rehabilitation program.

When his medical team heard of his decision to enter alcohol treatment, they tried to discourage it. They thought it would add too much stress to his life. However, John did go for treatment and has remained alcohol and drug free for 2 years. He feels that he has finally begun living and refers to his active drinking days as his life in the shadows.

During the course of his chemical dependency treatment, several issues relating to his HIV disease emerged. The first was setting treatment priorities. The counselor was concerned with John's recurrent focus on issues surrounding his HIV disease at the expense of confronting his alcoholism. There was an initial period of grieving the AIDS diagnosis and processing the feelings this evoked. Case management issues such as coordinating with health care agencies, social service agencies, and community support groups were discussed and arranged.

After the initial phases of treatment, John continued to talk more about HIV-related issues and less about issues of his recovery. John was vague about his recovery-related plans and began to consider his problem with alcohol a quirk and not a chronic problem. He viewed his main issue as learning to cope with AIDS. He began to question the need for attendance at Alcoholics Anonymous meetings and the relevance of group therapy sessions at the program. He claimed that his problems were so great that the program probably could not understand what he was going through.

The counselor acknowledged the special nature of John's problems at the same time that he reminded John of the difficulties that brought him into treatment. He stressed the need to work in several areas, including alcohol abuse. John's attitude, although understandable, placed him apart from other clients, isolating him from the help he could get from his peers at the program. The staff and his counselor began to refocus John's attention to issues in recovery, such as preventing relapse, creating a workable recovery plan, and incorporating activities promoting sobriety, as well as to health care needs. He connected with an Alcoholics Anonymous group that focused on persons living with HIV disease. This was a crucial point in John's treatment: He was able to get support from peers who were also struggling with staying abstinent from drugs and alcohol.

Another HIV-related issue was John's concern about how much to be self-revealing about his HIV status to other clients in treatment, to his friends and family, and to other social contacts. The counselor explored with John the advantages and disadvantages of revealing his chemical dependency, his sexual orientation, and his AIDS diagnosis in different settings. John began to get an idea of what was comfortable for him and became less isolated from this therapeutic community by taking chances and discussing his AIDS diagnosis and other concerns in group therapy sessions. The clients had been receiving AIDS information and training on an on-going basis, and fears of rejection based upon prejudice were fortunately not fulfilled. In fact, clients in the program rallied around John and were very supportive, almost to the point of avoiding confrontation of his issues and acting in a codependent manner toward him. The counselor pointed out in group therapy that key group members were very protective toward John, and this issue was discussed openly.

John completed treatment, building upon the support he received in the program from peers and relying on the on-going support of his Alcoholics Anonymous meetings. His counselor and other staff members clarified their roles in caring for clients with HIV disease.

In the process of treating John, staff learned more about AIDS, counseling issues related to AIDS, and resources in the community for persons living with AIDS. Additionally, they relied upon their skills in chemical dependency treatment to help them set priorities, maintain effective chemical dependency treatment goals, and connect John with recovery-oriented community resources to help him maintain his recovery goals.

John continued in individual counseling and group therapy for 2 more years. After completing his chemical dependency treatment program, the focus of his attention shifted to long-term recovery issues, such as rebuilding relationships with friends who were alienated by his active drinking behavior and grief about his AIDS diagnosis. Grief also was expressed at his loss of the use of alcohol, of what "used to be my only friend."

He learned ways of coping with triggers for relapse on an on-going basis. Anxiety over the course of his illness, difficulties with relationships, sexual attractions, and intimacy were raised in therapy. John began to learn how to initiate relationships, negotiate safer sex, and be self-revealing in appropriate circumstances, all while maintaining sobriety. He began to look at the spiritual aspects of his life, seeking quality friendships not quantity of friends. Medication and exercise became a part of his life, something he had not been interested in during his active drinking days.

His growth in recovery continued despite increasing physical weakness and other opportunistic infections associated with AIDS. As he became more debilitated, John focused on death and dying issues as well as pain management without relapsing into drinking. With support from his close Alcoholics Anonymous friends and community support volunteers from a community-based AIDS agency, he was able to maintain sobriety while coping with his impending death.

Summary

This chapter focuses upon common issues faced by lesbians and gay men with chemical dependency issues. It highlights the importance of evaluating substance abuse when counseling lesbians and gay men. Examples of effective counseling interventions with this population, using specific case histories, are included. This chapter's discussion of the evaluation, initial interventions, and referral of lesbians and gay men for chemical dependency treatment should help counselors and therapists in exploring these often neglected issues.

References

Delaney, M., & Goldblum, P. (1987). *Strategies for survival: A gay men's health manual for the age of AIDS.* New York: St. Martin's Press.

Faltz, B. (198). Substance abuse and the lesbian and gay community: Assessment and intervention. In M. Shernoff & W. Scott (Eds.), *The sourcebook on lesbian and gay health care.* Washington, DC: National Lesbian and Gay Health Foundation.

Faltz, B. (1989). Strategies for working with substance abusing clients. In J. Dilly, C. Pies, & M. Halquist, *Face to face: A guide to AIDS counseling* (pp. 127–128). San Francisco: University of California AIDS Health Project.

Finnegan, D. G., & Cook, D. (1984). Special issues affecting the treatment of gay male and lesbian alcoholics. *Alcoholism Treatment Quarterly,* pp. 85–98.

Finnegan, D. C., & McNally, E. B. (1987). The lonely journey: Lesbians and gay men who are codependent. In M. Shernoff & W. Scott (Eds.), *The sourcebook of lesbian and gay health care* (2nd ed., pp. 173–179). Washington, DC: National Lesbian and Gay Health Foundation.

Guilliani, D., & Schnoll, S. H. (1985). Clinical decision making in chemical dependence treatment: A programmatic model. *Journal of Substance Abuse Treatment, 2,* 203–308.

Lewis, C. E., Saghir, M. R., & Robins, E. (1982). Drinking patterns in homosexual and heterosexual women. *Journal of Clinical Psychology, 43,* 277–279.

Lohrenz, L. J., Connelly, J. C., Coyne, L., & Spare, K. E. (1978). Alcohol problems in several midwestern homosexual communities. *Journal of Studies of Alcohol, 39,* 1959–1063.

Morales, E. S., & Graves, M. A. (1983). *Substance abuse: Patterns and barriers to treatment for gay men and lesbians in San Francisco.* San Francisco Prevention Resource Center.

Pohl, M. (1988). Recovery from alcoholism and chemical dependence for gay men and lesbians. In M. Shernoff & W. Scott (Eds.), *The sourcebook on lesbian and gay health care* (2nd ed., pp. 169–172). Washington, DC: National Lesbian and Gay Health Foundation.

Ratner, E. (1988a). Treatment issues for chemically dependent lesbians and gay men. In M. Shernoff & W. Scott (Eds.), *The sourcebook on lesbian and gay health care* (2nd ed., pp. 162–168). Washington, DC: National Lesbian and Gay Health Foundation.

Ratner, E. (1988b). A model for the treatment of lesbian and gay alcohol abusers. *Alcoholism Treatment Quarterly, 5*(1/2), 25–46.

Wegscheider-Cruse, S. (1985). *Choice-making for codependents, adult children, and spirituality seekers*. Pompano Beach, FL: Health Communications.

Young, E. (1987). Co-alcoholism as a disease: Implications for psychotherapy. *Journal of Psychoactive Drugs, 19*(3), 257–236.

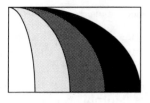

18

Helping Someone to Die

Fernando J. Gutiérrez, EdD
Marcia Perlstein, MFCC

One of the most difficult issues a counselor can be called upon to address is the issue of death and dying. Kubler-Ross (1969) identified several stages that the dying person goes through to reach acceptance of his or her death: (1) denial, (2) anger, (3) bargaining, (4) depression, and (5) acceptance.

The denial stage focuses on people's lack of acknowledgement that they have a terminal illness; the anger stage follows when people stop denying the illness and become angry about what has happened to them; the bargaining stage occurs when people acknowledge what has happened but are attempting to have the problem go away or to buy more time; depression sets in when people realize that they have no control over what has happened to them and that they are not able to avoid the impending outcome; and, finally, acceptance occurs after people adjust to what is occurring in their life.

Kubler-Ross's model is utilized throughout this chapter as we discuss the cultural and developmental issues faced by clients and counselors and as we identify the needs of the clients and the needs of the counselors. Counselor interventions are also discussed. Several case vignettes are woven into the text in order to illustrate the discussion.

The AIDS epidemic has made different demands upon the gay, lesbian, and bisexual communities. In these cultures, as in the mainstream culture, denial of death and dying exists; yet the emphasis on youth and physical attractiveness in the gay, lesbian, and bisexual cultures predominates (Murphy & Donovan, 1989), adding a burden to dying patients from these cultures.

AIDS has broken though this denial because, although AIDS in itself is not a terminal illness, people can die from complications of a weakened immune system caused by HIV infection. The physical emaciation and lesions formed by the skin cancer Kaposi's sarcoma can create a problem for a person's self-image.

The AIDS epidemic makes new demands upon counselors and challenges their sense of familiarity with clients' issues, thus creating a crisis for counselors. New skills need to be developed and old learnings reassessed. These demands can shatter a counselor's beliefs and values as well as his or her view of the world, especially with regard to death.

The AIDS epidemic also causes a developmental crisis for the client. Therefore, the counselor must assist the client in navigating through this developmental crisis and ultimately resolving it.

As gays, lesbians, and bisexuals break through the denial around death, they become more aware and sensitized to the fact that everyone also dies, whether from AIDS or such other causes as cancer and heart disease. For example, a San Francisco gay newspaper began an obituary column. This column not only includes the obituaries of people who are dying of AIDS but also the obituaries of men and women who have died of other causes. Before the AIDS epidemic, this column did not exist, and the issue of death was faced only privately by those who were close to the person who died.

As the issue of death and dying becomes more relevant to the gay, lesbian, and bisexual communities, it is imperative that counselors who work with these populations also become comfortable with the issue of death and dying and work through their countertransferences.

To examine the issue of death and dying, this chapter focuses on the cultural issues (Kluckhohn & Strodtbeck, 1961) that affect gays, lesbians, and bisexuals in coming to terms with their own deaths. This chapter also looks at the role of hospice care in changing the American value system regarding death and dying.

Death and Dying

Kluckhohn and Strodtbeck (1961) have identified value orientations held by different cultures with regard to nature: people view themselves as subjugated by nature, in harmony with nature, or as conquerors of nature. In American society people generally see themselves as conquerors of nature; therefore, in relationship to death and dying, the prolongation of life at all costs is promoted, even at times when individuals are in excruciating pain. One wonders how the taking of a horse's life can be justified as a compassionate gesture to relieve the horse of the pain of a broken leg, whereas the inhumane suffering of humans is allowed simply because life is valued and death is feared. Busick (1989) stated that it is because of our brains that humans want more control of our lives; however, she pointed out that we have little control over the process of life and are powerless to avert death.

Hospice care is changing the American value system around death and dying. It allows individuals to choose when they want to die and how they want to die. Weisman (1988) has developed the concept of appropriate death, which is defined as:

> a death one might choose, had one a choice ... dying in the best way possible, not only retaining the vestiges of what made life important and valuable, but surviving with personal significance and self-esteem, along with minimal distress and few intractable symptoms, as long as possible. (p. 67)

The view of hospice care is more in tune with the value orientation of being in harmony with nature. Rather than to prolong life at all costs, the goal is to utilize strategies that bring about relief, resolution, quiescence, equilibrium, and reward (Weisman, 1988). Weisman stated that the goal of hospice care is to let the client experience a death with less anguish, fewer regrets and left-over problems, clearer perceptions, and more acceptance. Allowing the client to maintain control of his or her life and participate in self-management and care and decision making is a goal of hospice care, according to Weisman. Murphy and Donovan (1989) added that the role of hospice caregivers is to control pain, subdue nausea, encourage appetite, and support weakness.

Another goal is to assist the client in maintaining his or her composure. Weisman (1988) stated that the goal here is to aid the client in the management of mood and emotionality so that the emotions can be kept within bounds and the client will not experience wide swings of anger, depression, anxiety, or bitterness. Thus, the client can achieve closure and become accepting of the allotment of time she or he has left.

Client Needs

Three client needs are important to address in the discussion of the dying client: (1) the resolution of conflict leading to forgiveness of self and others, (2) identity issues, and, finally, (3) grief.

Forgiveness and Conflict

This need seems to parallel the second stage in Kubler Ross's (1969) model, the anger stage. Murphy and Donovan (1989) identified the need for the client to put closure to unresolved conflicts and to work out issues of forgiveness. Some of the conflicts between the dying person and significant others may not become resolved. The client may have feelings of abandonment by family, friends, lovers, society, and God or his or her Higher Power. Significant others may be rejecting the client because of homophobia, fear of contagion, guilt, shame, anger, sorrow, or ambivalence (Murphy & Donovan, 1989).

Murphy and Donovan warned that the dying gay, lesbian, or bisexual client may have difficult questions for the counselor, which the counselor may feel unprepared to answer, such as "Is God angry with me?" or "Why is this happening to me?"

These questions represent the internalized homophobia with which the client grew up and which comes to the forefront all of a sudden. This was true of a client who called one evening in despair. He was grieving the loss of his lover who had died of AIDS complications, and he was scared because he has also been diagnosed with the AIDS virus. He was afraid that God is punishing him for his promiscuous lifestyle. The counselor's role is not necessarily to have answers for the client's questions because there may not be any answers. The counselor's role is to do what he or she was trained to do: listen supportively to the client and reflect what the client is saying so that the client can come up with his or her own answers.

Andersen and MacElveen-Hoehn (1988) suggested that the caregiver can facilitate the client's movement from a "Why me?" perspective to a "Why not me?" perspective. Illness happens, not because a person is being punished but because it just happens. Different illnesses are prevalent in different cultures. For example, sickle cell anemia is prevalent in the Black community; Tay Sachs is associated with the Jewish community; Latinos and Latinas have a higher prevalence of diabetes; and the incidence of alcoholism is higher among the Irish and Native

Americans. Yet society does not view these people as being punished by God.

Counselors are thus able to assist the client in reframing his or her perceived conflicts and resolutions so that the client can come to terms with the conflict and find peace and acceptance.

Identity Issues

Andersen and MacElveen-Hoehn (1988) pointed out the identity crisis in which the person with a terminal illness finds him- or herself. Gays and lesbians may still be in the process of developing a spiritual philosophy and belief at a time when they most need to draw upon this philosophy in order to find support and create meaning out of their diagnosis and suffering.

People with AIDS are often in their 20s and 30s. This is a time in the identity cycle in which they are beginning to deal with the nuclear conflicts of intimacy versus isolation or generativity versus self-absorption (Erikson, 1980). A potentially terminal illness thrusts the client into the final developmental stage of integrity versus despair at a time when the earlier stages may not have been resolved.

The issues of intimacy versus isolation are very real for gay, lesbian, or bisexual clients, who may still be dealing with issues of guilt and shame due to internalized homophobia or feelings of isolation due to societal discrimination and ostracism.

Spencer (1982) and Levinson (1978) identified the 20s as the time in the young adult's life when mentor relationships are formed, when people choose occupations and form love relationships. In a world in which mentors are closeted, there is little opportunity to have mentors. In a world in which people are not protected from employment discrimination, there is loss of hope for occupational success. In a world in which society causes so much damage to one's self-esteem because of homophobia, there is fear of forming love relationships. All of this blocks intimacy and reinforces isolation.

Spencer and Levinson identified the 30s as the stage in which adults correct the wrongs in their lives and identify the changes that are needed in the future. For the terminally ill client, there is no more future, no more opportunity to make corrections. Knowing this, the client may move to Kubler-Ross's (1969) third stage, bargaining, in an attempt to prolong his or her life and come to terms with the interruption of his or her developmental process.

During an individual's 30s, the developmental task to be resolved, according to Erikson (1980), is the conflict between generativity versus self-absorption. Generativity is not only a biological reproductive process. For gays, lesbians, and bisexuals generativity can take the form of a person's contribution to society. The terminally ill client has been robbed of the opportunity to complete this developmental stage. This can be particularly traumatic because society tends to define an individual based on the value orientation of doing versus being (Kluckhohn & Strodtbeck, 1961). The being alternative is also difficult for gays, lesbians, and bisexuals because society shames them for who they are. The client may then be thrust into Kubler-Ross's (1969) fourth stage, depression.

The terminally ill client must now face the developmental stage of integrity versus despair. At this stage, adults learn to accept their own life cycle and those of the significant others in their lives. If they do not, despair is the alternative. This despair is expressed in fear of death and contempt for self or for particular people or institutions. Resolution of this nuclear conflict depends on a successful grieving process.

Grief

The terminally ill gay, lesbian, or bisexual client goes through many losses, according to Murphy and Donovan (1989). The loss of physical health, appearance, weight loss, muscle atrophy, stamina; the loss of job, insurance, economic security; the loss of family, friends, significant others; and the loss of life.

The case of Barbara,[1] a 39-year-old lesbian dying of AIDS contracted through intravenous drug use, reflects these many losses and also illustrates the value of hospice care as well as a noteworthy difference between gay and lesbian patients. Recently Barbara was admitted to the hospice because she was extremely weak, could not take care of herself, and had a 3-month life expectancy. Barbara developed close bonds to the female members of the hospital staff. H. Parsons (personal communication, June 28, 1990) identified this close bond as a difference between male and female patients.

Women tend to form closer bonds with other women in the lesbian community. When they enter a hospice, these connections may no

---

[1]The authors want to thank Hillary Parsons, RN, case manager, Visiting Nurse Association Hospice of San Francisco, for the case vignette of Barbara.

longer be as close, for one reason or another. In Barbara's case, her friends were erroneously afraid of contracting AIDS so they withdrew from her. Patients depend on the hospital staff to replace that close bond. When Barbara's doctor left to have her baby, Barbara was overcome with a feeling of abandonment. She had become close to her doctor and depended on her for support.

Prior to her admittance, Barbara was visited by a close friend, who brought her favorite food and put it in the bottom shelf of the refrigerator. Barbara recounted to the nurse how angry and frustrated she had felt when she was not able to lift the serving dish out of the bottom shelf because of her physical weakness. She felt helpless and powerless. The nurse played a key role in being there for Barbara so she could vent her losses.

According to Busick (1989), "Grief is the response of the ego loosened from an essential identity mooring and cast adrift in uncertainty" (p. 92). Busick also stated that people utilize information from the environment as feedback in order to define who they are. She added that people grieve to the extent that their ego-identity is invested in the lost relationship, that is, in the significant other in their lives who has died or is dying, or in that part of themselves that is repressed. A person feels the loss of this role-defining element, resulting in temporary identity confusion. This loss triggers a process in which alternative information emerges from a person's unconsciousness around the roles a person plays. Busick explained that Jung called this unconscious the person's shadow side.

In the shadow lives the image of the person that she or he experiences as the true self, but is repressing. The person maintains this secret self to protect it from the messages received from others as to who she or he should really be. This concept is particularly relevant for gay, lesbian, and bisexual clients, who often must hide their true selves in order to avoid the confrontation of the true self with the hostile world in which they live.

Busick saw the incorporation of the shadow side into consciousness as the last task of redefinition of self. The person abandons the need for role playing and no longer seeks feedback from others in order to define him- or herself. This redefinition leads terminally ill clients into a period of growth and understanding that brings meaning and appreciation of the value of one's own and other's lives. This growth and appreciation assists the terminally ill in resolving the nuclear conflict of integrity versus despair and in becoming more in touch with their spirituality. A successful grieving process allows the dying person to reach Kubler-Ross's (1969) fifth and final stage in the grieving process: acceptance.

Counselor Needs

Working with the terminally ill can create a growth-producing experience for the counselor because it helps the counselor answer his or her own questions regarding his or her own mortality, spirituality, relationship to self, others, and one's Higher Power (Murphy & Donovan, 1989). In the process of obtaining these answers, however, the counselor may experience a crisis that interferes with his or her ability to focus on the client's needs and feelings. The counselor's own needs and feelings are intruding into the process.

Namir and Sherman (1989) have identified three types of crises that the counselor may experience when working with the terminally ill: (1) existential, (2) social, and (3) professional. The *existential crisis* involves the counselor's understanding of terminal illness, death and dying, and his or her reaction to the witnessing of the death of so many young people. The *social crisis* surfaces when counselors become involved in the political fight regarding AIDS and begin empowerment counseling with the disenfranchised members of society. The *professional crisis* is the counselor's perceived or actual lack of adequate knowledge and competence in working with the terminally ill.

Namir and Sherman also identified some situational factors for therapists who are not trained in a community psychology theoretical framework. The therapist's role requires him or her to leave the safety of the office and to visit the hospital, where the relationship with the client may take a secondary role to the medical needs and priorities of the medical staff, and where the counselor may be unfamiliar or uncomfortable with the medical equipment, procedures, and language.

The following case study illustrates the types of crises and some of the countertransference issues with which the male author dealt on his first assignment with a terminally ill person with AIDS.

Harold

A call came into the counselor's office on Friday from a person with AIDS at the county hospital who wanted to speak with a counselor. He had obtained the counselor's name from the local AIDS foundation. The counselor had never met him and did not know what the client wanted, except that he wanted to talk. The counselor had other persons with AIDS and HIV-positive clients in his practice, so dealing with issues around AIDS was familiar to him. Because he had been trained in a community psychology model, he was used to making home visits or to seeing the client in a setting other than his office.

Somehow this call felt different to the counselor, however. When he arrived at the hospital, he could not find a parking space, so he was irritable when he entered the hospital. He had displaced his anxiety regarding death and dying onto the fact that there was limited parking. The counselor was able to calm himself down on the way to the ward where the client was staying.

As the counselor arrived at the client's room, a door just inside the entrance to the room swung open abruptly. A young man who looked wasted away, a living skeleton like the pictures of prisoners of concentration camps, appeared at the door and began to yell, "Nurse, nurse!" He was obviously angry about something. He saw the counselor and became startled and asked, still in an angry tone, "Who are you?" The counselor introduced himself and offered to get the nurse for him. This was not only an intervention on the client's behalf. It also gave the counselor an opportunity to leave the room and deal with the shock of his first impression of the client.

As counselors, we are used to dealing with healthy-looking young, attractive, verbal, intelligent, and social (or YAVIS-type) clients in emotional pain. The ravages of AIDS forces us to face the total spectrum of life, including death. Even the persons with AIDS and HIV-positive clients that the counselor saw in his office had not prepared him to face this client's condition.

The nurse arrived, and it turned out that Harold had accidentally pulled out the intravenous needle from his arm as he was wiping himself after going to the bathroom. The counselor realized that he had intruded on the client's private moment of helplessness and embarrassment.

While the nurse went to get another needle and IV bag, the counselor was able to start to get to know Harold and ask him what he wanted to talk about. Harold said, "I want you to help me die. I'm tired and I can't fight it anymore." The counselor was stunned by the request and did not know how to respond. The counselor sensed a surge of anger at the perception that his training program had not trained him to deal with this particular problem. He felt professional incompetence. How does someone die? What is the role of the counselor in facilitating this process?

Harold's request was totally contrary to the way the counselor worked when counseling persons with AIDS. He was used to counseling them as one would counsel cancer patients. You fight until you beat it. The counselor had the typical caregiver fantasy (Weisman, 1988) that some-how he could rescue the client from death. But now this client was asking the counselor to help him die!

The counselor asked Harold what was stopping him from letting go. Harold responded that he and his lover David were intravenous drug addicts and that David depended on Harold financially and emotion-ally. Harold was worried about how David, who also had AIDS, could take care of himself if Harold died. The counselor helped Harold sort out what was his responsibility and what was David's responsibility regarding David. The counselor supported Harold as Harold learned to let go of David and let David take care of himself.

During the conversation, Harold's eyes began to roll back so that only the whites of his eyes showed. He was sitting on the edge of the bed slightly above the counselor. The counselor was afraid that Harold might die in his presence. He suggested to Harold that he might be more comfortable lying down.

The counselor watched Harold lying there. Harold had long hair and a beard, because he was too weak to get a haircut or shave. He had a sad and tired look on his face, and his eyes rolled up and down from time to time. Whatever was his past no longer mattered. This was a human being in need of help. It was then that the counselor felt a bond with Harold. He was no longer a stranger or just an ob-jectified intravenous drug user. He was a human being in pain who felt helpless and scared in his last moments of life and who wanted support as he risked letting go.

The nurse came with the IV bag. The counselor decided to go outside the room while the nurse tried, unsuccessfully, to put the IV needle in Harold's arm. Harold was so thin that the nurse was not able to find a vein. Harold began to yell at the nurse in frustration, so she desisted. The counselor and Harold were interrupted two more times by two different nurses who attempted to put the IV needle into Har-old's arm. Finally, the third nurse succeeded, to the relief of the coun-selor who is not comfortable around needles.

Harold was quite tired at this point. The counselor just sat with him for a while, watching him go in and out of consciousness. After Harold fell asleep, the counselor told the nurse to say good-bye to Harold for him and that he would come by after the week end (it was Friday). An hour had passed since the counselor had arrived at the hospital: To the counselor, it seemed much longer.

When the counselor went back to the office, fortunately his lover was there waiting for him so as to join a friend for dinner. His lover was able to comfort the counselor and listen to him as he recounted what he had just experienced—which was the most tender moment in his counseling career. The counselor was able to repress his feelings, and at dinner the friend was unaware of what the counselor had experienced not long before.

Harold died the following Monday. The counselor knew that he had done his job.

Looking back on that Friday, the counselor realized that he had known what to do and that his training had not been in vain. He had the tools that he needed to help Harold. What Harold needed from him was not answers or techniques in dying or specific knowledge about religion and one's relationship with God; he needed to have the counselor listen and be open to what Harold wanted to tell him. The counselor was able to put his own issues on death and dying aside so that he could focus on what was preventing Harold from letting go. The counselor also let go of his need to rescue Harold from death.

The counselor has reflected on his fear of Harold dying in his presence. He realized that he was treating "death" as something terrible and was feeling that if the client died he was somehow responsible. The counselor now realizes that if Harold had died in his presence, he could have said good-bye to someone who had moved him in ways that he had never been moved before.

The counselor also reflected on the irony of the nurse trying to place the IV needle into Harold's vein in order to continue his life just as the counselor was trying to help him let go and discontinue it.

After Harold died, the counselor simply went on with his life without grieving the loss of Harold. About a month later, the counselor had a personal disappointment at work. When he came home, in a grief reaction he threw the crystal mug he was drinking out of and watched it shatter into pieces on the kitchen floor. This was a grief reaction against all the losses with which the counselor had dealt personally and professionally, including Harold.

Shortly after his grief reaction, the counselor began to attend the support group for caregivers of persons with AIDS. He realized that when dealing with losses in such an intense and frequent manner, counselors are in need of their own support group. They must deal with their sense of loss in the course of their work so that they can maintain their own serenity and spirituality.

Spirituality can be defined as a sense of community and a sense of belonging. It is difficult to feel a sense of community and belonging when the community with which you are attempting to connect is dying. The support group can provide that sense of community and belonging as well as a sense of continuity.

Amenta (1988) defined spirituality as the center that integrates our identity, as the essence of self, as the God within. According to Amenta, spirituality is the part of us that longs for ultimate meaning, value, purpose, beauty, dignity, relatedness, and integrity. It is through our relationships with self, with others, and our Higher Power that we achieve spirituality. It is then that we can resolve grief. Referring again to Busick's (1989, p. 92) definition of grief: When we achieve spirituality, our ego will no longer be "loosened from an essential identity mooring and cast adrift in uncertainty."

From the discussion of the case of Harold, it is obvious that the AIDS epidemic has robbed people of time. Thus, a counselor's clinical decisions are different when working with persons with AIDS.

Counselor Intervention

In this section we take a look at four areas of counselor intervention that are relevant to this work: (a) bending the rule book, (b) shifting priorities, (c) employing techniques such as availability, homework, and advocacy, and (d) utilizing "straightforward talk" as a base line for all strategies.

The case of Ann, who came to counseling seeking help in dealing with her HIV-positive status, is used throughout this section to illustrate counselor interventions.

Bending The Rule Book

When the counselor went to the waiting room to greet Ann, Ann was waiting with her lover Tracy. The counselor asked Ann to follow her to the office, and when she turned around, she saw that Tracy and Ann were both sitting down on the office couch.

The counselor indicated to Tracy that she was welcome to wait in the waiting room. Ann, with a definiteness of purpose and an immediate, intractable set to her entire body and mouth, informed the counselor that Tracy would remain because she was intimately involved in the situation. The counselor responded immediately by bending the rule book and welcoming Ann's partner into Ann's therapy. The counselor realized that although separation and individuation were areas to address with Ann and Tracy under normal circumstances, this was not the time, although aspects would have to be addressed once a therapeutic bond was established.

As events occur in the therapeutic process with persons with AIDS, because of the client's changing health status the counselor must be able to shift the focus of the therapy sessions accordingly.

Shifting Priorities

The first session was different in other ways as well. The counselor did not take the thorough history that she traditionally does in the intake. She gleaned information as it was offered and concentrated on the distress over the HIV-positive diagnosis. Ann and Tracy's fears were intensified by their isolation because they had just moved to the San Francisco Bay area and had no friends nearby.

Other shifts took place during treatment in order to accommodate Ann and Tracy's needs: One was that when the diagnosis shifted from HIV-positive to full-blown AIDS, all other work stopped so that they could regroup and absorb the feelings and the ramifications of Ann's deterioration. A second was an intensification of the search for a son who had been taken away from Ann in his infancy and put up for adoption because of Ann's gayness. Ann realized she did not have much time left. The third was that the focus on some self-care techniques for both stopped when they lost their housing during the earthquake.

Employing Availability

In traditional counseling situations, counselors curtail their availability outside the 50-minute hour once per week to avoid client dependence, thus encouraging clients to call upon their own resources and develop a natural support network rather than rely solely on the therapist.

Because they were new in town and because of the seriousness of the illness as well as their lesbian status, which made their resources more limited, the counselor decided to adjust her stance on availability and offered to be accessible by phone. As the AIDS-related conditions worsened, she offered to make home and hospital visits. Often the client may be too weak to attend the sessions, so the counselor must adapt to the client's condition.

Employing Homework

The therapeutic process for persons with AIDS is an active process, and the counselor may become more directive. One manifestation of this directive is requesting homework assignments from the client.

Counselors working in the field of AIDS utilize a technique of helping the client to learn about living first and, when necessary, carrying that sense of empowerment toward facing death with full exercise of all his or her options.

The reality is that many persons with AIDS are facing death, but in living, they can exercise many options about the nature of the medical treatment they seek, the alternatives they are willing to consider to supplement traditional Western medicine (e.g., meditation, nutrition, acupuncture, and massage), the people with whom they want to be surrounded, and the issues that they want to confront or let go. The shortening of one's life can offer perspective and meaning to the time one has left.

Toward this end, the counselor assisted Tracy and Ann to work on the quality of their lives in the present while simultaneously making decisions about the future. The counselor assigned Tracy and Ann an activity of "making memories," which they were to report in their subsequent sessions. The therapeutic purpose of this assignment was to allow their bonding and concern for each other to offer them some solace in the present. Because they were so future oriented, the future was held out as the carrot that would be enjoyed more if they prepared for it now. It also afforded some balance to an otherwise bleak picture. It gave Ann and Tracy an opportunity to establish positive events that they could enjoy in the present, and Ann could feel that Tracy had positive memories of their time together.

After 2 years of this weekly assignment, practiced often in very simple and profoundly moving ways (even under conditions of frequent hospitalizations), they carried this principle to the height of its meaning for them in the decision to get married—the memory of all memories.

Employing Advocacy

AIDS can bring about many complicated issues and needs for the clients. These needs extend beyond the emotional sphere into the social, economic, and environmental. One of the roles of the counselor then becomes that of case manager. As a case manager, the counselor takes on an advocacy role.

Tracy and Ann had lost their housing during the earthquake, as mentioned earlier, necessitating their stay at a local shelter. The counselor intervened by putting Ann and Tracy in contact with a lesbian couple from the Midwest who had written to a local women's bookstore offering $200 to a lesbian who had suffered as a result of the earthquake. The counselor arranged for Ann and Tracy to receive the donation, enabling them to get an apartment of their own sooner than they could have otherwise afforded.

The contributors had wished to be anonymous, so Ann and Tracy sent their thanks through the bookstore along with information about themselves. The anonymous couple responded by sending their names and address to Ann and Tracy and a pen-pal relationship developed, with letters and occasional care packages. The couple flew out to the nuptial ceremony when Ann and Tracy exchanged vows.

Another advocacy role for the counselor can be to facilitate legal assistance in preparing durable powers of attorney for health care decisions as well as for disposition of the estate and for living wills. The case of Karen Thompson and Sharon Kowalski comes immediately to mind here (Thompson & Andrzejewski, 1988). Sharon became incapacitated in an auto accident, and her family of origin barred her lover, Karen, from seeing her.

Clients are encouraged to determine their wishes in advance, while they are healthy enough to think things through. Tracy and Ann moved on this suggestion within 24 hours of the discussion because they were both alienated from their families of origin and had already suffered deeply from homophobic legal battles initiated by ex-husbands and families of origin when Ann lost custody of her son because of her sexual orientation.

Utilizing Straightforward Talk

As the disease progresses, it may become important for the counselor to confront the client with his or her condition. The counselor may have to speak to the client in a very straightforward way.

This is one of the most painful strategies for both the client and the counselor, but it is often later reported as the most helpful.

An on-going thread in the early stages of the work with Tracy and Ann was that Ann often took to her bed when it was not medically necessary to deal with her fear. The counselor pointed out to Ann that the day would come when she would be bedridden and not have the choice to get up. The counselor encouraged Ann to exercise her choice to get up and take care of herself and enjoy what she could in the present.

The counselor worked with Ann to differentiate between experiencing fear and acknowledging it versus acting it out in inappropriate ways.

Conclusion

Working with somebody who is dying does not need to be anxiety producing for counselors as long as counselors have processed their own issues regarding death and dying.

Demystifying the process by recognizing that counselors do not have the answers to what is unknown about the afterlife can alleviate counselors' anxiety. This frees counselors from having to defend their lack of knowledge about something beyond their control and shifts the focus back to the client's anxiety about having to face the unknown.

Counselors can only offer what they have been trained to do: listen reflectively and support the client in the search for the answers that will bring him or her to a resolution of the last stage of life, integrity versus despair. Support for counselors through structured groups, individual counseling, consultation, or relationships with significant others is also an important part of the process of helping someone to die.

Resources

Brage, J. (1985). Terminal care: A bibliography of the psychosocial literature. *Hospice Journal 1*, 51–79.

Dilley, J., Pies, C., & Helquist, M. (1989). *Face to face: A guide to AIDS counseling.* San Francisco: University of California AIDS Health Project.

Fosters, L., & Paradis, L. (1985). Hospice and death education: A resource bibliography. *Hospice Journal, 1,* 3–61.

Monette, P. (1988). *Borrowed time: An AIDS memoir.* New York: Avon.

Wood, G., Marks, R., & Dilley, J. (1990). *AIDS law for mental health professionals: A handbook for judicious practice.* San Francisco: University of California AIDS Health Project.

References

Amenta, M. (1988). Nurses as primary spiritual care workers. *Hospice Journal, 4,* 47–55.

Andersen, H., & MacElveen-Hoehn. (1988). Gay clients with AIDS: New challenges for hospice programs. *Hospice Journal, 4*, 37–54.

Busick, B. (1989). Grieving as a hero's journey. *Hospice Journal, 5*, 89–105.

Erikson, E. (1980). *Identity and the life cycle*. New York: Norton.

Kluckhohn, F., & Strodtbeck, F. (1961). *Variation in value orientation*. Evanston, IL.: Row & Peterson.

Kubler-Ross, E. (1969). *On death and dying*. New York: Macmillan.

Levinson, D. (1978). *The seasons of a man's life*. New York: Knopf.

Murphy, P., & Donovan, C. (1989). Modern hospice care. In C. Kain (Ed.), *No longer immune: A counselor's guide to AIDS* (pp. 187–205). Alexandria, VA: American Association for Counseling and Development.

Namir, S., & Sherman, S. (1989). Coping with countertransference. In C. Kain (Ed.), *No longer immune: A counselor's guide to AIDS* (pp. 263–280). Alexandria, VA: American Association for Counseling and Development.

Spencer, A. (1982). *Seasons: Women's search for self through life stages*. New York: Paulist Press.

Thompson, K., & Andrzejewski, J. (1988). *Why can't Sharon Kowalski come home?* San Francisco: Spinsters/Aunt Lute.

Weisman, A. (1988). Appropriate death and the hospice program. *Hospice Journal, 4*, 65–77.

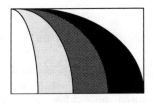

19

Bias in the Interpretation of Psychological Tests

Mark Pope, EdD

Little research has been published on the issue of how an individual's sexual orientation may affect his or her responses and, therefore, the interpretation of psychological tests (Gonsiorek, 1982). As a consequence, counselors are confused or unaware of the types of issues that may be important in the interpretation of psychological tests with the gay and lesbian client. Psychological testing has an aura of finality and mystery about it to the general public. It has been seen as having the ability to tell who you really are, and this can be dangerous. To clients who are either confused about or afraid of their sexual orientation, this can be the type of experience that may either be welcome or crisis provoking. It seems to depend on the perspective of both the client and the counselor. Interpretation issues for gay and lesbian individuals occur in the context of external societal intolerance and internal personal homophobia (Gonsiorek, 1984).

How can the counselor be better armed both emotionally and professionally to deal with the interpretation of these psychological tests? How can the gay or lesbian client know that this person is both accepting and sensitive to issues of sexual orientation? These are the keys to accurate test-taking responses and strategy as well as accurate interpretation.

The issue for many of these clients is whether or not this inventory will reveal their sexual orientation, which they do not want revealed as it might be used against them. There is no place in the research or clinical literature, however, that addresses the issue in this particular context with the specific psychological assessment instruments used here.

This chapter consists of case studies from the author's practice with gay and lesbian clients and their experiences with psychological testing. The instruments used in these cases include the Minnesota Multiphasic Personality Inventory (MMPI), California Psychological Inventory (CPI), Myers-Briggs Type Indicator (MBTI), Strong Interest Inventory (Strong), and Edwards Personal Preference Schedule (EPPS). Each of these instruments has one particular subscale that has been cited in the research literature as being more prone to the type of misuse referred to here (Campbell, 1971; Dahlstrom, Welsh, & Dahlstrom, 1972; Edwards, 1959; Wilson & Greene, 1971). Each of these instruments and their subscales are analyzed in the context of this chapter.

Minnesota Multiphasic Personality Inventory

Mark was studying for his master's degree in counseling and had taken the MMPI as part of the selection process for admittance into his academic department. He was so worried about his scores on the MMPI that he had difficulty sleeping. When he was asked why he was worried, he replied that he was afraid that the selection committee would not admit him. His admittance to this particular program was a key factor for him in his career, he reported. He had specifically asked for me when he telephoned for a counseling appointment at the testing and counseling center. The issue for Mark was that he had heard rumors from friends that this academic program had a prejudice against admitting homosexually oriented individuals. This had concerned him so much that when it came time to take the MMPI, he had lied on every item he thought related to "determining homosexuality." He was seen the first time before he had received his results on the MMPI or heard from the admission committee.

When he received his scores on the MMPI, they looked exceptionally "normal" with the notable exception of a high score (68) on Scale 9 (Hy—Hypomania), which the interpreter casually described as quite common for graduate students and dealt with issues of "impulsivity."

For Mark it was a relief. His Scale 5 (*Mf*—Masculinity-Femininity) score had been 59; his L Scale (*Lie*) had not been elevated significantly (44). He was ecstatic. Shortly thereafter he received his notification of acceptance into the program.

He returned later to discuss what to do about taking the MMPI again in his testing course. After much discussion around confidentiality and wanting to know his real scores, he decided to take it accurately this time. His results on the MMPI again were normal, but his profile had changed from only a high score on Scale 9 to only a high score on Scale 5 (87). His L Scale (46) was fine. This time he was told by the graduate teaching assistant for his testing course that lots of college males have high scores on this scale and that it is a measure of artistic and aesthetic interests. Mark had previously decided that his scores did not matter this time. He was going to be what he was.

In order to provide an accurate interpretation with lesbian and gay male clients, some historical and psychometric background on the development of Scale 5 is necessary. Dahlstrom, Welsh, and Dahlstrom (1972) discussed the development of this scale and stated that this scale:

> was designed to identify the personality features related to the disorder of male sexual inversion .... Persons with this personality pattern often engage in homoerotic practices as part of their feminine emotional make-up .... [B]asic response frequencies from the Minnesota normals were not available on these items. Special groups of normals had to be gathered for this scale construction work. The men were 54 soldiers and the women were 67 airline employees. The initial comparisons were based upon the normal men and a small group of carefully selected male sexual inverts. These latter cases were selected for their relative freedom from neurosis .... The cases were also carefully screened for psychotic disorders, since a few seriously disturbed patients may show homoerotic problems as an early or presenting complaint .... This careful pruning of the criterion cases left a rather homogeneous but disturbingly small number (13) of cases. Therefore, items in the preliminary scale were also studied to investigate the way in which they separated males from females .... An unsuccessful attempt was made to develop a corresponding scale (*Fm*) to identify female inversion by contrasting female patients and normal women. (pp. 201–202)

Factor analytic studies of the make-up of Scale 5 have had confused results, including an important finding in one study that only a small subset of the items in this scale effectively differentiated between two control groups of homosexual men and heterosexual men (Manosevitz, 1970).

Gough, McKee, and Yandell (1955) characterized men with high Scale 5 scores as psychologically complex, inner directed, and intellectually able and interested. They frequently take stands on moral issues and show a great deal of self-awareness and self-concern that is neither neurotic nor immature. Women with high Scale 5 scores see themselves as adventurous, as having physical strength and endurance, as poised, easygoing and relaxed, balanced and logical, and wise (Hathaway & Meehl, 1952).

Males with low Scale 5 scores are characterized as preferring action to contemplation, lacking originality in their approach to problems, showing stereotyped patterns of approach, lacking insight into their motives, having a narrow range of interests, being self-indulgent and unwilling to face unpleasant or troublesome situations (Gough, McKee, & Yandell, 1955; Hathaway & Meehl, 1952). Duckworth and Anderson (1986) have also provided alternate interpretations for a more normal population.

Greene (1980) summarized the literature on males who have high Scale 5s by stating that "there is little information on the empirical correlates of elevations on Scale 5 .... Scale 5 is a frequently occurring high point only in normal college-educated men with liberal arts majors and avowed homosexuals who are not trying to hide their homoerotic behavior" (pp. 134–135).

The research literature cited here should give counselors sufficient information to utilize Scale 5 on the MMPI effectively with a variety of their clients who may score high or low on Scale 5. The literature is clear on one point: This scale does not consistently and effectively differentiate between someone who is homosexually oriented and someone who is heterosexually oriented (Dahlstrom et al., 1972; Greene, 1980).

California Psychological Inventory

Linda wanted to be a police officer. She had been told that she had to take a battery of tests in order to be considered for the position. The battery of tests included both aptitude and personality, including the CPI. She had never taken the CPI or any other psychological inventory, but she had heard from various friends that these tests could identify her as a lesbian. She was afraid that if the police department officials found out that she was a lesbian, they would exclude her from consideration for the job.

Linda was living a very happy, suburban life on the West Coast with Elizabeth, her lover of 10 years who was a physician at a local hospital. Linda had been working at various part-time jobs for over 5 years since graduating from high school waiting for an opening in the police department. Linda had come from a long line of police officers (both parents were police officers as well as both grandfathers), and this position was very important for her. Her parents did not know that she was a lesbian, and they lived back in Peoria, Illinois. Her parents wanted her to become a police officer like them, and they had been hoping for this for several years. Linda was an only child and felt responsible for fulfilling her parents' career dreams.

The introduction of the idea that her sexual orientation might be identified through a psychological test and that this identification might cause her not to be accepted into the police training academy made her distraught. It was 3 weeks until she was scheduled to take the CPI. She was now eating desserts (she never had even liked desserts previously), had been snapping at her lover for no apparent reason, and was sleeping an additional 2 to 3 hours per night. She had been a client of mine prior to this for some basic career counseling, and we had addressed this issue somewhat, but it had not yet been a real issue. It was now suddenly very real and causing a great deal of distress.

In our discussions it was apparent that she had very little insight into what might have been causing all of these recent behavioral problems. She listed her familial history above without having an inkling that this might be a cause. With the realization of the importance of this career move in her life and the pressure that she was putting herself under to please her parents, she and I designed a short-term behavioral program to get her back into eating and sleeping properly and for lessening the angry outbursts at her lover.

To lessen her anxiety concerning the CPI's ability to identify her sexual orientation, I assured her that the CPI could not do so. An educational program was begun on what the CPI was designed to actually identify. Part of that process was the administration and scoring of the CPI along with the interpretation of her results. The interventions seemed to alleviate many of her behavioral symptoms.

Because the CPI is called by many counselors and referred to in the research literature as the "normal person's MMPI" (test development procedures were very similar and over 200 items from the MMPI are included on the CPI), issues similar to those presented in the preceding section on MMPI are at work here. The Femininity/Masculinity (F/M, CPI 1987 revised version, originally called Fe, Femininity) scale on the CPI is a scale that measures how much a person conforms to the sex role stereotype for either femininity or masculinity. These psychological constructs do not necessarily conform to physical or gender patterns in the research (Gough, 1969; Pope & Schulz, 1990).

Harrison Gough, the author of the CPI, has undergone a transition in his understanding of this scale as well. Gough (1952) reported that he was trying, with the Femininity (Fe) scale on the original version of the CPI, "to develop an instrument that is brief, easy to administer, relatively subtle and unthreatening in content, and which will, at the same time, differentiate men from women and sexual deviates from normals" (p. 427). Later, in the CPI manual (1963), he indicated that the purpose was to assess the subject's femininity or masculinity of interests. Then, in 1968, Gough stated that "the purpose of the Fe scale was not merely to distinguish between men and women but to define a psychological continuum which may probably be conceptualized as masculine versus feminine." (Gough, Chun, & Chung, 1968, p. 155). Although Gough began at first to try to measure "psychosexual deviation" or "sexual deviates," he now uses the term *amodal sexual preference* (Gough, 1987), responding to both the research and the times.

It can be seen that there was a progression in the thinking of the CPI's author on the issue of what was actually being measured by this empirically derived scale. This happens many times with scales validated using a factor analytic method. Factor analysis provides for the developer a cluster of items that group together because of a common theme, but the name of the theme cannot be identified by this statistical process. It is left to the intelligence and intuition of the developer to identify what all of these items have in common correctly and to provide an appropriate name for the scale. Test developers are never 100% certain that the overall scale name they have used captures the commonality ascribed to this particular grouping of items. The practice that both the MMPI and CPI use of attaching a commonly understood name for the factors that they are measuring can sometimes lead to a misunderstanding in interpretation by those who use these inventories on a daily basis. Megargee (1972) reported on the various factor analytic studies that have been done with the original CPI. He found that for the most part everyone agreed with the designation of "femininity and masculinity" but specifically cited Mitchell (1963) for creating the one truly original scale name for this scale: "emotional sensitivity versus masculine toughness."

For other reasons as well, this scale is an unusual and unique one for the CPI. All of the other CPI scales are constructed so that higher scores (T scores of 60 and above) or lower scores (45 and below) are considered to be more positive or negative, respectively. The F/M scale, however, is dichotomous or bipolar in nature, that is, higher scores are considered more stereotypically feminine and lower scores are considered more masculine, with the implicit assumption usually being made by many CPI users that there is, however, something wrong with men who score high on this scale or women who score low.

Gough addressed the issue of the dichotomous nature of the F/M scale by responding (in a personal communication to M. A. Torki, University of Kuwait, August 11, 1987) that this CPI scale does have a positive relationship with *observer* ratings of sex-role-stereotyped behavior, not self-ratings, and that is exactly what the CPI is designed to do. Further, if the F/M scale is broken down into its component items, two unipolar scales can be constructed, one measuring Masculinity (the items scored *false*) and the other measuring Femininity (the items scored *true*) (Babl, 1979; Kanner, 1976). The counselor can then get separate scores on this person's self-ratings of both Masculinity and Femininity, similar to the Bem Sex-Role Inventory (Bem, 1981) that allows for groupings of Masculine (high masculine, low feminine; Feminine (low masculine, high feminine); Androgynous (high masculine, high feminine); and Undifferentiated (low masculine, low feminine). This more complex way of looking at sex role behavior and attributes may not conform to the popular or folk ways that many people use to conceptualize sex roles but does seem to provide a more complete description of the actual behaviors.

Megargee (1972) noted that "a third goal [in the development of the CPI] was the detection of homosexuals; [however,] all studies reviewed ... have employed normal rather than clinical samples. Therefore, the Fe scale's usefulness in the detection of *sexual psychopathology* [italics added] is yet to be established" (p. 93). Megargee and his publishers did not even include the term *homosexuality* in their index and simply stated the research facts available in 1972. Later studies with the CPI have attempted to identify a psychological profile for lesbians and gay males (Freund, Langevin, Laws, & Serber, 1974; Siegelman, 1978; Wilson & Greene, 1971). Each of these studies was, however, looking at an overall pattern of responses and not at the issue of the validity of the items on the F/M scale for differentiating between a person with a homosexual orientation and a person with a hetero-sexual orientation. This scale does not seem to reliably differentiate either between gay and straight males or between lesbian and straight females.

Myers-Briggs Type Indicator

The MBTI focuses on Thinking and Feeling as two different ways of making decisions. Although women do tend to score more strongly in the Feeling direction and men do tend to have a preference for Thinking, in the MBTI schema there is nothing wrong with Feeling-oriented men and Thinking-oriented women. The remainder of the instruments discussed here all look specifically at the issues of fem-ininity and masculinity and sex role stereotyping in the context of the gay and lesbian client.

Clem, 16 years old, had just taken the MBTI and received his scores from his high school counselor. The counselor had told him that his personality type was either ESFJ (Extraverted Feeling with Sensing) or ESTJ (Extraverted Thinking with Sensing) because his Feeling prefer-ence score was only 1. Clem was slim and tall and had been described by the counselor as "having some fairly effeminate mannerisms." The counselor thought that he could make Clem more "masculine" by helping Clem develop his Thinking preference. The counselor told Clem that he was more likely to prefer Thinking because he was male. Clem was sure, after reading the descriptions of both, that he was a Feeling type; however, the counselor kept questioning this. Clem finally verbally accepted the counselor's description of him as an ESTJ and tried to be a dominant Thinking type for a long time, but it just was not him. He was very unhappy when he was referred to me.

Clem came to me to talk about career issues. He took the MBTI in a battery of psychological tests that I routinely give to my clients. Again, his score on the MBTI was ESFJ with a Feeling preference score of 2. During our interpretation session for the MBTI, I went through my regular type verification procedure with him and helped him identify that he in reality preferred Feeling. As he read the description of his type, everything spilled out. He began to cry and then to sob in a deep, cleansing way, seeming to take all of his pain from somewhere down deep inside himself and finally clearing it out. By the time he began to wipe away his tears, he also began to relate his history to me. Later, I talked with Clem's high school counselor.

Clem's sense of himself had been totally rejected by this counselor, and Clem had tried hard to be something he was not. Clem was obviously a Feeling-oriented male who happened to be gay; however, the counselor thought that if he helped Clem develop some more masculine behaviors, Clem would not "turn out to be gay" and Clem's life might be a little easier. The counselor was trying in his own way to "help" Clem. In reality, because of false and misleading information given to a young man who had trusted both his high school counselor and the counselor's interpretation of this respected psychological inventory, what this counselor had done was prevent Clem from, at an early age, accurately identifying his own personality preferences.

Of primary interest here is the fact that no major research has been performed with either gay males or lesbians using the MBTI. Further, well-designed research studies linking femininity with gay males and masculinity with lesbians are few and far between. The more popular ways of advancing these positions have been the psychodynamic case studies similar to those of Beiber (1965) and Socarides (1973).

Some of the best approximations of overall MBTI type patterns in the United States population come from research done by Myers (1957), coauthor of the MBTI, who administered the MBTI to students in 25 Pennsylvania high schools. In this group, 33% of the girls preferred Thinking and 40% of the boys chose Feeling. Although many researchers are exploring the issues of gender differences, this study helps to clarify the issue: Although most men are indeed Thinking types and, therefore, use logical and objective analysis of the facts in their decision-making style, and although a strong majority of women indeed use Feeling to make decisions and, therefore, use person-centered values with harmony and cooperation in their primary decision making, sizeable minorities of both sexes prefer not to follow the majority.

There is nothing in the research literature that suggests that the MBTI could be used to identify someone who is homosexually oriented. In the development of the MBTI, this question was never considered; the Jungian model on which the MBTI is based is relatively mute on this subject. Hopcke (1989) discussed Jung's references to sexual orientation and found them to be both small in number and limited in scope.

For the counselor in this case not to attempt honestly to verify Clem's true type and not to help Clem to understand his real psychological preferences was a misuse of the MBTI, or any other psychological instrument. It was also an unethical misuse of the MBTI. It is important for each of us as mental health professionals to identify our own issues and to deal with our clients in a professional and ethical manner.

Strong Interest Inventory

Tina, a college student at a large university in the western United States, had just recently taken the Strong Interest Inventory for career counseling at her university's testing and counseling center. She had an Infrequent Responses score of −3 and had been told by her counselor that her Strong was invalid. The counselor had her take another Strong, and her Infrequent Responses score changed to −2. The counselor did not know what to do, but knowing that I had worked as the psychological test specialist at Consulting Psychologists Press, referred her to me. Tina glanced around my office and noticed all of the books on homosexuality. The first thing she said was that she was a lesbian, the second was asking whether that was what was causing the problem with the Strong.

Tina was a political science major and taking a prelaw curriculum. She was active in the lesbian and gay alliance on campus and had been a speaker at various human sexuality classes for counselors. This was the first time that she had ever taken a psychological inventory. She enjoyed writing and sales as well as public speaking. Her scores on the Strong were consistent with her stated interests, with scores on the Lawyer Occupational Scale in the very similar range and scores on the Law/Politics Basic Interest Scale very high. She also had high scores on the Sales Basic Interest Scale. None of these had wavered between the two administrations of the Strong.

Her intuitive statement concerning her Infrequent Responses scores being a function of her sexual orientation was incorrect. The female Infrequent Responses Scale, however, is composed of items that females choose infrequently (approximately 5% of the total women in a general norming sample). The Strong User's Guide (Hansen, 1984) provides useful insight into this matter: "Responding 'Like' to a very unpopular item also can lower a score on the IR (Infrequent Responses) index; for example, a 'Like' response to *Boxing* is an unusual choice for women and results in a decrease in the female IR index. As long as the index remains positive, the profile is valid; *only a negative number indicates a problem.* Occasionally, in spite of a negative IR index, no problem exists with the profile; the person simply has unique interests. In cases like this, the profile can be interpreted just as it is" (p. 42). Items on the female normed version of this scale include responding *Like* to auto salesperson, life insurance salesperson, machinist, and military drill or *Dislike* to taking responsibility and entertaining others. Male items include responding *Like* to dental assistant, home economics teacher, office clerk, and typist or *Dislike* to taking responsibility and saving money. Scores are determined by subtracting one from a constant (8 for men, 7 for women) each time the individual selects an appropriate response on this scale. For individuals who have atypical sex role attitudes, behaviors, and responses, the counselor can expect negative values for this scale. This negative score does not, however, in and of itself invalidate the entire profile.

The earliest versions of the Strong Vocational Interest Blank included a scale to measure Masculinity-Femininity. It first appeared on the profile in 1936 and is the oldest nonoccupational scale. This scale, which was constructed of items that men and women answer differently, has been revised greatly over the years and was finally discarded in the most recent revisions. Campbell (1971) discussed this scale:

> A Masculinity-Femininity score can be troublesome to use, as men are prone to interpret the score as relevant to their virility—or lack of it. Counselors should be certain to dispel any such ideas. Educated men in particular score toward the feminine end, which usually means they like books and art, to go to concerts, to work inside and keep their hands clean, to be kind to others, activities that are typically "feminine" in society as a whole. Because of these problems, this scale should be used only by well-trained professionals who can integrate this score with the other information they have on their clients. (p. 236)

Edwards Personal Preference Schedule

Bob had taken the Edwards Personal Preference Schedule, which has a Heterosexuality scale. He had scored very high (standard score of 75) on this scale, but Bob was confused about the score as well as its strength. Bob had been the coordinator of the Gay Students Union at his college and had been active in the Harvey Milk Gay Democratic Club. He was openly and vociferously gay, and yet he had this score. Bob was referred to me by his college counselor.

The first task I did with Bob was to explore his response set—or style—when he took the EPPS. He talked about contrasting the two items and thinking that there were several pairs of items that were the same. Then he talked about his responses to several of the items that dealt with sexuality. He stated that he had interpreted those items as meaning human sexuality in general, and when the item had talked about the *opposite sex*, he had substituted the words *same sex*, answered the item appropriately, and moved on to the next item. He said that he was so used to "the heterosexist bias of psych tests" that he always did that. It was not that he was trying to fake a heterosexual orientation. He described himself as very comfortable with his sexual orientation, but was just tired of everyone always presuming that he and everyone else in the world were heterosexually oriented. This was his response set when he took the EPPS.

Is the EPPS truly measuring what it says it is measuring with a gay male or lesbian? How can a scale named *Heterosexuality* be interpreted with a homosexually oriented individual? The answer is that it depends on the response set of the client. For Bob, it was substituting *same sex* for *opposite sex* in each item; for some it will be to fake a heterosexual orientation; for others it will be to respond to the exact wording of each item. It is important for the counselor to explore the subjective response set of each client in order to interpret the scores correctly.

Although the authors of the MMPI and CPI were originally trying to measure homosexuality, Edwards took a different approach. The EPPS scale was named *Heterosexuality*. This scale as constructed by Edwards (1959) is based on the manifest need system proposed by Murray (1938). Items on the scale are to go out with members of the opposite sex, to engage in social activities with the opposite sex, to be in love with someone of the opposite sex, to kiss those of the opposite sex, to be regarded as physically attractive by those of the opposite sex, to participate in discussions about sex, to read books and plays involving sex, to listen to or to tell jokes involving sex, and to become sexually excited.

Because the EPPS is a theory-based instrument, there is no actual contrasting of a group of heterosexually oriented subjects with homosexually oriented subjects. In addition, this scale is not measuring some construct called *masculinity or femininity*. Instead, the items are based on the 15 needs taken from Murray's list of manifest needs. This is not an illness or clinical model that is designed to measure paranoia and hysteria (Anastasi, 1988).

Summary and Conclusions

The issues addressed in this chapter include fear of identification and exposure of sexual orientation (especially in the highly sensitive personnel selection area), bias and prejudice (heterosexism) of the counselor, appropriate interpretation based on identification of client response set, issues of sex role and sexual orientation stereotyping (male Feeling types and female Thinking types), and, generally, the appropriate interpretation of psychological tests with a gay male or lesbian client.

One of the real problems with much of the early research described here is the equation of distortions in masculinity and femininity with homosexuality. Somehow these scales concerning the sex role stereotypes of masculinity and femininity were supposed to differentiate reliably between homosexually oriented subjects and heterosexually oriented subjects. They never did. These research hypotheses, however, were born of the psychodynamic theoretic model that provided the underpinnings for much of the work of early personality psychologists. With the empirical evidence provided by well-designed research, these psychologists have had to face reality, and like true scientists, most have altered their conceptions of homosexually oriented men and women as well as heterosexually oriented men and women. Some of the truly hardcore psychiatrists who foisted this "disease" model of homosexuality on the professional community (Beiber, 1965; Socarides, 1968, 1973) have disregarded this research and still rely on the case studies of their own patients in order to reaffirm their own theories. This is an interesting type of cognitive self-eroticism that borders on unethical behavior in its distortions of scientific fact.

Finally, the issues of counselor bias toward heterosexual behavior and counselor prejudice about homosexual behavior are very important ones in relation to getting accurate test-taking response sets. Clients are sensitive to these issues, especially if they are their own. Gay and lesbian clients listen and watch for statements from their counselor to determine the attitudes of this mental health professional as they relate to the issue of sexual orientation. The use of heterosexually biased phrases like *wife* or *husband* can quickly communicate such bias to a client. Any or all of these issues may have an effect upon the response of the test taker and may potentially affect his or her test scores.

All of the instruments discussed here are also sensitive to and can be affected by the worries and concerns of everyday life. Any problem that the gay or lesbian client is having may affect his or her test scores. The fear of identification and exposure may result in depression and anxiety and be expressed in a general personality inventory (MMPI, CPI, EPPS). Especially in rural areas of the United States, where gay males and lesbians are often isolated from other gays and lesbians and are afraid of the exposure of their sexuality to the general population, they may present themselves in crisis to the local mental health professional—who also happens to be their own Sunday school teacher.

Awareness of the issues presented in this chapter will help the counselor to be better armed, both emotionally and professionally, to deal with these issues. To know that the counselor is both accepting and sensitive to issues of sexual orientation is especially important for the gay or lesbian client. These are the keys to accurate test-taking responses and strategy as well as to accurate interpretation. Although sexual orientation does not determine every aspect of our gay and lesbian clients' existence, it permeates their lives and thus deserves full integration into their lives.

References

Anastasi, A. (1988). *Psychological testing* (6th ed.). New York: Macmillan.

Babl, J. D. (1979). Compensatory masculine responding as a function of sex role. *Journal of Consulting and Clinical Psychology, 47,* 252–257.

Beiber, I. (1965). Clinical aspects of male homosexuality. In J. Marmor (Ed.), *Sexual inversion: The multiple roots of homosexuality* (pp. 248–268). New York: Basic Books.

Bem, S. L. (1981). *Bem Sex-Role Inventory: Professional manual.* Palo Alto, CA: Consulting Psychologists Press.

Campbell, D. P. (1971). *Handbook for the Strong Vocational Interest Blank.* Stanford, CA: Stanford University Press.

Dahlstrom, W. G., Welsh, G. S., & Dahlstrom, L. E. (1972). *An MMPI handbook: Vol. 1: Clinical interpretation* (rev. ed.). Minneapolis: University of Minnesota Press.

Duckworth, J., & Anderson, W. (1986). *MMPI interpretation manual for counselors and clinicians.* Muncie, IN: Accelerated Development.

Edwards, A. L. (1959). *Edwards Personal Preference Schedule manual.* New York: Psychological Corporation.

Freund, K., Langevin, R., Laws, R., & Serber, M. (1974). Femininity and preferred partner in homosexual and heterosexual males. *British Journal of Psychiatry, 125,* 442–446.

Gonsiorek, J. C. (1982). Results of psychological testing on homosexual populations. In W. Paul, J. Weinrich, J. Gonsiorek, & M. Hotvedt (Eds.), *Homosexuality: Social, psychological, and biological issues* (pp. 57–70). Beverly Hills, CA: Sage.

Gonsiorek, J. C. (1984). Psychotherapeutic issues with gay and lesbian clients. In P. A. Keller & L. G. Ritt (Eds.), *Innovations in clinical practice: A source book* (Vol. 3). Sarasota, FL: Professional Resources Exchange.

Gough, H. G. (1952). Identifying psychological femininity. *Educational and Psychological Measurement, 12*(3), 427–439.

Gough, H. G. (1963). *Manual for the California Psychological Inventory* (rev. ed.). Palo Alto, CA: Consulting Psychologists Press.

Gough, H. G. (1969). *Manual for the California Psychological Inventory* (rev. ed.). Palo Alto, CA: Consulting Psychologists Press.

Gough, H. G. (1987). *Administrator's guide for the California Psychological Inventory* (rev. ed.). Palo Alto, CA: Consulting Psychologists Press.

Gough, H. G., Chun, K., & Chung, Y. E. (1968). Validation of the CPI femininity scale in Korea. *Psychological Reports, 22,* 155, 160.

Gough, H. G., McKee, M. G., & Yandell, R. J. (1955). *Adjective check list analyses of a number of selected psychometric and assessment variables.* Unpublished mimeographed paper, Officer Education and Research Laboratory, Air Force Personnel and Training Research Center, Air Force Personnel and Development Command, Maxwell Air Force Base, AL.

Greene, R. L. (1980). *The MMPI: An interpretive manual.* Orlando, FL: Grune & Stratton.

Hansen, J. (1984). *The user's guide for the Strong Interest Inventory.* Palo Alto, CA: Consulting Psychologists Press.

Hathaway, S. R., & Meehl, P. E. (1952). Adjective checklist correlates of MMPI scores. Unpublished materials.

Hopcke, R. (1989). *Jung, Jungians and homosexuality.* Boston: Shambala Press.

Kanner, A. D. (1976). Femininity and masculinity: Their relationship to creativity in male architects and their independence from each other. *Journal of Consulting and Clinical Psychology, 44,* 802–805.

Manosevitz, M. (1970). Item analyses of the MMPI *Mf* scale using homosexual and heterosexual males. *Journal of Consulting and Clinical Psychology, 35,* 395–399.

Megargee, E. I. (1972). *The California Psychological Inventory handbook.* San Francisco: Jossey-Bass.

Mitchell, J. V. (1963). A comparison of the first and second order dimensions of the 16PF and CPI inventories. *Journal of Social Psychology, 61,* 151–166.

Murray, H. A. (1938). *Explorations in personality.* New York: Oxford University Press.

Myers, I. B. (1957). Sample of 11th and 12th grade high school students from 27 Pennsylvania high schools tested with Form D2. Reported in I. B. Myers and M. H. McCaulley (1985), *Manual: A guide to the development and use of the Myers-Briggs Type Indicator.* Palo Alto, CA: Consulting Psychologists Press.

Pope, M., & Schulz, R. (1990). Sexual attitudes and behavior in midlife and aging homosexual males. In J. A. Lee (Ed.), *Gay midlife and maturity* (pp. 169–177). New York: Haworth.

Siegelman, M. (1978). Psychological adjustment of homosexual and heterosexual men: A cross-national replication. *Archives of Sexual Behavior, 7,* 1–11.

Socarides, C. (1968). *The overt homosexual.* New York: Grune & Stratton.

Socarides, C. (1973). Findings derived from 15 years of clinical research. *American Journal of Psychiatry, 130,* 1212–1213.

Wilson, M. L., & Greene, R. L. (1971). Personality characteristics of female homosexuals. *Psychological Reports, 28,* 407–412.

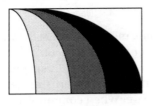

20

Coming Out in a Men's Group: Exploring Some Issues and Concerns

A. Michael Hutchins, PhD

Coming out is often a difficult process for gay men. At times, this process can involve disclosing information about one's sexuality, for the first time, in the group setting. Such self-disclosure may have a very important impact on the self-disclosing individual, other group members, and the group as a unit. In this chapter, some of the experiences involved in disclosing one's sexual orientation in a group setting are explored.

The reader is invited to observe part of the group session in which members first openly begin to address issues of sexuality and sexual orientation. This view of the session sets the stage for a more in-depth discussion of issues that often arise.

The Group

The group formed when a number of men came together to explore ways of experiencing a new sense of masculinity. These men were either self-referrals or referred by the counselors with whom they had been working. The men in the group are all interested in coming to a greater understanding of the different roles men play in contemporary society and in becoming more creative in the way they live and manage their lives. The focus of the group is on taking creative responsibility for the way one's life is developing. In keeping with this focus, group members are exploring such concerns as developing a healthy male identity; becoming clearer when communicating; exploring their emotional selves; making changes in their lives; clarifying their relationships with other men; developing healthy relationships with women; exploring intimacy and sexuality; grieving and letting go in cases of loss; exploring their roles in families as fathers, sons, and partners; clarifying what *career* means in their lives; and "putting it all together." Additionally, each of the men has specifically identified a desire to explore issues related to sexuality and sexual identity.

The group members have agreed to participate for a minimum of 24 sessions. These sessions occur weekly and are 2 hours in length. The particular session described here is session 6, which focuses on sexuality and sexual identity. In preparation for this session, group members were encouraged to read articles and books related to sexuality and intimacy. (Specific articles and chapters are assigned weekly and are related to the topic to be discussed.) In each session group members briefly "check in" and share with others how they are feeling and what concerns they wish to have addressed in the session. Because the reading for this session has focused on sexuality and intimacy, group members have been asked to focus on these as primary concerns.

The role of the facilitator can be defined as that of keeping group members on track and encouraging the completion of one topic before another is introduced. The group has also reached the stage in its development in which participants monitor the Gestalt norms (Zinker, 1977) introduced in the initial session. These norms include using "I language"; relating in the "here and now"; making distinctions between cognitive processes, affective processes, and behaviors (thinking, feeling, doing); distinguishing between "can't" and "won't"; using "what?" and "how?" to replace "why?"; and being responsible for one's own learning.

The Setting and Members

Jeffrey, a college-educated man of British-Irish descent, sits quietly in the group. He struggles to decide if and when he should speak. He has been coming to the group for 6 weeks now, at the encouragement of his counselor. Initially, he sought counseling because he was feeling "depressed" and was having trouble dating. His vision is to be more open and honest in relationships with others and to feel more comfortable with who he is. He has listened to others in the group discuss their difficulties relating to other people and acknowledges that, at age 33, he has some of the same difficulties.

Something else bothers him. He is aware that he wants to get to know Bob, another group member, better. In fact, he has dreams about Bob. It frightens him to think about the dreams or to admit that he finds Bob attractive.

At times during the previous sessions, Jeffrey has thought about dropping out of the group. He tells himself that the only reason he continues to come to the sessions is that he has made a commitment to Michael, the group leader, to attend for 24 sessions. What Michael thinks and how well Michael accepts him have become very important to Jeffrey. "It is not just that Michael is the group facilitator," Jeffrey thinks, "It is like he is the older brother I've never had."

Bob grew up in a midwestern, Lutheran household. At age 32, he sought out the group because he has been unhappy with his life for the past couple of years. He has read that men's support groups have been forming to help men become more comfortable with each other and with what it means to be a man. He believes that he is a sensitive person who responds to others and acknowledges that his sensitivity sometimes gets him into trouble with other men because they interpret this as gay. He wonders if he can be sensitive and masculine at the same time.

Because he grew up in a wealthy Jewish family, Paul sees himself as being very different from the other men in the group. As a 42-year-old recently divorced father, he is feeling the loss of a relationship with his former wife and with his children. For a while, he drank heavily, but now he has given that up. He frequently wonders if the other men in the group feel as isolated as he does. Paul wants to feel connected to other men in a meaningful way, but he does not always understand what this means.

Ricardo has joined the group because he saw a television show focusing on male depression. He believes that he may be depressed because his life is not what he wants it to be, and at 45, he has begun to feel unsatisfied with his sexual relationship with his wife of 15 years. It seems that his sex drive is becoming weaker, and he is embarrassed to even question himself. He acknowledges that in his Latino culture there are images he needs to live up to, and he believes that he is not doing so. He has also visited an adult bookstore recently, a visit that embarrassed and terrified him. He knows he cannot share this information with anyone, even the members of this group, who are men he is beginning to trust. Ricardo wants to trust himself and others and wants to come to some resolution about integrating sexuality into who he is.

John has recently been hospitalized for 10 days in a psychiatric facility. At 35, he committed himself to the facility because he believed that he had "lost control" of his life and because he was "feeling suicidal." As a result of his hospitalization, he has become aware of his anger and fear of life. John left home at age 15 because his father's "hot Italian temper," as John describes it, "pushed people away." John believes that he can be very much like his father. Since his release, John has felt healthier but recognizes that he has much more work to do before he can accept himself, again. In the hospital, John became "very close" to his roommate before finding out that his roommate was homosexual. John is ashamed and embarrassed and does not understand homosexuality. He believes that it is sinful and abnormal. He feels safe in this group because none of the participants appear to fit any of the stereotypes he has about homosexual men. John's goal is to be less angry and fearful and to have a sense of centeredness and personal power in his life.

Ed, a social worker from an Irish-Catholic family, is the senior member of the group. He thinks of himself as the group mentor. At 55, he has recently begun to consider retiring from his career and is not quite certain of what his life will be like if he does retire. He knows that he wants "more out of life" but has not defined what *more* means. He has begun the discussion of *intimacy* because he is not certain of what the word means. For many years, he has equated intimacy with sex and sex with sexuality. After reading some books about masculinity, he is beginning to question these definitions and wonders if the other men in the group have the same questions.

David became a member of the group because he had "lost sight of who he is." He has been in a relationship with Todd for 10 years. They tell their friends that they are very happy, but David is also aware that he does not tell other people that he is gay and that he and Todd refer to themselves as roommates. At 31, David is afraid that if people at work find out about his relationship with Todd he will lose his job and not be able to support himself. David would like to tell other group members that he is gay but is afraid that they will not want him in the group. He believes that he has worked very hard, as a Black professional, to get where he is in life. He has told himself that if others knew that he is not only gay but that he also has a White lover, both of their lives could be destroyed. He has read about homophobia and recognizes the effect it has on his life. Whenever the group comes close to discussing sexual issues, David changes the subject. David wants to overcome his own homophobia so that he can make genuine contact with other men.

The discussion has stopped, and a sense of expectation and tension exists. Michael, the group leader invites discussion with a summary of what has been occurring during the session and invites members to "explore what is going on for each of you, right now." The group is silent.

The Sharing

One of the men in the group is discussing troubles he has with intimacy. As the discussion progresses, Jeffrey feels more and more uncomfortable. Usually he says something humorous to take the stress off the discussion. Tonight he can think of nothing to say. He is afraid that someone is going to notice his silence and discomfort. Worse yet, someone might ask him what is going on for him.

Jeffrey looks up, red-faced, and with some hesitation and stammering begins to speak:

> I have something I think I want to share and I'm really scared. I'm afraid of what you guys will think of me and I'm terrified of what may be happening to me. I've read the assignments for this week, and I kept coming back to the sections about homosexuality. I ... I ... I think I may be gay. I've never been, you know, WITH a man, but I have thought about it ... and ... and ... and I think I might like to try it. (He begins to cry.)

The others in the group remain quiet. Bob wants to respond but is afraid that if he appears to be "too sensitive" others in the group may think that he, too, is gay.

Paul doesn't know what to say or do. He's never even thought about homosexuality and believes that he "doesn't even know any gay people." He would like Jeffrey to know that he is supportive and doesn't know how to communicate this. He feels some of what he believes is Jeffrey's isolation. Paul feels frightened and alone, again.

Ricardo is stunned. He remembers his visit to the bookstore and the men he saw there, one of whom tried to "put the make on" him. He was disgusted when this happened. This is the only contact he has had with "faggots," and he now feels some of the disgust. He is also confused because he has gotten to know and like Jeffrey, and Jeffrey is not like the man in the bookstore at all. Adding to his confusion are all of the religious messages. "For some reason," Ricardo thinks, "I feel guilty about what Jeffrey is talking about." He also questions whether he can trust Jeffrey, though he would really like to.

John is angry. He thought he was safe in this group, and now one of the men is gay. His first response is to leave the group immediately. He convinces himself that he knew that Jeffrey was gay "by the way he spoke." He looks at Jeffrey with anger. Ed is confused. He's not certain what gay really means. He questions, again, what sexuality is all about: Does a person choose to be gay or straight? Is sexuality more than what you do in bed? How does a person get to be gay? Will Jeffrey come on to him? What if he does? Could he be gay and not know it? He thinks of himself as the group's mentor, believes he needs to do something, but does not have anything to say.

David feels the stress of indecision. He greatly respects Jeffrey for sharing this struggle, and he understands it well. He knows what it is like to feel isolated and lonely and assumes that Jeffrey feels these feelings very strongly, at the moment. He also knows what it is like to love and be loved by another man. He knows that being gay is "more than what a person does in bed." He also believes that being gay could destroy a person's life. David struggles with his hiddenness and decides it is time for him to come out in the group, too. He hopes that his self-disclosure will also help Jeffrey. David responds:

> Jeffrey, I want to tell you how much respect I have for you and for what you just did. You see, I'm gay, and I've had a hard time letting other people know that. Also, I've had a lover for 10 years, and it's a very special relationship. Some problems, but everybody has those! I was afraid to tell people here about it because I was afraid nobody would accept me and my lover . . . .

The group continues . . . .

Some Group Issues

Risk

Jeffrey appears to be in an early stage of exploring his sexual orientation. His questions may, in fact, be even more basic than his sexual attraction; he may be about to investigate what it means to be sexual at all. He reports that he has not acted out in any sexual way with men, unlike others in the group, although he has thought about doing so. He is questioning himself and his attractions. He is at a stage in which he recognizes that information about homosexuality may have relevance to him. At this point in his life, this information can be very threatening.

It is important for the group facilitator to recognize the amount of risk involved in sharing the information that Jeffrey has shared. Additionally, it is important to recognize that Jeffrey is taking a step toward connectedness with others and out of his isolation and secrecy. At this point in his development, Jeffrey needs reassurance that he is valued as a person and that he is taking appropriate steps toward his vision of being open and honest about who he is.

It is also important, for Jeffrey to receive some affirmation from the group leader who has become a figure of authority for him. As a group facilitator, Michael needs to be clear about his own sexuality at this time as well as understand the struggle that Jeffrey is experiencing. The group leader needs also to recognize that Jeffrey's self-disclosure is not merely an event but part of an on-going process. As the group facilitator, Michael can support Jeffrey's self-disclosure verbally and encourage other group members to share their feelings and responses, as David has. At this time in the group, it becomes important for Michael to encourage the sharing in a manner that will affirm each member and that will acknowledge the legitimacy of the responses. The facilitator, at this point, can clearly enforce the Gestalt norms of ownership, focus on the here and now, and distinguish between feelings, thoughts, and behaviors (Zinker, 1977).

Attractions

When working with a client who is exploring his sexuality and sexual orientation, it is very important for the counselor to be aware of the dynamics between the client and the counselor. As indicated in the group description, Jeffrey has become aware that he has an attraction to Michael, the group's facilitator. He defines this relationship as "more than being a facilitator" and as "like a brother." Jeffrey, on some level, indicates that acceptance by the facilitator is a very important piece of the growth process for him. Additionally, it will be important for Michael to be supportive and accepting as Jeffrey continues his exploration. If Jeffrey is to come to a healthy understanding of himself as a sexual person and perhaps as a gay man, Michael may need to help Jeffrey know that he is attractive and capable.

As the facilitator, Michael can encourage a discussion of the attraction group members share for each other and for the facilitator as the group becomes more intimate. The facilitator can affirm each member's feelings and responses and share information about the development of intimacy and the way members create this intimacy as the group develops. As the facilitator, Michael can acknowledge Jeffrey's risk taking openly and support him for doing this in a capable manner. He can also verbally acknowledge Jeffrey as an attractive and capable member of the group.

Understanding Identity

At this point in his coming out, Jeffrey may be defining his sexuality in terms of behavior leading to orgasm rather than in a more integrated and comprehensive manner (Berzon, 1988; Isay, 1989; Kus, 1990). As a result of this approach, he may be focusing on behavior and attempting to find a way of relating to himself in terms of this behavior, although he may not even know what it is. It can be helpful for him, and for the other group members, to explore an expanded definition of sexuality.

Several of the group members have been sorting through their own concerns about sexuality and sexual orientation. They have not necessarily verbalized this in the group yet; and the group facilitator needs to be aware of sexual concerns whenever a group is developing. When one group member begins to explore his understanding of his own sexuality, other group members also begin to explore their sexual concerns. For some clients, this exploration may be relatively smooth and harmonious; for others, it may shake the very foundations of their belief systems (Berzon, 1988; Clark, 1987; Fortunato, 1987; McNaught, 1988). A common response to the sharing of sexual information is to understand sexuality in terms of behavior, particularly in terms of behavior leading to orgasm. Several of the men in this group appear to have this limited concept of sexuality. As sexual information is generated, it is important to clarify the definitions of sexuality. Are clients limiting their understanding to behavior or are they able to discuss the spiritual, emotional, psychological, affective, cognitive, social, cultural, and ethnic aspects as well as the physical aspects? When the counselor can facilitate the discussion of all aspects of sexuality, safety can be enhanced in the group. As the facilitator, Michael can invite the group to explore their definitions of *sexuality* and can encourage the members to explore how these definitions are reflected in the feelings they have for each other. Initially, the discussion may focus on more general responses, and the facilitator's responsibility may be in bringing the focus onto group issues. Additional information from the reading assignments may become relevant to the discussion, although not the focus of discussion. Assisting each group member in safely coming to a clearer definition of himself as a sexual person may be the group leader's primary responsibility during this discussion.

Internalized Homophobia

David's response to Jeffrey's self-disclosure provides additional information about the coming out process (Berzon, 1988). David recognizes that being gay is more than physical attraction. He has been in a long-term relationship and recognizes that some of the concerns in same-sex relationships are similar to, and in some cases the same as, those of people in heterosexual relationships. Others are quite different. David further recognizes and shares that there are opportunities for growth as a healthy gay man. David is also able to recognize his own homophobia. He acknowledges this when he acknowledges his fears about what would happen for him personally and professionally if his relationship with his lover was disclosed. He even struggles with this self-disclosure in the group. David reflects a common concern for many men, both gay and straight: learning to trust himself and others with personal information. Some of David's fears may be well founded; others may not be. It becomes important for the group facilitator to recognize the different stages of coming out (Berzon, 1988) experienced by David and Jeffrey and to further recognize the importance of exploring issues of fear and trust (Berzon, 1988; Clark, 1987, 1988; Fortunato, 1987).

David has defined himself as different from the rest of the gay community. This is a common experience for many gay men who have grown up feeling different from others. This, again, may be a subtle form of the homophobia that David has identified in other areas of his life. It may be important for David and for other group members to explore the difference between information that is *private* and information that is *secretive*. The distinction may be that private information is merely information that need not be shared with others, and the nonsharing has no effect on the relationship, whereas secretive information is information that when not shared creates a barrier of mistrust for one or more of the people within the relationship.

At this point, it is important for the facilitator to be clear about his response to homosexuality. Many of the signals of internalized homophobia are very subtle. The facilitator can encourage the discussion of private versus secret parts of oneself. He can encourage group members to discuss openly their fears and their sense of isolation. As identified earlier, several group members have fears based on misinformation and confusion. The facilitator can encourage open discussion and the clearing up of misinformation.

Intimacy Versus Sexuality

Jeffrey's self-disclosure may be even more important than it appears to be on the surface because it can open up a discussion focusing on the meaning of *intimacy* as well as of *sexuality*. The confusion about intimacy and sexuality is frequently a concern to men in group settings and is shared by other members of this group, although it may not have been identified as such yet. Relatively little distinction has been made historically between intimacy and sexuality, particularly for men (Nelson, 1988). Much in our upbringing has reinforced that physical contact is the same as sexual contact (McCarthy, 1988; Nelson, 1988). For many men, experiencing an emotional connection with others becomes sexualized and either attractive or frightening. This leads to much confusion. As indicated in the group description, this is a concern for several members of this group. The discussion of intimacy may have prompted Jeffrey's self-disclosure. The self-disclosure most certainly will lead to a discussion of intimacy and sexuality if facilitated by the group leader.

The group leader can facilitate the distinction between intimacy and sexuality by focusing on the relationships that are developing in the group. As members share more personal information concerning their inner selves, the group is becoming more intimate. If sexual aspects are involved in the development of this intimacy, and the atmosphere is one of safety, group members can discuss their responses with the assistance of the facilitator who acknowledges and affirms open, caring interaction.

Labeling

Another issue that may be brought up as a result of Jeffrey's self-disclosure is that of labeling a person's sexual orientation. Group members may wish to label a person as *homosexual, heterosexual,* or *bis-*

exual with the expectation that this will somehow or other provide a sense of safety for each person. Group members may believe that by categorizing themselves and others in the group, they will clarify sexual feelings and behaviors and be able to include or exclude themselves and others from a category. Again, this categorization happens more readily if sexuality is conceived of only in terms of acting-out behavior. If it is conceived of as an integration of physical, emotional, psychological, affective, cognitive, spiritual, cultural, ethnic, and social factors, it becomes more difficult to categorize. Group participants can be encouraged to define sexuality in broader terms and not to force sexuality into tightly defined categories.

As a counselor, it is important to be clear about one's own sexuality and sexual orientation. Clients, like Jeffrey, can invite a counselor to be even clearer about himself and his beliefs by challenging the counselor's beliefs, encouraging the counselor to gather more information about what it means to be gay and stimulating the counselor to explore sexual issues in his own supervision and counseling. It is especially crucial to understand one's own beliefs about homosexuality and bisexuality. Merely accepting a client's homosexuality may not be sufficient and, in fact, may be a cue to overt or covert homophobia. Many counselors believe that they are accepting of different lifestyles, but when confronted with self-disclosure by a client in the group setting, they may find that it is extremely important to support the individual for who he is assertively. Covert homophobia can easily be detected or feared by an uncertain client with low self-esteem who is struggling to accept himself. The counselor's clarity becomes even more important in the group setting when other group members may be frightened, angry, and threatened. As evidenced in the group described here, Jeffrey's self-disclosure has a different impact on each of the group members. For some, Jeffrey's self-disclosure serves as an invitation to explore their own concerns about sexuality and intimacy more openly, either verbally or internally; for others, this self-disclosure may, initially, reinforce defensiveness and stereotyping. The counselor's ability to support Jeffrey's sharing openly is essential to inviting further self-disclosure and acceptance.

Stereotyping

For many clients, the introduction of homosexuality into the group setting stirs up many stereotypes of what being gay means. Members may conjure up visions of the gay lifestyle, which may be viewed in terms of anonymous sex, the "bar scene," stereotypical professions, lack of monogamous relationships, and a multitude of sexual partners. Within the group setting it becomes important to provide information concerning changes occurring in society and within cultures. Partly in response to the AIDS epidemic, and in response to other changes in society, more and more gay men are making commitments to "healthier" lifestyles. Although being gay once meant living alone in secrecy and fear, it no longer necessarily means this. Support for developing open and honest relationships does exist, and clients may need to know this. In many communities, more and more resources are available as support systems for gay men and lesbians. It becomes increasingly important for counselors to be familiar with the resources available in their communities. In communities where local resources are less available, counselors may obtain access to national associations that provide a variety of services. Although the group facilitator may not, necessarily, share this information in the group setting, it can be very helpful to clients in conjunction with the support provided in the group setting.

Religion and Sexuality

As indicated in the group description, several of the group members are struggling with religious concepts and sexuality. It is very important for the group facilitator to acknowledge this struggle at some point in the exploration of developing a healthy sexual identity. Group members have had different religious experiences, and several have indicated, at least to themselves, the desire to reconcile their religious upbringing with their growing sense of who they are as sexual people. At least one group member, John, has strong conflicting experiences, feelings, and beliefs related to sexuality. If John is to remain in the group, he must learn that the group is a safe place to explore these and continue to be accepted by group members. At this point in the group's development, John may become the center of group conflict, and ground rules for conflict may need to be clearly acknowledged and enforced.

As a counselor, it becomes important to be aware of the religious structures within which group members live. Communities throughout the country have specific religion-affiliated groups to which gay men can belong. It can be most helpful to gay clients if referral to these organizations can be made.

Cultural Diversity

The men in the group come from a variety of ethnic, cultural, religious, and social backgrounds. As a result, they bring with them many different ideas and values about what it means to be sexual as well as homosexual and bisexual. It is important for the growth of all members of the group that these differences in background be acknowledged and clarified. However, in the process of recognizing the individuality of group members, it is also crucial to recognize their common purpose. All of the group members have acknowledged, to themselves if not to others in the group, the desire to be more open, to make more meaningful connections with others in the group, to feel safer and more trusting with each other, and to feel less isolated, secretive, and alone.

The men have also shared their desire to develop a greater, clearer sense of what it means to be a man in contemporary society. In order to attain this vision of greater integration and synthesis, the men in the group need to acknowledge their common basic purpose. This purpose is to learn to live their lives in a loving manner. At times, this course may seem difficult. Perhaps what they have that is most important is the opportunity to follow their own paths, and to share with others in the group as they grow. As counselors working with groups, we become traveling companions for a walk along the path. It may become increasingly exciting to acknowledge the role of traveling companion within the group setting. Clients may need reinforcement in recognizing that learning to integrate a healthy sense of sexuality into their lives means taking many different paths to a common destination, and in recognizing that each of the paths provides the opportunity to learn something special about what it means to be unconditionally loving.

Conclusion

Within the context of a group, the issues of sexuality and homosexuality frequently become relevant. It is important for the group facilitator to have an understanding of coming out as a process and not as an isolated event. It is also important to understand that the disclosure of one's sexual orientation in the group setting introduces a variety of issues that may not arise otherwise.

A. Michael Hutchins

References

Berzon, B. (1988). *Permanent partners*. New York: Dutton.

Clark, D. (1988). *As we are*. Boston: Alyson.

Clark, D. (1987). *The new loving someone gay*. Berkeley, CA: Celestial Arts.

Fortunato, J. (1987). *Embracing the exile: Healing journeys of gay Christians*. New York: Harper & Row.

Isay, R. (1989). *Being homosexual*. New York: Farrar, Strauss, Giroux.

Kus, R. (1990). *Keys to caring: Assisting your gay and lesbian clients*. Boston: Alyson.

McCarthy, B. (1988). *Male sexual awareness: Increasing sexual satisfaction*. New York: Carroll & Graf.

McNaught, B. (1988). *On being gay: Thoughts on family, faith, and love*. New York: St. Martin's Press.

Nelson, J. (1988). *The intimate connection: Male sexuality, masculine spirituality*. New York: Harper & Row.

Zinker, J. (1977). *Creative process in Gestalt therapy*. New York: Random House.

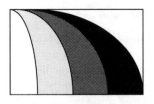

21

Empowering the Counseling Professional to Work With Gay and Lesbian Issues

Reese M. House, PhD
Elizabeth L. Holloway, PhD

Counselors' attitudes toward gay men and lesbians have changed dramatically over the 17 years since professional organizations stopped labeling homosexuality as a form of mental illness. As a result of this change, it is reasonable to assume that counseling practices should reflect a view of homosexuality as an acceptable lifestyle and that counselors should model gay- and lesbian-affirmative attitudes and behaviors (Corey, Corey, & Callanan, 1988). To be gay- and lesbian-affirmative is to value homosexuality and heterosexuality equally as natural or normal attributes (Krajeski, 1986).

Such a gay and lesbian positive stance is, however, at odds with the prevalent view in American society that condemns homosexuality as a perversion or morally wrong. Therefore, it cannot be assumed that all counselor supervisors and supervisees are gay and lesbian affirmative (Buhrke, 1989; Clark, 1979; Garfinkle & Morin, 1978; Gattrell, 1984; Thompson & Fishburn, 1977). Some counselor supervisors and supervisees make such comments as, "I have never known anyone who is gay" or "I will not be working with lesbian clients" or "I have no intention of having gay clients on my case load." Whether they are aware of it or not, all counselors, regardless of their work setting, have clients who are gay and lesbian. Since all counselors have gay and lesbian clients, supervisors must help supervisees in becoming knowledgeable and aware of gay and lesbian clients and the issues they bring to counseling.

To become effective, counselors must overcome the negative societal messages about same-sex activity. Many counselors have absorbed misinformation and myths about homosexuality. Such mythology, misinformation, and ignorance may interfere with accurately identifying the etiology of the problems presented by gay and lesbian clients (Silberman & Hawkins, 1988). Many counselors function under the myth that all clients are heterosexual, when at least 10% of the population has a same-sex orientation. Comments like "You couldn't possibly be gay," "I am sure I can help you change your sexual orientation," or "I am sure you could become interested in the opposite sex if you just tried" have a clear heterosexual bias and deny the sexual orientation of clients. When counselors believe and act on myths about gays and lesbians, they perform a disservice to these clients (House, 1991).

Supervisors and supervisees need to understand that gay and lesbian people live in a homophobic culture. Cultural homophobia is manifested in those individuals who downgrade, deny, stereotype, or ignore the existence of gays and lesbians. These homophobic reactions create a devalued minority in a hostile society and are inconsistent with such primary tenets of counseling as acceptance and tolerance. Cultural homophobia goes hand in hand with heterosexism—the assumption of normality and superiority by heterosexuals. Heterosexism is the societal norm in the United States against which gays and lesbians must struggle. It includes the subtle and indirect ways that the system reinforces heterosexuality as the only acceptable and viable life option. For example, most parents automatically expect that their children will marry a person of the other sex. Typically, the only positive and satisfying relationships portrayed by the media are heterosexual. Teachers often presume all of their students are heterosexual and conceal the homosexual identity of many artists, politicians, and other public and famous figures. Homophobia and heterosexism are the two faces of discrimination that gays confront daily in their lives.

Most often, gays and lesbians bring concerns to counseling that are no different than those of heterosexuals. Even though the concerns may be no different, however, the issues are exacerbated by the ignorance, prejudice, oppression, and homophobia that gays and lesbians must address (McWhirter & Mattison, 1984). Heterosexual counselors who down play the importance of societal homophobia may fail to maintain empathy with gays and lesbians (McCandlish, 1985). The lack of practical knowledge about gays and lesbians and their lifestyle is a major obstacle to satisfactory counseling. Counselor educators and supervisors have an obligation to reeducate themselves about homosexuality so they can provide responsible, relevant training and supervision to the next generation of counselors (Norton, 1988). In this chapter the authors present four different supervisory cases that illustrate some of the basic issues that supervisors and supervisees face when addressing the needs of gay and lesbian clients. Each case is followed by a brief dialogue between the supervisor and supervisee and a case analysis of each supervisory dilemma.

Empowering the Supervisee:
A Framework for the Supervisory Process

The goal of supervision in counseling practice is the enhancement of the supervisee's effective professional functioning. Essentially, the supervisor's task is to provide a learning environment that empowers the supervisee. Two primary factors contribute to the empowerment of the supervisee: (a) the acquisition of a skill and knowledge base relevant to the counseling profession and (b) the experience of personal power within the supervisory and counseling relationship. To work effectively with gay and lesbian clients, knowledge and acceptance of homosexuality must be included in the supervisory process (Buhrke, 1989). Since gays or lesbians are disempowered by the discrimination and prejudice of the society at large, it is critical that the supervisory relationship provide an experience of support and empowerment for both gay and lesbian supervisees and for all supervisees working with gay and lesbian clients.

Many different elements of the supervisory process influence a supervisor's goal of empowerment. The definition and clarification of these supervision aspects can provide a basis for understanding supervisory situations relevant to working with gay and lesbian supervisees. A map of supervision (Figure 1), developed as an heuristic tool by Holloway and Dunlap (1990) provides a framework for analyzing such supervisory situations. The case dialogues, issues, and analyses illustrate how gay or lesbian issues can be positively addressed within the supervisory context.

Figure 1

Aspects of the Supervisory Process

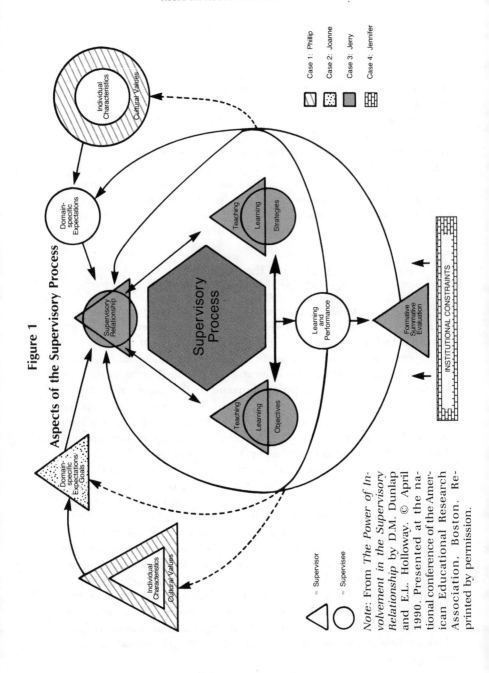

Note: From *The Power of In-volvement in the Supervisory Relationship* by D.M. Dunlap and E.L. Holloway. © April 1990. Presented at the na-tional conference of the Amer-ican Educational Research Association, Boston. Re-printed by permission.

Individual Characteristics and Cultural Values

Supervision typically entails two individuals coming together to form a working relationships in which one person has the role of supervisor and the other the role of supervisee. Both bring to supervision their own interpersonal characteristics, knowledge, abilities, and cultural values (see the double circle representing the supervisee and the double triangle representing the supervisor in Figure 1). The cultural values of both the supervisor and supervisee include attitudes and beliefs about homosexuality in our society. Because the individual characteristics and values of each participant form the foundation on which the relationship is based, it is critical that supervisors address their own and their supervisee's values regarding homophobia and heterosexism and their expression of the resulting attitudes. Addressing these issues is necessary with supervisees who are gay or lesbian or supervisees who counsel gay and lesbian clients.

Case 1

Client. Phillip is a well-known lawyer in a large metropolitan city. He is in his late 40s and has been working in a prominent law firm in the area of criminal law. He is gregarious and well respected by his colleagues. He is a gay man who has not come out or been in a longstanding relationship. In the last 2 months he has been experiencing frequent panic attacks and has been using alcohol in an effort to relax.

Context and Dialogue. The following dialogue takes place in a private practice setting. A heterosexual female supervisor is working with a gay male supervisee who is working on postdegree licensing hours and counseling Phillip. The dialogue illustrates the dilemmas posed by a supervisor making heterosexist assumptions and a supervisee making homosexual assumptions.

> *Supervisee:* I would like to talk to you about my personal relationship with my partner because I think that is is relevant to my work with my client, Phillip.
> *Supervisor:* Go ahead.
> *Supervisee:* Well, I am wondering if my client might be gay. I am concerned, though, that I might just be projecting on him. I don't want to do that. . . . I need some help sorting out me from him.
> *Supervisor:* I don't think that I understand what you are trying to tell me. My understanding is that he is pretty anxious

and using alcohol as a refuge. He is a successful fellow in a high-stress job. His symptoms are not surprising. What does this have to do with him being gay? Are you overidentifying with his situation?

Supervisee: I'm not sure. But there are a lot of things that he has said or hinted at that give me the feeling that he is testing me out to see if I will accept him as a gay person. I'm trying to test him out and wondering if I should tell him I am gay. We're playing cat and mouse in there. It's very frustrating.

Supervisor: I'm confused. I didn't know that. . . . Are you telling me that you are gay and your partner. . . . I don't know what to say. I never thought of the possibility of either you or your client being homosexual.

Supervisee: Now I'm feeling really uncomfortable that somehow our supervisory relationship is going to be different because of what I've told you.

Issues. How are the assumptions made by the supervisor and supervisee affecting the supervisory relationship? Is the client being assisted by these assumptions? How open are the supervisor and supervisee to discussing these issues in spite of their assumptions? How much of the personal lifestyle of the supervisee does the supervisor address?

Case Analysis. It is evident in this supervisory vignette that the supervisor has made fundamental cultural assumptions regarding the heterosexuality of the supervisee and client. These assumptions have prevented her from understanding more fully the counselor's dilemma of countertransference and thus jeopardized the client's care. The supervisee's last comment reflects his own sense of vulnerability in the supervisory relationship as he confronts his supervisor's heterosexism. At this moment the supervisory relationship is in jeopardy. The supervisee is directly questioning his acceptability to the supervisor and the degree of support and trust that exists between them. The supervisor at this point needs to acknowledge her own issues of heterosexism. It would be helpful for the supervisor to engage the supervisee in a discussion of cultural homophobia and her own homophobic reactions as well as the influence of this discussion on their supervisory relationship. If the supervisor ignores the issues of homosexuality in both the counseling and the supervisory relationship, she undermines both the counselor's ability to function effectively with the client and her effectiveness as a supervisor.

Goals for Professional Counselors

Supervisors have goals that relate to their understanding of the attitudes, skills, and knowledge supervisees must acquire to be professional counselors (single triangle, left, Figure 1). Similarly, supervisees have a set of performance expectations as counselors based on preparation and practice (single circle, right, Figure 1). Supervisors have a responsibility to insure that supervisees both understand the issues and develop effective strategies in working with gay and lesbian clients. As a matter of course, supervisors can introduce the issues of cultural homophobia, heterosexism, and the influence of these societal norms on individuals in our society. Supervisors can also demonstrate their commitment to these issues by including gay and lesbian books in their library and loaning them to students, posting supporting articles about gay and lesbian issues on bulletin boards, and rejecting and challenging antigay and antilesbian language and jokes. Case 2 illustrates how supervisors can either avoid or attend to gay and lesbian issues with naive supervisees.

Case 2

Client. Joanne is a woman in her mid-30s. She is a single parent with two children and teaches high school English. She has been divorced for 6 months and is very relieved to be out of her marriage. The last month she has been spending time with a woman friend from work and has enjoyed this relationship; however, her friend has left for her summer home for 2 months, and Joanne is feeling very despondent.

Context and Dialogue. A male heterosexual supervisor has been working with a female heterosexual supervisee for 3 months in a community mental health setting. During a weekly supervision session the supervisee discusses Joanne, who is a new client.

> *Supervisee:* I saw a new client today. She is a very bright woman in her mid-30s who teaches at a local high school. She teaches English. I really think that I am going to be able to work well with her.

Supervisor: I am pleased to hear your excitement about the client. What does she want to work on in counseling?

Supervisee: Well, she is divorced and she has two kids. She's just coming out of a relationship. She's feeling depressed, lonely, and can't concentrate at work.

Supervisor: Do you think she is suicidal?

Supervisee: Oh no. She is just feeling down. I'll talk with her about places to meet men. I am newly single and have had to figure out how to cope with all of this.

Supervisor: Well, that might be helpful in a later stage in counseling but right now let's focus on the meaning of the client's depressed feelings.

Issue. In this last response the supervisor and supervisee ignore the sexuality of the client. What are the consequences for the client? What effect will this avoidance have on the professional development of the supervisee?

Case Analysis. Neither the counselor or the supervisor know at this point whether or not the client is lesbian. In fact, the client may not understand her sexual orientation. However, if the supervisor has explored his own heterosexist assumptions and accepts the significance of these values in the counselor role, then he can use this situation as an important teaching opportunity. Rather than the last comment, the supervisor could say:

Supervisor: I understand your need to be helpful to this client in the sense that you really identify with her situation. However, let's for a moment think about the possibility that your client is not interested in a heterosexual relationship. You have assumed that she is heterosexual when perhaps she is not. Let's explore this possibility and it's meaning to your work as a counselor with her.

This comment reflects the supervisor's proactive stance in challenging heterosexist assumptions and supports the possibility that the client is a lesbian.

The Supervisory Process

The interplay among the supervisory relationship of objectives and strategies is an integral part of the supervisory process (Figure 1, center). This interplay reflects a learning alliance between supervisor and supervisee that represents an equality of influence, shared goals, and a common understanding of the learning process. This learning alliance is used as a vehicle to establish teaching and learning objectives specific to the supervisee's level of skill and the client's needs. The nature of the client's issues influences the objectives of supervision. For example, if a supervisee is working with a gay or lesbian client, the supervisor has the opportunity to establish learning objectives that encourage the supervisee's exploration of his or her own homophobic reactions or heterosexist assumptions. Case 3 presents a situation in which the objectives of the supervisor and supervisee are at odds and thus threaten the supervisory process.

Case 3

Client. Jerry is a 23-year-old college senior. He has maintained a 3.4 grade point average as a student at a state university. Recently he has been feeling depressed and is unable to motivate himself to finish his senior year in college. He has few friends and lives alone in a residence hall room. He has dated sporadically throughout college but has not developed either a long-term or significant relationship. As he talks with the counselor in the campus counseling center, he never uses specific pronouns to identify his dating relationships. As the counselor explores this issue with Jerry, the counselor discovers that Jerry is wondering about his sexuality and that all of his dates have been with other men.

Context and Dialogue. The supervisor, the director of a university counseling center, in this case is a gay male supervising a heterosexual male supervisee. The supervisee is an intern in the counseling center and the director is his immediate supervisor. The following dialogue takes place in their weekly supervision session.

> *Supervisee:* My client is really experiencing a lot of stress, has anxiety attacks, and is feeling guilty. I think that he has felt suicidal and tries to mask his feelings. I really want to help this fellow. I can understand why he feels guilty. He has had several sexual relationships with men. And he is in a lot of pain because he feels hopeless about fitting in to this world.
> *Supervisor:* I am interested in knowing how you are going to intervene here.
> *Supervisee:* The bottom line is this guy would be a lot happier if he could change. No one can be happy when they are

gay, and we have got to help him get sexually involved with women.

Supervisor: I'm concerned to hear you so intent on changing Jerry or believing that all gays are maladjusted.

Supervisee: But I am sure this guy is not really homosexual, and I know I can help him to get things clear.

Supervisor: I find myself upset at your insistence that Jerry is really heterosexual in spite of his expressed needs and behaviors. We need to talk about some of your ideas regarding gays and lesbians.

Issues. How much do the supervisor's own issues enter into this situation because he is gay? Should the supervisor tell the supervisee that he is gay? How can the supervisor form an effective learning alliance with the supervisee? Is the supervisee open to understanding his own reactions to this client? Is the supervisee able to consider different goals for the client? Is the supervisee willing to work with the supervisor on alternative views of homosexuality? Is the supervisee appropriate for counselor training? Should the supervisor insist that the client be referred?

Case Analysis. The supervisor must consider several factors in deciding how to proceed with this supervisee. His first task is to examine his own feelings regarding this supervisee's adamant need to make his client heterosexual. This insistence in the face of the supervisor's own sexual orientation is bound to engage the supervisor's own attitudes, beliefs, and personal vulnerability. As important is the supervisor's responsibility to the client. Exploration of the supervisee's homophobia is the first step in determining a course of action.

The supervisor may choose to tell the supervisee that he is gay. This disclosure will most likely have a substantial impact on the supervisee and the character of the relationship. It may enhance the opportunity for the supervisee to work through his homophobia if he has a strong positive connection with the supervisor. Or it may cause the supervisee such dissonance that he will flee the supervisory relationship. In any event, the supervisor must closely monitor the supervisee's openness to personal change. If the supervisee's individual characteristics of rigidity prevent a transformation of attitude and values, then the client must be referred. The removal of a client from a supervisee's case load is a serious statement about that supervisee's performance and has important repercussions for the supervisory relationship. The supervisor should make every effort to continue to work with the supervisee and thus provide an opportunity for learning and resolution. However, in some cases it becomes evident in the process of supervision that the supervisee needs more in-depth psychological understanding of his beliefs and behavior. It may be incumbent on the supervisor in these circumstances to refer the supervisee for personal counseling. Addressing these issues directly with the supervisee is a process that leads to the evaluation aspect of supervision.

Evaluation

Supervisors must evaluate the supervisees' performance as a part of their professional role (triangle at the base of Figure 1). This evaluation process helps supervisees understand how their attitudes, beliefs, and values affect clients in the counseling process. Supervisors need to influence supervisees who are ignorant, misinformed, or homophobic about gays and lesbians. The authors believe that supervisees must adopt a gay- and lesbian-affirmative stance so that gays and lesbians feel comfortable as clients or as professionals. When supervisors inform supervisees about their issues of homophobia and heterosexism as a part of the evaluation criteria, supervisees then have the opportunity to understand how important it is to accept gays and lesbians. Both supervisor and supervisee attitudes and beliefs about homosexuality affect the evaluation process. Case 3 might eventually have the following dialogue as part of the evaluation process:

> *Supervisor:* It seems that you are unwilling to explore other alternatives to heterosexuality.
>
> *Supervisee:* Well, frankly, I think that you're just as biased in your need to make this guy gay because you are gay. It is pretty mean spirited on your part to want this guy to be gay, given the kinds of obstacles that it will create in his life. Why can't you just give me the opportunity to make a relationship with a woman work for him? Why can't you hope for something better for him than you have for yourself?
>
> *Supervisor:* Because you speak to me with such vehemence and insistence, I am even more troubled that you are unable to work with this client with objectivity or unable to have him make a decision about his own goals. Frankly, I am not able to trust your capacity to work effectively with this client. Since it is my responsibility to safeguard the client's welfare, I will

begin the process of referral for this client to another counselor in the center. I do not want you to see this client again.

Supervisee: This is pretty outrageous. Do you mean to tell me I am going to get kicked out of here?

Supervisor: No, I did not say that. I did say that I will reassign this client. However, I do want us to talk further about your personal intensity around the issue of homosexuality, and if I am not satisfied with your openness to different lifestyles with your clients then I will recommend that you receive personal counseling. You should also know that I consider that it is part of your professional responsibility as a counselor to accept diversity, and that includes different sexual lifestyles.

Issues. What effect will this confrontation have on the supervisory relationship? By taking such a strong stance is the supervisor endangering his position? How easy would it be for the supervisor to take such a stand?

Case Analysis. The referral of a client from a supervisee's practice is a critical step for a supervisor and must be embarked upon with careful consideration of the client's welfare and the supervisee's training experience. It is not easy to construe such a reassignment as empowering for the supervisee. However, the supervisor's responsibility to the client must take first priority under circumstances as depicted in Case 3. As the supervisee broadens his world view, he becomes more effective with clients exploring or dealing with their sexual orientation and ultimately enhances his professional effectiveness. Indeed, it may be difficult for this supervisee to accept the value in this approach to his training. The supervisor has recommended personal counseling, and it appears that such an option might well be the best approach in helping this supervisee move beyond his homophobic views. The supervisor might also need to recommend a leave of absence from clinical practice if the supervisee is unable to perform adequately during his internship while addressing homophobia issues.

The supervisor must also face the prospect of providing a summative evaluation of the supervisee's practice. The supervisor must ask himself, "Is this counselor able to practice independently without supervision?" "Should this counselor be permitted to remain in his position with such strongly entrenched homophobic views?" In making this decision the supervisor is also making a critical decision for the profession and the society as a whole. Does the counseling profession tolerate and thus promote the existence of heterosexism and homophobia in the profession? To take a stand that such attitudes and beliefs cannot be tolerated is to also take a risk. This supervisor is gay, and if he works in an environment that does not support the tenets of affirmative action, he puts his own position and personal reputation in jeopardy. The support of his heterosexual colleagues will be essential in this case. The issues of institutional constraints play an important role in determining the kinds of options and consequences for supervisors facing such critical decisions.

Institutional Constraints

At the foundation (the base of Figure 1) of every supervisory relationship lie the constraints of the institution, including guidelines, bylaws, legalities, policies, regulations, and norms. Often these formal and informal institutional norms reflect nonacceptance of gays and lesbians (for elaboration on dealing with institutional norms and values, see Gutiérrez, 1991). Counselors cannot ignore the cultural and societal context in which their clients live and need to help change societal views to an acceptance and understanding of gays and lesbians (Loulan, 1986). As professional role models, it is particularly important for supervisors to advocate tolerance and understanding of gays and lesbians (Buhrke, 1988). Supervisors need to teach counselors, as change agents in the communities in which they live, to support positive public and institutional policy decisions regarding homosexuality. Counseling supervisors need to adopt this role as an ethical and professional obligation. Counselors trained with this knowledge and skill can then encourage tolerance in educational settings and advocate for nondiscriminatory measures. Case 4 presents some of the difficulties in facing these issues.

Case 4

Client. Jennifer is a 17-year-old high school junior who has clearly identified herself as lesbian. She has come out to her mother, several friends, and a few teachers at school. She attends a gay and lesbian support group on a nearby college campus. She is beginning to push for gay-related activities to be held at the high school. The administrators and members of the local community react negatively to any mention of gay or lesbian issues on the school grounds. A counselor in training has been asked to discuss these issues with Jennifer.

Context and Dialogue. The supervisee is a heterosexual female counselor in training at a medium-sized high school. The supervisor is a male heterosexual director of counseling services in the school district. The counselor in training has come to her supervisor to discuss Jennifer and the implications for the high school.

> *Supervisee:* I've been thinking about Jennifer and what she is trying to do here in this school, and I am really worried about her.
>
> *Supervisor:* Why? What do you think might happen?
>
> *Supervisee:* I am afraid kids are really going to harass her and might even beat her up. You know this community thinks gays and lesbians are next to dirt. I've seen it out there.
>
> *Supervisor:* Well, I'm afraid you are right about the community, and I appreciate your concern for Jennifer's safety. We need to think not only about what is best for Jennifer but also what is best for this school. This is a delicate situation.
>
> *Supervisee:* I don't know what we can do about this school. I sense that the teachers and principal don't want to deal with this issue, but the issue is with us since Jennifer has just announced her candidacy for senior class president and has publicly stated that she is a lesbian.
>
> *Supervisor:* It is really clear that we as counselors are caught in the middle of this.
>
> *Supervisee:* Yes, and I can't afford to get publicly involved since my certification is at stake.
>
> *Supervisor:* I understand your fear, and everyone here, including the school, Jennifer, you, and I are in a bind. I think that we need to talk about the meaning of our roles as counselors in this community. It might help us in formulating an intervention.

Issue. How do the supervisor and supervisee address the constraints placed on them by the community and the school? How do they address the homophobia in the community? What steps should they take to assist Jennifer and other high school students who come out? What ethical standards need to be considered in this dilemma?

Case Analysis. Both the supervisor and supervisee are facing the reality of homophobia in American society. The risk of advocating for acceptance and change is evident from the supervisee's expressed fear of how such action may jeopardize her professional advancement. The supervisor faces this reality directly in his desire to discuss the political and ethical issues that are involved in being advocates for Jennifer within the school. This is an important learning opportunity for the supervisee in both ethical decision making and professional responsibility. This dilemma depicts vividly the importance of understanding supervision in the context of the institution in which the supervisor works and points out the need for the counseling profession to address the value of diversity in our society. Unless the counseling profession provides the leadership necessary, counselors may not have the kind of support needed to be effective in creating positive change within institutions regarding gay and lesbian rights. Acceptance of diversity needs to be reflected in counselor training programs, in supervision, and in mental health and school counselor settings, and it needs to become a part of the criteria for competency of professional counselors.

Conclusion

Counselor training and supervision need to include the advocacy of diversity and thus support lesbians and gays (Buhrke, 1989). This position is a clear statement of the professional commitment to the promotion of human growth and development in our society and consistent with the ethical standards of the profession (American Association of Counseling and Development [AACD], 1988). Supervisees need to be educated in training and supervision to understand issues of heterosexism and homophobia (Buhrke, 1989). The cases presented in this chapter illustrate the difficult decisions that supervisors need to make if they intend to uphold the values of diversity and nondiscrimination in the training of counselors. Not only is the immediate supervisory relationship often at risk, but also the supervisor's own professional identity within the institution or agency may be at risk. Supervisors have a professional responsibility to accept these risks if the profession as a whole is to progress toward acceptance of gays and lesbians in society.

A part of this acceptance in society is the recognition and nuturance of gay and lesbian counselors. Until recently it was assumed that heterosexuality was the only suitable orientation for counselors (Rochlin, 1985). However, publicly identified gay and lesbian mental health professionals are growing in number. The gay or lesbian professional who comes out serves as an important resource for the gay and lesbian community, serves as a role model for gays and lesbians, provides security for those who want to see a gay or lesbian counselor, and acts as a resource consultant for other counselors (Woodman & Lenna, 1980). Supervisors need to encourage gay and lesbian supervisees to recognize their sexuality and acknowledge the strengths they have to offer when they function as gay and lesbian professionals.

Supervisors have an important role to play in empowering all counselors, whether they are gay, lesbian, or heterosexual, to work effectively with gay and lesbian issues. As role models, supervisors are in a powerful position to influence the next generation of counselors. Their own awareness of individual characteristics and cultural values regarding sexual orientation as well as their inclusion of these issues in the supervisory process are important first steps in promoting informed and gay- and lesbian-affirmative counseling. Without examining their own values and beliefs regarding gays and lesbians in the culture, supervisors risk passing on damaging stereotypes to supervisees. Such values reinforce stereotypes that undermine the development of confident, capable, and contributing members of our society: a consequence in direct conflict with the goals of our profession (AACD, 1988). However, counselors who are sensitive to gay and lesbian issues, who have examined and challenged the heterosexist and homophobic assumptions of our culture, and who have confronted their own values can assist all clients who are addressing gay- and lesbian-related issues.

References

American Association for Counseling and Development. (1988). *Ethical standards* (rev. ed.). Alexandria, VA: Author.

Buhrke, R. A. (1988). Lesbian-related issues in counseling supervision. *Women and Therapy, 8,* 195–206.

Buhrke, R. A. (1989). Incorporating lesbian and gay issues into counselor training: A resource guide. *Journal of Counseling & Development, 68,* 77–80.

Clark, M. F. (1979). Attitudes, information, and behavior of counselors toward homosexual clients. *Dissertation Abstracts International, 40,* 5729A.

Corey, G., Corey, M. S., & Callanan, P. (1988). *Issues and ethics in the helping profession* (3rd ed.). Pacific Grove, CA: Brooks/Cole.

Garfinkle, E. M., & Morin, S. F. (1978). Psychologists' attitudes toward homosexual psychotherapy clients. *Journal of Social Issues, 34* (3), 101–112.

Gattrell, N. (1984). Combating homophobia in the psychotherapy of lesbians. *Women and Therapy, 3,* 13–29.

Gutiérrez, F. (1991). *Managing the campus ecology of gay and lesbian students on Catholic college campuses.* Santa Clara, CA: Santa Clara University Counseling Services and Programs. (ERIC Document Reproduction Service No. ED324612).

Holloway, E. L., & Dunlap, D. M. (1990, April). *Cross-disciplinary exchange: Power and involvement in the learning alliance.* Paper presented at the annual meeting of the American Educational Research Association, Boston.

House, R. M. (1991). Counseling with gay and lesbian clients. In D. Capuzzi & D. Gross (Eds.), *Introduction to counseling: Perspectives for the 1990s* (pp. 353–387). Boston: Allyn Bacon.

Krajeski, J. P. (1986). Psychotherapy with gay men and lesbians: A history of controversy. In T. S. Stein & C. J. Cohen (Eds.), *Contemporary perspectives on psychotherapy with lesbians and gay men* (pp. 9–25). New York: Plenum.

Loulan, J. (1986). Psychotherapy with lesbian mothers. In T. S. Stein & C. J. Cohen (Eds.), *Contemporary perspectives on psychotherapy with lesbians and gay men* (pp. 103–137). New York: Plenum.

McCandlish, B. M. (1985). Therapeutic issues with lesbian couples. In J. C. Gonsiorek (Ed.), *A guide to psychotherapy with gay and lesbian clients* (pp. 71–78). New York: Harrington Park.

McWhirter, D. P., & Mattison, A. M. (1984). *The male couple: How relationships develop.* Englewood Cliffs, NJ: Prentice-Hall.

Norton, J. (1988). Gay and lesbian populations. In N. A. Vacc, J. Wittmer, & S. Devaney (Eds.), *Experiencing and counseling multicultural and diverse populations* (pp. 61–88). Muncie, IN: Accelerated Development.

Rochlin, M. (1985). Sexual orientation of the counselor and therapeutic effectiveness with gay clients. In J. C. Gonsiorek (Ed.), *A guide to psychotherapy with gay and lesbian clients* (pp. 21–29). New York: Harrington Park.

Silberman, B. O., & Hawkins, R. O., Jr. (1988). Lesbian women and gay men: Issues for counseling. In E. Weinstein & E. Rosen (Eds.), *Sexuality counseling: Issues and implications* (pp. 101–113). Pacific Grove, CA: Brooks/Cole.

Thompson, G. H., & Fishburn, W. R. (1977). Attitudes toward homosexuality among graduate counseling students. *Counselor Education and Supervision, 17,* 121–130.

Woodman, N., & Lenna, H. (1980). *Counseling with gay men and women.* San Francisco: Jossey-Bass.

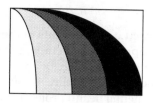

22

Some Ethical Considerations When Counseling Gay, Lesbian, and Bisexual Clients

Sari H. Dworkin, PhD

This chapter differs from previous chapters in its emphasis on theoretical considerations rather than practical applications, although case material from previous chapters is referred to for illustrative purposes. Ethical codes are designed as guidelines for behavior and responsibility and serve to solidify professional identity (Mabe & Rollin, 1986). For the mental health professions these guidelines have been formulated to attempt to ensure protection of the client. Ethics differ from morals in that morals tend to relate to God and what is perceived by many as "natural law" (Tripp, 1987), whereas ethics are related to the personal rights of people. It is within ethics that arguments for the rights of minorities are addressed, for example, the right to be able to choose any profession one wants. In chapter 2 on career counseling, Russell had to deal with anger about the necessity of having to consider how his sexual orientation might affect his choice of a career. He was also angry that his sexual orientation affected others' perceptions about his competence.

This book is concerned with the rights of the gay and lesbian client population to receive appropriate therapeutic care. Until recently appropriate care has not been available for a variety of reasons. Moral or natural law that defines homosexuality as "sin" or "sickness" has historically pervaded the mental health professions (Dworkin & Gutiérrez, 1989). Homosexuality, bisexuality, and heterosexuality are morally neutral, and yet this has not been recognized until recently by our field (Dworkin & Gutiérrez, 1989; Pharr, 1988). Ethical standards of the mental health professions have maintained the status quo by not addressing specifically the ethics involved in the counseling of oppressed groups (American Association for Counseling and Development, 1988). The status quo is also maintained by the guideline found in the ethical code of the American Psychological Association that admonishes psychologists to be aware of and comply with community values (Brown, 1985). This often has meant complying with patriarchal values (Brown, 1985) that enforce heterosexuality, homophobia, and biphobia (Pharr, 1988). Current psychological theories that affect the practice of counseling have trapped practitioners into a binary system of classification of sexual orientation (Ross, 1987) that appears to be bound to western culture and does not account for homosexual behavior across cultures. This binary system ascribes critical importance to the selection of partner by gender. Bisexuality calls this into question because for the bisexual person the gender of the partner is not the crucial variable. If the therapist working with John in the chapter on bisexuality (chapter 12) subscribed to this binary system, he or she would have had difficulty with John's heterosexual and homosexual attractions. According to Ross (1987), this binary system decreases the examination of sexual feelings as falling on a continuum and happening for a variety of reasons. Theories influence practitioners—and then the care received by bisexual, heterosexual, lesbian, and gay clients. The quality of care rests on the general training of the caregiver and the specific training to work with gay, lesbian, and bisexual clients received by counselors. This specific training has been nonexistent to inadequate (Dworkin & Gutiérrez, 1989; Iasenza, 1989). Appropriate therapeutic care requires responsibleness on the part of counselors. According to Tennyson and Strom (1986), this responsibleness "... entails an attitude toward others based on moral principles of respect, fairness, and freedom. Inherent in this attitude is a positive, practical concern for others that extends to all persons, no matter how different they may be" (p. 299).

Culture and Counseling

As Dworkin and Gutiérrez (1989) have stated, it is important to view the history of oppression and survival tactics generated to deal with that oppression as forming a psychological culture for gay, lesbian, and bisexual people. This psychological culture interplays with other cultures such as ethnicity (see chapters 8, 9, and 10 on Latino and Latina, Asian-American, and African-American gay, lesbian, and bisexual clients). The counselor must be aware that the salient cultural identity of a client may change even within the context of a single interview (Pedersen, 1990). Maria (in chapter 9) is Puerto Rican, a lawyer, a lesbian, and part of a couple. At any point within counseling, one or another of these identities may be the most salient cultural identity. If the counselor assumes that the identity of a client remains constant at all times, then there is danger of stereotyping. Ethically a counselor must guard against stereotyping and must ascertain the culturally learned assumptions of the client and the cues, signals, and patterns of the client in order to interpret the behavior accurately (Pedersen, 1990). This will be more difficult for a counselor who is culturally different from the client. The therapist in the chapter on psychotherapy with physically disabled lesbians (chapter 11) felt a kinship with Jan because they were both visually impaired, both had adult daughters, and both were lesbians. This gave the therapist a grounding in the learned assumptions of the client. Therefore, without a thorough grounding in the lifestyle and culture of gay, lesbian, and bisexual people, heterosexual counselors may have difficulty in accurately interpreting the behaviors of this population (see Gutiérrez, 1989, for an elaboration of the etic versus emic view of sexual orientation). That is not to say that there are not problems with gay, lesbian, or bisexual counselors working with this population, and this will be addressed later.

Ethical guidelines are rarely specific enough to address the necessity for the counselor to know and appreciate the belief system of the client (Cayleff, 1986), but guidelines certainly address the importance of protecting the client's welfare. Cayleff (1986) believed the ethical counselor needs to consider beneficence and autonomy when working with minority clients. *Beneficence* means to act in a way that not only avoids harm to the client but actually benefits the client. This is difficult if the counselor is unaware of a client's culture and belief system. Michael, in chapter 20, on coming out in a men's group, knew that coming out is a difficult process and that the men in his group to whom this was an issue were in different places in this process. He respected where they were and let them make their own decisions. Autonomy is allowing the client to make choices based on complete information. Sometimes counselors slant information in the belief that the counselor is acting in the best interest of the client. If Michael had been a counselor who believed that coming out was absolutely necessary for the mental health of all gay men, he might have slanted information about the risks involved in the coming out process. Slanting information is paternalistic and compromises the client's autonomy. Western culture has acted paternalistically toward minorities throughout history; and counselors, as a part of the larger society, have sometimes perpetuated this paternalism (Cayleff, 1986; Dworkin & Gutiérrez, 1989).

Special Issues

I want to address some issues that I think are of particular importance when working with the gay, lesbian, and bisexual population. Some of these issues are of concern to any therapist working with this population, and other issues are of particular concern when both the therapist and client are of the same sexual orientation. The issues to be explored are diagnosis, confidentiality, discrimination against those clients who fit stereotypes, transference and countertransference, and dual relationships and boundary violations. This is by no means a comprehensive discourse on ethical issues in general or on these areas in particular.

Diagnosis

It sometimes becomes difficult to separate psychological issues from political ones. The struggle to remove homosexuality as a pathology and to practice gay- and lesbian-affirmative counseling has led some counselors away from diagnosis (Gonsiorek, 1982). Sometimes a client manifests pathology that results from difficulty in accepting a gay or lesbian identity. Sometimes the issue is severe pathology and not a reaction to coming out and oppression. Sometimes it is a combination of both. Sometimes homosexual rumination is a symptom of pathology and has nothing to do with sexual identity. These points are briefly discussed in chapter 12 on bisexuality and chapter 6 on the male couple. I direct readers to John Gonsiorek's (1982) article entitled "The use of diagnostic concepts in working with gay and lesbian populations" for a complete discussion. Ethical practice with these populations involves combining affirmative therapy with traditional psychological concepts (Gonsiorek, 1982). In chapter 6 on male couples, the therapist realizes that some of the hostility in the case of Bob and Allen might be symptoms of issues from family of origin dysfunctions and not from their sexual orientation.

Confidentiality and Privilege

Confidentiality is essential to any counseling relationship. Confidentiality takes on even more significance because the populations that this book deals with are populations that still face prejudice and discrimination. It is the client's choice whether or not sexual orientation is kept private (Kain, 1989; Shannon & Woods, 1991). Earlier I discussed paternalism. In helping a client decide whether or not to come out, it is important for the counselor to also remember beneficence and autonomy when exploring these issues. Other areas where confidentiality is crucial are in the knowledge of HIV antibody status, AIDS, and AIDS-related diagnoses (Shannon & Woods, 1991). One struggle now facing counselors is the dilemma around confidentiality and the duty to warn when a client is HIV positive and knowingly infecting others (Johnston, 1989; Wood, Marks, & Dilley, 1990). Counselors need to keep abreast of the latest thinking around these issues by professional organizations and the latest laws passed within their states.

Issues of confidentiality and privilege are important to consider when dealing with gay or lesbian custody cases. It is unclear whether or not counselors can claim privilege if asked about sexual orientation in these cases because privilege is voided when the client's mental status has been placed in the court as an issue by the client (Bernard, 1986). Counselors need to keep up with state laws, and clients need to be informed when and how the law might affect them. Consultation with an attorney may be warranted.

We, as counselors, try to be as gay and lesbian affirmative as possible, but we have to remember that in half of the states in this country it is still illegal to have same-sex genital contact (Herek, 1989). The constitutionality of these sodomy laws has been upheld by the Supreme Court (*Bower v. Hardwick*, 1986, cited in Herek, 1989). So, in effect, by affirming gay and lesbian relationships but primarily gay relationships and keeping these relationships confidential, we are also helping our clients to break the law in many areas of the country. This becomes a matter of civil disobedience.

Sari H. Dworkin

Discrimination Against Stereotypic Behavior

As mentioned earlier, counselors, whether gay, lesbian, or nongay, are not immune to the attitudes of society. Penelope (1986) discussed discrimination within the lesbian and nongay communities against women who are more masculine looking: "Feminine lesbians, who come closer to looking like women, are perceived to be 'more normal' than masculine lesbians" (p. 72). To my knowledge there is no research on this. But there has been enough written on homophobia and sexism and the inability for society to tolerate those who violate patriarchal sex roles to assume some validity for this position (Pharr, 1988). I hypothesize that this discrimination generalizes to more feminine looking gay men and to those gay men who are drag queens. In fact, in chapter 19 on bias in the interpretation of psychological tests, one of the clients, Clem, tested higher on the Feeling dimension than on the Thinking dimension of the MBTI, and his high school counselor believed Clem would do better in life if he could develop the more masculine Thinking preference. Not only may feminine looking gay men face more discrimination than more masculine looking gay men, but those gay men who show feminine characteristics on psychological tests may also face more discrimination than those gay men showing the preferred masculine characteristics. This certainly has implications for ethical counseling with those gay and lesbian people who are stereotypical in appearance and behavior, and this needs to be examined further.

Transference and Countertransference

Transference and countertransference are important in any counseling relationship, but when the therapist is also gay, lesbian, or bisexual, there may be some special considerations. Most of the therapeutic process operates independently of the sexual orientation of either the client or the therapist (Schwartz, 1989) (although, as this book attests, sexual orientation certainly is a factor). According to Schwartz (1989), when clients want to know the sexual orientation of the counselor they are usually trying to assess the therapist's views about homosexuality. It is rare for a therapist to initiate discussion about his or her sexual orientation because such self-disclosure is rarely appropriate and results from countertransference issues of the counselor. Unless a client has particularly chosen a therapist because the therapist is known to be gay or lesbian, most clients make the same heterosexist assumptions that society makes about the sexual orientation of people.

Matching a gay client with a gay therapist or a lesbian client with a lesbian therapist may introduce overt sexuality into the relationship, and erotic transference may sometimes be prolonged (Anthony, 1985; Schwartz, 1989). Erotic transference needs to be acknowledged and handled. Again, in chapter 20 on coming out in a men's group, Michael knows that Jeffrey is attracted to Michael, the group facilitator, and Michael also knows that Jeffrey is in the beginning of his coming out process. It is important for Michael to be supportive and accepting so that Jeffrey can know that he is attractive and capable. In addition to sexual attractions, for a gay therapist working with a gay client there may be similar concerns about health issues (HIV infection, AIDS, AIDS-related diagnoses), and countertransference can arise (Schwartz, 1989). In chapter 18 on helping someone to die, the counselor working with Harold was aware of his countertransference regarding death and was able to deal with it effectively so that it did not interfere with his work with Harold.

Another area of concern is the therapist's own internalized or latent homophobia causing mutual client and counselor blind spots that could affect the therapist's capacity for beneficence (Cayleff, 1986; Schwartz, 1989).

Dual Relationships and Boundary Violations

Ethical codes in the helping professions have frowned on dual relationships in an attempt to diminish the abuse of the power of therapists (Berman, 1985). Whether or not counselors want to admit to their power, counseling is a hierarchical and powerful relationship (Cayleff, 1986). It is important that we use our legitimate power in responsible ways (Brown, 1989). Dual or overlapping relationships are virtually impossible for the gay or lesbian therapist to avoid unless he or she is willing to completely isolate from the gay and lesbian community (Anthony, 1985; Berman, 1985; Brown, 1989; Shannon & Woods, 1991). Many gay and lesbian clients choose therapists they see at political events or community events precisely because they expect these therapists not to be homophobic. It is important for therapists to explore with clients how the clients want these outside meetings to be handled. The therapist must deal with his or her own feelings about being under scrutiny when in public. Under no circumstances should the therapist try to meet the social needs of the client or have the client meet his or her social needs.

Brown (1989) discussed some interesting issues in terms of boundary violations. Very often lesbian (and gay) therapists are leaders in their communities. Therefore, when a lesbian (or gay) therapist is engaging in unethical behavior, the impact of the harm may be greater than it is for a heterosexual therapist because it might mean the loss of a leader and role model in the gay and lesbian community. Thus, it may be more difficult to confront the therapist. Another point Brown (1989) made is that people generally believe "men violate boundaries and women are violated" (p. 16). Thus it may be hard to believe that some women therapists violate boundaries, making it difficult to confront the lesbian therapists who are violating boundaries. Our own oppression sometimes engenders a sense of powerlessness that also makes necessary confrontations difficult. This sense of powerlessness may also cause an overidentification with the powerless client and become a rationalization for a boundary violation with a client (Brown, 1989). All of us are capable of boundary violations with clients, and these boundary violations fall on a continuum as to their seriousness (Brown, 1989).

Conclusion

As counselors we struggle to be competent and ethical in what we do. When working with an oppressed, minority group such as the gay, lesbian, and bisexual population, there are some specific concerns relating to ethical practice. This chapter has explored some of these issues. In order to be ethical we must understand the client from the client's world, which means recognizing the impact of culture (Dworkin & Gutiérrez, 1989). We must also be aware of, acknowledge, and explore our own potential for unethical behavior (Brown, 1989). When examining what we are doing within the counseling relationship, we must ask ourselves whether we are enhancing or diminishing client power (Pedersen, 1990). Ultimately, as Cayleff (1986) has stated, ethical practice is based on the "principles of beneficence, autonomy, justice, and welfare" (p. 346). If we bear these principles in mind when working with our gay, lesbian, and bisexual clients, we will rarely go wrong.

References

American Association for Counseling and Development. (1988, March). *Ethical standards*. Alexandria, VA: Author.

Anthony, B. D. (1985). Lesbian client-lesbian therapist: Opportunities and challenges in working together. In J. C. Gonsiorek (Ed.), *A guide to psychotherapy with gay and lesbian clients* (pp. 45–57). New York: Harrington.

Berman, J. R. S. (1985). Ethical feminist perspectives on dual relationships with clients. In L. B. Rosewater & L. E. A. Walker (Eds.), *Handbook of feminist psychotherapy* (pp. 287–296). New York: Springer.

Bernard, J. L. (1986). Confidentiality. In A. E. Moses & R. O. Hawkins, Jr. (Eds.), *Counseling lesbian women and gay men* (pp. 181–185). Columbus, OH: Merrill.

Brown, L. (1985). Ethics and business practice in feminist therapy. In L. B. Rosewater & L. E. A. Walker (Eds.), *Handbook of feminist therapy* (pp. 297–304). New York: Springer.

Brown, L. S. (1989). Beyond thou shalt not: Thinking about ethics in the lesbian therapy community. *Women and Therapy, 8*(1/2), 13–25.

Cayleff, S. E. (1986). Ethical issues in counseling gender, race, and culturally distinct groups. *Journal of Counseling and Development, 64*(5), 345–347.

Dworkin, S. H., & Gutiérrez, F. (1989). Counselors be aware: Clients come in every size, shape, color, and sexual orientation. *Journal of Counseling & Development, 68*(1), 6–8.

Gonsiorek, J. C. (1982). The use of diagnostic concepts in working with gay and lesbian populations. In J. C. Gonsiorek (Ed.), *A guide to psychotherapy with gay and lesbian clients* (pp. 9–20). New York: Haworth.

Gutiérrez, F. (1989, August). *Gays and lesbians: An ethnic minority identity.* Paper presented at the annual convention of the American Psychological Association, New Orleans.

Herek, G. M. (1989). Hate crimes against lesbians and gay men. *American Psychologist, 44*(6), 948–955.

Iasenza, S. (1989). Some challenges of integrating sexual orientations into counselor training and research. *Journal of Counseling and Development, 68*(1), 73–76.

Johnston, M. W. (1989). *AIDS issues and answers for university counseling center staff.* Long Beach: California State University Counseling Center.

Kain, C. (Ed.). (1989). *No longer immune: A counselor's guide to AIDS.* Alexandria, VA: American Association of Counseling and Development.

Mabe, A. R., & Rollin, S. A. (1986). The role of a code of ethical standards in counseling. *Journal of Counseling and Development, 64*(5), 294–297.

Pedersen, P. (1990). The constructs of complexity and balance in multicultural counseling, theory, and practice. *Journal of Counseling and Development, 68*(5), 550–554.

Penelope, J. (1986). Heteropatriarchal semantics: Just two kinds of people in the world. *Lesbian Ethics, 2*(2), 58–80.

Pharr, S. (1988). *Homophobia, a weapon of sexism.* Inverness, CA: Chardon Press.

Ross, M. W. (1987). A theory of normal homosexuality. In L. Diamant (Ed.), *Male and female homosexuality* (pp. 237–259). New York: Hemisphere.

Schwartz, R. D. (1989). When the therapist is gay: Personal and clinical reflections. *Journal of Gay and Lesbian Psychotherapy, 1*(1), 41–51.

Shannon, J. W., & Woods, W. J. (1991). Affirmative psychotherapy for gay men. *The Counseling Psychologist, 19*(2), 197–215.

Tennyson, W. W., & Strom, S. M. (1986). Beyond professional standards: Developing responsibleness. *Journal of Counseling and Development, 64*(5), 298–302.

Tripp, C. A. (1987). On morals and ethics. In L. Diamant (Ed.), *Male and female homosexuality* (pp. 271–282). New York: Hemisphere.

Wood, G. J., Marks, R., & Dilley, J. W. (1990). *AIDS law for mental health professionals*. San Francisco: University of California AIDS Health Project.

Epilogue:
Where Do We Go From Here?

Sari H. Dworkin, PhD
Fernando J. Gutiérrez, EdD

Now that you have come to the end of this book, it should be apparent that gay, lesbian, and bisexual clients have complex lives, of which their sexual orientation is but one factor. It is easy to recognize that many of the issues faced by the clients in the case studies presented are issues that the mainstream heterosexual client may also face.

The added variable for the clients presented in this book, however, is the factor of an identity that is stigmatized and fairly invisible. The culture of these clients must be understood by the counselor, if the counselor is to be effective in the diagnosis of problems and in the intervention strategies that will assist the client in resolving the problems based on the cultural norms of the group (Dworkin & Gutiérrez, 1989). It is only then that a counselor can become gay and lesbian affirmative.

The role of the counselor working with the gay, lesbian, and bisexual community must catch up with the rest of the field of mental health. Almost 30 years ago, in Swampscott, Massachusetts, the field of community psychology was born. The Boston Conference on the Education of Psychologists for Community Mental Health Committee (Anderson, Bennett, Cooper, Hassol, Klein, & Rosenblum, 1966) had this to say:

> Today the mental health frontier is shifting from the treatment of illness to its prevention, and to the positive promotion of mental health. Increasingly, the mental health professions

335

are delivering services to the community—not just responding to the onset of pathology. A broad spectrum of professional activity is emerging, generally characterized as
community mental health. It involves active participation in
community affairs on the part of mental health personnel,
preventive intervention at the community level, and collaboration with responsible laymen in reducing community tensions. (p. 1)

The Boston conference committee also advocated the mental health
professional's role in initiating and advancing legislation as well as in
influencing decisions and execution of public policy. This advice must
be heeded by counselors working with gays and lesbians. We must
respect the current scientific knowledge that supports gayness and
lesbianism as a difference rather than a pathology. Mental health
professionals must stand up and inform our lawmakers and government administrators setting public policy about the reality of the gay,
lesbian, and bisexual population in order to prevent decisions being
made based on fears or erroneous stereotypes. The editors believe that
a truly gay-, lesbian-, and bisexual-affirmative counselor will actively
advocate for the civil rights of this population.

At a minimum, this activism entails involvement with the divisions,
committees, or special interest groups of professional organizations
that are involved in the study of gay, lesbian, and bisexual issues.
Although this sounds easy, it means overcoming external homophobia
for the nongay or lesbian counselor. Belonging to these groups means
possibly being perceived as gay, lesbian, or bisexual. For the gay, lesbian, or bisexual counselor, involvement means overcoming internalized homophobia.

The American Association for Counseling and Development should
follow the lead of the American Psychological Association in establishing a division for the study of gay, lesbian, and bisexual issues as
well as for the education and training of gay-, lesbian-, and bisexual-
affirmative counselors. APA's Division 44, the Society for the Psychological Study of Lesbian and Gay Issues, has over 800 members.

The American College Personnel Association has a Standing Committee for Lesbian, Gay, and Bisexual Awareness. This committee is a
positive model of what an organization can do to address lesbian, gay,
and bisexual issues.

Involvement in professional organizations, such as the Association
for Gay, Lesbian, and Bisexual Issues in Counseling (AGLBIC) and the

Association of Lesbian and Gay Psychologists (ALGP), can be another way of contributing. These organizations have chosen to remain autonomous, with affiliative status to the mainstream organizations in order to have the freedom to act politically.

The best weapon to counteract the oppression by specific interest groups is research. It has only been within the last 20 years that investigation of homosexuality and bisexuality could examine anything other than interventions to change a client from homosexual to heterosexual.

At a panel on lesbian research held at the 1989 annual convention of the American Psychological Association, there was overwhelming recognition of the need for qualitative studies describing the ordinary lives, relationships, and families of lesbians. The same is needed for gay men and bisexuals. Too often psychological theory is based on client populations and then generalized to the mainstream group. Research must investigate the characteristics and needs of gay, lesbian, and bisexual people who use therapeutic services. Research must also investigate the needs and characteristics of those who cope with life stresses in other ways.

The editors are encouraged by forthcoming dissertations such as *Peer Relationship of Adolescent Children of Gay Men* (Rogers, 1991) and *Lesbian Identity Development* (Holmes, 1991) coming out of the California School of Professional Psychology. These works are positive examples of the type of research needed to help counselors understand the gay and lesbian worlds.

Participation in professional organizations and conducting research is not enough to undo the psychological harm that oppression causes nonheterosexuals. As agents of social change and advocates for the rights of gay, lesbian, and bisexual people, it is important for counselors to become activists locally, statewide, and nationally. Public schools are still ignoring the fact that there are gay and lesbian adolescents in need. Although not every community may be able to initiate a Project 10, as Los Angeles, or a Harvey Milk High School, as New York, counselors can at least work with school boards to demand inservice training on the needs of gay and lesbian youth.

Counselors can assist in the struggle for recognition of gay and lesbian couples and families by supporting bills that provide equality for gay and lesbian couples, such as the domestic partnership bill recently passed in San Francisco. These bills protect equality in the areas of custody, health insurance, wills, finances, property, and the rights of a partner to be involved in health care decisions when the partner is incapacitated. Mental health professionals can also assist by removing bias based on sexual orientation in the evaluation of gay and lesbian parents during custody evaluations.

Some states, such as Connecticut and California, are working to include sexual orientation as a protected status within employment and housing statutes. There is a national movement primarily operating on college campuses to change the discriminatory policies of the military against gay and lesbian people. Another movement is involved in the change of immigration policies based on sexual orientation.

The gay and lesbian community is shoring up for a major struggle as we seek the enactment of a National Lesbian and Gay Civil Rights Act (Morin, 1991). The interdisciplinary work among mental health professionals, attorneys, and lawmakers will be crucial in this struggle.

The work of AACD's Government Relations Office will also be significant. We must challenge with scientific evidence regarding the mental health of gays and lesbians the unfounded arguments being proposed by certain lobbying groups.

Counselors of all sexual orientations who consider themselves gay, lesbian, and bisexual affirmative must become involved in these struggles.

Finally, the editors want to leave you with the words of a song popular at many Latino church services that expresses the beauty of the "loves of many colors." For us, the words symbolize the celebration of lesbian, gay, and bisexual love:

De Colores	Of Many Colors
De colores, De colores brillantes y finos se viste la aurora, De colores, de colores son los mil reflejos que el sol atesora.	Of many colors, of many colors brillant and fine, is the dawn, Of many colors, of many colors are the thousand reflections treasured by the sun.
De colores, de colores es el arco iris que vemos lucir, y por eso los grandes amores de muchos colores me gustan a mi ...	Of many colors, of many colors is the rainbow that, shining, we see And that is why the great loves of many colors are appreciated by me ...

Y por eso los grandes amores de
muchos colores me gustan a mi ...

References

Anderson, L., Bennett, C., Cooper, S., Hassol, L., Klein, D., & Rosenblum, G. (1966). *Community psychology: A report of the Boston Conference on the Education of Psychologists for Community Mental Health.*

Dworkin, S.H., & Gutiérrez, F.J. (1989). Counselors be aware: Clients come in every size, shape, color, and sexual orientation. [Introduction to special issue]. *Journal of Counseling & Development, 68*(1), 6–8.

Holmes, R. (1991). *Lesbian identity formation.* Unpublished doctoral dissertation proposal, California School of Professional Psychology, Fresno.

Morin, S. (1991). Removing the stigma: Lesbian and gay affirmative counseling. *The Counseling Psychologist, 19*, 245–247.

Rogers, L. (1991). *Peer relationships of adolescent children of gay men.* Unpublished doctoral dissertation proposal, California School of Professional Psychology, Fresno.

Professional Associations and Resources for Lesbians, Gays, and Bisexuals

Affirmation (Gay and Lesbian Mormons)
Box 26302
San Francisco, CA 94126
(415) 641-4554

Affirmation (United Methodists for Gay and Lesbian Concerns)
Box 1021
Evanston, Il 60204
(312) 475-0499

American Association of Physicians for Human Rights
Box 14366
San Francisco, CA 94144

Asian Pacifica Lesbian Network
c/o Shamakami
PO Box 460456
San Francisco, CA 94146-0456

This list was partially compiled by Lynn Milburn, University of Texas at Austin, in March 1988 and Fernando Gutiérrez, EdD, in July 1991.

Portions of this list appeared in C. Hetherington and A. Orzek (1989), Career Counseling and Life Planning With Lesbian Women, *Journal of Counseling & Development, 68*, 52–57; and in K. Ritter and C. O'Neill (1989), Moving Through Loss: The Spiritual Journey of Gay Men and Lesbian Women, *Journal of Counseling & Development, 68*, 9–15.

Association for Gay, Lesbian, and Bisexual Issues in Counseling
  (AGLBIC)
PO Box 216
Jenkintown, PA 19046

Association of Lesbian and Gay Psychologists (ALGP)
2336 Market Street No. 8
San Francisco, CA 94114

Bay Area Lawyers for Individual Freedom
PO Box 1983
San Francisco, CA 94101

Bay Area Network of Gay and Lesbian Educators (BANGLE)
c/o Billy De Frank Community Center
175 Stockton Street
San Jose, CA 95126

Bay Area Physicians for Human Rights
2940 16th Street, No. 309
San Francisco, CA 94130

Black Gay and Lesbian Leadership Forum
3924 West Sunset Boulevard
Los Angeles, CA 90029

CALM: Custody Action for Lesbian Mothers
Box 281
Narberth, PA 19072

Concerned Insurance Professionals for Human Rights
Box 691006
Los Angeles, CA 90069-9006
(713) 247-0426

Couples National Network, Inc.
Box 26139
Tempe, AZ 85285-6139

Dignity, Inc. (Catholic)
1500 Massachusetts Avenue, N.W., Suite 11
Washington, DC 20005

Directory of Homosexual Organizations and Publications
Homosexual Information Center
4758 Hollywood Boulevard, Suite 208
Hollywood, CA 90028
(213) 464-8431

Domestic Partnerships Commission
114 15th Street, N.E.
Washington, DC 20002
(202) 543-0298

Education in a Disabled Gay Environment (EDGE)
PO Box 305, Village Station
New York, NY 10014
(212) 246-3811, ext. 292

Evangelicals Concerned
c/o Dr. Ralph Blair
311 East 72nd Street
New York, NY 10021
(212) 517-3171

Family Diversity Project
Box 65756
Los Angeles, CA 90065
(213) 258-8955

Fathers for Equal Rights
PO Box 010847, Flagler Station
Miami, FL 33101
(305) 895-6351

Federal Lesbians and Gays (government employees)
584 Castro, Suite 464
San Francisco, CA 94114
(415) 695-9174

Federation of Parents and Professionals for Friends of Lesbians and
  Gays (P-FLAG)
PO Box 24565
Los Angeles, CA 90024

Friends for Lesbian and Gay Concerns (Quakers)
Box 222
Sunneytown, PA 18084
(215) 234-8424

Gay and Lesbian Parents Coalition International
Box 50360
Washington, DC 20004

Gay Asian Pacific Alliance
1841 Market Street, 2nd Floor
San Francisco, CA 94103

Gay Fathers' Coalition
PO Box 19891
Washington, DC 20036

Gay Married Men Who Are Gay Parents
PO Box 50360
Washington, DC 20004

Gay Media Task Forces
2172 Moreno Drive
Los Angeles, CA 90039

Gay Public Health Workers
c/o Herbert
1801 Clysdale Place, N.W.
Washington, DC 20009

Gay Rights National Lobby
PO Box 1892
Washington, DC 20013

Gay Theatre Alliance of Gay Plays
JH Press
Job 294, Village Station
New York, NY 10014

Gray Panthers of San Francisco
1182 Market Street, Suite 203
San Francisco, CA 94102

Handicapped Gay Correspondence Club
Para-Amps
PO Box 515
South Beloit, IL 61080

High Tech Gays
PO Box 6777
San Jose, CA 95150

Human Rights Campaign Fund
1012 14th Street, N.W., Suite 600
Washington, DC 20005
(202) 628-4160

International Bisexual Conference
584 Castro, Suite 422
San Francisco, CA 94114

International Gay and Lesbian Archives
PO Box 38100
Los Angeles, CA 90038
(213) 662-9444

International Gay Information Center
PO Box 2, Village Station
New York, NY 10012

Lambda Legal Defense and Education Fund
666 Broadway
New York, NY 10012

Lesbian and Gay Caucus of the Democratic National Committee
1742 Massachusetts Avenue, S.E.
Washington, DC 20003
(202) 547-3104

Lesbian and Gay People in Medicine
c/o American Medical Student Association
1910 Association Drive
Reston, VA 22091

Lesbian Mothers National Defense Fund
Box 21567
Seattle, WA 98111
(206) 325-2643

LLEGO Nacional
PO Box 44483
Washington, DC 20036

National Association of Black and White Men Together
584 Castro Street, Suite 140
San Francisco, CA 94114

National Association of Gay Gerontologists
1853 Market Street
San Francisco, CA 94013
(415) 349-4537

National Association of Lesbian and Gay Alcoholism Professionals
(NALGP)
204 West 20th Street
New York, NY 10011

National Center for Lesbian Rights
1663 Mission, 5th Floor
San Francisco, CA 94103
(415) 621-0674

National Family Register:
Human Rights Campaign Fund
1012 14th Street, N.W., No. 607
Washington, DC 20005
(202) 332-6483

National Gay and Lesbian Families Project
1517 U Street, N.W.
Washington, DC 20009
(202) 332-6483

National Gay Health Education Foundation
Box 784
New York, NY 10036
(212) 563-6313

National Gay and Lesbian Task Force
1517 U Street, N.W.
Washington, DC 20009
(202) 332-6483

National Organization for Gay and Lesbian Scientists and
    Technical Pros
PO Box 39582
Los Angeles, CA 90039-0582

NETGALA (college and university alumni associations)
1442 Q Street, N.W.
Washington, DC 20009-3908

New York Bankers Group
PO Box 973
Rockefeller Center Station
New York, NY 10185

PARTNERS: Newsletter for gay and lesbian couples
Box 9685
Seattle, WA 98109

SAGE: Senior Action in a Gay Environment
208 West 13th Street
New York, NY 10011
(212) 741-2247

Seventh Day Adventist Kinship International, Inc.
Box 3840
Los Angeles, CA 90078-3840
(213) 876-2076

Unitarian Universalists for Lesbian/Gay Concerns
25 Beacon Street
Boston, MA 02108
(617) 742-2100

Universal Fellowship of Metropolitan Community Churches (MCC)
5300 Santa Monica Boulevard, No. 304
Los Angeles, CA 90029
(213) 464-5100

World Congress of Gay and Lesbian Jewish Organizations
Barrett Brick, Executive Director
PO Box 18961
Washington, DC 20036
(202) 483-4801

Note: Your local phone book may have additional organizations that could be useful, such as Equal Rights for Fathers organizations.